LIVING ABROAD IN
COSTA RICA

ERIN VAN RHEENEN

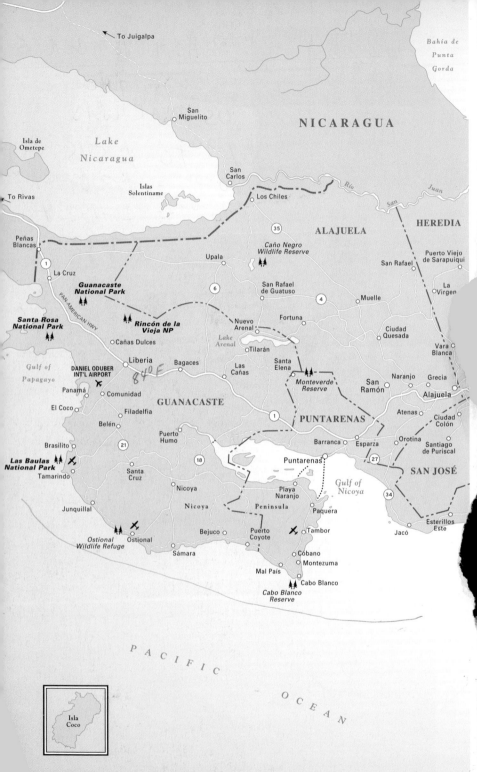

COSTA RICA

174 mi wide

99 mi

298 mi

Caribbean Sea

Barra del Colorado

Tortuguero

Tortuguero National Park

LIMÓN

79° F

Las Horquetas

Guácimo

Matina

Moín

Puerto Limón

4

32

Guápiles

Siquirres

Los Canales

Cahuita National Park

Puerto Viejo

Cahuita

Manzanillo

Gandoca-Manzanillo Wildlife Reserve

Bribrí

Sixaola

Chirripó National Park

73° F

Turrialba

10

LIMÓN

CARTAGO

Heredia

SAN JOSÉ

JUAN SANTAMARÍA INT'L AIRPORT

Cartago

Tapantí

La Amistad International Park

PANAMA

Aserrí

Cañón

San Ignacio de Acosta

2

San Gerardo de Rivas

San Gerardo de Dota

San Isidro de El General

Buenos Aires

PUNTARENAS

Parrita

82° F

Savegre

Platanillo

Paso Real

San Vito

Quepos

Manuel Antonio

Dominical

Uvita

Manuel Antonio National Park

Palmar Norte

2

Ciudad Neily

Coronado Bay

Palmar Sur

Sierpe

PAN-AMERICAN HWY

Rio Claro

To Santiago

Golfito

84° F

Paso Canoas

Drake Bay

Drake

Sweet Gulf

Zancudo

Isla Caño

Corcovado National Park

Puerto Jiménez

(Golfo Dulce)

Pavones

Sirena

Carate

Osa Peninsula

0   50 mi

0   50 km

Are you ready for a change? Is it time to trade

your old life for one that's a little more *livable?*

Costa Rica, long known for ecofriendly vacations, is also a great place to live. In the most peaceful and stable country in Central America, everyday life ambles along at a decidedly human pace. Enjoying nature and spending time with family and friends will be at the top of your to-do list, if indeed that list survives the move.

Because Costa Rica imposes its own agenda, one that persuades rather than insists. It humbly invites you to enjoy the simple pleasures of life, like peeling a mango or watching the waves roll in.

One of the country's most potent charms is the ability to get up close and personal with nature, re-awakening forgotten senses. There's nothing like coming face to face with a howler monkey perched in a nearby tree, chewing contentedly on a dinner of leaves. You may glimpse a jaguarundi (a small wildcat)

tree on Caño Island

along a forest path, or spot a pair of scarlet macaws on the wing. And the landscape here is as alive as the animal kingdom: Catch a wave on the beaches at Puerto Viejo, raft the thundering whitewater of the Reventazón River, or make your way through the tropical tangle of the Osa Peninsula's coastal rainforest. Clip onto a zipline and fly above the canopy, or tend the orchids in your own backyard.

If you're off the beaten track — a place just down the road from the overrun — you'll be amazed by how untamed this country still is. In 2006, the nation's environment minister was lost for three days in Corcovado National Park on the Osa Peninsula, which *National Geographic* calls the "most biologically intense place on earth." Menaced by a tapir, the minister fell down a ravine, and then wandered alone for three days before a search plane spotted him. If the man in charge of Costa Rica's environment can get lost in his own backyard, it's a good sign that parts of this country are still pretty wild.

painted oxcart wheel from the town of Sarchí

Many areas in Costa Rica still have a wild west feel — places where the gap between law and enforcement, between intention and actuality, is as wide and deep as the country's notorious potholes. Despite the inconsistently enforced laws, many people breathe a sigh of relief to be in place where not everything is regulated. This rawness can be both liberating and exasperating. Along hiking trails, for example, there are no signs warning you away from cliffs. It's taken for granted that people look where they're walking and have a vested interest in taking care of themselves.

If you want to sleepwalk through your days, don't come here. Being alert is the price you pay (and, of course, the reward) for not being told at every turn what to do. For those who adapt well to it, this is an ideal place to lead a rich, independent life.

That independent spirit coexists here with a level of human warmth that has all but disappeared from many more-developed nations. Human interaction is far and away the most important

Rodrigo Miranda surfs Playa Junquillal.

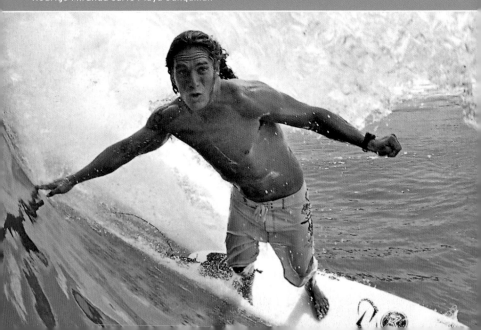

value, and people take time to say hello to neighbors or to make small talk with clerks and taxi drivers. This is true even in the relatively fast-paced capital city, but it is much more pronounced in small towns. Expats who stay here for a while and then go home for a visit are shocked all over again by the fact that "nobody talks to anyone else back there." It's a commonplace that is nevertheless true: In many countries these days, people live to work; in Costa Rica, they work to live.

Costa Rica is immensely appealing, for all the charms it possesses but also for all that is *doesn't* have: While other countries in the region suffer civil strife or military dictatorships, Ticos (Costa Ricans) visit the polls for peaceful multiparty elections. People come here from all over the world for security, a stable business environment, high-quality and affordable health care, a lower cost of living, and a very high quality of life.

The nation is no utopia, of course, and is by no means undiscovered. Costa Rica's new national bird may well be the

waterfall near Dominical

construction crane. It's boom time here, at least in certain areas. But even in the hot spots filling up with international expatriates, your life will be radically unlike the one back home. To say that the pace is slower and the language and culture very different only scratches the surface of the new worlds you'll encounter.

Beyond all the quantifiable factors, there are more mysterious reasons why people come to Costa Rica. I've spoken with a surprising number of expatriates who speak of being "called" here. These are often average North Americans – which is to say logical, restless, and driven. It's just that they've chosen to pay attention to the signals we all get but usually ignore: to slow down, open up, and to go to a place where life slows down enough to let you jump onboard. The bottom line is, if a voice is telling you to come to Costa Rica, why not listen? However crazily you come to it, it may be the sanest choice you ever make.

church in the town of Orosí

Contents

PRIME LIVING LOCATIONS 285

RESOURCES 391

INDEX 435

WELCOME TO COSTA RICA

INTRODUCTION

At an outdoor café in downtown San José, the capital of Costa Rica, a tourist is talking about his travel plans. "I want to get out of the city," he says. "See the rest of the island."

A few hours north, in the town of La Fortuna, another visitor walks into a tour agency within sight of perfectly conical Arenal Volcano. "What I need to know," she says, "is when they turn the volcano on."

For all its popularity, Costa Rica draws many people who have a somewhat distorted view of what this lovely country has to offer. If you've picked up this book, chances are you know that, despite lucking out with a disproportionate amount of coastline for such a small nation, Costa Rica is not an island. And only the truly Disneyfied would imagine that the natural wonders of this mecca of biodiversity can be switched on and off at will.

But you may have subtler biases, like thinking a life in Costa Rica will resemble a vacation in Florida or Hawaii. Or that you can breeze into this

WHAT I LOVE ABOUT COSTA RICA

- Waiters and shopgirls call me *mi amor* (my love) or *mi reina* (my queen).

- Fathers (and mothers!) here are so affectionate with their kids.

- You can buy single cigarettes at kiosks and *pulperías*, thereby pretending that you're not really a smoker.

- Roses and hibiscus, palm trees and pine, all grow in the same Central Valley backyard.

- Good seats at a play in a venerable old theater cost around US$6.

- Even on crowded city sidewalks, Ticos manage not to run into each other or poke each other with dripping umbrellas.

- Fresh-squeezed orange juice costs about US$.35 from a streetside cart.

- You'll never catch this country declaring war.

backwater with your first-world moxie and make a killing in real estate or tourism or teak farming.

Dreamer beware. Costa Rica is no Florida, and it's no backwater banana republic. One of the most politically and economically stable nations in the region, it has long attracted international investors. It's easy for a foreigner to start a business here—you can even do it on a tourist visa. Running a successful business is another story, and it requires the same skill and luck such an endeavor requires anywhere in the world. In fact, doing business here—or just successfully hanging out—may demand more of you than you might expect. No one thrives here without humility, a fully functioning sense of humor, and a degree of flexibility that would amaze the most accomplished yogi.

Of course, the country lives and breathes contradictions. Costa Rica has made the right choices, eliminating its army and creating a thriving nation with enviable national parks, high education levels, and health care for all. And yet, this is still a wild place, especially outside of the heavily populated Central Valley. Harvey Haber, author of the early editions of the *Insight Guide to Costa Rica,* agrees that there's still an outlaw quality to Costa Rica. "Totally straight people and outright criminals won't last here," says Harvey. And while he may be joking, I think he's hit on something. Costa Rica is not for the faint of heart, nor for those who insist on imposing an old order on a new experience. "If you want to come here and make it just like home," I've heard from a variety of sources, "just stay home."

On the other hand, if you're ready to take this country on its own terms, and to trade your golden dream for a reality of a more complex alloy, your move to Costa Rica could be one of the most satisfying things you'll ever do.

But you need to be prepared. This book will show you the nitty-gritty of life in a foreign country: working, shopping, banking, buying or building a house, dealing with immigration, and arranging for the best health care. It describes the different parts of the country, from the dry northern Pacific coast to the luxuriant Zona Sur. You'll read the many case studies of people like you who've made the move and are happy to be here. And of course you'll come and visit. When you step off the plane into the balmy Costa Rican air, you'll start to know in your skin and bones whether or not this is the place for you. Do your research, soak up the atmosphere, then make your own decision. The independent attitude you'll need to thrive here can start right now, as you move through myths and misconceptions and into the heart of the real Costa Rica.

The Lay of the Land

Talk about centrally located. Picture the bent elbow of land that connects North and South America: Costa Rica rests in the crook of that arm, at the northern edge of where North America funnels down into a narrow isthmus separating the Pacific and the Caribbean.

The country lies at the hub of two continents and at the crux of two geographic plates—the Cocos and the Caribbean. In millennia past, the isthmus served as a land bridge, allowing flora and fauna to come up from the south and trickle down from the north. The resulting diversity of plant and animal life is staggering. Imagine 1,400 species of orchids and more than 100 kinds of bats and you get a taste of the huge feast spread on this small table of a country.

At 50,000 square kilometers (19,305 square miles), Costa Rica is the second-smallest country in Central America, after El Salvador. Its Caribbean coastline is a mere 160 kilometers (99 miles) long, while the Pacific coast, with more bays and peninsulas, measures 480 kilometers (298 miles) from the Nicaraguan border to Panama. At its widest—280 kilometers (174 miles)—Costa Rica is still a narrow country that can be traversed in a few hours.

The country doesn't feel so small when you're clanking along a rutted back road at 15 kph, wondering when you'll hit the next gas station, but it feels very intimate in terms of people. Sometimes the whole country feels like a small town. When I first arrived in San José, I met a North American named Jay who worked as a builder in the northern province of Guanacaste. He said he'd be happy to talk to me about his profession and his adopted country. When later I traveled to Guanacaste, I had, of course, left Jay's number in my San José apartment. But when I looked up a friend of a San Francisco friend, it turned out he was working construction, and his boss was… Jay. Guanacaste, let me add, is not a small town. At around 10,000 square kilometers (3,861 square miles), it's Costa Rica's second-largest province, with a population of about 280,000.

This wasn't an isolated case. The Italian woman I bummed a cigarette from in a San José café? A month later I walked into a yoga class in the Pacific beach town of Nosara, and there she was. Even in the capital city I would often run into friends and acquaintances. And if you live in a small town (most of Costa Rica seems to be made up of small towns), you'll see people you know about seven times a day. "After a while," one local admits, "you just smile and nod. How many times can you ask after someone's kids, their mate, or their health?" But the fact that people do ask after your family and your health, and that they do smile and nod, makes Costa Rica a very friendly place indeed.

COUNTRY DIVISIONS

Costa Rica is divided into seven provinces: San José, Heredia, Alajuela, Cartago, Puntarenas, Guanacaste, and Limón. In every province except Guanacaste, the province and its capital share the same name (Guanacaste's provincial capital is Liberia). San José, with nearly two million inhabitants, is by far the most populous province, while Puntarenas, which accounts for most of the country's Pacific coastline, is the largest. The provinces of San José, Cartago, Heredia, and Alajuela fan out from the Central Valley; the latter two stretch north all the way to the Nicaraguan border.

Each province is divided into counties, of which the country has 81. Counties are divided into districts; there are 449 districts in Costa Rica.

Locals also divide the country into "zones," which have less precise boundaries. There's the Zona Norte (Northern Zone), composed of the northern parts of Heredia and Alajuela, along with some of inland Guanacaste. From misty mountain towns to fiery Arenal Volcano to Caño Negro's flocks of roseate spoonbills and snowy egrets, the Zona Norte is nothing if not varied.

The Zona Sur (Southern Zone) is best known for spectacular Corcovado National Park, Costa Rica's Amazon, which takes up much of the Osa Peninsula. But the zone also includes inland marvels like Cerro Chirripó, at 3,819 meters (12,530 feet) the highest peak in the country, as well as cool and verdant towns like San Vito, not far from the Panamanian border. The large and placid Golfo Dulce (Sweet Gulf) is part of the Zona Sur, as are the fabled beaches along that gulf's eastern edge: Playa Zancudo and Pavones are the best known of the seemingly endless number.

The Zona Caribe (Caribbean Zone) is almost, but not quite, synonymous with Limón province—the zone is mainly the Caribbean coast, while the province extends inland into mountain ranges like the mighty Talamanca. Many tourists know of the sea turtle migrations at Tortuguero National Park, some have heard of the famed Salsa Brava wave at Puerto Viejo, but only a select few have visited the indigenous reserves and the vast unexplored wilds inland from Costa Rica's lesser-known coast.

The Central Valley, sometimes called the Meseta Central or Central Mesa, is the heart of the country. Measuring about 80 by 40 kilometers (50 by 25 miles), the area is ringed by a series of steep-sloped volcanoes, some of them still active. The capital city of San José lies at the center of the Central Valley, and at 1,150 meters (3,772 feet) it enjoys year-round temperatures between 21°C and 26°C (70°F and 80°F).

WEATHER

Great weather is one of the country's big draws. Those who've had it up to their wool turtlenecks with cold and snow find relief in Costa Rica's tropical sun and balmy breezes. The northern province of Guanacaste in particular is a sun-worshipper's dream, with hardly a drop of rain falling between December and May. The green season brings more rain, but even then showers are usually confined to afternoon and evening hours, with mornings as glorious as ever.

But if you've never been a beach person, don't worry. Even those who prefer cooler climes will thrive here. Temperature in Costa Rica is less a function of season than altitude, and you can fine-tune your weather by going up or down a few hundred meters. If you like an occasional bite in the air, just look for an emerald-green lot on the side of one of the (inactive) volcanoes, where the sun shines brightly at midday but where dawn and dusk bring cooling mists. At higher elevations you'll see pine trees alongside vine-draped tropical hardwoods.

The variety of climates means that the natural world is one of the most varied you'll ever see. Of course it helps that Costa Rica has set aside a quarter of its territory in parks and reserves where rare animals still roam freely. Jaguars, tapirs, sloths, and monkeys call this country's rainforests home, and get ready for a stunning variety of birds, including 50 species of hummingbirds, various toucans, parrots, and macaws, and the elusive resplendent quetzal,

JUST HOW HOT IS IT?

If you're among that minority of world citizens who thinks 32 degrees means you'd better bundle up, it's time to learn about Celsius. Thirty-two-degree weather in Costa Rica means you'd better break out your bathing suit – it's almost 90° Fahrenheit.

To go from Celsius to Fahrenheit, multiply by 1.8, then add 32. To go the other way (Fahrenheit to Celsius), subtract 32, then divide by 1.8.

Below are the average temperatures in major Costa Rican cities on a day in late March.

CITY	CELSIUS	FAHRENHEIT
Alahuela	25	77
Golfito	29	84
Liberia	29	84
Limón	26	79
Puntarenas	28	82
Quepos	29	84
San José	23	73

with the male's iridescent green tail feathers more than three times the length of its body.

EARTHQUAKES AND VOLCANOES

Costa Rica is the child of a volatile but enduring relationship between sections of the earth's crust that both want to have—or rather *go*—their own way. The Caribbean and Coco plates come together just off Costa Rica's coast, and the resulting clash produces pent-up geological energy that finds release in earthquakes and volcanic eruptions. Of the county's many volcanoes, at least five are still active. Watching truck-sized hot rocks tumble down Arenal Volcano's perfect cone is a sight not soon forgotten, but even the wisps of smoke issuing from Rincón de la Vieja are impressive reminders that the earth's surface is still very much a work in progress.

Earthquakes have also played their part in teaching Ticos to respect the "fire down below." The colonial capital of Cartago was destroyed by quakes in 1841 and again in 1910. More recently, in 1991 a 7.5 earthquake rocked the Caribbean and South-Central zones, destroying the San José–Limón railroad and countless roads and bridges. More gentle quakes are common, and geologists say the frequent tremors serve as relief valves to postpone the next really big one.

Volcanic peaks help make up the country's four major mountain ranges. In the north, the Cordillera de Guanacaste rises up in a series of peaks that includes Rincón de la Vieja, 1,895 meters (6,217 feet) high and the centerpiece of a national park of the same name. The Cordillera de Tilarán is dominated by Arenal Volcano, one of the most active in the world. Hemming in the Central Valley to the east is the Cordillera Central, which includes Poás, Irazú, Barva, and Turrialba Volcanoes. To the south of the valley surges the Cordillera Talamanca.

A GREEN REPUBLIC

The varied terrain makes for an amazing number of microclimates, each with its own complicated ecosystem. Incredibly, less than 20 percent of this biodiversity has been scientifically identified, making it all the more important to preserve the land until scientists can catch up with nature. Who knows if a cure for Alzheimer's or a solution to world hunger lies in the depths of the disappearing rainforest? The National Institute of Biodiversity (INBio), a joint public/private venture, is working hard to find out.

Costa Rica is devoted to protecting its own environment—more than 25 percent of national territory is set aside in parks and reserves. Still, there are serious challenges. The country doesn't have the money or human resources to enforce laws or patrol preserves. Poachers and lumber companies continue to chip away at the land ringing the protected areas, even making forays into national parks when they think they can get away with it. Another problem has been the government's inability to pay landowners for the territories expropriated for national parks. Sometimes these uncompensated landowners return to their land and continue farming, mining, or logging it.

Still, with all its problems, Costa Rica is teeming with life, and the country knows that it's this life that draws tourists. And since tourism is a huge business, there's yet another incentive to pass—and enforce—laws that protect the environment.

It's not only the land that boasts so many species; Costa Rica has 10 times as much protected territory underwater as it does on land, and is working hard to protect everything from its giant sea turtles to its shark populations, recently threatened by the practice of finning—removing fins for the Asian markets in which they are a delicacy, while leaving the rest of the mutilated shark to a watery grave.

On a happier note, the Tourism Institute has created a Bandera Azul (Blue Flag) program to recognize beach towns that commit to cleaning up their act. Program assessors not only look at whether there's trash on the beach,

THE MYSTERY OF THE SPHERES

In the southern Pacific region of Costa Rica are found perfectly spherical sculptures made of granite, andesite, and sedimentary stone. Some you can hold in your hand; others are up to 16 tons and 7 feet in diameter. These *bolas* are found nowhere else, and it has long been a mystery how these apparently ceremonial objects – found along riverbeds and in cemeteries – were transported up to 30 kilometers from the source of the stone to where those remaining now stand like sentinels to a lost world.

Theories abound and are all over the map. Erich von Daniken, in his *Chariots of the Gods,* proposes that they came from extraterrestrials; others have speculated that the spheres were shaped and polished at the base of thundering waterfalls, tumbling like ball bearings until smooth and perfectly round. Whatever their origin, they are now a symbol of Costa Rica and can be seen in parks, museums, and wealthy homes. Some can still be visited at their original sites, in places like Caño Island off the Osa Peninsula.

© HOUMAN PIRDAVARI

but also judge waste disposal, security issues, and environmental education efforts. More and more beaches, on both the Pacific and Caribbean coasts, are working to be green enough to fly the blue flag.

Local newspapers are filled with accounts of struggles to balance industries like fishing, mining, large-scale agriculture, and oil exploration with protection of the land. Some call Costa Rica hypocritical for billing itself a "green republic" while still allowing some exploitation of its natural resources, but it seems inevitable that there will be conflict and compromise along the road to balancing all the country's needs. Those who lament the sometimes slow progress and backsliding often take matters into their own hands, joining forces with national and international conservation organizations or even buying up land so developers won't be able to get their hands on it.

NATIONAL PARKS

The strength and importance of the National Conservation Area System (SINAC) is all the more impressive when you realize it began very recently—in the 1970s. And Costa Rica's 25 national parks are just the tip of the iceberg; there are also at least 135 reserves and refuges that seek to protect varied habitats and ecosystems for both present and future generations.

By far the most popular park is Manuel Antonio on the central Pacific coast, with its beaches bordered by wildlife-rich rainforest and its location only a few hours from San José. Also popular and even closer to the capital are Braulio Carrillo, a teeming, dripping forest that you can see via aerial tram if you'd rather not get your shoes muddy; and stunning Irazú Volcano, from which on a clear day you can see both coastlines. More effort is required to get to two other popular parks: the Caribbean coast's Tortuguero, with its canals, crocs, turtles, and teeming bird population; and Corcovado, on the lushly wild Osa Peninsula. After you've visited the big guns of the system, it's a pleasure to start exploring the lesser-known and less-visited reserves, where you might see no one on the path for hours or even days.

entrance to Tortuguero National Park

© ERIN VAN RHEENEN

One exciting development in the park system is the founding of international reserves. Parque Nacional la Amistad (Friendship Park) is a 622,000-hectare (1,537,000-acre) tract of remote forest that straddles the Costa Rica-Panama border. Up north, Sí-a-Paz (Yes to Peace) Park seeks to protect one of the last great stands of rainforest, shared by Costa Rica and Nicaragua. Extending even farther and involving more nations, the MesoAmerican Biological Corridor aims to create a protected passageway from Mexico all the way to Colombia. The isthmus once served as a land bridge for migrating species; the hope is that soon it will be able to serve that function once again.

GETTING AROUND

With all the wild and rugged corners of this country, you might imagine that to get anywhere you'd need several weeks and a pair of seven-league boots. Not so. Costa Rica is small enough that you can snorkel the Caribbean in the morning and surf the Pacific in the afternoon. And if you choose to fly instead of drive, puddle jumpers will speed you to places that used to require a full day (or two) of journeying. A 40-minute flight from San José puts you in Golfito (an eight-hour drive) for a day of sportfishing, then you can hop back up for a gourmet dinner in San José.

Those on a budget will appreciate the extensive network of buses that take you anywhere in the country for no more than US$12. Buses run often, they run on time, and most are at least as comfortable as the Greyhounds you've ridden back home.

Renting a car is another option. A four-wheel drive will be your best bet, so that you won't be denied if a highway suddenly peters out into rutted track. It's exhilarating to stop at nothing—not even a river—to get where you want to go. For those accustomed to glassy-smooth interstates, Costa Rica's roads will come as a shock, but soon enough you'll be four-wheeling with the best of them. Getting back on an easy track even starts to be somewhat of a disappointment, like eating a hot dog after you've been chewing on a char-grilled steak.

Oh, and getting to Costa Rica is easy. You don't need a visa—just a valid passport. Airfares from the United States and Canada are quite reasonable (typically US$400–700, depending on your departure city) and sometimes downright cheap. At the airport you'll get a stamp on your passport saying you have up to 90 days in the country. And if you have no interest in San José, international flights now speed you to Liberia, only half an hour from some of the best beaches in Guanacaste.

Social Climate

"Stay a week and you think you know a country," goes the old adage. "Stay a year and you know you never will." When you first arrive in Costa Rica, you may be struck by how similar it is to the United States, especially in and around the capital city of San José. You'll see the same fast-food franchises, like McDonald's and KFC; the same stores, from Foot Locker to Office Max; and the same products in U.S.-style supermarkets, even Häagen-Dazs ice cream and Celestial Seasonings teas. Food labels are almost always in Spanish and English, and at ATMs you can opt for instructions in English.

When there's a problem here, people dial 911, just like in the States. On TV, many programs and even commercials are in English. In U.S.-style multiplex theaters in U.S.-style malls, you'll see trailers for the latest Hollywood movies as you munch on overpriced hot dogs and popcorn. And just like back home, you can drink the water—probably one of the most profound differences between Costa Rica and its Latin American neighbors. Somehow that small fact looms large, and is one of the many reasons North Americans feel comfortable here.

Stay a little longer and you start to notice the differences. "The idea that we're all the same is a myth," opines Joy Rothke, a freelance writer who moved to La Fortuna in 2002. "Sure, there may be superficial commonalities, but deep down, Costa Rican culture is very, very different from U.S. culture." This is doubly true for towns outside of the populous Central Valley.

STANDARD OF LIVING

Newcomers to Costa Rica are often surprised that the country doesn't have that third-world, shanty-town look that they were expecting of a Central American "banana republic." Indeed, Costa Rica is a relatively well-off nation that takes care of its own much better than many more developed countries. Everyone here has access to decent health care and education, which makes for infant mortality rates up there with Canada and the United States, and literacy rates that rival those of Europe. People look healthy, and even those with little money take care to dress in clean, new-looking clothes. If you see someone with holes in his jeans, he's almost certainly a tourist, affecting a down-and-out look while no doubt having more money in his pocket than the smartly dressed locals.

Life here is not dirt cheap, but it's a lot less expensive than living in the United States or Canada—from 30 to 50 percent cheaper, depending on your

WHAT'S A TICO?

Costa Ricans love nicknames; they even have one that covers the entire population of their country. They call themselves Ticos, after the local habit of adding the diminutive to as many words as possible. While other Spanish speakers are likely to add "ito" to make a word like *chico* (small) even smaller (*chiquito*), Costa Ricans would say *chiquitico*. "*Ya voy en un minutico*," is Tico for "I'll be there in a tiny little minute." Of course, another Tico habit is lateness, so that tiny little minute may be closer to a big fat hour.

lifestyle. A couple can live frugally but not without a few frills for US$1,500 a month. Travel within this small but wondrously varied country could be one of those frills, since buses are a bargain, and there are plenty of reasonably priced beachfront or mountaintop hotels.

Real estate is affordable, much more so if you stay away from the hottest markets, like well-known beach towns or upscale suburbs of San José. Many of the local financial institutions that were paying out astronomical interest rates to expats have recently gone belly up, bad news for investors but good news for those looking for a reasonably priced house or lot.

POLITICAL AND ECONOMIC STABILITY

Costa Rica enjoys one of the most stable democratic governments in all of Latin America and an economy that has long attracted foreign investors. Multinational corporations with branches in Costa Rica include Intel, Johnson and Johnson, Colgate-Palmolive, Monsanto, and Pfizer. All the baseballs used in the Major Leagues are sewn by hand in one small Costa Rican town called Turrialba, and even Wonderbras are assembled here. The United States is Costa Rica's most important trade partner, and the government here offers generous incentives to foreign businesses, including tax breaks and exemptions from some export tariffs. Big and small companies come to Costa Rica because of the solid telecommunications network, a very educated workforce, and a high standard of living.

It's easy for a foreigner to start a business here—you can do it even if you only have a tourist visa. Many expats work successfully in the burgeoning tourist sector, starting restaurants, hotels, and tour companies. Many say that although there are of course regulations to learn about and follow, in general there exist fewer constraints on businesses here than in their home countries.

UNIVERSAL HEALTH CARE

In 2007 an estimated 47 million U.S. citizens were without health insurance, and the number seems to be increasing every year. Costa Rica has made a commitment to provide health care to all of its residents, and even visitors can take advantage of the high-quality, low-cost care. For a small monthly fee (under US$100), residents can be a part of the public system that includes everything from drugs to dentistry, as well as care in public clinics and hospitals. For a little more each month, anyone (not just residents) can sign on with the INS, the state insurance provider—this route lets you choose your own doctor. International policies like Blue Cross/ Blue Shield are accepted at the excellent private hospitals and clinics. If you have no insurance and don't want to join up with the public system, you can pay out-of-pocket and still spend a third less than you would in the United States.

And if you're cringing, thinking of third-world hospitals with poor hygiene and badly trained staff, think again. The University of Costa Rica has one of the most respected medical schools in all of Central America and the Caribbean, and many doctors do further study in Europe, Canada, or the United States. Hospitals often have up-to-date equipment, like Hospital CIMA's open MRI, the only one in Central America. Confidence in the system is expressed by the number of people who come to Costa Rica just to have surgery, whether a facelift or a triple bypass.

AWARD-WINNING FRIENDLINESS

It's long been agreed that Costa Ricans are exceptionally friendly, but a few years ago science confirmed that impression. A study published in *American Scientist* revealed that, of 23 cities worldwide, San José ranked number two in Latin America in terms of friendliness (Rio de Janeiro came in first). The six-year study measured "simple acts of kindness," ranging from whether passersby returned a dropped pen to whether a blind man got help crossing a street. The Costa Rican capital received consistently high marks in every category. Robert Levine, the head of the study, commented that the cities with the friendliest inhabitants were ones where the pace of life was slower, and where the culture emphasized the value of social harmony.

And if San José qualifies as one of the friendliest cities in the world, then outside of the urban area, where life is slower, people are even friendlier. In small towns, everyone greets everyone else on the street, and citizens pitch in when their neighbors need help. Need to get to a bigger town? Start walking and you'll almost certainly get offered a ride. Need someone to look after your kids? Small-town folks routinely and casually trade child-care duties. If your car gets stuck in the mud, before you know it you'll have half a dozen people there to help you push it out. And the more generous you are, the more it comes back to you. Social scientists would call it reciprocity. Whatever you call it, it makes Costa Rica a very nice place to live.

WHY PEOPLE COME TO COSTA RICA

More and more North Americans are looking for a place to start a new life—whether it's for retirement, a career change, or plying one's current profession in a new market. Millions are choosing to live abroad, with many drawn to the physical beauty and lower prices of places like Costa Rica.

Many North American workers have been "made redundant" by ongoing corporate efforts to reduce operating costs. Other workers retain jobs that they feel are sucking the life out of them, and they dream of a time when they can get back in touch with themselves and with simple pleasures. Many fantasize about a place where the living is cheaper and the pace more humane. Parents of young children may long for an environment where kids can be immersed in another language and culture, one that emphasizes basic human values over relentless accomplishment and acquisition.

And for those approaching retirement age (or already there), places like Costa Rica are looking better and better. Persons over 65 make up one of the fastest-growing segments of the U.S. population, and many hit retirement with modest pensions and little savings. For those on a budget Costa Rica is a place to live well for less.

Of course Costa Rica is no paradise, and in fact may be a victim of its own popularity. Tourism has mushroomed into an industry sometimes at odds with environmental protection. The influx of foreign visitors and residents can strain basic infrastructure in this country with a population of about four million. "We weren't ready for all of you," laughs Anabelle Furtado, a Costa Rica native who works for the Association of Residents of Costa Rica (ARCR). Economic hard times have meant cuts in previously flush social services, and locals complain that foreigners, with their easy spending habits, drive up prices on everything from pineapples to a four-bedroom house. And as in most countries of the world, crime and other social ills are on the rise.

Still, the benefits outweigh the problems. Costa Rica has an immensely appealing combination of the exotic and the familiar. It's a far-off land less than three hours by air from Miami, an international destination with a decidedly local feel, a sophisticated place where life is still fueled by basic human warmth.

HISTORY, GOVERNMENT, AND ECONOMY

For nearly a century Costa Rica has been an island of stability in an often turbulent sea. Though the country has much in common with its Central American neighbors, the differences are perhaps even more striking. Costa Rica has an enviable political and economic climate, a high standard of living, and a commitment to peace underlined by the abolition of its army.

Travel further back in time and we see a pre-Columbian crossroads where cultures from the south and the north met and merged. Fast forward a few centuries and we find ourselves in one of the poorest backwaters of the opulent and cruel Spanish colonial empire—a territory that, ironically, became the most prosperous of Central American nations.

One of modern-day Costa Rica's big drawing points is its political stability. Since 1948 power has changed hands peacefully and democratically. Ticos elect a new president every four years, just as in the United States, and Costa Rica has a similar system of checks and balances, composed of the executive, judicial, and legislative branches of government. The economy is

© ERIN VAN RHEENEN

steady and strong enough to attract a host of multinational corporations—from Abbott Labs to Intel. This stability and the fact that Costa Rica works in ways familiar to North Americans makes it an attractive place for expats to live and do business.

History

Tens of thousands of years ago, early settlers in what is now Costa Rica hunted mastodon and giant sloth, tracking their prey through dripping tropical forests. Between 8000 and 4000 B.C., these nomadic bands learned to domesticate plants, and around the start of the Christian era, they made the transition to farming. Sedentary life brought on a more complex social hierarchy and division of labor. Instead of making only tools for hunting, like stone spearheads and knives, people began creating farming implements and vessels to cook and store their food.

Located on an isthmus between two great continents, Costa Rica was a meeting place for cultures from the south and the north. From South America came yucca, sweet potatoes, coca leaves for chewing, and Andean gold-working techniques. Tribes from the southern forests and Caribbean coast of Costa Rica traded with the peoples of Panama, Colombia, and Ecuador. Other parts of the country—especially the Gran Nicoya, located in what is now Guanacaste—were more influenced by Mesoamerican cultures to the north. From Mesoamerica came corn, beans, jade, hieroglyphic books, the practice of filing teeth to points, and certain pottery styles still in use today.

There were cultural and linguistic differences among the many indigenous groups, but the tribes also had a lot in common. Most were matrilineal, and some—including the Chibchas and the Diquis—are said to have been matriarchal. Religious beliefs pivoted on the conviction that not only animals and plants were alive but that even natural phenomena like rivers and stones were animate and possessed their own spirit. Funeral rites implied a belief in an afterlife—ritual objects and even slaves were buried with the bodies of powerful women and men.

Tribes congregated in large and small settlements, and the village was, according to Molina and Palmer in *The History of Costa Rica,* "the axis of everyday life, which was taken up by agriculture, crafts, commerce, and war." Tribes and villages banded together to form *cacigazcos* (chiefdoms), and *cacigazcos* might unify into larger political and military alliances called *señoríos.*

In the Pacific Northwest of what's now Costa Rica, the *cacigazcos* of the Gran Nicoya, influenced by Maya, Aztec, and Olmec culture, practiced human sacrifice and cannibalism. Three times a year, on dates coinciding with the corn harvest, the nobility dressed in their finery, drank *chicha* (corn liquor), and presided over the ritual murder of five or six preselected women and men. These chosen few had their hearts cut out, their heads chopped off, and their bodies rolled down the side of the temple—to later be eaten as the most sacred of food.

War was widespread and was waged for a variety of reasons: to expand or defend territory, to gain access to trade routes, or to take prisoners for slave labor or, in the case of women of childbearing age, to serve as breeders. In some areas, like the Diqui region in southern Costa Rica, both men and women went into battle together.

Remnants of the Past

The National Museum estimates that in Costa Rica today, there are at least 2,000 archaeological sites, most of which are still buried in deep forest or under mounds of earth. The region that was the Gran Nicoya, now in Guanacaste, has the most sites, but the most accessible and fully excavated site is Guayabo, now a national monument. Located on the southern flank of Turrialba Volcano in the Central Valley, Guayabo shows us the remains of a settlement at its height between 1000 B.C. and A.D. 1400, when an estimated 10,000 people lived in its conical structures and walked its cobblestoned streets. An aqueduct system built more than 2,000 years ago still functions today.

Other sites take more effort to find and visit. Until Costa Rica can devote time and expertise to more excavations, locals will probably continue to stumble upon old stone roads and pre-Columbian artifacts half-buried in cattle pastures or strewn along centuries-old jungle paths.

One type of relic that is *puro Tico* (purely Costa Rican) is the *bola*, stone spheres found mostly in the southern part of the country near the Valley of Diquis. Researchers still can't say for sure how they were made or what their function was, but some of these strangely moving

pre-Columbian ruins at Guayabo National Monument

© ERIN VAN RHEENEN

sculptures measure more than two meters across and weigh several tons. There are a few at the Museo Nacional, which may whet your appetite to see others in their original context, like the ones on Caño Island off the Osa Peninsula. Since the spheres are found nowhere else in the world, they have become a symbol for Costa Rica, and you'll see the *bola* motif worked into the architecture of government buildings and upscale homes.

Indigenous Culture Today

For years it was thought that as few as 30,000 people were living in Costa Rica when the Spaniards arrived. This figure supported the myth that the country has little indigenous heritage, but more recent scholarship puts the number at between 400,000 and 500,000.

The half million people here when Columbus landed in 1502 were reduced to 120,000 by 1569 and whittled down to 10,000 by 1611, mostly due to infectious diseases brought by the Spaniards. The 2000 census counted 63,876 indigenous persons, but one of the few books on indigenous Costa Rican culture by indigenous authors, *Taking Care of Sibö's Gifts,* by Paula Palmer, Juanita Sánchez, and Gloria Mayorga, says that fewer than 25,000 people here "retain a cultural identity as indigenous people." Whatever the true figure, native peoples make up only about 1 percent of the national population. Many live on one of 22 reserves, which collectively make up about 6 percent of national territory.

Quite a decline, to be sure. But some aspects of indigenous culture have survived since the arrival of Europeans, and other features are being revived. The largest tribes are the Cabécar and the Bribrí, concentrated on the Caribbean coast and in the Talamanca mountains. Both groups actively work to maintain and revive their language and customs, as well as adapt tourism to their own needs, allowing a few visitors onto their reserves for cultural and natural history tours. When I took a tour of the Kèköldi Reserve (within which Cabécares and Bribrí live), a native guide walked us through mud and heavy brush to a spectacular waterfall deep within the reserve, stopping along the way to point out trees and vines traditionally used for medicinal purposes.

In the 1970s, legislatures passed the Ley Indígena (the Indigenous Law), establishing autonomous governing structures within the existing indigenous reserves. During the same period, CONAI (the National Commission for Indian Affairs) was established, but indigenous people felt it did not represent them and so created their own organization in 1981, the Pablo Preserve Indigenous Association. Members of both organizations work to forge alliances between various indigenous groups within Costa Rica and to reach out to similar groups throughout the Americas. They also try to maintain the reserves, which are

WHITE PEOPLE ARE LEAF-CUTTER ANTS

In the book *Taking Care of Sibö's Gifts*, coauthor Gloria Mayorga, of the Kèköldi Indigenous Reserve on Costa Rica's Caribbean coast, writes of the mythic origin of white people:

The origin of white people is the King of Leaf-Cutter Ants. Just look at the leaf-cutter ants, how they all work together cleaning and clearing the land around their nests. Where the leaf-cutter ants live, all the vegetation is gone because they cut every last leaf and take them back to their big nests. That's how the white man is. He works very hard, but he destroys nature. He chops down all the trees to make his cities, and where he lives all the vegetation is gone. There is nothing there. The white man cuts down everything that is green, and where he lives there are no trees, no rivers, no animals. He destroys everything in his path.

threatened on all sides: by mining and lumber companies, hydroelectric projects, tourism, and nonindigenous peasants who want land to farm. The government still holds deed to all reserves and has been known to cut deals with outside companies at the expense of indigenous land and autonomy.

Besides trying to revive their customs, indigenous groups are also looking to their economic future. In 1995, for example, the Cabécares and Bribrí created their own bank, the Banco Indígena de Talamanca, which they say is "neither a private nor state bank. It is a bank of and for Indians."

In Costa Rica today there are at least seven indigenous cultures (Bribrí, Cabécar, Guaymi, Térraba, Malecu, Huetar, and Chorotega) speaking six languages.

Afro-Costa Ricans in History

A small number of people of African descent were brought to Costa Rica as slaves shortly after the Spanish conquest of the territory, but it wasn't until around 1870 that the black community in Costa Rica began to grow by leaps and bounds. At that time a large number of Jamaicans (and smaller numbers of other Caribbean islanders) were hired to build the Atlantic railroad, which has since fallen into disuse.

Migrations continued into the 20th century and included Jamaican Marcus Garvey, who arrived in 1910 and worked briefly on the United Fruit Company's banana plantations in Limón. Garvey would later found the Black Star Line and become an international icon in the movement for black nationalism and self-reliance (known in the 1920s as the "back to Africa" movement).

The Black Star Line was an all-black steamship company that transported cargo and passengers between Costa Rica, Jamaica, Panama, Haiti, Cuba, and the United States. The Costa Rican headquarters was in Puerto Limón, and the Black Star Line building there did double duty as Costa Rica's branch of Garvey's Universal Negro Improvement Association (UNIA).

Garvey's stay on Costa Rican soil was short but memorable. It was while working on Limón plantations that he was reinforced in his belief that black people were victims of prejudice on a worldwide scale. Garvey encouraged workers here to form unions and start newspapers, to make public the struggles of workers in general and black workers in particular. Within a year of his arrival, Garvey was expelled from Costa Rica. Some accounts say it was for harassing the British Consul, while others maintain it was his activism that got him ousted.

The Black Star Line building still stands and is a now one of Limón's most important cultural centers, the venue for many of the events that culminate in Black Culture Day every August 31.

Puerto Limón is the city with the highest Afro-Costa Rican population, which is estimated to be about 35 to 40 percent. In the province of Limón, the figure is around 15 percent, while nationwide the black population is given at anywhere from 2 to 5 percent.

THE COLONIAL ERA

On his fourth and final trip to the New World, Cristóbal Colón (Christopher Columbus to English speakers) landed in September 1502 at what is now Puerto Limón on Costa Rica's Caribbean coast. His four ships had been damaged by storms, and his crew of 135—a third of whom were young men between 13 and 18—badly needed a break.

The indigenous people of the area welcomed the new arrivals, swimming out to the ships with gifts of finely woven cloth and pendants made of tumbago, an alloy of copper and gold. These necklaces, among other finds, convinced arriving Europeans that the area was rich in mineral deposits, and later the region was christened Costa Rica, or Rich Coast.

In fact, Costa Rica turned out to be one of Spain's poorest colonies, and this lack of wealth made it a backwater of the empire for the next several hundred years. Thick forests, impassable mountains, and raging rivers didn't help matters. Settlers had a rough time of it, and they often lived like the "savages" they had come to conquer, dressing in clothing made of pounded bark, employing native farming methods, and using cacao beans as money when the paper bills and metal coins ran out.

Early Settlements

Sixty years after Columbus's arrival, Juan de Cavallón founded what was to become the first permanent settlement in Costa Rica, christened Garcimuñoz in 1561 and located in what is now the Río Oro de Santa Ana region of the Central Valley. Towns had been founded earlier on both coasts, but most didn't last long, as settlers battled harsh conditions, lack of supplies, infighting among the townspeople, and attacks from pirates and what were then called *indios bravos* (wild Indians). Garcimuñoz was moved and renamed several times, until it ended as Cartago, which would become the colonial capital.

In *The Ticos,* coauthors Mavis, Richard, and Karen Biesanz characterize Spanish Costa Rica as "the Cinderella of Spanish colonies, [which was] taxed, scolded, ignored, and kept miserably poor. An isolated and neglected province of the captaincy general of Guatemala, it was unable to raise enough revenue to pay its own administrative expenses. Its clergy was subordinate to the bishop of León in Nicaragua, who rarely visited."

In addition, the colonial practice of *encomienda,* in which European invaders

WILLIAM WALKER AND JUAN SANTAMARÍA

An egomaniacal mercenary from Nashville, Tennessee, ended up playing an unexpectedly large role in the formation of Costa Rican national identity. The man's name was William Walker, and he dreamed of ruling over a Central American empire that would be a fresh source of slaves for the United States.

As crazy as the idea sounds, Walker had an army and the backing of several U.S. industrialists, and he had some success, first taking Nicaragua and then invading Costa Rica. The year was 1856, not far into the first decades of a fledgling nation in which people still felt more identified with their city or region than their country. Cutting across these regional identities, President Juan Rafael Mora called together a ragtag army to drive Walker's forces from the northern province of Guanacaste.

The Costa Rican army, some of them armed with little more than farming tools, chased Walker into Nicaragua, where, at the town of Rivas, a young soldier, Juan Santamaría, set fire to Walker's barracks before collapsing under a hail of bullets. Costa Rica thus reclaimed its territory and also got its first national hero, who now has his own holiday, celebrated most fervently in Santamaría's hometown of Alajuela. Santamaría's nickname was El Erizo, "The Hedgehog," for his thick hair that stood straight up.

were granted land that didn't belong to them and allowed to extract labor or tribute from the true owners (indigenous people), never really took hold in Costa Rica, in part because the indigenous peoples either died from disease, headed for the hills, or offered up armed resistance to the idea that they should become slaves on their own land.

So instead of the vast *encomiendas* found elsewhere in Central America, in Costa Rica small, family-owned farms were more the norm, and even governors were said to work their own land. This was less true in Guanacaste, where enormous cattle ranches were worked by not only indigenous but also black slaves. Guanacaste was part of the richer colony of Nicaragua until just after both countries declared independence from Spain, when it chose to ally itself with poor but peaceful Costa Rica over wealthy but war-torn Nicaragua.

Many historians believe that Costa Rica's poverty during the colonial era actually helped to lay the foundation for a democratic nation of equals, where all struggled just to survive and where class differences were not as pronounced as elsewhere.

INDEPENDENCE AND EARLY NATIONHOOD

When in September 1821 the captaincy general of Guatemala declared independence from Spain, Costa Rica didn't receive word until a month later. The news sparked confusion in a land that was less a nation than a loose collection of rival city-states. Some Costa Ricans wanted to become part of the powerful Mexican Empire, while others wanted to help create a federation of newly free Central American states. Still others suggested that Costa Rica become part of Colombia, which then included present-day Panama and was ruled by the "Great Liberator," Simón Bolívar.

The four most powerful Costa Rican cities—San José, Cartago, Alajuela, and Heredia—all had different plans for newly liberated Costa Rica, and they backed up their ideas with guns. A side issue was which of the cities should be the capital; for a while the honor was rotated among the cities, and then a battle decided the issue in San José's favor.

Those who wanted Costa Rica to become a state in the Central American Federation won out, but a few decades later, when it was obvious the experiment had failed, the country became its own republic in 1848.

The first head of state after independence was Juan Mora Fernándes, who founded the country's first newspaper, expanded public education, and established a judicial system. Braulio Carrillo, remembered as a heavy-handed dictator who nonetheless fostered national unity, ruled from 1835 to 1842; he presided over Costa Rica's withdrawal from the federation of Central American states and its emergence as an independent country. Carrillo is also known for planting the seeds of the nation's coffee economy—he offered free land to those who would reap and sow the glossy-leafed crop.

The 1880s brought a succession of liberal governments that made far-reaching and lasting changes, most involving the separation of church and state. Presidents during this period secularized schools, making primary and secondary education free and obligatory; shut down the church-run University of Santo Tomás; and expelled the Jesuits and one Catholic bishop. They also allowed for civil marriage and divorce, secularized the cemeteries, and abolished the death penalty.

A PIVOTAL DECADE

During the volatile 1940s, two larger-than-life political figures fought each other for power, war was declared on Nazi Germany, and Costa Rica suffered through its own 40-day civil war. The constitution drafted after that battle (in 1949) provided the basis for what was seen at the time as a new nation.

The decade began with the election of Rafael Ángel Calderón Guardia, who gave workers' rights a huge boost with reforms such as a guaranteed minimum wage, unemployment compensation, and paid vacations. Calderón's administration was responsible for the Labor Code of 1943, a lengthy series of constitutional amendments that is still in effect today.

During Calderón's tenure the country declared war on Nazi Germany, just one day before the United States did the same. Germans in Costa Rica lost their property and were sent to internment camps, many located in the United States.

When Calderón lost the 1948 elections, his government cried fraud; the resulting conflict erupted into a battle that killed 2,000 people, most of them civilians. Jose María ("Don Pepe") Figueres Ferrer and his National Liberation Party emerged victorious, and Don Pepe became head of the Founding Junta of the Second Republic of Costa Rica, pushing through reforms such as nationalizing banks and insurance companies, abolishing the army, and finally giving blacks and women full citizenship, including the right to vote.

THE MODERN ERA

Don Pepe's National Liberation Party (Partido de Liberación Nacional, or PLN) ruled Costa Rica from the late 1940s to the late 1970s, consolidating the reforms of its early days and building an even larger bureaucracy to promote social justice through a welfare state. A growing middle class began to undercut

WHERE PEOPLE COME TO DISAPPEAR

Costa Rica gained independence from Spain in 1821. For the next two decades, four rival cities — San José, Alajuela, Heredia, and Cartago — vied for the privilege and power of being the new country's capital city. Sometimes the three Central Valley cities fought together against Cartago, which had the historical claim, having been the colony's administrative center, with responsibilities that included conducting a census of the country's inhabitants. San José had the nation's first mint, where the first truly Costa Rican coins were produced, and was the center of most trade. San José was also where coffee, which almost immediately began to play a large role in the country's economy, was first planted in 1830. The "golden bean" was first exported to Chile and then shipped around the Horn to an ever-growing market in Britain.

The four cities battled for primacy, and one battle, between Cartago and forces from San José, Alajuela, and Heredia, demonstrated that from its very beginnings Costa Rican history has been shaped by it being a place where people come to disappear.

"Even before independence," says Dr. Arturo Condo, professor and dean at INCAE business school, "with Costa Rica at the southernmost border of the Guatemala captaincy" (the Spanish colonial jurisdiction to which Costa Rica belonged), "it drew outlaws who wanted to be as far as possible from the Spanish authorities" — people who wanted to fall off the edge of the map. "Their agenda was to not be noticed."

These aren't the kind of people who would let the Cartago-based census takers find them. The battle of Ochomogo, in which Cartago fought the other three cities, was much shorter than expected. When Cartago marched to the battle, in a field halfway between San José and Cartago, the Cartago forces were surprised by the number of people coming from the valley.

"They should have known," points out Dr. Condo. "The census was one of the only things they did at that time. That, and taxes. So they should have known how many people would be fighting against them, but they didn't have a clue. That's because so many people came here and didn't register, didn't want to be noticed."

San José won the fight to become the capital, and people still come to Costa Rica to fall off the edge of the map.

the power of the traditional elite, such as coffee barons, even as the government worked to attract foreign capital to help industrialize the country.

In the late 1970s and the early 1980s, the bill for big government came due, and at a time of worldwide economic crisis. In 1981, Costa Rica was forced to suspend debt payment to its creditors and had to ask for help from lenders like the World Bank and the International Monetary Fund (IMF). Costa Rica got its loans, but at a price: The country had to promise to cut government spending and begin to privatize its economy.

This puzzle—of how to maintain the best parts of the welfare state while still cutting costs and moving toward privatization—is still being pieced together today.

Government

The Costa Rican constitution of 1949 guarantees a host of rights for residents and foreigners alike. These rights include freedom of speech, press, and assembly, all of which are exercised on a daily basis and underline Costa Rica's enviable place among its neighbors. Unlike many other Latin American nations, Costa Rica has no standing army, no guerrillas, and no political prisoners. For more than half a century, power has changed hands peacefully.

The voting age is 18, and the country is a democratic republic that elects a new president every four years. Though the presidency is a powerful position, the constitution guards against concentration of power in any one of the three branches of government: executive, legislative, and judicial.

EXECUTIVE BRANCH   PRESIDENTE

The president coordinates government programs, commands the police, and directs national and international policy. He or she exerts considerable power through ties to all manner of ministries, but must also answer to the party that sponsored his or her candidacy, to labor unions, and to public opinion. There also are two vice presidents and a 15-member cabinet that includes one of the vice presidents.

Since 1969 presidents had been limited to one four-year term, but in 2003 the Costa Rican high court brought the law back in line with the 1949 constitution, which states that ex-presidents may run for reelection after they have been out of office for two presidential terms (eight years). Many former presidents had been waiting for just such a development, and in 2006 Nobel Peace Prize winner Oscar Arias Sánchez, president from 1986 to 1990, was elected once again.

LEGISLATURE

Fifty-seven elected *diputados* (deputies) serve four-year terms in the Asamblea Legislativa (Legislative Assembly); they can seek reelection after a term spent out of office. The legislature makes, amends, and repeals laws, and imposes taxes. It also has some say on budget issues, including foreign loans negotiated by the president, which it must ratify by a two-thirds majority. Deputies may run for reelection after sitting out one four-year term.

JUDICIAL SYSTEM

"Costa Rica has the best judicial system in the region," says Dr. Arturo Condo, professor and dean of INCAE, a business school with campuses in Costa Rica and Nicaragua. "A trial here doesn't depend on bribing the judge or what political party you belong to."

The legislature chooses the Supreme Court's 22 magistrates, who serve for eight years and then, usually, renew their term. The Supreme Court in turn appoints judges for civil and penal courts. The Supreme Court itself oversees electoral issues, from the functioning of political parties to the actual counting of votes. A recent poll showed that Ticos, more and more cynical about politicians, still hold the Supreme Court in high regard.

BIG GOVERNMENT

There's no denying that Costa Rica has opted for big government. It's estimated that 90 percent of public expenditures go to paying the salaries of public employees. Besides the three branches discussed above, autonomous institutions like ICE, the state electricity monopoly, exert influence over national policy and everyday life. Along with ICE (pronounced EE-say), the Caja (Social Security) and RECOPE, the state oil agency, are important players on this field.

Government not only controls utilities and a large part of health care, it also has monopolies on liquor production and insurance and majority interests in banking and tourism. Both Ticos and foreign residents complain of the inefficiency of the bureaucracy. Often an agency's budget goes almost

© HOUMAN PIRDAVARI

state workers on strike

entirely to salaries and operating expenses rather than to the purpose—say, alleviating poverty—for which the agency was created.

Sometimes it's all but impossible to know which institution does what, and people who enter the system (to obtain residency, for example) can be shunted from one office to the next. The authors of *The Ticos* acknowledge that "the public sector includes such a bewildering maze of agencies that it is often difficult to know who is responsible for making what decisions—and who actually does make them. And therefore, it is easier to understand why some decisions are slow to be made and why many others are made only symbolically, if at all."

Political Parties and Elections

Political parties and electoral process may seem to many people about as interesting as reruns of school board meetings on late-night cable. But a look at the differences between the Costa Rican and U.S. systems provides an interesting lesson in what might make people more likely to participate in the political process.

Although the basic outlines of electoral politics in Costa Rica and the United States look similar, some differing details mean that smaller, "third" parties thrive in one system while languishing in the other. Part of the political apathy in places like the United States comes from the belief that we have very few choices, and that the dominant parties seem to be coming to resemble each other more and more, like an old married couple.

The relative political diversity in Costa Rica may explain why people seem more politically engaged here than in the United States. Jacqueline Passey, a self-described "election nerd" who covered the 2006 Costa Rican elections on her blog, noted that:

> Voter turnout was predicted to be much lower than usual due to voter apathy over dissatisfaction with their candidate choices and the apparent inevitability of Oscar Arias's victory. But after what I saw today I have to say that if this is their idea of "apathy," I'd be scared to see them when they're enthusiastic!!! It was totally crazy. Hundreds, perhaps thousands, of people were gathered in the park [Parque Central, in San José] and on the sides of the street, and hundreds more in cars were driving slowly by to show off their party flags and the loudness of their horns. There were also several makeshift floats, drummers, and other performers.

THE BASICS

In Costa Rica, third, fourth, and even fiftieth parties seem to have a good shot at being part of the governing structure of this country of four million. Including the local parties that field candidates for local city councils (municipalities), there are about 50 political parties here.

There are 449 electoral districts in seven regions (which correspond to the seven provinces). Though the president is elected through a national popular vote, the 57 seats in the National Assembly are elected by proportional representation. Seats are allocated to districts by population: San José has 20, Alajuela has 11, Cartago has 7, Heredia has 5, Limón has 5, Puntarenas has 5, and Guanacaste has 4.

WHY PROPORTIONAL REPRESENTATION MATTERS

Proportional representation in Costa Rica means that instead of voting for individual *diputados* (deputies) to represent them in the National Assembly, people vote for a party list. The assembly seats are allocated to the parties according to what percentage of the vote each party wins. If a party wins enough of the vote to garner two seats, it will send the first two candidates on its list to the assembly.

In 2006 the Partido Movimiento Libertario (Libertarian Party), for instance, won 9.17 percent of the popular vote, which translated into 6 seats in the 57-seat National Assembly.

Historically, the two largest and most powerful parties have been the National Liberation Party (Partido de Liberación Nacional, or PLN) and the Social Christian Unity Party (Partido de Social Cristiana, or PUSC). The PLN was founded in the middle of the last century by "Don Pepe" Figueres,

ETHNIC MAKEUP OF COSTA RICA

ETHNIC GROUP	% OF POPULATION	NUMBER
Indigenous	1.68	63,876
Black	1.91	72,784
Chinese	0.21	7,873
Other *(mestizo)*	93.66	3,568,471
Unknown	2.55	97,175

– from 2000 census

who in 1948 dissolved Costa Rica's army, expanded social welfare programs, gave women the vote, and nationalized banks, A coalition of parties opposing the PLN has been around for a long time and became the PUSC in the 1980s. The current president, Oscar Arias, is a PLN member, and the former president, Abel Pacheco, was with PUSC.

But political winds shift often, and in the 2006 presidential election, though the internationally known Oscar Arias was expected to win by a landslide, Ottón Solís of the Citizens' Action Party (Partido Acción Ciudadana, or PAC) almost beat him.

POLITICAL DIVERSITY AND GENDER AND RACIAL EQUALITY

There are many powerful "third" parties in Costa Rican politics, and proportional representation appears to allow for a greater political diversity, especially in the powerful National Assembly, which is roughly equivalent to the U.S. House of Representatives. The 2006 elections in Costa Rica saw the country's National Assembly peopled with politicians from eight parties, and many more parties received votes but not enough to earn them a seat. In this system people don't think they're "wasting" their vote on nondominant parties, because nondominant parties have a better chance of winning seats.

While the National Assembly can boast of a diversity of political parties, it doesn't have much to be proud of in terms of racial diversity. Not one of the deputies elected for the 2006–2010 term was Afro-Costa Rican (there were three Afro-Costa Ricans in the previous four-year term), and none were of indigenous heritage. There was a first in the 2006 election, however: Epsy Campbell, a black woman, was the vice presidential candidate for the Citizens' Action Party (PAC). Afro-Costa Ricans make up about 2 percent of the total population of Costa Rica, while indigenous peoples make up a little less.

Women have fared better, mostly because of a 1996 electoral reform requiring that political parties have at least 40 percent women on their election roster (though the women tend to be relegated to the bottom of the list, which means that they don't always win seats in the assembly even if their party wins; see the discussion of proportional representation). One of President Oscar Arias's two vice presidents is Laura Chinchilla. And in 2006, 22 of the 57 (or 38.6 percent) of the seats in the Costa Rican National Assembly went to women, a figure that makes Costa Rica number one in Latin America and third in the world in terms of women's participation in national politics. Number one in the world in 2006 was Rwanda, with 48.8 percent female participation in national politics, mostly because political violence had all but decimated that country's male population. For that same year, only 15.2 percent of legislators in the U.S. Congress were women. Odd that a so-called *machista* society like Costa Rica has so much more female participation in politics than a nation that boasts of equal opportunity for all.

It's just these seeming "anomalies" that get expats thinking about the world they live in and the assumptions they've made about it. And for that reason alone—that the experience opens your mind to other, often better ways of doing things—living abroad makes you a better international citizen. And if and when you go back to your home country, you may find yourself a lot more political and informed (even about your own country) than you were when you left.

Economy

COFFEE, BANANAS, AND BEEF CATTLE

Costa Rica will forever be associated in the world's imagination with both the *grano de oro* (golden grain, a.k.a. the coffee bean), which wakes up half the world every morning, and the yellow fruit that became synonymous with Central American backwaters ("banana republics"). Historically the country's primary exports have been agricultural, principally coffee—so well-suited to the rich volcanic soil and mild climate of the Central Valley—and bananas, which thrive in the wet coastal lowlands. Of the two crops, coffee is perhaps most tied up with the national identity, but bananas are more lucrative. After Ecuador, Costa Rica is the second-largest banana exporter in the world. Pineapples are another important crop.

Though farming is still vitally important, the country's economy is now much more diversified. Cattle ranching began in the early colonial period, and in the 1960s many more Ticos invested in beef cattle. By 1975, there were almost as many cows as people in Costa Rica. These "locusts with hooves" have not been kind to the environment or the economy. Demand for beef waned in the 1980s—fast-food chains up north were ordering less as North Americans became more health conscious. Forest converted to pasture causes drought in many regions (like Guanacaste), and ranching puts people out of work—it takes fewer people to work a herd then to work fields planted in crops. But, as Mavis, Richard, and Karen Biesanz report in *The Ticos*, "Ticos still see cattle as a profitable and prestigious investment. Over two-thirds of agricultural land (and 40 percent of the national territory) was pasture in 1994; only 7 percent was devoted to crops."

NEW INDUSTRY

Starting in the 1990s, electronic components, furniture, and pharmaceuticals (among many others) became important exports. Multinational pharmaceutical companies—such as Abbot Labs, Bristol-Myers Squibb, Johnson and Johnson, Colgate-Palmolive, Monsanto, and Pfizer—have branches here. Tech giant Hewlett Packard employs at least 4,000 people here in Costa Rica; many of them provide tech support in English to callers from the United States and Canada. The textile industry has also grown by leaps and bounds, from 14,000 workers in 1986 to 43,000 in 1996. In some years textiles bring more foreign exchange than the all-important banana.

Tourism, the "industry without smokestacks," also exploded in the 1990s, with the number of foreign tourists going from 376,000 in 1989 to more than a million in 2000 and then to about 1.5 million in 2004. Tourism has now surpassed all other moneymakers and is the number-one source of income for Costa Rica.

Another recent and dramatic change to the economy came when Intel, based in Santa Clara, California, began to build assembly plants here in 1997. The big daddy of foreign investors, Intel has three sprawling plants in Costa Rica, which churn out a third of its worldwide production of computer chips and provide thousands of jobs. In 1998, the company's exports accounted for 8 percent of the country's GDP (gross domestic product; in Spanish, PIB, for *producto interno bruto*). In 2005, Intel opened a new financial services center in San José. For better or worse, more and more North America-based companies are outsourcing jobs to the "Switzerland of Central America."

U.S. INFLUENCE

The United States is Costa Rica's most important trading partner, buying up about 30 percent of its exports in recent years. Of the goods that it imports, Costa Rica has been buying about 40 percent from the United States. Add to that the fact that U.S. companies account for

San José residents watch the 2003 U.S. invasion of Iraq.

© ERIN VAN RHEENEN

well over half of foreign investment in Costa Rica, and you'll see why the United States plays a disproportionately large role in the Costa Rican economy.

Almost every day, the local press reports on the ins and outs of this crucial relationship, like when CEOs of U.S.-based companies with branches in Costa Rica threaten to take their business elsewhere unless the government agrees to give them more tax breaks. Articles on the state of the U.S. economy also appear daily, since activity up north can have a dramatic effect on countries like Costa Rica that are so closely tied to the world's biggest economic engine.

THE PRICE OF A LOAN

The United States exerts its influence in other ways as well. In the 1960s and 1970s, Costa Rica borrowed large sums of money—mostly to improve infrastructure and social services—from international lending institutions, many of them based in the United States. When the country had trouble repaying the loans, the lenders—United States Agency for International Development (USAID), the International Monetary Fund (IMF), the World Bank, and the Inter-American Development Bank—offered up easier repayment terms in exchange for what in essence became their greater control of the Costa Rican economy. Other developing countries were in similar positions, and similar deals were struck around the world, as the lending institutions saw their "opportunity to convert the world's many state-managed and protectionist economies into free-market systems," as coauthors Mavis, Richard, and Karen Biesanz explain in *The Ticos.*

In 1985 Costa Rica signed the first of many structural adjustment pacts (PAEs) with these lenders. The PAEs require increased imports, reduced external tariffs, and the privatization of some state agencies. That last requirement is especially onerous to Costa Rica, whose national identity is largely based on its strong state-run agencies. Some industries, like banking, have already been at least partially privatized, but there are others, like the state electricity utility (ICE) and the national oil company (RECOPE), that politicians and the public alike vow will remain state-run and strong.

GOVERNMENT MONOPOLIES, FREE TRADE, AND CAFTA

Costa Rica is generally considered very open to international trade and foreign investment. Foreign franchises flourish here; first-time North American visitors may be surprised to see so many familiar names, from Taco Bell to Hertz to Best Western. The rules regulating foreign businesses are for the most part the same as those that govern Tico-owned enterprises.

There are, however, sectors that have traditionally been government monopolies and are thus closed to foreign investment, like electrical power, telephone service, and insurance. Other sectors—like health care and banking—have a strong state-sponsored element but are also open, with caveats, to private sector competition.

The national health care system (the Caja), for instance, provides health care for the majority of Ticos, but there are also private clinics like CIMA in Escazú and Bíblica in downtown San José. Often individuals practice *medicina mixta* (mixed medicine), combining private and public services according to their needs. Your private doctor, for instance, might operate on you in one of the public hospitals, to take advantage of its better equipment.

In banking, the three state banks have some differences over their 15 or so private counterparts. State banks can never be forced into bankruptcy, but they are also occasionally obliged to serve as development banks and to fund public-interest projects deemed necessary for the country.

Right now, many previously state-owned sectors are in flux, mostly due to the Central American Free Trade Agreement (CAFTA, this region's NAFTA). The treaty (whose signatories are the United States, Costa Rica, El Salvador, Guatemala, Honduras, Nicaragua, and the Dominican Republic) obliges Costa Rica to begin to open up some of those government-controlled sectors, namely telecommunications and insurance.

CAFTA is very controversial in Costa Rica, and though the country signed the pact in 2004, it was three years before the treaty was put to a national referendum. The issue has sparked dozens of protests, and fierce debate continues as to whether the treaty is good for the country and for the average Costa Rican.

Foreign businesses may welcome the opportunity to invest in previously off-limit sectors, and some Ticos and expats think the increased competition will bring better services and lower prices, especially in cell phone technology and Internet access. But others see the coercive hand of the United States at work, forcing changes in the country's economy that only Costa Rica itself should be deciding. In fact, for some CAFTA has become symbolic of imperialism and globalization in general, and some of the anti-CAFTA protests have a decidedly anti-U.S. feel.

CAFTA proponents say it will allow Central America to "speak with one voice," to band together to negotiate better trade opportunities with North American markets. Others say that Costa Rica cannot compete with the United States on this so-called level playing field and will come out the loser in any battle. "It's like a fight between a wild tiger and a tied-up mule," says one critic of the plan.

GAMBLING

Some commercial sectors in Costa Rica are more open than they are in other countries. Gambling, for instance, is legal in Costa Rica, and is big business. There are an estimated 200 sportsbooks, or online betting services, operating in Costa Rica, employing about 10,000 people. Row upon row of workers sit at their computer terminals, speaking into telephone headsets, taking calls from all over the world and arranging bets in dozens of languages. Callers to the sportsbooks bet on sports, of course, but they also bet on elections and even on the romantic lives of movie stars.

Sportsbooks are attracted to Costa Rica in part because there are fewer regulations to comply with here, and those that exist are often not enforced. There's more than a whiff of underworld in this business; a few sportsbooks have been linked with mob activity in New York. It's also unclear how long sportsbooks' commitment to Costa Rica will last—probably until the Costa Rican government starts imposing more taxes on gambling proceeds. Or until the long arms of the U.S. agencies that battle gambling begin to regularly reach down this far. Already some online gambling operations here have been targeted by U.S. officials, who say that as long as these sportsbooks take money from U.S. customers, they fall within the jurisdiction of U.S. laws. But despite U.S. legislation aimed at prohibiting the credit card and electronic fund transactions U.S. players often use to settle online bets, most Costa Rican sportsbooks seem to be going strong.

STABILITY

On balance, Costa Rica is still a good place to live and do business. It has one of the most stable economies in all of Latin America, a fact that draws many foreign companies here, further anchoring the economy. Top foreign investors include Intel, Dole Fruit, Chiquita, Abbott Laboratories, Baxter Healthcare, Hanes Underwear, Scott Paper, PriceSmart, Payless Shoes, McDonald's, and Bechtel.

Compared to its neighbors, Costa Rica has a fairly high per capita gross domestic product (GDP), a figure often used to measure a country's standard of living. In 2005 Costa Rica's per capita GDP was US$11,100, while Panama's was US$7,200 and Nicaragua's US$2,900. For comparison to wealthier, more developed countries, the U.S. per capita GDP for the same year was US$41,800 while Canada's was US$34,000.

Sure, there are problems. Devaluation of the *colón* is as sure as afternoon rain in the green season, averaging about 10 percent per year. The country is battling a large foreign debt, trying to impose IMF-mandated austerity measures while continuing to provide the social services its people have come to expect. Free education and health care are priorities for Costa Rica, and they don't come cheap. But for the moment, at least, Costa Rica is still erring on the side of maintaining a high level of health and education services, while offering incentives to foreign businesses so that they might come here and provide jobs for Ticos.

PEOPLE AND CULTURE

Though the Tico national identity is as hard to pin down as any other, one current that runs through the culture is the belief that Costa Rica is unique. Ticos define themselves against their neighbors, in ways that range from the "whiteness" of their racial makeup to the pacifism that does indeed distinguish this country from others in the region. Since 1948 Costa Rican leaders have come to power not through violence or fraud but via more or less honest elections. Ticos are proud of this democratic heritage, and many see theirs as an egalitarian society relatively free of class and racial distinctions. Costa Ricans are also justifiably proud of the fact that 25 percent of their national territory has been set aside in parks and reserves, and that the country has a commitment to preserving its natural heritage even as it encourages economic development.

Of course there's always a gulf between a culture's defining myths—what it wants to believe about itself—and the society's day-to-day reality. But there's no argument that Costa Rica has its heart in the right place and is hard at work negotiating the contradictions of its character.

© ERIN VAN RHEENEN

Ethnicity and Class

WHO IS *PURA TICA*?

As recently as the early 1990s, a Costa Rican president (Rafael Calderón, on a visit to Spain) was claiming publicly that there had been no indigenous people in his country when Columbus arrived. Of course there had been—perhaps as many as 500,000—but only lately have Ticos begun to assimilate that truth into their national consciousness. And until very recently, tourist literature mentioned the overwhelmingly "European" blood of the country's inhabitants as one more plus for prospective visitors.

Whiteness has been, and still is to some extent, a national preoccupation. This is not so very different from some other nations on the American continent, where indigenous and African influences are not much celebrated, and where darker-skinned peoples tend to be overly represented in the lower socioeconomic strata. But because there's a kernel of truth in the Tico myth of whiteness—Costa Ricans *do* tend to be lighter-skinned than, say, Nicaraguans or Mexicans—the country seems slower than most to embrace the mixture of ethnicities present in even the lightest-skinned Tico.

In 1995, and utilizing five decades' worth of research, University of Costa Rica (UCR) geneticists Ramiro Barantes and Bernal Morera declared that almost all Costa Ricans are *mestizos* (mixed bloods) with varying combinations of the general population's gene pool: 40–60 percent white, 15–35 indigenous, and 10–20 percent black. The census tells a different story (see the sidebar *Ethnic Makeup of Costa Rica* in the *History, Government, and Economy* chapter), in part because "race" here, as elsewhere, is often less a matter of ancestry than of culture. A Guanacasteco with a fair share of African blood, for instance, may or may not think of himself as black, depending on his cultural affiliations. And though there is pride among minority ethnicities, there are also plenty of incentives to assimilate into the mainstream.

After all, the word *indio* here is still usually an insult, and many "white" Ticos think blacks aren't "real" Costa Ricans. During the 19th century, the elite boasted of their pure European stock and slandered their rivals with racial epithets. Presidential portraits often showed the men as lighter-skinned than they actually were. And when in the 1930s the United Fruit Company moved its banana plantations from the Caribbean to the Pacific coast, President Ricardo Jiménez forbade the transfer of "colored" employees, saying the move would "upset racial balance" and cause "civil commotion" in Costa Rica. The decree was repealed in 1949. In recent decades, the influx of an estimated one to two million Nicaraguan immigrants has rekindled Tico resentment against darker-skinned outsiders. Ask any taxi driver why violent crime is on the rise in Costa Rica, and he will have an easy answer: It's the Nicaraguans, so accustomed (goes the prejudice) to bloodshed.

Chinese, Jews, and members of other immigrant groups are often not considered *pura Tica,* even if their families have been here for generations. Twice—in 1862 and again in 1896—the government prohibited immigration of "Orientals," claiming "that race is hurtful to the progress of the Republic." The laws were quickly repealed when cheap labor was needed, as when in 1873, 600 Chinese were allowed to immigrate and then were paid one-fifth of the going wage to help build the Atlantic railway.

Despite the fact that the country is populated almost entirely by *mestizos* (a word you almost never hear in Costa Rica), to this day the nation is dominated by a handful of families who trace their ancestry back to the Spanish *hidalgos* (aristocrats) who arrived during the colonial period. No matter that many of the Spaniards were poor and had to work their own land, or that because most settlers were men they coupled with non-Spaniards, setting into motion the genetic mixing of Spanish, indigenous, and African blood that has made Ticos who they are. But even today, the perception of "European" blood seems stronger in Costa Rica than the *mestizo* reality.

Still, Costa Rica has done much to combat racism. The 1949 constitution declared that anyone born in Costa Rica has the full rights of citizenship, which meant that blacks, women, and members of other marginalized groups finally had the right to vote. In 1992, President Calderón (the same man who had claimed his country had no indigenous people) signed the United Nations Treaty on Indigenous Populations and Tribes, which puts indigenous sovereignty above national law and guarantees indigenous people bilingual education and health care. Academics study indigenous language and culture, and encourage "average Ticos" to value their indigenous heritage rather than separate themselves from it by calling it "pre-Columbian culture." And while past tourism campaigns showcased the country's whiteness, now you'll often see indigenous and black people pictured in ads.

Increasingly, cultural festivals celebrate black and indigenous culture. At a 2003 exhibition of paintings by a group called Divas Afrolatinas, academics from the University of Costa Rica announced the formation of a group that would study *cultura afrocostarricense* (Afro–Costa Rican culture). In his enthusiasm for the project, then-president Abel Pacheco told the assembled guests, "There is a kind of black, one that wants to sing with more feeling— that is the black we all carry inside of us." Although to North American ears Pacheco's comments may sound a little off, they nevertheless suggest that

Ticos—all the way up to the president—are making efforts to embrace their multicultural heritage.

COSTA RICA'S MIDDLE CLASS

While racial and ethnic biases may be on the wane, economic inequities seem to be on the rise. One of Costa Rica's claims to fame has been its large middle class, the group thought to stabilize a country economically and politically. Historically, Costa Rica was a poor Spanish colony, less a society of land barons and peons than surrounding states. When in the 1880s coffee began dominating the national economy, the tradition of small independent landowners persisted in a core of small coffee growers that made up a significant middle class. And although economic frustrations led to the 1948 civil war, for three decades after the war far more Ticos climbed up the class ladder than slid down it.

Beginning in 1979, worldwide recession and a sharp devaluation of the *colón* had a chilling effect on the economy. Between 1980 and 1983, the number of poor families doubled, and buying power was so severely reduced that even nominally middle-class families began to feel poor.

Taxes also played their part in widening the gap between rich and poor. In the 1980s, revenue from direct taxes (such as income and corporate taxes) fell from 44 to 19 percent. Revenue from indirect taxes (such as those on goods and services) shot up from 47 to 71 percent, putting a greater burden on those who could least afford it.

The Costa Rican economy has recovered from the hardest hits of the last few decades, but there is still a sense that the middle class—not to mention the working class—is hurting. The increasing availability of credit and the pressures of consumerism don't help matters. An influx of relatively well-off foreign residents has also driven prices up, especially in real estate, making it harder for Ticos to buy property.

Still, a newcomer to Costa Rica who has traveled in other Central American countries will see far less evidence of dire poverty here than elsewhere. However humble, most homes are in good repair, with healthy children playing in well-tended yards.

Customs and Etiquette

More than one observer has noted the similarities between Asian and Latin American cultures: Both emphasize social harmony and saving face. To North Americans, who often value honesty above harmony, the Costa Rican method of preserving accord and personal honor can sometimes look a lot like lying. Ticos don't much like our version of honesty, however, thinking it clumsy and rude.

What you see here is not what you get. Ticos are known as "icebergs" because often only a fraction of their true selves is visible; it's easy to crash into the 95 percent hidden beneath the surface. The smiling exterior of a Tico acquaintance may conceal many things, including that you just offended her deeply. Attempts to get things straight—to speak perhaps uncomfortable truths for the good of the relationship—don't find much favor in this culture.

Things do get communicated, but to the uninitiated, the language in use might as well be code. In the rare instances I manage—with the help of locals—to gain insight into problematic situations, from giving the wrong gift at a child's birthday party to the proper way to issue dinner invitations, I hear comments like, "I thought you knew," or "But wasn't it obvious?"

No, it wasn't obvious. When you're new to a culture, what's obvious to natives is not obvious to you. One consolation is that you're expanding your awareness of your own assumptions, as well as opening your eyes to the fact that there are dozens of ways in this world to solve the same problem. Keen observation, good will, and a boundless sense of the absurd will serve you well as you adapt to your new environment. The process brings unexpected gifts of self-knowledge, as you discover what parts of yourself you're willing and able to change, and which are more bedrock aspects of your character. If all else fails, remember the old saying: What doesn't kill you makes you stronger.

HOUSEHOLD HELP

Having servants is more common in Costa Rica than in North America, and many expats of even relatively modest means hire a cook, a gardener, or a housekeeper. Nannies, often from Nicaragua, are common in both expat and Tico households, especially those in which both parents work. Wages for household help are low but are strictly regulated by the government. As with any employee, employers are required to provide holiday and vacation pay for household help. For more information, see the *Labor Laws* section of the *Employment* chapter.

PERSONAL SPACE

You're on a crowded bus, and you've been lucky enough to get a seat. In the press of bodies, the señora in the aisle has her behind smashed up against your arm, the kid in the seat behind you is playing with your hair, and a man leans over, a few inches from your face, to pull the cable that signals the driver to stop. No one says *perdón,* no one even glances your way to acknowledge that they are—by North American standards at least—making serious incursions into your personal space.

Whether you think this normal, charmingly different, or downright rude will depend on your culture and upbringing. It's one of my pet peeves, in part because my response to it is so very physical. I can explain away other cultural differences, but this one makes me feel like a dog with her hackles up. A local told me to think of it as a sort of compliment—a collective hug, welcoming me to the extended family.

This reduced margin can also be seen in the way Ticos drive. They pull out into traffic that would give others pause, pass even if a truck is bearing down from the other direction, and cut off cars so closely you're amazed that there aren't even more accidents.

EARLY (AND NOISY) RISERS

Most Ticos are up before six in the morning, and they aren't tiptoeing around, trying not to wake the gringos who sleep till eight. Señoras bang pots, kids squeal, and the buses that pick up schoolkids honk at every door. Construction crews hammer away, leaf blowers are turned on high, and even the birds get up early to contribute to the racket.

If you can't fight them (and you can't), you may as well join them. You will be much, much happier if you adjust to Tico hours, which means getting up with the sun and going to bed as early as 9 or 10 o'clock. Out in the country there's little to do at night, and even in cities things are usually quiet by midnight. After the adjustment period you may even find that you really like being up for the sunrise.

Love, Marriage, and Family

WOMEN AND MEN

Officially speaking, women and men in Costa Rica enjoy absolute equality. The 1949 constitution says as much, and a 1966 constitutional amendment prohibits discrimination based on sex, race, or religion. The 1974 family code stipulates that husbands and wives share equal rights and responsibilities, and that a woman can do everything from inherit property to form a corporation on her own. There are laws on the books against sexual harassment and gender discrimination. The far-ranging 1990 Ley sobre la Igualdad Real de la Mujer (Law for Women's True Equality) was intended to help close the gap between women's legal rights and their "true" lives. It provided for a host of reforms, including that schools were supposed to modify materials that promote sexist stereotypes, like books that state: "Mother kneads the dough while Father reads the paper."

Husbands for Rent: We do anything

© HOUMAN PIRDAVARI

Traditions Die Hard

Sound like a feminist utopia? Not exactly. Traditions die hard, and Costa Rica is still a *machista* society, where little girls are taught to serve their brothers at table. In hiring, men are more likely to get high-level positions. Recently, the Institute of Social Studies in Population (IDESPO) reported that Costa Rican men earn, on average, 40 percent more than women. Only 32 percent of the women in the workforce hold service-related jobs (16 percent in retail/sales and 16 percent in professional, technical, and clerical positions), leaving the remaining 68 percent to work in low-paying agricultural, domestic, and manufacturing positions. There are more women than men currently enrolled in most of the country's universities, though it is still common for women to give up their studies or careers once they marry.

Marriage and Kids

Most Ticos are married by the age of 25, though those who are studying for advanced degrees tend to wait longer. Increasingly, both husband and wife work, and often a nanny or female relative spends more time with the children than their parents do. In 2006, the fertility rate was 2.24 children per woman, fairly low for a developing country, probably due in part to the high levels of education and income in Costa Rica. A study by the Institute for Social Assistance showed that between 1986 and 1996, the number of women heads of household grew 57 percent, while the number of male heads of household grew only 8 percent in that same period.

Despite Costa Rica being a Catholic country, out-of-wedlock births have grown common; the 2000 census (the latest taken) showed that a whopping 53 percent of children born that year were born out of wedlock. The law deals with this trend by insisting that both parents, whether the couple is married or not, are responsible for their children. But when a deadbeat dad skips town, there are no official resources to track him down.

Another recent study showed that a majority of women in active sexual relationships used contraceptives, at least some of the time. Abortion is illegal (except when the mother's life is at stake), though it is widely available in private clinics for those with money, and in back alleys for those without.

I've heard from several Tico sources that the single most important piece of advice a father can give his son is, *"Hijo,* you can't expect to sleep with every woman in the world. But you've got to at least *try!"* Sure, it's a joke, but like many jokes it has a large grain of truth in it. Men here are expected, to a certain extent, to proposition every eligible woman they meet, and there's still a strong double standard when it comes to fidelity. A man who strays expects to be forgiven by his long-suffering partner; a woman had better not expect the same indulgence.

On the Street

More day-to-day cultural differences will make themselves known to you as you go about your daily life. Where you live in Costa Rica (and who you hang out with) will largely determine what you see, with the rural, far-flung communities more traditional and the urban areas more "westernized." But almost everywhere you go, it seems, women—even grandmothers—dress more provocatively here than in North America. Pants can be almost comically tight, heels high, and blouses revealing. The attitude seems to be, if you have it, flaunt it, and if you don't have it, flaunt that too.

As in other Latin American countries, Costa Rica has a tradition of the *piropo,* something between a compliment and a catcall. Attractive women get plenty of attention on the street, with men hissing and murmuring sweet (and not-so-sweet) nothings under their breath. While many men in the street will offer up to passing women a reptilian *psssst!* or a porcine grunt, others are a bit more creative, saying something like *si la belleza fuera delito, yo te hubiera dado cadena perpetua* (if beauty were a crime, you'd get life in prison).

THE FAMILY

In Costa Rican society, it's all in the family, with the law backing up generations of tradition. Slights of honor against family members—even long-dead ones—are punishable by law. A person who murders a relative may get a longer jail sentence than one who kills a stranger. Adults are legally responsible for not only their spouses and children but also other family members in need, such as a disabled sibling.

Relatives who live outside the city may come to live with urban relations in order to find better work or attend school. Children are more likely to play with their siblings or cousins than "outsiders." Many adults count their siblings among their best friends and spend most of their social time with family members. Families go into business together, and government officials hand out prime jobs to family members.

What does this mean to the newcomer? Many North Americans leave home at an early age, perhaps settling far from their family of origin. They create a new sort of family out of good friends and community. That happens much less in Costa Rica, where people tend to stay put and are more insular and clannish.

It can be hard to break into these clans, and although Ticos are known as polite and welcoming, the welcome often stops at the front door—literally. Especially in the country, visitors are not often asked to come inside, though you may be invited to sit on the front porch and have a lemonade. Long-term expats joke that if you're lucky enough to have a Tico invite you to his house, he won't tell you how to get there. Ticos may also be wary of people who they think will be here today and gone tomorrow.

It's not impossible to make Costa Rican friends, but it takes time and effort. Start by being as polite as you know how, and try not to take offense if your friendly overtures are not reciprocated as you would like. If you have children, you're one step ahead—you'll have a door into Tico families with kids the same age as yours. If you work with locals, that's another way in. And remember, there are plenty of other foreign residents who are in the same boat, and more than happy to commiserate about it. Enduring friendships have been based on less.

WHAT'S IN A NAME?

Let's say your new friend introduces herself as María José Mora Pacheco de Vargas. Before you roll your eyes in exasperation and wonder why anyone would need five names, let's dissect her monikers and see what we can find out.

María – first name
José – second name; like our middle name (middle names can go against gender)
Mora – first surname; comes from María's father
Pacheco – second surname; comes from María's mother
de Vargas – married name; comes from María's husband

Confused yet? Okay, let's take a step back. First of all, like other Latin Americans, Costa Ricans trace descent through both their mother and father. The father's last name is the child's *primer apellido* (first surname); the mother's last name is the child's *segundo apellido*, or second surname.

María's father's name is Wilbur Álvaro Mora Espinoza; his first surname becomes his daughter's first surname (as for the "Wilbur," English names are popular in Costa Rica). María's mother's name is Soledad Berta Pacheco Molina; her first surname becomes María's second surname. María's husband's name is Victor Hernán Vargas Salas; his first surname is sometimes appended to María's

parade of names, preceded by "de" (of) to denote that she is married to him. But for most purposes, including legal documents and medical files, María will not use the "de Vargas."

If she wants to be quick, María may write her name María J. Mora P., spelling out the most important names (first name, first surname), while abbreviating the less important names (second name, second surname). If she works with North Americans, she might call herself María Mora, knowing that nonnatives sometimes get confused by the Costa Rican carnival of names. Poor gringos, she might be thinking, with so few names.

If you meet someone with two identical *apellidos*, like Julio Ricardo García García, either both Julio's parents had the same *primer apellido*, or his father is "unknown," and they repeated his mother's surname twice on the birth certificate.

For official records, which are set up to require two surnames, clerks may try to solve the inconvenience of a one-surname foreigner by repeating her surname twice. Thus I became Erin Kathleen Van Rheenen Van Rheenen for Social Security purposes. My documents are sometimes filed under *V*, sometimes under *R*, and often not filed at all because no one can figure out why the gringa has not two surnames but four.

EXPAT SOCIAL LIFE AND ROMANCE

The unspoken motto in many of this country's far-flung, sometimes incestuous expat communities seems to be "all's fair in love and real estate." The subject of conversation is most often the selling of land or the switching of romantic allegiances. On the real estate side, most people who've been down here for a while get into that game on some level—from becoming developers to feeding a local real estate agent clients and getting a small cut of the deal.

On the love side: Couples who move here together sometimes thrive, but just as often the big life change puts all sorts of new stresses on the relationship. People adjust differently—maybe one partner loves the place immediately, and the other takes a while to warm up to it, or never does. A move to a totally new culture also shows you things about your partner that you may never have known—that she treats employees badly, for example (maybe you never had any employees before, so it didn't come up), or that he can't go a day without complaining that there's nothing to do here.

Some couples who arrive together split up and then start looking among the local singles for a new partner. Some stick to the expat world, reasoning that relationships are hard enough without additional language and cultural barriers. Others, noting that their ex spoke English perfectly but that they never understood what she or he was saying, reason that communication is about more than language. These folks expand their field of vision and might take up with a local or an expat from another country.

THE LURE OF THE TICA

There's a definite contingent of North American and European men, often quite advanced in years, who come to Costa Rica expressly to meet and sometimes marry a Tica (Costa Rican woman), often half or a third their age. Some will tell you Ticas are unencumbered with feminist notions, don't care about a man's age or attractiveness, and that they "spoil their men rotten" without asking for anything in return. If that sounds plausible to you, you're in for a few surprises. Those who know a variety of Ticas and have observed Tica-gringo relationships know the situation is significantly more complex. As in other aspects of Costa Rica, you should be suspicious of extravagant claims that the rules that apply everywhere else are somehow suspended in Costa Rica.

FOR WOMEN ONLY

Women seeking adventure will most likely find it, as Tico men are often on the lookout for new conquests. Those hoping for something more lasting may find that Costa Rican men can be less egalitarian and faithful than North American women are accustomed to. Many of the single expat women I meet go out with fellow expats, not necessarily from their own country.

Some women, especially middle-aged and older, complain of a dearth of eligible men here. Margie Davis writes on www.welovecostarica.com that "even

EXPAT LOVE: HOW THEY MET

¿Hablas Español?

In 2002 Gerald Aust moved from Nebraska, where he'd been a professional pilot, to his mother's dairy farm on the shores of Lake Arenal. One day as he waited in the truck outside a feed store in the nearby town of Tilarán, Sara Murillo, a Tica from a well-known local family, crossed the street to talk to him.

¿*"Hablas español?* she asked.

"Un poco," he replied.

These days he speaks a lot more Spanish, and he and Sara are inseparable. Gerry still works with his mother and brother on the farm, and he and Sara run Toucan Realty (www.toucanrealty.com).

Scott and Isaac

Scott Pralinsky came to Costa Rica on vacation in early 2004. He found the people here so friendly (especially compared to folks back home in Hollywood) that he decided to stay for good. Though Scott knew he wanted to be in Costa Rica, actually being here was a bit of a shock. He wondered if he'd made the right decision.

Then Scott met Isaac Garcia, a Tico, at a local dance club. Nine hours later they were off to the beach for the weekend. Not much later they were sharing a farm in Cartago, overlooking the Orosí Valley. In 2006 they founded Tropical Adventures (www.tropicaladventures.com), a cultural enrichment program that arranges for visitors to study Spanish by volunteering in local communities.

"Being gay in Costa Rica is really a non-issue," says Scott. "Most people here (both Ticos and expats) are very discreet about their sexuality. But we certainly don't hide anything and have never run into any kind of friction. I feel more comfortable in Costa Rica being myself than in most places I've lived in the U.S."

Robyn and Henry

On Robyn White's first visit to Costa Rica in 2001 she hired a guide to show her around. That guide was Henry Kantrowitz, an American who'd been in Costa Rica since 1989. They kept in touch after Robyn went back home to California, even when Henry moved to the remote Osa Peninsula. He could only get to an Internet café once a week, but that didn't slow down their burgeoning romance. "We made each other laugh so much it was uncanny," says Henry.

In a more serious moment, Henry wrote that he wondered whether Peggy, his wife of 22 years who had died the year before, had anything to do with their meeting. Robyn wrote back saying she'd been waiting for him to ask her that, because she thought she'd been sensing some sort of message from Peggy.

Dubious, Henry says he "decided to throw her a curve ball." He replied that if Robyn was talking to Peggy, she should know their password, a word that no one else knew, not even their kids.

When Henry returned to the internet cafe a week later, Robyn's reply

© LAINE HARRIS

Isaac Garcia and Scott Pralinsky

was waiting. She wrote that she'd tried to open herself to any possible message. First she got the letter *p*. And then a word came to her, a laughable and unlikely word, she thought: *pumpkin*. "I'm sorry," she wrote, "but that's all I got."

Henry sat in the internet café, staring at the screen. "I just about died right there," he says. "Peggy's and my password was pumpkin."

A few months later Robyn moved from California down to the Osa to be with Henry. Years later and still together, they live near Punta Leona on the central Pacific coast.

Sandy and Roger
Writer Sandy Shaw Homer came to Costa Rica in 1990 with her husband; after they split up, Sandy took up with Roger Eichholz, a windsurfer and craftsman who arrived in the Lake Arenal area in 1992.

"How'd you meet?" I asked them. They looked at each other. "It's slim pickings up here," he smiled. Sandy nodded, adding, "He was the only good-looking single guy on the lake."

Online Romance
Jacqueline Passey, creator of a popular blog (www.jacquelinepassey. com), found her Costa Rica companion through an online personal ad. Noting that she was interested in the politics, history, and culture of the places she visits, she cautioned, "I'm really not a lay-on-the-beach-drinking-margaritas-and-reading -trashy-paperbacks kind of traveler."

She got more than 50 responses, one of whom became her boyfriend.

"For people who are looking for something really specific or who are a little weird," says Jacqueline, "online personals really work."

though I love my life in Costa Rica, there's one big gaping hole—I have no one to date. I am attractive with a petite body, yet I can't find a suitable man to ask me out. When I moved down here I left a 17-year marriage, and getting into another relationship was the last thing on my mind. But now that I've been here and gotten on with my life, I want to date again. I've had three dates in 13 months. I am not alone in this situation. My single gringa and Tica women friends in their 40s, 50s and 60s have the same lament."

I'd have to agree with Margie at least in part. Wherever I go in this country, when I speak with single women expats the conversation usually rolls around to "do you know any eligible men around here?" But then again, conversations about the lack of viable dating options are no doubt going on right now all over the world, among both women and men.

A SMALL POND

There's a rueful saying around here that many of the expats who arrive in Costa Rica are either "wanted or unwanted." (For the "wanted" part of that equation, think of the posters on U.S. Post Office walls.) Expat communities (even in the well-populated Central Valley, but especially outside of it) are small, so there's not a lot to choose from. Just as when you're traveling you end up hanging out with people you might not be able to tolerate at home, when you are part of a small expat community, you might end up dating or being friends with people who back home wouldn't have been your cup of tea. This isn't necessarily a bad thing—one of the great things about living in Costa Rica is that you'll probably make friends with all sorts of people from many different countries. In the end I think it's a positive thing to be compelled to let more (and different) people into your heart.

Those looking for same-sex partners will find their pool of applicants even further reduced. But many a great love is based on exceptions to all sorts of rules, so never say never.

GAYS AND LESBIANS

San José is known as a gay-friendly city. There are many openly gay bars in town, lots of gay-friendly restaurants and guesthouses, and in 2003 the city organized its first "Pride" festival, which attracted more than 2,000 people. One speaker at the festival joyfully proclaimed that Costa Rica had come out of the closet, but it's clear that most Tico gays still live a fairly closeted life, especially if they are in positions of power. Guides to gay Costa Rica stress that the country is a fairly tolerant place as long as you're not "openly affectionate" in public. Gay men, by the way, are far more visible than gay women, and there is a big transvestite community, with cross-dressing sex workers much in evidence along some downtown streets.

Around the country, there are pockets of gayness; Manuel Antonio (near Quepos, on the Pacific coast) is one of the best-known. In general, though, outside of the Central Valley, more traditional mores hold sway, and gays should be as aware as they'd be in the less-tolerant areas of their own countries.

Legally speaking, homosexual activity is not a crime between consenting adults (over 18). There have also been court rulings prohibiting police raids and harassment at gay locales.

There are many resources for learning more. Check out Uno@Diez at Calle 3 and Avenida 7 in San José (tel. 506/258-4561, www.1en10.com). It runs a GLBT information center. The Sexual Diversity Cultural Center of Costa Rica (800/247-2227, www.cipacdh.org) sponsors the June Gay Pride festivities and organizes events to mark World AIDS Day each December 1. It also has counseling and support groups for gay, lesbian, and transgendered persons. The Agua Buena Human Rights Association (tel. 506/234-2411, www. aguabuena.org) concentrates on AIDS activism.

Look for copies of the magazines *Gente 10* (www.gente10.com), *Gayness,* and *Manuel Antonio Circuit.*

Search for gay-owned and gay-friendly lodging, restaurants, or tour agencies at www.gaycostarica.com, which has everything from news to personal ads.

For information on Costa Rica's lesbian community, check out www.mujerymujer.com.

Religion

CATHOLICISM

Costa Rica is a visibly Catholic country, and the great majority of Ticos call themselves Catholic. Churches are everywhere, and shrines to the Virgin can be seen in parks, public buildings, and even taxicabs. Most Ticos are baptized and married in the church, and everyday speech is full of religious phrases. Ask a Tica how she is, and most likely she'll reply, *"muy bien, gracias a Dios"* (very well, thank God). A fair number of people cross themselves when passing a church or beginning a journey. Religious festivals are often national holidays: The country all but shuts down during Easter week, and on August 2, hundreds of thousands of Ticos make the pilgrimage to the Cartago cathedral that houses the Virgin of the Angels, Costa Rica's patron saint. (See the sidebar *La Negrita's Gifts* in the *Central Valley and Beyond* chapter.)

Even so, Costa Ricans are not necessarily devout. Catholic influence here seems almost more cultural than religious, with people observing the outward rituals but lukewarm to the Catholic precepts that don't fit with their individual philosophy. Premarital and extramarital sexual activity is common, out-of-wedlock births are on the rise, and contraception is promoted by the government and embraced by the people. Holidays, whether secular or religious, often seem to be an excuse to drink and carouse.

This lukewarm faith is nothing new. In 1711, the bishop in charge of Costa Rica was so appalled by low church attendance and nonpayment of church fees that he ordered chapels built in every town and man-

Basílica de Nuestra Señora de Los Angeles, Cartago

dated that fees be paid before any marriage or funeral could be performed. His decree had little effect.

The country's first constitution specified Catholicism as the state religion, but in 1853 a visiting German Catholic noted that Ticos "attend church more from hereditary custom than from individual impulse .... Above all, they do not want to give much money to the church." Although Ticos have historically been less than pious, neither have they been anticlerical, perhaps because the church was never powerful enough to thwart secular desires. Still, the church is the strongest nongovernmental organization, and Roman Catholicism remains the official religion.

OTHER FAITHS

Just over 10 percent of Costa Ricans identify themselves as Protestants, and most belong to one of the approximately 100 small evangelical sects active here. Most of the country's blacks arrived in this country as Protestants and remain so today.

Denominations include Baptists, Methodists, Mormons, Seventh Day Adventists, and Jehovah's Witnesses. As elsewhere in Latin America, Protestant fundamentalism is on the rise, in part because converts feel a greater sense of community in their small sects than in the often-impersonal state-sanctioned

Catholic Church. Many Protestants belong to missionary orders, and sometimes you'll see the faithful going door-to-door or performing concerts or plays in local parks. At my local park there are occasional Christian rap concerts, with Christ-centered lyrics and heavy bass booming through our quiet suburban streets.

Two synagogues in San José serve the city's Jewish community of about 3,000. Some Jews are new arrivals, many from North America; others are descended from families that came from Europe in the early 20th century. Many Jewish children attend the Weizman Institute in San José, a trilingual school with classes in English, Spanish, and Hebrew.

Many Ticos of Chinese descent have converted to Catholicism, though some still practice Buddhism or Confucianism. There is a small Quaker community, mostly living in the northern mountain town of Monteverde. As in the United States, many Ticos study yoga, Zen, or Asian martial arts, and they may shoehorn a bit of Eastern spirituality into their mostly Catholic or secular worldview.

Expats will have a wide choice of services to attend, some in English. The weekly *Tico Times* lists the various options. There is also plenty of new age spirituality on offer, from indigenous-inspired rites to a Course in Miracles.

The Arts

For such a small country, Costa Rica gives a lot of support to its arts. The Ministry of Culture, Youth, and Sports sponsors music and dance performances in towns throughout the country, workshops for kids, and an annual international arts festival. The government subsidizes the House of the Artist, founded in 1951 and offering free painting and sculpture lessons—many Tico artists began their careers here. Musicians and dancers have the Conservatorio Castella (started in 1953), and the state-subsidized Editorial Costa Rica (founded in 1959) publishes local writers and sponsors yearly writing awards.

There is also the National Symphony Orchestra, until the early 1970s a small ensemble playing a few poorly attended concerts each year. President Pepe Figueres sparked the revitalization of the orchestra, asking "Why should we have tractors if we lack violins?" Now the orchestra is first-rate, featuring famous international soloists but still staying true to its roots, playing not only in the elegant National Theater but also in small-town plazas throughout the country. When musicians are hired (often from outside the country), they know they must not only play but also teach: The "second orchestra" is one of the few state-sponsored youth orchestras in the world.

The National Dance Company is also on the upswing, as are all sorts of theater groups, including expat troupes that perform works in English. During one recent week in San José, arts lovers could choose among flamenco dance, Tibetan music, a monologue about Nicaraguan immigrants, many broad comedies in Spanish, *You're a Good Man, Charlie Brown* put on by an expat theater group, and all sorts of popular music and dance concerts. Tickets are usually very reasonably priced (often under US$5). Check listings in the English weekly *Tico Times* or the Spanish daily *La Nación*.

Private financing of the arts is also on the rise, with some of the larger multinational corporations supporting mostly music and theater, and *La Nación* sponsoring yearly writing awards.

Film here is pretty much a Hollywood import, with blockbusters shown at multiplexes not unlike the ones back home. In San José, there is the occasional foreign film festival, and two venues—Sala Garbo and the Teatro Laurence Olivier, right next door to each other near Paseo Colón—regularly show foreign and independent films. There is a Centro de Cine that sometimes organizes film series, like a recent series of Cuban films. The Costa Rican film industry is in its infancy, though business forces are trying hard to sell the country as a beautiful and economical movie location.

Almost all of the cinemas in the country are in San José. Outside of the capital, the cultural pickings in general can be slim, though you could always start your own theater group, film club, or chamber orchestra.

CRAFTS

Tourists looking for crafts may be disappointed to find that many of the "souvenirs" in Costa Rica are made in Indonesia—beach towns in particular offer up a glut of batiked sarongs and colorful bikinis from halfway across the world. You'll also see street vendors—often itinerant South Americans—selling handmade jewelry and head-shop paraphernalia. Costa Rica lacks the rich tradition of native crafts enjoyed by nearby countries whose African and indigenous arts have been preserved and/or absorbed into a hybrid of old- and new-world forms. Still, small pockets of indigenous cultures—like the Cabécar and Bribrí on the Caribbean coast—continue to create the colorful wooden masks and other crafts that their ancestors fashioned centuries ago.

Increased tourist demand and a growing pride in the country's pre-Columbian heritage have led to the revival of some other traditions, and now you may see reproductions of pre-Columbian stone statues and pottery that resuscitate ancient techniques and designs. The towns of Guatíl and San Vicente on the Nicoya Peninsula have become the center of an exciting revival of Chorotega ceramics (see the sidebar *Revival of a Pre-Columbian Past* in the *Guanacaste and the Nicoya Peninsula* chapter).

One craft that is *pura Tica* is the kaleidoscope-bright painting of wooden oxcarts, based in the Central Valley town of Sarchí. Even in the mid-20th century, oxcarts were still used daily to transport coffee and other crops. Farmers would decorate their carts in patterns resembling Tibetan mandelas or Pennsylvania Dutch motifs. You'll still see the occasional cart in use today, though mostly they've been taken out of circulation and put in people's front yards, as North Americans might have flamingos or garden gnomes. Miniature painted carts are now popular in tourist shops.

Costa Rican craftspeople also make full use of the tropical hardwoods found here. Some of the objects—from bowls to chairs to keychain figurines—are crudely carved by hopeful amateurs, while other items are true works of art.

LITERATURE

Despite the high literacy rate here, Costa Rica is not a country of readers. The lack of public libraries attests to this, and, apart from newspaper journalists and advertising copywriters, Costa Rican authors might win prizes but are unlikely to make a living at their craft.

Even so, there are plenty of Tico writers who have made their mark on popular culture. (All works mentioned here have been translated into English unless otherwise noted.)

Carmen Lyra is known for her 1920 collection of folkloric short tales, *Los cuentos de mi Tía Panchita (My Aunt Panchita's Stories),* still read today.

Carmen Naranjo is a writer, visual artist, activist, and stateswoman. She was the first woman appointed to a cabinet post (in the Ministry of Culture, Youth, and Sports, in 1974), was ambassador to Israel, and has published dozens of novels, plays, essays, and books of poetry. Her best-known works are the novel *Diario de una multitude (Diary of a Crowd,* 1974), a book of short stories titled *Ondina* (1983), and *Mujer y cultura (Women and Culture,* 1989), essays that take on cultural myths relating to gender.

Carlos Luís Fallas is known for *Mamita Yunai* (1976), a lively novel about banana workers in the early 20th century.

Quince Duncan, a descendant of English-speaking West Indian blacks, is known for his two novels, *Los cuatro espejos (The Four Mirrors,* 1973) and *La paz del pueblo (The People's Peace,* 1978). Eulalia Bernard also explores the black Costa Rican experience with her books of poetry, including *My Black King,* written in a medley of Spanish, standard English, and Jamaican English.

Anacristina Rossi takes on the environmental destruction wrought by foreign investment and tourism in her novel *La loca de Gandoca (The Crazy Lady from Gandoca,* 1992). *El expediente* (not translated, 1989), by Linda Berrón,

TIME AND SPACE FOR ARTISTS

"Ask the bus driver to let you off at the *bomba* [gas station]," said Bill White, directing me to the arts colony he'd founded just outside of Ciudad Colón. "Turn left at the narrow bridge," he continued. "The road will turn to dirt and start to climb."

I'm glad that my first approach (back in 2002) to The Julia and David White Arts Colony, the only arts colony in Costa Rica, was on foot. I got a chance to appreciate the vines and brilliant flowers threading in and out of fences along the rutted country road, and to look closely at the enormous ficus trees along the way, their exposed roots like gnarled fingers on a giant hand. And when I finally made it to the top of the hill, panting and sweating, the colony seemed all the more like a refuge, the cool glass of water Bill offered emblematic of what the place offers artists. What it offers is the most basic artistic nourishment: time and space to work.

Arts Colony director Royce Slape

© ERIN VAN RHEENEN

This haven didn't come easily. It was, in fact, born of pain. In 1994, Bill's daughter Julia killed herself in Seattle, and 17 months later his son David died in Spain. Both were in their 20s, and both had been aspiring artists – Julia a writer and David a musician.

The shock of losing not one but both of his children sent Bill into a downward spiral. He started to emerge from the fog of grief, he says, when he realized he needed to create a place that would commemorate and celebrate his children's lives, the lives they had led and the ones that they might have had. He wanted a place, he decided, that would contribute to a more peaceful and humane world. He would do this by supporting working artists, whom White considered "the visionaries and innovators who remind us of our common humanity."

Shortly after he arrived in Costa Rica in 1990, Bill had bought 17 acres of land for US$84,000. Now he set about building an enclave on his property that would welcome six artists at a time: two writers, two visual artists, and two composers. The colony welcomed its first artists in 1998. Soon after, local expats were coming to the colony for chamber music concerts or to the monthly salons where visiting artists would showcase their work.

Bill died in February 2005, a much-loved fixture among Central Valley expats. But the colony lives on, now under the capable direction of Royce Slape, a writer from

Portland, Oregon, who came to the colony as Bill's assistant in 2002.

"I saw an article about the colony in *Poets & Writers*," says Royce. "I'd been wanting to simplify my life, make time to finish my first book of poetry. I emailed Bill, and we corresponded for a few months before the idea of me working here came up. I submitted creative writing as well as my resume because Bill wanted whoever worked here to be not just an administrator but a working artist as well."

When Royce arrived, he not only helped Bill run the colony but also did his own work, often sharing poems-in-progress with the visiting artists. He'd also sometimes read from journal entries about growing up with a mother who suffered schizophrenic delusions and who joined a Pentecostal cult hoping it'd be able to cast out the demons that plagued her. The other artists and writers at the colony told him this material had real power, and with their encouragement Royce changed his focus from poetry to the writing of a memoir. He finished the first draft of *Are You My Son?* in late 2006.

"Needless to say," says Royce, "the contacts I've made here – writers who've already gone where I want to go, who have agents and contracts – have put me in a much better position that I would have been, say, sitting in Powell's Books [in Portland, Oregon], with a first draft, thinking, My God, what am I supposed to do with this?"

Meanwhile, Royce has also been at the helm of the colony, steering the ship in the direction Bill wanted it go, and also trying to make some changes, like forging stronger bonds with local arts organizations.

"The municipal building in Ciudad Colón is now also the Casa de Cultura. They're doing wonderful things, offering affordable classes. We donated a baby grand piano, which they restored and painted a bright, lacquer blue – so Costa Rica. We've also been inviting local arts students and their families to the colony, and now I'd say that about a third of the people who come to our arts events are Ticos. That wasn't the case before.

"We're also starting a kind of artists' time share – there are five or six homes on the property, and when they become available, a group of artists can get together and rent the place for, say, six months, deciding who gets to come when. We're also thinking about maybe letting people build on the property, if they would contribute to the colony. All sorts of things are in the works," Royce concluded.

Whenever I go up to the colony, I think of that first time, and I think of Bill. I remember him saying, "When you pay attention to what's going on, even just a little bit, how many interesting people you can meet! I've met all kinds of people just because I ask, 'Who are you? What are you doing here?'"

I asked Bill who he was and what he was doing here, and I will always remember his answer – the answer being his whole life, which culminated in his founding an arts colony in Costa Rica. "I love living in Costa Rica," he told me. "I can't ever imagine living in the U.S. again, or any country that makes wars. I'm an atheist, I don't believe in any fairy-tale stuff. But I do believe in humanness, in people being empathetic, because we're all the same, we're all human."

shows the comeuppance of a compulsive womanizer. Jaime Fernández Leandro writes of the life of petty bureaucrats in *Aquel fue un largo verano* (not translated, 1993).

Author José León Sánchez wrote several novels, the most famous being *La Isla de los Hombres Solos* (literally "The Island of Lonely Men," but available in English under the title *God Was Looking the Other Way)*, a fascinating and fictionalized account of the author's incarceration on San Lucas Island, Costa Rica's notorious island prison.

Playwright Alberto Cañas has been enormously influential, both through works like *En agosoto hizo dos años (Two Years Ago in August,* 1966) and through his work as Secretary of the Ministry of Culture, Youth, and Sports, where he did much to bring the arts to a wider audience.

Jorge Debarvo, who died in 1967 at the tender age of 29, is one of Costa Rica's most famous poets. He gives his name to Jorge Debarvo Day, January 31, otherwise known as National Poetry Day.

PAINTING AND SCULPTURE

The best-known Costa Rican artist is probably the sculptor Francisco Zúñiga (1912–1998), whom many people mistakenly believe to be Mexican because he lived much of his life in that country. Zúñiga left his homeland in anger after critics said that his *Maternity* sculpture, placed outside a San José hospital, looked more like a cow than a woman. As is often the case in the art world, the artist had to go into exile before his work began to be appreciated at home. Now Ticos claim Zúñiga as a native son, and his work can be seen in many public spaces.

Sculpture has a long tradition in Costa Rica, both in stone and, especially, in wood, as artists take advantage of the gorgeous tropical hardwoods their native land has to offer.

In painting, Tico artists looked to Europe for their inspiration until around 1920, when a homegrown movement called *costumbrista* was launched. Up north in Mexico something similar was happening, as artists like Diego Rivera, David Alfaro Siquieros, and Frida Kahlo rejected European models and embraced their national roots. Here in Costa Rica, artists painted scenes from daily life—farmers in their fields and tile-roofed rural houses were favorite subjects. In the 1950s, Tico artists moved toward the abstract, rejecting as corny the *casitas* (little houses) favored by their predecessors. More recently, Costa Rican artists have followed the international trend of exploring new media, from film to performance art to holographic sculptures.

MUSEUMS AND THEATERS

Most of the country's museums are in San José. They include the National Museum, housed in a pleasant colonial-style building with breezy tiled verandas and a good view of downtown. The museum's small but interesting collection of archaeological artifacts refutes the notion that this country has little pre-Columbian history. So, too, the Gold Museum houses a remarkable collection of pre-Columbian gold pieces, while the Jade Museum has the western hemisphere's largest collection of jade sculptures.

Smaller museums include the Insect Museum, on the UCR campus, Barrio Amon's Museum of Contemporary Art and Design, and the Costa Rican Art Museum, located at the eastern end of Sabana Park.

There are many theaters in San José; the most architecturally interesting of the bunch are the splendid National Theater, in the heart of downtown, and the nearby Melico Salazar. Both host highbrow music, theater, and dance performances, and both have lovely cafés in their lobbies.

See the *Resources* section for contact information of museums and theaters.

MUSIC AND DANCE

From the heel-toe stomping of the Punto Guanacasteco (the national folk dance) to the sinuous rhythms of cumbia, salsa, lambada, and merengue, Ticos love to dance. And if you want to see how the pros do it, there are dozens of dance companies, most in the capital city, that perform everything from ballet to tango. San José has a hot dance and music scene, but Ticos wanting to shake a leg or be moved to tears by a ballad will not be denied anywhere across the country. Whether it's reggae in Puerto Limón, a traditional love song in Guanacaste, or deep house in the capital city, there's no shortage of music in Costa Rica. Ticos are great dancers, and a party isn't a party until the first couple takes the floor.

In 1970, Costa Rica's National Symphony Orchestra burst on the scene, and now internationally known soloists and conductors often appear with the "home team" at the National Theater in downtown San José. In 1989 singers from two state universities came together to form the Sura Chamber Choir, the first professional choir in Central America.

In terms of contemporary music, Editus, a trio of guitar, violin, and percussion, won two Grammies for collaborations with Panamanian legend Rubén Blades. Cantoámerica is known for its Latin-Caribbean music; La Orquesta de la Papaya is composed of musicians from different Central American countries. Manuel Obregón, Mal País, and El Sexteto de Jazz Latino all offer up their versions of Latin-flavored jazz. The king of Costa Rican calypso is

Walter Ferguson. Tico rock and punk is well represented by bands such as San Lucas (the name of Costa Rica's notorious island prison), Ghandi, Cabuya, Nada, Esimple, and Xpunkha.

Music festivals abound; the examples that follow only scratch the surface. The Monteverde Music Festival brings internationally acclaimed classical, jazz, and Latin musicians to that mountain town, but the new Monteverde Amphitheater means that you'll have a good chance of seeing class acts any time of year. The last week of January sees the Guanacaste String Festival at Tamarindo Resort in Tamarindo. March and April bring the Caribbean Music Festival in Limón and other Caribbean coast venues. The International Music Festival enlivens San José in August. The National Baroque Festival comes the second week of October to Santa Ana's church. November's International Arts Festival in San José has a strong musical component, and early December brings the Christmas Choir Festival at the National Theater.

Sports and Recreation

SPORTS

To understand sports in Costa Rica, you only need to know three words: *fútbol, fútbol,* and *fútbol.* You might know it as soccer, but this sport has a stranglehold on the nation, with little boys taught to play before they're potty-trained, and almost half of all front-page newspaper photos pertaining to recent matches. In taxicabs you'll be treated to games broadcast at full volume, the familiar "goooooooal!" eliciting cheers and the honking of horns from half the drivers on the road, the waving of banners, and, in some cases, drunken revelry and mayhem. The streets often empty out during important matches. Though he's not much of a fan, Arturo Condo, professor and dean at INCAE business school just outside of San José, kept all the 2006 World Cup matches noted in his Palm Pilot because you couldn't schedule important business meeting during important matches.

No, it's not on the level of countries where spectators pull guns on rival fans, but it's still a very big deal. In fact, soccer seems to excite more passion in Ticos than anything else, including love and politics. A columnist in *La Nación* called it "a functional alternative to the violence of more militaristic peoples."

Boys kick the ball around in the streets, fishermen play impromptu matches on the beach as they wait for the tide to turn, and bus drivers play a little game before their shifts. Towns and neighborhoods organize their own teams, and most villages have at least one scheduled weekly *mejenga* (match), not to mention countless pickup games.

It used to be that soccer was the province of young men, but now there are leagues for girls, women, and older men. Ticos, in fact, are much more active than they were just a decade or two ago, and if you get up early enough (while it's still cool), you'll see men and women of all ages jogging at the nearby *polideportiva* (sports center) or walking briskly along city streets, dressed in sneakers and sweats.

Basketball, baseball, and volleyball all have their fans here, and bicycling is surprisingly popular, given the state of the country's roads and the plumes of car exhaust riders must inhale. Tennis and golf are played mostly at private clubs, with golf courses multiplying as well-heeled tourists and foreign residents arrive wanting to wield their clubs. There's one polo field (at Los Reyes, a gated community near San José), with another being built on the central Pacific coast.

RECREATION

There are so many recreational opportunities in this country that you could spend years sampling them all. In fact, most visitors to Costa Rica come with outdoor fun in mind, from surfing world-renowned waves to rafting tumultuous rivers.

Surfing is first-rate on both coasts, with especially potent waves at places like Puerto Viejo on the Caribbean and Pavones on the Pacific. As soon as you've met a few planes at the San José airport and seen how many travelers arrive lugging board bags, you'll realize that Costa Rica is an internationally known surf spot. One plus is that the tourist low season (the rainy season, May–October) also happens to be the best time to find good waves.

Fishing is also a huge draw, especially in Quepos, Golfito, and out of northern Guanacaste beaches like Flamingo and Tamarindo. Head out into the Pacific for sailfish, wahoo, or the hard-fighting blue marlin. Inland you'll find *trucha* (trout), *machaca* (a kind of shad), and *mojarra* (a bluegill with teeth), among many others. The Caribbean side has excellent tarpon and snook action. Fishing lodges abound, and it's easy to find a captain willing to take you out at a moment's notice.

White-water rafting devotees have dozens of put-ins to choose from, with the Reventazón and Pacuare Rivers the most popular choices. Tour companies big and small offer trips that take rafters through Alpine-like territory at higher elevations and through steamy rainforests closer to sea level.

Windsurfers can try Bahía Salinas, on the northernmost Pacific coast, or head inland to Lake Arenal, considered one of the best freshwater windsurfing spots in the world.

Scuba diving and snorkeling are good on both the Pacific and Caribbean coasts when big waves aren't churning things up, and excellent at places like Caño Island off the Osa Peninsula. Dive boats take the truly dedicated on 10-day excursions to Cocos Island, 500 kilometers (311 miles) off Costa Rica's Pacific coast and one of the world's best dive spots. There you'll share the water with huge populations of white-tipped and hammerhead sharks, manta rays, and whales.

For those in search of more land-bound pleasures, there's hiking, from the challenging ascent of Chirripó (at 3,819 meters/12,530 feet, the highest mountain in the country) to strolls through easy but gorgeous territory like Manuel Antonio National Park.

Serious bird-watchers have to make a pilgrimage to Costa Rica at least once in their lives, to check off some of the fifty species of hummingbirds here, or to catch a glimpse of the resplendent quetzal, with its three-foot iridescent green tail feathers. There are nearly as many bird species here as there are in all of North America.

PLANNING YOUR FACT-FINDING TRIP

The only way to know if Costa Rica is the place for you is to come here, as many times as possible, for as long as your life will allow. But there's always a first time, or the first time you visit with the possibility of living here lurking in the back of your tourist brain.

A trip in which you're window-shopping for a new life will be different from one in which you just want to see volcanoes erupt and hear monkeys howl. That doesn't mean you can't take in some of the best-loved sights and have a little fun—in fact, it would be a shame not to take full advantage of what Costa Rica has to offer, even as you assess the country for its longer-term potential.

The trick will be to strike a balance between hurrying around and see-ing every area, and staying long enough in each place to get a sense of more than the airport or bus station. Below I've outlined several itineraries: a 10-day whirlwind tour to sample as many areas as possible; a two-week trip that has you narrowing down to two areas, and suggestions to make the most of a monthlong stay.

If you're trying to squeeze in both relocation research and the best of the tourist circuit, remember not to overbook in the activities department. A day hanging out and talking to locals is at least as valuable for your purposes as one spent whizzing above the treetops on a zipline. Hotel and restaurant owners—often expats themselves—are excellent sources of information, and life is slow enough that you needn't worry about "wasting" people's time. Talk is what people do here instead of going to the movies, since in most parts of the country there are no cinemas.

And when you find the place that speaks to you—that murmurs *you could be happy here*—well, it's never too soon to book your next trip.

WHEN TO GO

Costa Rica's tourist high season runs from early December through the end of April. This is the country's dry season—or summer, if you like—though temperatures remain fairly constant year-round, with variations more a function of altitude than season. In the Central Valley, for instance, temperatures usually stay around 21°C–26°C (70°F–80°F) throughout the year, while beachside temperatures are most often in the 20s Celsius (80s Fahrenheit). The difference between Costa Rica's "winter" and "summer" is rainfall, and most rain falls between May and November, with the fiercest storms often in September or October. November and May are good times to come—they are relatively untouristed months in which the rains are either just beginning or just tapering off.

There are regional variations, of course. In Guanacaste and on the Nicoya Peninsula, the dry season is bone-dry—hardly a drop falls between December and April. On the Caribbean coast (a different world, climatically speaking), you may find rain at any time of the year, with somewhat drier times to be had in February, March, September, and October.

Rain here can feel like one of the seven wonders of the world, with *aguaceros* (downpours) no umbrella can stand up to. But even when the rains are at their heaviest, it's rare that they come down all day long. Each microclimate has its patterns, to which you quickly adjust. During the Central Valley's rainy season, for example, the mornings are glorious, the rain comes after lunch (just in time for siesta), and most often the evenings are clear again.

The winter, or wet season, has been dubbed the "green season" by tourist promoters, and it can be a great time to come to Costa Rica. Sometimes there are deals on airfare or hotels during that time, though most hoteliers I spoke with said that they really have two high seasons—December through April

NATIONAL HOLIDAYS

Official holidays in Costa Rica are listed below, but these are just the beginning of the revelry. Ticos also celebrate with fairs, festivals, and carnivals, not to mention the *festejo* that each town has to honor its patron saint.

January 1:	New Year's Day
April 11:	Juan Santamaría Day
May 1:	International Day of the Worker
July 25:	Annexation of Guanacaste
August 2:	Virgin of the Angels Day (Costa Rica's patron saint)
August 12:	Mothers' Day
September 15:	Independence Day
October 12:	Day of the Cultures (Columbus Day)
December 25:	Christmas

The week before **Easter Sunday** is an unofficial vacation time. Much of the country shuts down. On Thursday and Friday of this week, only essential services function; even many of the public bus routes cease operation.

and again in June and July, the northern hemisphere's summer, when kids are out of school and families take their vacations.

I've traveled during each and every month, and I've never had a bad trip. One caution: If you're heading to remote areas, the rains may turn unpaved roads into impassable stews of mud and streams into raging rivers that no sane person would attempt to ford. In the more developed areas, however, the rain doesn't have to slow you down. One Oregonian who'd relocated to lush Lake Arenal put it this way as we sprinted for cover: "You're not made of sugar—you're not going to melt!"

Preparing for Your Trip

LEARN A LITTLE SPANISH

Of the many things you can do to enhance your trip to Costa Rica, the most important is to study Spanish, even if you learn just a few basic phrases. The country will open up to you in direct proportion to how open you yourself are to it, and making an effort to communicate with locals just shows basic respect. Learning a language well is a lifetime endeavor, but even small efforts will yield great rewards.

How to begin? A class—perhaps at a nearby university or community college—is a good investment, but don't stop there. Rent movies in Spanish, watch

SPEAKING COSTA RICAN

Sure, Ticos speak Spanish, and you'll find a portable Spanish-English dictionary worth its weight in gold if you plan to converse with anyone outside of gringo enclaves. But Ticos also speak Costa Rican, using terms that you'll never hear in Madrid or Mexico City. Here are a few *tiquismos* (Costa Rican expressions) to get you started.

adios: The word for "good-bye" can also (especially in rural areas) mean "hello."

bomba: a gas station

chunche: 1) thingamajig, thingee; 2) car or bus

con gusto: literally means "with pleasure." The phrase is often used in response to "thank you," instead of *de nada* (you're welcome).

maje: pal or buddy – kind of like *dude* in the United States or Mexico's *güe*. *Maje* is most often pronounced with the *j* (equivalent to the *h* sound in English) swallowed; the omnipresent term ends up sounding like the English *my*.

matar la culebra: literally means "to kill the snake." Use this phrase when you want to say "to kill time."

un montón: literally, a mountain; often used to mean "a lot." For example, *Habia un montón de gente en la fiesta* means "There were a lot of people at the party."

paco: a policeman

porfa: short for *por favor* (please)

tuanis: good or fine. It is thought to derive from the phrase "too nice," from the English patois-speaking Caribbean coast.

upe: Anyone home? Called out at someone's door; sounds like "ooo-paay!"

If you ask *Como esta?* (How are you?), they may say:
Muy bien, por dicha. Very well, fortunately.
or **Muy bien, gracias a Dios.** Very well, thank God.
or they may answer with the national phrase: *¡Pura vida!* Great!

Some Costa Rica *dichos*, or sayings:
Mas largo que un domingo sin plata: Longer than a Sunday without money.
Mas pesado que un mal matrimonio: Heavier than a bad marriage.
Mas incomoda que dormir con la suegra: More uncomfortable than sleeping with your mother-in-law.

Spanish-language TV, and listen to Spanish radio stations. At first it may all sound like gibberish, but without even realizing it you'll be absorbing the tone and rhythm of the language. In many parts of the United States, there are large communities of Spanish-speaking residents. Perhaps a recent arrival from Central America would like to meet regularly to practice English. You could converse half the time in Spanish, half in English, and you'd both be learning a great deal. Or look for children's books in Spanish—the basic vocabulary is about the right speed for beginners, and the illustrations will help fix the vocabulary in your mind.

READ UP

Also read about Costa Rica, from guidebooks to short stories (see *Suggested Reading* in the *Resources* chapter). Internet resources are extensive, including online discussion groups like Yahoo's GalloPinto (www.groups.yahoo/group/gallopinto) and CostaRicaLiving (www.groups.yahoo/group/costaricaliving), the bulletin board at www.discoverypress.com, or more general sites like Lonely Planet's Thorn Tree (http://thorntree.lonelyplanet.com). Wondering if there's a good vet in Playas del Coco or a fun bar in Puerto Jiménez? Post your question and you'll get a variety of replies, often from foreigners living in Costa Rica.

STUDY MAPS

Some people are map lovers and others aren't, but even if you don't know true from magnetic north and your refolded maps look like origami swans, get a map of Costa Rica and put it on your wall. As you read about the country, try to find the places mentioned. Soon you'll know by heart that Guanacaste is up north and Osa down south, and that the oft-mentioned town of Escazú is just west of San José. You'll know that the volcanoes closest to the capital are Poás and Irazú (not to be confused with Escazú!), and that the Caribbean coastline is much shorter and straighter than the Pacific coast.

ASK AROUND

Hit up friends, relatives, and colleagues for their experiences in Costa Rica or for the names of people they know who have visited—or have made the move. Most people will be happy to talk about their vacation or to share their knowledge of living here. That said, don't expect folks you don't know to write a 10-page treatise for you on the country's politics or to offer their house for your upcoming visit. Costa Rica is a real place, not just a vacation destination, and people here (even foreigners) lead real lives.

CHECK YOUR DOCUMENTS

Citizens of the United States or Canada don't need visas to enter Costa Rica, but they do need a passport, valid for at least three months after your arrival date. Remember that visitors have been known to ignore their ticket home and to stay on longer than planned.

WHAT TO TAKE

Besides your passport, your plane ticket, and money in a variety of forms, pack as light as possible. You may be taking buses or flying in small planes with luggage restrictions. Even with a car, you'll be happier if you don't have to pack up four large suitcases every time you change hotels.

It's seldom truly cold here, so don't worry about heavy sweaters or jackets, though a lightweight fleece jacket and a light, breathable raincoat will come in handy. Take beachwear, of course (two or three swimsuits may seem excessive, but you'll be happy to not have to put on a wet suit). Remember that in bigger towns beachwear will mark you as a clueless tourist—adult Ticos just don't wear shorts in the capital, for example, no matter how hot it is. Take at least one lightweight, wrinkle-resistant, nicer outfit for dinners out and to feel at home in bigger towns.

Even if you're not a beach lover, take gear to protect you from the sun:

- hat

- long-sleeved, lightweight shirt

- sunglasses

- sunscreen

Other items to consider:

- camera (a good way to document different landscapes, housing types, and even road quality in the areas you might move to)

- small notebook and pen (you'll be learning so much it'll be hard to remember it all without writing it down)

- insect repellent

- sturdy shoes if you plan to hike, though lightweight running shoes will be fine for most purposes

- sturdy flip-flops

- a travel alarm clock—few of the clocks you see will have the right time. Because most areas of Costa Rica have regular power outages, electric clocks (in hotels, banks, government offices, and on church towers) are almost always wrong. It won't matter until you try to make a flight on time.

- your own washcloth (or one of those thin bath gloves, which dry faster than washcloths) and soap, especially if you're staying in bare-bones hotels—but even some nicer lodging options won't necessarily provide washcloths

- a clothesline and clothespins (things get wet here, and they take a while to dry)

- extra medication (and your prescription, so that customs officers won't think you're transporting illegal drugs)

- extra contact lenses or an extra pair of glasses

- flashlight and extra batteries

- Ziploc plastic bags of various sizes (to protect your things from rain or humidity; once you've had a notebook full of hard-won information bleed into a one-tone watercolor, you'll always keep your notebook in plastic)

- duct tape (to fix a window screen or a snorkel, hold your backpack together, and even do emergency repair on your shoes)

- all the cables you think you'll need for your computer—Ethernet, telephone line, etc. You can get them here but it'll be easier if you have them to begin with.

Currency

Gone are the days when travelers carried all their money in travelers checks. Nowadays, diversification is the name of the game. A thin packet of travelers checks is still a good idea, if only for backup, but credit and debit cards are your best bet. Credit cards are widely accepted, especially in tourist areas, and debit cards allow you to get money out of ATMs, which are abundant, especially in larger towns. You can also get an advance of cash on the credit card, of course. Before you go, make sure you have PINs for both your credit and debit cards, so that you can use both in ATMs. I also like to bring some cash with me, maybe a few hundred dollars in twenties. If there's a problem with the banks or ATMs nearby, you won't be left high and dry. U.S. dollars are accepted in the more touristed areas, and you can usually pay for a taxi in San José with dollars.

And speaking of diversification, it's a good idea to keep your money in a variety of locations—pockets, purse, backpack, and suitcase—so that if one stash gets lost or ripped off, you'll still have the others.

Arriving in Costa Rica

CUSTOMS AND IMMIGRATION

U.S. and Canadian citizens don't need visas to travel to Costa Rica, but they do need valid passports. Children traveling with one parent are required to provide official permission from the other parent. You won't always be asked for it, but it's a good idea to have a notarized letter on hand.

Going through customs is usually fast and painless. At the San José airport, you'll be asked to push a button. If the light turns green, you're on your way without a hitch. If you get the red light, your bags will be searched. More people come up green than red.

If you know you'll be here for a while, bringing possessions in as regular luggage is the fastest and easiest way, even if you have to pay for the extra weight. For details on bringing children, pets, or possessions into the country, see the *Making the Move* chapter.

TRANSPORTATION

Taxis are easy to come by and relatively cheap. There's a taxi stand at the San José airport; you can even pay with dollars. A cab to the center of town will cost around US$15.

Tip: Consider *not* picking up your rental car at the airport (and don't have the car rental representative meet you there and then take you to the rental lot). You've just flown in, it may be dark, you're tired, and you may never have driven in Costa Rica before. This is not the time to start learning. Have your hotel pick you up from the airport (most do that for free or for a small fee). Then ask your car rental company if it'll deliver your rental car to your hotel; most will if the hotel isn't too far outside the main Central Valley area. That way you don't have to try to find your hotel in a country where few roads have names and drivers play fast and loose with traffic laws. It's fun to gradually learn the ins and outs of driving in this country of beautiful (if potholed) backroads, but for your first few hours (or days) here, give yourself a break and let others do the driving.

If your trip includes a chunk of time in the Central Valley, I would advise *not* renting a car for that time—it's much easier to take taxis or to hire your own driver (your hotel can usually suggest a good person) for a very reasonable fee by the hour, day, or trip. You'll reduce your stress level by at least 73.5 percent if you don't have to drive around San José and its suburbs.

Later, rent that car. Renting here isn't cheap but can be an excellent investment, especially if you want to explore off the beaten track.

© ERIN VAN RHEENEN

Slow down and share the road.

Buses are one of Costa Rica's great bargains, and they go just about everywhere. Small planes fly throughout the country and are a good bet if you have more money than time. A one-way flight from San José to the Guanacaste beach town of Tamarindo, for instance, will cost about US$60 on Sansa (Costa Rica's national domestic airline), more on other carriers. You'll get there in 40 minutes, be treated to spectacular views, and save yourself a five- or six-hour road trip.

Although Costa Rica is a small country, getting where you need to go can take a while. All roads lead to San José, and often it's quicker to return to the capital and venture out again, rather than try to get from one outlying area to the next.

You'd think, for instance, that going from the southern Pacific coast to the southern Caribbean coast would be easy. In practice, it's all but impossible. There are no roads, and small planes don't usually make the trip. Your best bet is to return to San José, by air or overland, and then either fly or take the well-traveled highway from the capital to the Caribbean coast.

For more detailed information on transportation to and within Costa Rica, see the *Travel and Transportation* chapter.

TIPPING AND TAXES

Since a 10 percent service charge is included on all restaurant bills, most Ticos leave no tip. If service has been exceptional, you might want to leave another 5 percent, but it's not required or expected. There will also be a sales tax—13 percent—added to restaurant bills, making the final bill 23 percent more than you were expecting.

That 13 percent sales tax applies to all goods and services except fees to independent professionals like doctors and lawyers. The sales tax on airline tickets is 5 percent. The sales tax on hotel rooms is the usual 13 percent but with an additional tourist tax of 3.9 percent, for a total of 16.9 percent.

Taxi drivers are not tipped, while bellboys, hotel maids, and tour guides are. For more information, see the *Finance* chapter.

SAFETY PRECAUTIONS

Crime is on the rise, especially in the capital city of San José. Costa Rica still has less violent crime than the United States and is safer than most of its Central American neighbors, but visitors need to be alert. Petty theft is common, and tourists are easy targets. Keep your bags close, your money in deep pockets or tucked into a money belt, and your wits about you. Make photocopies of important documents—passport, plane tickets, drug prescriptions, address book—and keep the copies separate from the originals.

Another option is to scan or take digital photographs of all your travel documents (and any important prescriptions for medication), then email those files to a web mail address that you can access from Internet cafés. That way you'll always have online copies of crucial documents in case you lose your luggage.

If you're traveling by bus, try to make sure that your luggage stays in sight (all the more reason to travel light, with one or two small bags). If you're driving, don't leave anything in your car, and make sure you find a safe place to park it overnight. Keep your doors locked while driving.

For more on safety, see the *Health* chapter.

Sample Itineraries

There are two basic approaches for your fact-finding trip: Either cast a wide net, seeing as much as possible, or settle in for the duration, soaking up daily life in one or perhaps two places.

The 10-day itinerary below casts the net as wide as possible for the time allowed; the two-week tour encourages you to narrow your focus down to two areas, choosing from four; the month-long stay can be spent either all in one area (if you've chosen the area you'd like to live in) or on a more leisurely tour of the entire country.

Wherever you go, take the time to see with a resident's eye. Is this neighborhood safe after dark? Are there schools nearby for your kids? Where would you shop for food if you lived in this remote beach town? What are three-bedroom houses going for up that hill with a killer view? Where is the nearest medical care?

Check in with real estate agents and ask them to show you around. Find where the expats congregate and make a point of hanging out there. Ask them what it's like to live here. What do they miss most? What brought them here? Is life in Costa Rica what they expected?

Do things you'd do if you lived here. Get a haircut. Attend a church service. Read the local paper (there are many English-language papers if you don't yet speak Spanish; the most widely read is the weekly *Tico Times*). See if there's an English-language reading group or an AA meeting in town. Go shopping for fresh fruit and vegetables. Sit on the beach and try to name all the colors of the sunset.

You can find more about the areas listed here in the *Prime Living Locations* section; the appropriate chapter is listed with each area. *¡Buen viaje!*

10 DAYS: A WHIRLWIND SAMPLER OF EXPAT HOT SPOTS

Ten days will fly by in Costa Rica, especially if you're trying to catch a glimpse of many different parts of the country. The itinerary below won't leave much down time, but it will give you a taste of both coasts, the Central Valley (where most expats live), and the country's most active volcano. This tour hits on many of the most popular tourist areas as well, so you can surf or snorkel in the Pacific and the Caribbean, visit the much-loved Manuel Antonio National Park, and soak in the hot springs below Arenal Volcano.

The three big tourist guns this tour leaves out are the mountain town of Monteverde, known for its cloud forest preserve and its Quaker community; the Osa Peninsula, Costa Rica's answer to the Amazon and home to Corcovado National Park; and Tortuguero National Park on the northeast coast, with its crocodiles, sea turtles, and even manatees. You could substitute Monteverde for Arenal on this 10-day itinerary, but to do justice to the Osa or Tortuguero, you'd want at least three days for each. Neither Tortuguero nor the Osa qualifies as an expat hot spot, though some hardy souls have braved these remote areas and now make their homes there.

In terms of transportation, if you feel confident about driving in unfamiliar territory, rent a car in San José and drive to all of the places mentioned. This approach has the added benefit of allowing you to see the hidden-away towns and striking landscapes between the more well-known destinations.

But if the thought of driving Costa Rica's fabled roads makes you anxious,

FINDING YOUR WAY

Whether you're driving on a dirt road deep in the jungle or walking along a crowded city street, finding your way in Costa Rica can be a real challenge. Roads – even major highways – are often not signed at all, and even main streets will have no indication of what they're called. Most buildings have no numbers, and a mailing address (and directions to the place) may look like this:

de la Farmacia San Francisco
100 e, 200 n, 75 e
Casa izquierda, rosada, dos pisos
La Pacífica, San Francisco de Dos Ríos
San José, CR

Translation, please. Your starting point is the pharmacy in the San Francisco section of the city of San José. From there you go 100 meters (109 yards) to the east, then 200 (218 yards) to the north, then 75 (82 yards) to the east. One hundred meters is a block, so the above would mean 1 block east, 2 blocks north, and three-fourths of a block east. "Casa izquierda, rosada, dos pisos," means "house on the left, pink, two floors." La Pacífica is a section of San Francisco de Dos Ríos, which in turn is a neighborhood in San José.

If you think that's confusing, consider that many "addresses" aren't even that specific. Some use landmarks that you probably won't know; some of the landmarks used to be there but aren't any more. Addresses and directions in Costa Rica are definitely geared toward long-term locals – who would know that "Coca Cola" means where the Coca Cola bottling plant used to be 20 years ago. Some addresses take as their reference point a tree (god help you if it's been cut down) or the

---

with a little planning you can piece together short flights, bus or minivan travel, and taxi rides. All of the places listed on this itinerary are popular enough that such services will be easy to arrange. See the *Travel and Transportation* chapter for more detailed information on getting around the country.

Days 1 and 2: San José and Environs

Fly into Juan Santamaría airport just outside of the capital city. Stay in town the first night, exploring some of the city's better neighborhoods (like Los Yoses and San Pedro in the west, Rohrmoser and La Sabana to the north). Get a sense of city life by walking the downtown pedestrian mall (the Paseo Colón), have coffee and read the *Tico Times* at the café in the historic National Theater, and check out the nearby Gold Museum. For your second night, stay in a hotel outside of the city, to the west if the next day you'll explore the western suburbs (Escazú, Santa Ana, Ciudad Colón) or to the north if you want to get a sense of cities like Heredia and Alajuela or towns such as Sarchí

© ERIN VAN RHEENEN

The good news: There's a sign. The bad news: It's on the ground.

big house where the doctor killed himself. I'm not kidding.

But people here are friendly and anxious to help. Asking for directions may not come easily to some people, but you'll need to learn to do it, again and again, if you want to get where you're going in Costa Rica.

As a taxi driver once told me, *"Preguntando, llegamos a Roma."* (Asking [for directions], we get to Rome.)

and Grecia. Give yourself a break and don't try to see both the towns west of San José and the northern ones. Leave time for a leisurely lunch and gossiping with the taxi driver or waitress. Take time, too, to see what's for sale in the omnipresent supermarkets and malls. The Central Valley is where the whole country comes to shop.

Even if you have rented a car, this part of the trip might be more enjoyable if you leave your car parked in the hotel lot and hire a driver. It takes some time to figure out how to get around San José and its environs; you don't want to spend all your time getting lost or cursing the traffic. Ask at your hotel for a car and driver, or negotiate with a taxi driver to hire him or her for a few hours or the entire day. Ten dollars an hour is not an uncommon price for such services—cheaper than letting the meter run. (These services would most likely cost more outside the Central Valley, where there's less competition among drivers and the roads are worse.)

Another option is to rent a car the day you want to leave the San José area, relying on taxis or hotel shuttles until then. For more information about this area, see the *Central Valley and Beyond* chapter.

Day 3: Zona Norte

Drive, take a small plane, or ride a bus, minivan, or taxi north to the town of La Fortuna. Nearby you'll find Lake Arenal, famous among windsurfers, and active Arenal Volcano, with the luxurious Tabacón Hot Springs at its base. The trip from San José to La Fortuna winds through some lovely scenery, and the Arenal area itself is lushly gorgeous. There's an ever-growing community of expats clustered around the lake, people who appreciate the cooler weather and the low-key vibe.

For more information about this area, see the *Central Valley and Beyond* chapter.

Days 4 and 5: Northern Guanacaste Beaches

Drive or fly to Playas del Coco or Tamarindo. Playas del Coco will be of interest to visitors drawn to the convenience of the area (less than an hour from Liberia's international airport, and on good roads) or who'd like to take a look at all the condos going in there. The Mapache group (www.grupomapache.com) is behind many of the more affordable developments; check out the website and stop in to its Playas del Coco office. Visit nearby Playa Ocotal, less hectic than Coco and one of the nicest little coves around, and head north to Playa Hermosa, another expat hot spot.

Tamarindo will appeal to the partying set or to those who want to surf or see giant seas turtles laying their eggs. Once a little fishing village, these days Tamarindo is growing so fast you can hear its bones creak.

For more information about this area, see the *Guanacaste and the Nicoya Peninsula* chapter.

Day 6: The Nicoya Peninsula

Drive or fly to either the Nosara/Playa Sámara area (halfway down the Nicoya Peninsula) or the Montezuma/Mal País area (at the southern tip of the peninsula). Both areas are far less developed than northern Guanacaste beaches like Tamarindo or Playas del Coco, though these southerly areas, too, are experiencing their own smaller booms. Nosara has the Nosara Yoga Institute and good beaches for swimming and surfing; Sámara is a more typical low-key resort popular with Ticos, with a beach good for learning to surf.

Montezuma is a pretty little alternative-flavored town popular with the backpacking set but also providing services for more luxury-minded travelers.

Mal País (and nearby Santa Teresa) is a surfer's haven that lately has seen a lot of growth to its one-strip wonder of a town.

Between Montezuma and Mal País is Cabo Blanco Reserve, worth a day's visit—walk through the forest for a few hours and arrive at a pristine white-sand beach where you may be the only one there. Both areas have growing international expat communities.

For more information about these places, see the *Guanacaste and the Nicoya Peninsula* chapter.

Day 7: Central Pacific Coast

Drive or fly to the mega-popular beach town of Jacó or to Quepos and nearby Manuel Antonio National Park, the most-visited park in all of Costa Rica. In both areas you are in high tourism mode, which may be a bit of a shock after laid-back Montezuma and Mal País. If you drive, you'll need to take the car ferry from the tip of the Nicoya Peninsula (Paquera) to Puntarenas, then drive south on the coast road. Jacó comes first, and it's easy to feel overwhelmed there. Literally hundreds of condos are in the works as we speak, and the town is getting more and more rambunctious, with partying of all kinds on the rise. But it's good to see the place, if only for comparison. Check out the condo prices here, compare them to houses for sale in out-of-the-way towns, and marvel at the huge difference.

Quepos, an hour south, is slightly less overwhelming. It's the gateway to Manuel Antonio National Park. Although crowded in high season, the park is also beautiful. Tangled jungle spills down the hill to meet white-sand beaches, and the trees are full of monkeys and sloths.

For more information about these places, see the *Central and South Pacific Coast* chapter.

Day 8: Dominical Area

If you stay one night in Jacó and another in the Quepos area, skip Dominical, which is another hour south of Quepos on the coast. The farther south you go, the less touristy it gets. Dominical has a long beach where the waves pound in—great for surfers, not so great for swimmers. Nearby Ojochal is a little French-Canadian–infused haven with stylish hotels and a few excellent restaurants.

For more information about these places, see the *Central and South Pacific Coast* chapter.

Days 9 and 10: Southern Caribbean Coast

If you drive, you'll take the road inland from Dominical, pass through San

Isidro de General, then head north toward San José (driving time would be 3–4 hours, depending on road conditions). From the San José area to the Caribbean coast is another 3–4 hour drive. If you fly, you'll fly from Jacó or Quepos to San José, then from San José to Limón (each flight is under an hour). This coast has a very different feel than the Pacific coast. It's wetter and less developed, and real estate is cheaper. It also has more racial diversity than the rest of Costa Rica; most of the country's blacks and indigenous people live in the Zona Caribe.

Check out Cahuita and its lovely beachside national park, then surf, party, and take long flat bike rides in Puerto Viejo. Down the road from Puerto Viejo is Gandoca-Manzanillo National Wildlife Refuge, one of the less-visited jewels in the national park system. You can also visit indigenous reserves.

For more information about these places, see the *Caribbean Coast* chapter.

TWO-WEEK ITINERARY: DIGGING DEEP

If you have two weeks, you could either do the 10-day itinerary above at a slower pace, add another one or two destinations to that tour, or choose two areas and explore both of them fully. The following describes a week in the four areas of the country most popular with expats. Depending on your tastes, choose two and get ready for a more in-depth experience of Costa Rica living.

A Week in the Central Valley

There's a reason so many expats live in the Central Valley. For those who don't do well with heat and humidity, the area's year-round springlike climate is a real plus. It also has most of the country's infrastructure, including major shopping centers and malls, respected private medical clinics, government offices, and every imaginable cultural activity, whether you want to stay within the English-speaking expat community or branch out into the larger Spanish-language world.

Stay in only one or two hotels the whole week, so you can really settle in and not have to worry about moving every other day. Staying a bit outside of the center of San José will be more relaxing than being in the thick of things, but even if you're sure you don't want to live in San José, do spend some time here. Visit the bustling University of Costa Rica (UCR) in the neighborhood of San Pedro—there are often lectures or events open to the public, sometimes in English. Walk the Paseo Colón, the pedestrian mall, and explore the Mercado Central, with its little stalls offering up everything under the sun.

Have lunch or dinner at one of the many upscale restaurants in the suburb of Escazú to see that the food here goes way beyond *gallo pinto* (the national dish of rice and beans). Check your email at a local Internet café and see who else is doing the same.

Read the newspapers, especially the invaluable *Tico Times,* which has its finger on the pulse of Costa Rica's expat community. See what events are on offer the week you're there. Maybe you'll catch a concert at the National Theater, attend an English-language play put on by the Little Theater Group, check in with the local Democrats Abroad chapter, or join in an ultimate Frisbee game.

Talk to a few different real estate agents and see what they have on offer. Ask them to take you around the areas you're most interested in. Take a half-day trip or two to outlying areas like San Ramón (with its growing expat community and its convenient location, midway between San José and the Pacific coast); Cartago to the east (one of the oldest cities in the country); or Atenas (on the road to the Pacific coast), which according to *National Geographic Magazine* has the best climate in the world.

/ Visit one of the private clinics such as CIMA in Escazú or Clínica Bíblica in downtown San José, perhaps making an appointment for a tour or to ask about the insurance they accept or the prices of particular procedures. Both places have English-speaking staff available, especially if you arrange the visit ahead of time.

If you're in San José the last Thursday and Friday of any month except December, consider attending the relocation seminar given by the Association of Residents of Costa Rica (the ARCR; see the *Resources* chapter). It costs US$50 for the two days (US$25 if you are a member; membership is US$100/year). If you keep in mind that many of the presenters—lawyers, real estate agents, and the like—want your business and have a vested interest in getting you to move to Costa Rica, you can extract a lot of usable information from the gentle hype. Even better, you'll meet some people who live here and lots more who are thinking of making the move.

If you aren't here at the right time of month or if you choose not to devote two full days to sitting inside a conference room, you could visit the ARCR office (near La Sabana Park in San José) and talk to the staff about what membership would provide you. I know many people who feel that the ARCR has helped them a great deal.

For more information about this area, see the *Central Valley and Beyond* chapter.

A Week in the Arenal Area

The Arenal area is a beautiful mountainous zone with mild weather, great for those who don't want to live at the beach or in the highway-laden bustle of the

San José area. Arenal is high enough to avoid the worst of the heat, though the perennial green here comes at the price of lots of rain.

Your week in Arenal will be significantly more laid-back than your week in the Central Valley—there's a lot less to do here. For some that will be hard; for others it will be a dream come true. A two-day side trip to nearby Monteverde will give you a glimpse of another lush mountain town, this one settled in the 1950s by draft-resisting Quakers from Alabama.

Expats are scattered all around the stunning artificial Lake Arenal (there's a town, or what's left of it, at the bottom of that body of water). Some expats base themselves in La Fortuna, the lively small town from which tourists take off for volcano hikes, trips to the swinging bridges in the jungle, horseback riding, or visits to nearby waterfalls. Others are secreted away in the folds of the hills surrounding the lake; some are in the towns of Nuevo Arenal and Tilarán.

Do advance research to discover some of the local community groups, and attend a meeting or two. There's Fuentes Verdes, which tries to keep an eye on the development in the region; groups that work to spay and neuter stray animals; and of course more purely social groups that meet for lunch or a game of tennis. The *Tico Times* Community Connections page has news from each area; look for the Arenal report, with its roundup of various community groups and their activities.

For more information about these places, see the *Central Valley and Beyond* chapter.

A Week in Guanacaste and the Nicoya Peninsula

The northern Pacific region of Guanacaste is one of the hottest expat areas in the country. Its beaches draw surfers, sport fishers, and divers. It is the driest and sunniest part of the country, with nary a drop falling between December and April. The Daniel Oduber International Airport in Liberia has begun to receive more and more international flights, and it's only about an hour from the coast (flying in to San José means a four- or five-hour drive to northern Guanacaste). For all these reasons, the area is in the middle of a massive building boom.

Start in the Playas del Coco area, where a string of beach communities—Playa Hermosa, Playa Panama, and Playa Ocotal—are no more than 30 minutes from Coco, which has the most amenities of the lot: a bank, a post office, and a few supermarkets. You might want to drive an hour north to see the impressive and very isolated new Four Seasons Resort on the Gulf of Papagayo.

Head south down the coast, stopping in at Playa Flamingo with its full-service marina and sportfishing and diving opportunities. If you have school-age children, visit the Playa Potrero branch of the Country Day School, a highly regarded bilingual private school and one of the few such institutions outside of the Central Valley. (See the *Language and Education* chapter for more about schools.)

Spend a day or two in Tamarindo, and see how a fishing village can mushroom into a well-equipped resort area while still having atrocious roads. There is no shortage of real estate agents in the area who will show you what's available, and check in with the Tamarindo Improvement Association, a dedicated group of expats and locals who want the best for their town in terms of sustainable development.

Then breathe a sigh of relief and leave the mixed-blessing bustle behind, striking out into less congested areas.

Head south, either just meandering where the road takes you (this is more possible in the dry season) or settling for a few days in the Nosara/Playa Sámara area, midway down the peninsula, or at the tip of the Nicoya, in the Montezuma/Mal País/Santa Teresa area.

For more information about these places, see the *Guanacaste and the Nicoya Peninsula* chapter.

A Week on the Central and South Pacific Coast

If you start in Jacó and head south, ending up in the surf haven of Pavones or on the rainforested Osa Peninsula, you'll see the full range of Pacific coastal habitats, from hyper-developed to Way Out There. In general, land prices drop and amenities disappear the farther south you go.

In and around Jacó, marvel at the hundreds of condos on offer and the hundreds more being built. A few miles north of Jacó lies the five-star Marriott Los Sueños resort, marina, and golf course, which is definitely worth visiting, if only for its feeling of being inside a luxurious bubble. Continuing in that vein, have a drink at the nearby and over-the-top Hotel Villas Caletas, where the prices are nearly as stunning as the view.

Come down to earth and sit in a café or ice cream parlor in downtown Jacó, watching the parade of surfers, backpackers, locals, and tourists throng the sidewalks of this burgeoning beach town.

In Quepos and along the road to Manuel Antonio National Park, take in the lovely hotels and homes perched on the forested hills with views of the beaches below.

Drive south and check in at Dominical, sometimes called a "tropical Big Sur." See if you can spot any whales at the Ballena Marine National Park (*ballena* means "whale"). Stop for lunch or dinner at one of the excellent international restaurants near the French-Canadian stronghold of Ojochal. Set aside some time for surfing, visiting waterfalls, diving, birding, or kayaking—this area is gorgeous and not nearly as heavily touristed as Jacó and Manuel Antonio.

Farther south still, you'll need to decide whether to head on to the Osa Peninsula, basing yourself in Puerto Jiménez, with its enviable position right on the Golfo Dulce, or head to the scrappy port city of Golfito and on to the end-of-the-road surf town of Pavones, with its legendary left-breaking wave. Either way you'll get a taste of this tropical wild west, great for those who want to really get away from it all. This part of the trip will be harder in the rainy season—ask about weather and road conditions. If you don't want to be denied, drive a powerful and high-clearance four-wheel drive if you're traveling between May and November. But even the most impressive vehicle can't cross a raging river, so be prepared to be flexible about where you'd like to go.

On your way back to San José for your flight home, you can either retrace your steps along the coast or head inland at Dominical and pass through San Isidro de General, an agrarian crossroads town with its fair share of amenities and a very different feel from the coast.

For more information about these places, see the *Central and South Pacific Coast* chapter (San Isidro is covered in the *Central Valley and Beyond* chapter).

ONE MONTH: SEEING IT ALL OR SETTLING IN

Ah, a month in Costa Rica. If you're considering a stay of a month or longer, you may already know where you think you'd like to live. If so, I encourage you to spend the entire trip in that one place. Only then will you start to get a sense of the town or city's day-to-day rhythms. And if you're going to be one month in one place, this may be the time to sign up for Spanish classes. Learning Spanish is the single most important thing you can do to prepare for a move to Costa Rica.

If you're still in shopping mode, however, the itinerary below will give you a lot of information as you try to decide where in this beautiful country to make your new home. A car (it's best to rent a high clearance four-wheel drive) will make most of this trip much, much easier, though the last part of the trip (on the Caribbean coast) could easily be done without one.

Days 1-5: San José and Environs

Visit the towns mentioned in the 10-day itinerary: Los Yoses and San Pedro in the west, Rohrmoser and La Sabana to the north, the western suburbs of

Escazú, Santa Ana, Ciudad Colón. Travel farther north to get a sense of Heredia and Alajuela or Sarchí and Grecia. Dine in Escazú, read the papers, talk to real estate agents, and sample some of the other activities mentioned in *A Week in the Central Valley.*

Days 6-8: Zona Norte

Travel north to La Fortuna and explore Arenal Volcano, Lake Arenal, Nuevo Arenal, and Tilarán. Spend a day in lush Monteverde. For more ideas, see *A Week in the Central Valley* and *A Week in the Arenal Area.*

To spend more time in San José and Zona Norte, see the *Central Valley and Beyond* chapter to decide which other neighborhoods and towns you'd like to explore.

Days 9-16: Guanacaste and the Nicoya Peninsula

Start north in the Playas del Coco area and drive down the coast to the southern tip (Mal País), exploring towns along the way. The unpredictable roads are best tackled during dry season (December–April), and there's a stretch—from Playa Sámara south—where you'll need to leave the coast and take inland roads.

To explore the area further, see the itineraries *A Week in Guanacaste and the Nicoya Peninsula* and *A Week in the Central Valley,* and consult the *Guanacaste and the Nicoya Peninsula* chapter.

Days 16-22: Central and South Pacific Coast

Take the car ferry from Paquera (on the southern Nicoya Peninsula) to Puntarenas, then head south to Jacó. Quepos and Manuel Antonio are an hour or so from Jacó. Dominical is another hour from Quepos.

Head south for the Osa Peninsula and beyond. Choose a few but not all of the following: Drake Bay, Corcovado National Park, Puerto Jiménez, Golfito, Playa Zancudo, Pavones.

To explore the area further, see *A Week on the Central and South Pacific Coast* and *A Week in the Central Valley* itineraries, and consult the *Central and South Pacific Coast* chapter.

Days 22-24: San Vito and San Isidro

On your way from the Pacific coast back up to the San José area (you need to go this way to get to the Caribbean coast, your next and last stop on this itinerary), pass through the southern inland valley, stopping at San Vito, a mountain town with an Italian flavor, and San Isidro de General, a growing crossroads town that is *puro Tico.*

Days 25-29: Caribbean Coast

Take in Costa Rica's less-visited coast, starting up north in Tortuguero (no cars here—you must fly or take a boat), then heading south for Cahuita and Puerto Viejo. Spend a few days surfing in Cahuita before biking through Puerto Viejo.

There are more details about Cahuita and Puerto Viejo, and more information about the larger area, in the *Caribbean Coast* chapter.

Day 30: Back to San José

As you return to the capital city for your flight home, how does it feel now that you've seen the rest of the country? Some will appreciate all the amenities San José has to offer even more; others will find the urban chaos even less tolerable now that they've seen the remote beauty of some of the rest of the country.

Whatever your response, you'll go home with a wild assortment of vivid impressions that you'll need a while to absorb. If you've taken photos and recorded important points in a notebook, it'll help you continue to sort through your experiences even after you're back at work and your Costa Rica trip seems like a dream you can barely remember. Keep those memories alive, and come back soon.

GOING BACK

If you stay in Costa Rica for a while and then go home for a visit or to stay, you may find that reverse culture shock can be even more jarring than culture shock. In a new culture, you expect to feel out of place, but you don't expect to feel that sense of dislocation in what used to be home.

Brenda Burnside went home to Las Vegas for a three-week visit after a year and a half of living in the Pacific coast town of Nosara. "I was miserable," she said. "People there don't know how to live. You say hi to them and they look at you like, 'What do you want?' My friends had all the best new electronic equipment, flat-screen TVs, and killer stereos – all in these dinky little apartments. They work all the time to be able to afford the stuff. I went to see a friend and she didn't – even have time to talk to me – she was too busy showing off her new TV.

"I'd rather have nothing, but have time to sit around and talk to my friends."

Gina Hyams, who returned to Oakland after four years in the Mexican state of Michoacán, has some interesting things to say about going home. In her essay, "Before and After Mexico," in the book *Expat: Women's True Tales of Life Abroad*, she writes: "Perhaps we've become permanent expatriates – neither fish nor fowl, forever lost no matter our location. But the fluidity also means that we're now like mermaids and centaurs – magic creatures who always know there's another way."

Practicalities

Notes and Tips

A *soda* in Costa Rica is somewhere between a café and a full-fledged restaurant. *Sodas* usually serve economical, Tico-style meals, including the omnipresent *casado,* a cheap lunch or dinner plate that includes meat, rice, salad, and sometimes a drink and dessert. Most *casados* cost under US$5.

When booking a hotel (especially if you're right there at the front desk), offering to pay cash can sometimes get you a discounted rate, usually around 16 percent, which is the total tax on hotel rooms (13 percent sales tax and 3 percent hotel tax). Be aware, too, that some hotels will quote you the cash price and then charge extra when you pay with a credit card. Try to nail everything down ahead of time.

Because Costa Rica is a country under construction, email hotels to ask if there's going to be construction going on during your visit—you don't want to wake up to hammering or power tools at 6 A.M. In fact, you should ask that everywhere you make reservations, especially in the low season (May–November), when most places do any necessary repairs or expansions. Ask too if there are any construction projects going on next door.

SAN JOSÉ AREA
Accommodations

The small **Hotel Le Bergerac** (tel. 506/255-3322, fax 506/221-2782, www .bergerachotel.com, US$60–120 not including taxes) in western San José is blissfully quiet, a small miracle given its location a block south of the main road from downtown San José to San Pedro (the university district). This boutique hotel has bright and airy rooms, cool tile floors, cable TV, Internet access, and big, firm, comfortable beds. Some rooms have views of the mountains; some have balconies or private patios. The staff is friendly and helpful (many speak English and/or French). There's secure parking, and the front desk can hail you a cab or you can walk downtown or to San Pedro in 10 minutes. Complimentary full breakfast is included, which you'll want to eat at a garden table if the weather is fine. The hotel's French restaurant, **L'Île de France,** is very well regarded. The hotel is at Calle 35, 50 meters south of the first entrance to Los Yoses (coming from downtown San José).

Outside of San José but still convenient to the airport is the lovely and luxurious **Hotel Alta** (tel. 506/282-4160, U.S. tel. 888/388-2582, fax 506/282-4162, www.altatravelplanners.com, $170–390). Twenty-four rooms cascade down a gentle hillside in Santa Ana, near Escazú. Spanish colonial-style

© ERIN VAN RHEENEN

San José street

architecture creates a graceful, old-world ambience, with red tiled roofs, terra-cotta floors, and lovely handmade tile in the bathrooms. Ground level rooms 1–5 have their own patios, made semiprivate by a profusion of tropical plants. Room 1 is closest to the pool. Most of the higher-up rooms have their own patios with sweeping views of the valley below. Each room has a coffeemaker, minibar, DSL hookup, telephone, and cable TV. The top floor can be rented out as a "penthouse," which would include three guest rooms, a meeting room, a common area with fireplace (yes, it can get chilly here), and a balcony with valley views. La Luz, the hotel's restaurant, is considered one of the best in the country for continental fare—I've had excellent meals there with very attentive service. The front desk can arrange tours, airport shuttle service, and cell phone rental. From Escazú, Hotel Alta is on the old road to Santa Ana.

Hotel Aranjuez (U.S. tel. 877/898-8663, Costa Rica tel. 506/256-1825, fax 506/223-3528, www.hotelaranjuez.com, $50 per night, cheaper with shared bath) is a popular budget option in Barrio Aranjuez, on Calle 19 between Avenidas 11 and 13. It's within walking distance of downtown San José. This labyrinthine hotel sprawls across five contiguous houses in a quiet, historic, and somewhat run-down neighborhood. Rooms can be cramped and dark but are clean and satisfactory given the low price. Amenities include voicemail in each room (very handy if you're trying to connect with others in town), free Internet access, and luggage storage for a few weeks if you want to travel light for the rest of your trip. Great common areas (you'll meet lots of fellow travelers if you so choose) include an open-air dining room set in lush gardens and offering a big breakfast that's included in the nightly rate. Make reservations as early as possible—this place books fast.

If you'd like to be based north of San José, a good choice is the **Hotel Bougainvillea** in Heredia (tel. 506/244-1414, fax 506/244-1313, www.bougainvillea .co.cr, $80–120), a midpriced hotel set amid extensive and well-designed grounds. For what it offers—nice (if generic) rooms, conference facilities, great views across the valley, easy airport access, tennis courts, whirlpool tub and sauna, pool, restaurant, plus a free shuttle to downtown San José—the rates are quite reasonable. It's in Santo Tomás de Heredia, 100 meters west of the Escuela de Santo Tomás. Confirm your reservation, especially if you're arriving late in the day—they may rent your room out from under you if they think there's a chance you won't show.

B&Bs are great places to stay for people looking to relocate. Often run by expats who know a lot of the other expats in the area, they can be gold mines of information and contacts. Just outside of San Ramón, on the road to Arenal, is the **Angel Valley Farm Bed and Breakfast** (tel. 506/456-4084 or 506/308-7357, AVF1@hotmail.com, www.angelvalleyfarmbandb. com, $35–60), a modest and homey place set amid misty rolling hills and in close proximity to an ever-growing enclave of expats. Angel Valley also offers cooking classes that make use of the farm's fresh produce, and they recently began to lead relocation tours. Angel Valley Farm is in Los Angeles Sur, San Ramón de Alajuela.

Food and Drink

Machu Picchu (Calle 32, between Avenidas 1 and 3, tel. 506/222-7384), a reasonably priced Peruvian restaurant in the Paseo Colón area of San José, offers great ceviche and Pisco sours. Open Monday–Saturday 11 A.M.–3 P.M. and 6–10 P.M. It's 150 meters (164 yards) north of KFC (Pollo Frito Kentucky) on Paseo Colón. There's another Machu Picchu in San Pedro, 150 meters (164 yards) south of Mas x Menos (tel. 506/283-3679).

San José's inexpensive **Lubnan** (Paseo Colón, between Calles 22 and 24, tel. 506/257-6071) serves good Lebanese food, and the cool bar stays open until 1 A.M. Closed Sunday and Monday.

Places that try to do too much usually get into trouble, but **Tin Jo** in downtown San José (Calle 11, between Avenidas 6 and 8, in front of Teatro Lucho Barahona, tel. 506/221-7605) takes on a full range of Asian cuisines, from Japanese tempura to Indian curry, and is the delicious exception to the rule. Highlights include moderate prices, creative cocktails, vegetarian-friendly offerings, and real cloth napkins! Open Monday–Saturday 11:30 A.M.–3 P.M. and 5:30–10 P.M. (Fri. and Sat. hours are extended until 11 P.M.), and Sunday 11:30 A.M.–10 P.M.

Inexpensive **Vishnu** (San José) is a chain of eight vegetarian restaurants with locations all over San José; try the one on Avenida 1 between Calles 1 and 3, a few blocks east of the big downtown post office (tel. 506/256-6063).

Vishnu serves fruit plates, filling *platos del día* (soup, salad, entrée, and dessert) for about $3, and excellent smoothies. At the front counter you can get good whole-grain bread. It's open daily 8 A.M.–9:30 P.M.

At **Café Mundo** (tel. 506/222-6045), eclectic international cuisine is served in a former colonial mansion in a historical district. It's on Avenida 9 at Calle 15, or 200 meters (219 yards) east and 100 meters (109 yards) north of the INS building in downtown San José. Pasta, pizza, and Asian-inspired dishes abound. The slightly bohemian crowd belies the prices, which are moderate to expensive. Open Monday–Thursday. 11 A.M.–11 P.M., Friday 11 A.M.–midnight, Saturday 5 P.M.–midnight.

Café Britt del Teatro Nacional (Avenida 2 at Calle 3, San José, tel. 506/221-3262, moderate) is a lovely high-ceilinged café tucked inside the architecturally stunning National Theater. It serves espresso drinks, desserts, and light meals. Open Monday–Saturday 10 A.M.–6 P.M.

Calle de la Amargura is a short San José street near UCR (University of Costa Rica) that's lined with bars and packed on weekends with a university crowd. Tell the taxi driver the name of the street and then take your pick of loud or louder places to eat and drink. One of the nicer places, in an old house, is La Villa (tel. 506/280-9541).

El Bochinche (Calle 11 between Avenidas 10 and 12, tel. 506/221-0500) is a popular gay-friendly hangout with good drag shows in downtown San José.

Shops and Activities

Costa Rica Expeditions (tel. 506/257-0766, fax 506/257-1665, www.costarica expeditions.com) is based in San José but operates throughout the country. This venerable tour agency is the one to beat, offering great packages to its Corcovado Tent Camp or Tortuga Lodge on the Caribbean coast, wonderful guides, and high safety standards. Its San José office is on Calle Central at Avenida 3, a few blocks from the main post office.

The **North American Cultural Center** (tel. 506/207-7500, fax 506/224-1480, mercadeo@cccncr.com, www.cccncr.com), in San José's Bario Dent, is an attractive complex of classrooms, galleries, the Mark Twain library (books, magazines, and newspapers in English and Spanish), and the Eugene O'Neill Theater (with plays in English). Definitely worth a look—and one of the city's few bowling alleys is right across the street!

In Escazú, **Biesanz Woodworks** (tel. 506/289-4337, fax 506/228-6184, woodworks@biesanz.com, www.biesanz.com) sells exquisite (and expensive) wooden bowls and boxes made of tropical hardwood. It's not easy to find; call ahead for directions.

The **Museo de Insectos** (tel. 506/207-5318) is a small and rather odd museum, but fascinating if you like bugs. Even the location is unlikely—it's in the basement of the music building on the UCR campus, in the San Pedro area of San José. Closed weekends; call ahead to make sure of the hours.

ZONA NORTE
Accommodations
Between San Ramón and La Fortuna, **Tierras Enamoradas** (Lands in Love, tel. 506/475-1351 or 506/475-1082, fax 506/475-1084, U.S. tel. 408/351-2656, reservations@landsinlove.com, www.landsinlove.com, $100 per night with breakfast included) has a name that sounds better in Spanish than in English. This expansive resort-style motel lies on the very scenic road from San José to Arenal Volcano, about 30 kilometers northwest of San Ramón. Lands in Love is a good base from which to explore the cloud forest, go horseback riding, do the seriously exciting zipline just up the hill, or take a half-day excursion to the volcano and nearby hot springs. There are 35 pleasant, well-appointed rooms in 1950s hotel-style blocks a short walk or drive from the main reception/restaurant area. Each room has queen and double beds, cable TV, a minifridge, coffeemaker, telephone, and WiFi (and bidets in the bathroom). Out your front door are comfortable wooden chairs for sitting and admiring the view—the heavily forested folds of a steep valley—or seeing how many birds you can spot. Run by a friendly

© ERIN VAN RHEENEN

The Río Tabacón, near Arenal Volcano, runs hot.

and efficient group of Israelis, the complex also has a pool, Jacuzzi, yoga and meditation classes, excellent vegetarian cuisine, conference rooms, dog boarding, and signed jungle trails. They can help you look for property to buy, sharing their land-hunting experiences with you (they looked in many different countries and all over Costa Rica).

At **Arenal Observatory Lodge** (reservations tel. 506/290-7011, lodge tel. 506/695-5033, fax 506/290-8427, info@arenal-observatory.co.cr, www.arenal observatory.co.cr), if the clouds clear, some rooms in this converted vulcanology research station let you lounge in bed and watch the antics of an active volcano, which is fortunate since rooms have no phones or TVs. This lodge near Arenal Volcano has come a long way since scientists bunked together in cramped dorms. Now there's a horizon pool, a Jacuzzi, and paths and bridges through the extensive and well-maintained grounds. Take a guided hike (to the lava fields or a nearby extinct volcano, Cerro Chato) or wander in the rainforest on your own. You'll probably eat most of your meals at the lodge dining room, since getting to a town (La Fortuna is the closest) takes 30 or 40 minutes over bone-jarring dirt roads. Rates vary considerably depending on room and time of year—check the website.

Casa Mañana Bed and Breakfast (tel. 506/693-1234, fax 506/693-0009, casamanana@msn.com, www.casamananabedandbreakfast.com, $40–60) is on the Tilarán side of Lake Arenal. Alex Murray runs this small and stylish B&B with an excellent view of Lake Arenal. Alex seems to know just about everyone in the area, and his place, not far from the mountain town of Tilarán, is peaceful, nicely decorated, and full of books. He's involved in many community groups, including those promoting sane and sustainable development, and he can give you the scoop on real estate in the area.

Food

La Choza de Laurel (tel. 506/479-9231, chlaurel@sol.racsa.co.cr, inexpensive) in La Fortuna has great *típico* food in a rustic, open-air setting a few blocks west of the town square. Try the chicken, roasted to perfection in a brick oven. Call for business hours.

With a charming outdoor patio overlooking Lake Arenal, **Toad Hall** Gallery and Restaurant (between La Fortuna and Nuevo Arenal, tel. 516/692-8020, fax 516/692-8001, www.toadhall-gallery.com, inexpensive) is an unassuming little roadside place with a lot to offer: fresh juices, smoothies, espresso, and healthy and tasty breakfasts and lunches. The owner, originally from Colorado, has also created a small but well-stocked gift store and gallery, with local arts and good road maps (hard to come by around here). Don't miss the macadamia nut brownies, denser even than the surrounding foliage. Call for their business hours. There's also a Toad Hall in Playas del Coco. **Tom's Pan** (tel. 506/694-4547, inexpensive) in Nuevo Arenal is an excellent German bakery that also serves enormous lunches. Enjoy strong coffee and delicious pastries on the funky terrace. Call for business hours.

Shops and Activities

About five kilometers (3.1 miles) south of La Fortuna lies **La Fortuna Waterfall,** a stunning cascade that plummets into a steep ravine. You can walk or drive from town, then (after paying a small entrance fee) make your way down a slippery trail (use the handrail!) to the falls. The pool at the base of the falls is lovely, but it's best not to go for a dip in the churning waters; swimming is safer a little ways down the river (follow the path). If you're going to walk all the way, it's best to start relatively early in the morning, thus avoiding the midday heat.

Tabacón Hot Springs (tel. 506/256-1500, fax 506/221-3075, sales@tabacon .com, www.tabacon.com) is near La Fortuna, at the base of Arenal Volcano. For soothing tired muscles or just taking in the exquisite tropical gardens, nothing beats these hot springs, 13 kilometers (8 miles) west of La Fortuna. A naturally warm river has been guided into pools and even trained over a small falls, which will drum the tension right out of your shoulders and neck. The entrance fee is up to about US$30 per person (US$10 less after 7 P.M.), but if you're a hot springs fan you shouldn't miss this Shangri-La experience. There's also a big pool with a slide for the kids and a swim-up bar for adults, a well-regarded restaurant, massage and spa treatments, and a hotel up the hill. If you stay at the hotel (42 rooms, moderate to expensive), entrance to the springs is free. Visit at night for the full effect, when you can sometimes see lava tumbling down the flanks of nearby (*very* nearby) Arenal Volcano. The springs are open 10 A.M.–10 P.M.

ZONA SUR (THE INLAND VALLEY)
Accommodations

At **Wilson Botanical Garden** (tel. 506/240-6696, fax 506/240-6783, re-serves@ots.ac.cr, www.ots.ac.cr, US$70 s/US$125 d, meals included) in San Vito you can stay in rustic luxury amid extensive and varied gardens, and eat family-style with students, researchers, and other nature-loving tourists. Book through the Organization for Tropical Studies, which oversees the garden.

Food

At **Taquería México Lindo** (tel. 506/771-8222, inexpensive) in San Isidro de General you get real Mexican food made by real Mexican cooks. After a few dozen *casados,* you'll be more than ready for some tacos or a spicy *mole.* It's on the west side of the main square, in a little mall that also has a good Internet café. Open Monday–Saturday 11 A.M.–8 P.M.

Partake of San Vito's Italian heritage at **Pizzería Liliana** (tel. 506/773-3080, inexpensive), which serves great pasta and pizza. Decent red wine is available by the glass. It's just up the hill from the tiny main square (actually, it's more of a triangle). Call for business hours.

GUANACASTE AND THE NICOYA PENINSULA
Accommodations

These accommodations are listed from north to south.

In Playas del Coco, **Hotel Puerta del Sol** (tel. 506/670-0195, fax 506/670-0650, $55–110) is far enough off the main drag to be quiet. This moderately priced Italian-run boutique hotel is utterly charming, and the best food in town can be had at its alfresco Restaurant Sol y Luna—excellent pasta, fish, and meat, plus a good wine list and a dozen kinds of beer. There are free scuba lessons in the small hotel pool, and breakfast is included in the price of a room. Rooms have air-conditioning, cable TV, good reading lamps, and big, comfortable beds. From the main drag, just west of Hotel Coco Verde, take a right. Go about 200 meters (two blocks), take another right, then go about 100 meters (one block). It's on the left.

On a cliff above lovely Ocotal Beach, comfortable **Hotel El Ocotal Beach Resort** (Playa Ocotal, tel. 506/670-0321, fax 506/670-0083, reservations@ ocotalresort.com, www.ocotalresort.com, $100–285) has it all: view rooms with little balconies, air-conditioning, minifridge, phones, and cable TV. Villas are also available. There are pools, tennis courts, and a nice meandering path down to the beach, where you can arrange diving or fishing trips. Rates include full buffet breakfast, in an open-air dining room with a truly stunning view of the ocean. They do weddings here as well.

Not in Tamarindo proper but on nearby Playa Langosta, **Villa Alegre Bed and Breakfast** (tel. 506/653-0270, fax 506/653-0287, vialegre@racsa.co.cr, www.villaalegrecostarica.com, $150–230) is an expansive Spanish-style house with five rooms, two villas, and a pool. Linger over an extravagantly delicious breakfast then amble down the garden path to the beach—a narrow strip of sand and volcanic rock that when the tide is low creates perfect little sun-warmed pools for soaking. Owners Barry and Suzye Lawson, formerly of California, also plan and host weddings.

Café de Paris (tel. 506/682-0087, fax 506/682-0089, www.cafedeparis.net,

© ERIN VAN RHEENEN

The northern Guanacaste coast – also called the Gold Coast – is becoming more and more popular with expats.

$60–120) in Nosara is not just a popular bakery (expats congregate here) but a good, centrally located hotel as well. It's on the main road into Nosara, just where you turn for Playa Guiones. Some of the pleasant, high-ceilinged rooms have kitchenettes; all have air-conditioning. Tables set out under thatched lean-tos invite a game of outdoor chess, while the hammocks beckon at siesta time. Pool, game room, restaurant, and bar. Book rooms early; when Nosara Yoga up the hill is having one of its monthlong teacher-training courses, they board their students here.

Hotel Trópico Latino (tel. 506/640-0062, fax 506/640-0117, troplat@racsa. co.cr, www.hoteltropicolatino.com, $85–175) is one of the better beachfront options in Santa Teresa (near Mal País, at the southern tip of the Nicoya Peninsula). Eight bungalows and three rooms are reached down white stone paths that wind through beautifully landscaped and maintained grounds. Garden bungalows are two per building, but their staggered front porches make them feel private. The two beachfront bungalows are each freestanding, a touch smaller than the garden bungalows but with more charming details (like mosaic floors), not to mention that from your front porch you can watch the waves roll in to one of the nicest white-sand beaches in the area. Rooms have coffeemakers, air-conditioning, screened windows, high ceilings, and safes. There's also a good restaurant, a pool, and a lovely shaded area right on the beach, with hammocks, chaises, and rustic tables and chairs—great for a game of cards or finishing that novel.

Food

These establishments are listed from north to south.

In Playas del Coco, **Restaurant Sol y Luna** (tel. 506/670-0195, fax 506/670-0650, moderate) serves excellent Italian food on the modest covered patio of Hotel Puerta del Sol. From the antipasto plate to the daily fish specials, everything is prepared with care. It's two blocks north and one block east of the main road; turn right after Hotel Coco Verde and before you get to the beach. Call for business hours.

An old open-air favorite right off the main traffic circle in Tamarindo and on the beach is **Nogui's Sunset Cafe** (tel. 506/653-0029, inexpensive to moderate). Everyone else will be there; you'd better go, too. Nogui's has great breakfasts as well as good salads, sandwiches, and quiches for lunch, and you *must* go at sunset to have a drink and chat up the expat crowd. There's also a low-key bar where you can watch the game. It's open all day, but call for the exact hours.

At **Playa de los Artistas** (tel. 506/642-0920, moderate) in Montezuma, dig your toes into the sand while feasting on creative Mediterranean cuisine. Enjoy surprisingly sophisticated food, including grilled fresh fish, in a funky beachside ambience. The restaurant is open Monday through Saturday, 5–10:30 P.M.; reservations are recommended. It's about one kilometer out of town on the road to Cabuya and Cabo Blanco, across from Hotel los Mangos.

Nectar at the Flor Blanca Hotel (tel. 506/640-0232, fax 506/640-0226, florblanca@expressmail.net, www.florblanca.com, expensive) in Santa Teresa is *the* place to go for a high-quality splurge at the southern end of the Nicoya Peninsula. The menu offers inventive international cuisine, plus a great selection of beer, wine, and liquor. Enjoy alfresco dining at this very exclusive beachfront hotel, where presidents and rock stars hole up in the lovely villas. See if you can spot a Kennedy or a DiCaprio. Call for business hours.

Shops and Activities

Topsy Bookstore (tel. 506/642-0576, joelledelaney@hotmail.com) in Montezuma was opened in 1987 by a Connecticut native. This cozy little shop allows you to both buy and rent "wicked good books" in a variety of languages.

Cabo Blanco Nature Reserve near Montezuma is Costa Rica's oldest nature reserve. It was brought into being by two Scandinavian expats (see the *Montezuma* section of the *Guanacaste and the Nicoya Peninsula* chapter for more information). It's about 11 kilometers from Montezuma; you can either walk (a long and rather dusty—or muddy—trek), drive, or find a taxi in Montezuma.

There are two trails—one a two-kilometer loop through primary forest, the other a four-kilometer (one-way) walk through forest to the pristine and oft-deserted beach. Howler monkeys call from the trees, and brown pelicans glide on the updrafts. Simply lovely.

CENTRAL AND SOUTH PACIFIC COAST
Accommodations

These accommodations are listed from north to south.

If you want to base yourself in Jacó to scope out the surrounding area, **Apartotel Girasol** (tel. 506/643-1591, cgirasol@racsa.co.cr, www.girasol.com, $100–150, better deals by the week) is a good place to stay. The small grounds are landscaped with flowers and pejibaje palms, and the hotel's front yard gives directly onto the beach. Spacious, breezy one-bedroom suites with nice decor sleep four. There are fully equipped kitchens and full-sized refrigerators. The sitting area has comfortable rattan furniture and a TV; the dining area has a glass table with four chairs. Downstairs suites have a patio, upstairs suites a small balcony with two chairs and a table. High ceilings in the upstairs suites, air-conditioning in the bedroom, lots of screened windows, and ceiling fans allow for good airflow. Maid service is daily. Most suites look onto the small but enticing swimming pool; room 21 (upstairs) is the closest to the beach, though your view is somewhat blocked by a venerable old tree. Girasol is far enough away from the main drag to be quiet, close enough to walk to bars and restaurants. Nightly, weekly, and monthly rates are available. From Mas x Menos supermarket on the main street, go 300 meters (three blocks) south, then 75 meters (three-fourths of a block) west (the street dead-ends at the beach). Girasol is on your right.

The white-walled, red-roofed bungalows at **Casitas Eclipse** (tel. 506/777-0408, fax 506/777-1738, eclipse@racsa.co.cr, www.casitaseclipse.com, $100–320) in Manuel Antonio cascade down a verdant hill. Rooms are simple but elegant, with tile floors and spacious bathrooms. Paths lead to not one but three swimming pools, one with stunning views of the coastline below. The hotel's Gato Negro restaurant serves Italian food. The hotel is located about midway between Quepos and Manuel Antonio.

Pacific Edge (tel. 506/787-8010 or 506/381-4369, pacificedge@pocketmail .com, www.pacificedge.info, $50–125) is four kilometers (2.5 miles) south of Dominical. One kilometer up a steep gravel road (four-wheel drive recommended), owners George and Susan Atkinson have built a series of rustic *cabinas* and more deluxe bungalows. All have absolutely gorgeous ocean views, along with kitchenettes and front porches perfect for lounging. There's also a pool, a small open-air restaurant, and a bird-watching platform that affords even more astonishing views than the bungalows.

At **Villas Gaia** (tel. 506/786 5044 or 506/363 3928, fax 506/786 5009, San José office tel. 506/244 0316 or 506/382 8240, fax 506/244-9205, info@villasgaia.com, www.villasgaia.com, $60–85) on Playa Tortuga, choose from 11 charming and spacious bungalows, well placed amid densely landscaped grounds, as well as a two-bedroom house. Awe-inspiring views spread out from the hilltop swimming pool, and a very good international restaurant offers everything from Greek salad to Thai curry. Moderate prices. Villas Gaia is about 30 kilometers (18.5 miles) south of Dominical.

La Paloma Lodge (tel. 506/239-2801, fax 506/239-0954, info@lapalomalodge.com, www.lapalomalodge.com, moderate to expensive) in Drake Bay on the Osa Peninsula is a very popular lodge where you'll meet your fellow guests at mealtime in an open-air dining room with long communal tables. Potted palms, ceiling fans, and cloth napkins make you think you're back in the British raj, but the stunning views of Drake Bay and beyond are *pura Tica*. Spacious bungalows, modestly furnished, dot the hillside and share in the view; some are big enough to accommodate whole families. Bungalows 1 and 3 are especially nice. The lodge arranges all manner of tours—to Corcovado National Park and Caño Island, among others—and its guides are excellent—ours knew just where to look for the giant sea turtles, manta rays, and sharks that scared us halfway out of our snorkels. Rates include meals; also look into the packages ($1,050–1,800), which include tours.

Corcovado Tent Camp (tel. 506/257-0766, fax 506/257-1665, www.costaricaexpeditions.com /Lodging/corcovado/, $45–85 per person with meals included) is in Carate on the Osa Peninsula. Fly by light plane to Carate, then walk along the shoreline for half an hour to get to this seriously relaxing spread on a long, beautiful beach. Don't let the word "tent" throw you—these tents are basically raised cabins with flexible walls, with beds and tables and little front porches. The camp has good access to Corcovado National Park. Meals are family-style, bathrooms are shared (but kept scrupulously clean), and there are guided hikes and horseback rides. Rates include meals.

At the end of the supposedly maintained road from Puerto Jiménez to the tiny town of Carate, **Luna Lodge** (tel. 506/380-5036, U.S. tel. 888/409-8448, information@lunalodge.com, www.lunalodge.com, $125–255) sits atop a heavily wooded hill above the Carate River and adjacent to Corcovado National Park. It is 2.5 kilometers up a rough road from the Carate airstrip. Charming individual bungalows with traditional Sarchí rockers on the front porches are set in a wonderland of tangled jungle and plunging waterfalls. The lodge's Wellness Center offers many different kinds of massage, as well as yoga on a spacious platform overlooking the sea. Meals, which make liberal use of fresh fruit and vegetables, are included.

Oasis on the Beach (tel. 506/776-0087, jay@oasisonthebeach.com, www .oasisonthebeach.com, $40–80) in Playa Zancudo is first on the road into town and a good option for laid-back elegance. The raised wooden *cabinas* have comfortable queen-size beds, table and chairs, spacious bathrooms, and nice front porches from which to watch the waves break. Also available are more traditional motel-style rooms (with air-conditioning but not as close to the beach) and condos with beach views. Either way, you're only a few steps from the open-air bar and restaurant, which serves up specialties like brick-oven pizza and grilled ribs with Jack Daniels sauce. Owner Debbie Walsh is friendly and knowledgeable about the area; surfing, fishing, or horseback-riding tours can be arranged. Discounts are available during low season and for longer stays.

Several blocks (though there are no blocks here) south and then uphill from downtown Pavones is **Casa Siempre Domingo Bed & Breakfast** (tel./fax 506/775-0631, heidi@casa-domingo.com, www.casa-domingo.com, $80), where you can share the lofty hilltop home of Greg and Heidi Norris and their son, Winston. With soaring hardwood ceilings and cool tiled floors, four immaculately maintained rooms have at least two comfortably firm beds, private baths, and ceiling fans. The common area, where guests are served breakfast,

© ERIN VAN RHEENEN

the very laid-back Playa Zancudo

has one of the most amazing views I've seen, with the Golfo Dulce to the right and a sweep of open ocean to the left. Check out the spiraling outdoor shower, studded with mosaic tiles and shells.

Food

These eateries are listed from north to south.

Steve-n-Lisa's Restaurant (La Pita, Tarcoles, tel. 506/637-0594, moderate) is a beachside open-air restaurant serving fish, lobster, ceviche, tacos, hamburgers, pasta—just about everything you can think of. The atmosphere is casually elegant—they've got tablecloths but you can come in your flip-flops. Have a daiquiri from the full bar and listen to the waves break a few feet from your table. Note: Less than a kilometer south of Steve-n-Lisa's is a restaurant on the non-beach side of the road whose name is the Pargo Rojo, but oddly, they've added the words "Steve-n-Lisa's" to their sign, perhaps to capitalize on the real Steve-n-Lisa's excellent reputation. Remember that the restaurant you want is on the beach side of the highway, 15 kilometers (9 miles) north of Jacó. They're open for all meals, but call to confirm hours.

Caliche's Wishbone (tel. 506/643-3406, inexpensive tot moderate) in Jacó is right on the main drag, with outdoor tables for those who want to watch the human parade. Caliche's is an excellent choice for Asian-inspired noodle dishes, Mexican-inflected *platos,* homemade pizzas, and fresh fish (try the lightly seared tuna with wasabi dressing). Huge portions incorporate quality ingredients. Inside there's a bar with a TV showing surf videos. The restaurant is open Thursday to Tuesday, 11:30 A.M.–3 P.M. and 5:30–10 P.M.

Café Milagro (tel. 506/777-1707, fax 506/777-2272, info@cafemilagro.com, www.cafemilagro.com, inexpensive to moderate) has locations in Quepos and Manuel Antonio and serves excellent espresso drinks, hot and iced, along with homemade muffins, bagels, and sandwiches. Open daily 6 A.M.–10 P.M.

Exo-Tica (no phone, moderate to expensive) in Ojochal is 35 kilometers (21.7 miles) south of Dominical. Down an unlit dirt road is this gem of a French restaurant, one of the best around. Lucy from Quebec makes the luscious desserts, while a Belgian, Marcela, works her magic with the entrées, from classics like beef bourguignon to innovative curries full of locally caught fish. The funky, open-air elegance includes candles lining the path to the dining area. Open Monday–Saturday 11 A.M.–9:30 P.M.

La Manta Club (no phone, inexpensive) in Pavones serves good Mediterranean food—hummus, falafel, fresh fish kabobs—in an open-air, thatch-roofed restaurant. Every evening, footage of the day's surf action is projected hugely on a white wall. Wall-dwelling geckoes seem to be part of the picture, riding the waves or perching on an unsuspecting surfer's shoulder. BYOB. Open Monday–Saturday 11 A.M.–9:30 P.M.

Shops and Activities

At **Shooting Star Yoga Studio** (tel. 506/393-6982, info@shootingstarstudio .org, www.shootingstarstudio.org) in Pavones, Amy Khoo presides over a thatch-roofed, open-air studio with a view of the beach, leading classes in bikram, ashtanga, and "yoga for surfers." She also hopes to host yoga workshops soon.

CARIBBEAN COAST
Accommodations

This section lists accommodations from north to south.

You won't regret booking a day or two at **Tortuga Lodge** (tel. 506/257-0766, fax 506/257-1665, www.costaricaexpeditions.com, $90–150) in Tortuguero, a lovely riverside lodge right next to Tortuguero National Park. Run by well-respected Costa Rica Expeditions, the lodge is a class act, with rustically elegant rooms and excellent food. It employs some of the best guides, who will show you the boas, caimans, crocodiles, and turtles that call the area home. Birds abound, and if you're really lucky, you may see a manatee. Package deals are available.

In Tortuguero, near the Catholic church, is **Casa Marbella** (tel. 506/833-0827 or 506/709-8011, fax 506/709-8094, safari@racsa.co.cr, http://casa marbella.tripod.com, $30–45). If you want to see Tortuguero the independent way, leaving behind lodges and package tours, try this in-town option run by guide extraordinaire Daryl Loth (originally from Canada) and his Tica wife Luz Denia Loth. In these modest but appealing accommodations right on the river, guests can use the communal kitchen, and breakfast is included. Daryl's tours come highly recommended; he plies the waterways in a stable, flat-bottomed boat equipped with a quiet, environmentally friendly four-stroke motor and a silent electric motor (less likely to scare away the wildlife). Turtle tours are also fascinating; nesting leatherbacks can be seen March–May, green turtles July–October.

Centro Turístico Brigitte (tel./fax 506/755-0053, brigittecahuita@hotmail. com, www.brigittecahuita.com, $20–45) in Cahuita is 50 meters (55 yards) inland from the Playa Negra road. Swiss-born Brigitte Abegglen runs a small but pleasant complex with three budget *cabinas,* a small restaurant, and a few computers with Internet access. Horseback riding and bicycle rentals are also available. They'll pick you up from the bus station for free if you give them advance notice.

along the canals of Tortuguero

Cabinas Casa Verde (tel. 506/750-0015, fax 506/750-0047, www.cabinas casaverde.com, $40–110) in Puerto Viejo is a good in-town choice. Well-maintained rooms are set among front and back gardens with hammocks and lush gardens. Rene from Switzerland and Carolina, who is Costa Rican, run a nice little place. Options include private or shared bath.

Cabinas la Costa de Papito (tel. 506/750-0080 or 506/750-0704, costa papito@yahoo.com, www.lacostadepapito.com, $40–70) in Puerto Viejo has pretty all-wood bungalows with appealing porches and hammocks in lush grounds. Features include a simple café, bicycle rentals, and a walk to a nearby beach. It's just south of Puerto Viejo, on the right-hand side of the road.

Food

These eateries are listed from north to south.

At **La Casona Restaurant and Bakery** (no phone, inexpensive) in Tortuguero, San José–born Jenny Madden, her son Andrés, and his young son Michael make this cozy restaurant a family affair. Jenny offers up "alternatives to the usual rice and beans," and the traveler weary of that sacred combo can feast on pasta, fish, or delicious banana pancakes. Eat inside or out on the patio, where beach finds like weathered paddles and turtle shells hang helter-skelter on the walls. La Casona is right next to the town soccer field.

Sobre las Olas (tel. 506/755-0109, inexpensive to moderate) in Cahuita is on the Playa Negra road (a short walk north of town). Right on the beach, this Italian-run place lets you dine alfresco on creative cuisine. Lots of fish, of course, but also Italian treats like bruschetta. Closed Tuesday.

Cha Cha Cha (tel. 506/394-4153, inexpensive to moderate) in Cahuita offers delicious international cuisine—from hummus to grilled shrimp—a block west of the main plaza. Open noon–10 P.M.; closed Monday.

Miss Sam's (tel. 506/750-0108, inexpensive) in Puerto Viejo is always full, and for good reason. Afro-Caribbean specialties come at very reasonable prices. Sometimes Miss Sam runs out of the excellent rice and beans cooked in coconut milk—arrive early, and BYOB if you want to drink with your meal (there's a liquor store down the street). Closed Sunday. Hours are flexible, but it's usually open for dinner.

Pan Pay Café and Bakery (tel. 506/750-0081, inexpensive) in Puerto Viejo has good coffee, pastries, and sandwiches; books for rent; and indoor and outdoor tables. It's an excellent place to hang out and people-watch. You might just find yourself here every morning and most afternoons. It's near Johnny's place, across from the police station and two blocks from the bus station. Call for hours.

Shops and Activities

The **Caribbean Conservation Corporation** (CCC) runs John H. Phipps Biological Field Station (tel. 506/710-0545, www.cccturtle.org/volunteer-researchprograms.php?) in Tortuguero. This one-room but very informative museum features fascinating displays on the sea turtles that give the area its name (*tortuguero* means turtle hunter). To get there you walk north on an overgrown path from the town center.

Look up guide **Barbara Hartung** (tel. 506/842-6561, tinamon@racsa.co.cr, www.tinamontours.de) in Tortuguero. Barbara is a German-born biologist and guide who has lived in Tortuguero for many years.

ATEC (Talamanca Association for Ecotourism and Conservation, tel./fax 506/750-0191, atecmail@sol.racsa.co.cr, www.greencoast.com/atec.htm) in Puerto Viejo is a grassroots group working hard to promote responsible tourism. Its Puerto Viejo office is a community center of sorts, offering Internet access and tour information and booking.

Long-time Manzanillo resident and guide **Florentino (Tino) Grenald** (tel. 506/759-0619 or ask for him at the ATEC office in Puerto Viejo) helped plan and administer the Gandoca-Manzanillo reserve early in the reserve's history. He grew up here and knows the reserve and surrounding areas like few others. To list all the flora and fauna Tino pointed out on our walk through the lowland jungle would take pages, but here's a small sampling: cacao trees, wild turmeric, a sloth, a spectacled owl, toads, tree crabs, bats, and three eyelash vipers.

DAILY LIFE

MAKING THE MOVE

So you're all set. You've visited Costa Rica (preferably many times), done your homework, and you're still feeling the love. Your friends either think you're crazy or tell you to make sure your new house has a guest room. If you're making the move with family or friends, they are as ready as you are. And you've thought about what it will take—financially, logistically, and emotionally—to make the move of a lifetime. You're good to go.

But there are a few things to think about even before you get here.

First, consider what kind of residency status you'd like to have. Maybe you'll be content to begin as a perpetual tourist, leaving Costa Rica every three months to maintain your legality. Or perhaps you'll want to plant your roots a little deeper right from the start, applying for *rentista, pensionado,* or *inversionista* status. All three categories require that you start the application process from your home country, working with the nearest Costa Rican consulate (see *Resources* for a list of Costa Rican consulates in the United States and Canada). Those interested in permanent residency or citizenship will be

in for a longer haul, unless they take the relative shortcuts of either marrying a Costa Rican citizen or having a child in Costa Rica.

Next, think about what you want to bring with you and how best to do so. What might you be better off leaving behind? Examine the relative merits of bringing your possessions into the country as checked baggage on the plane, as air cargo, or by ship.

Even as your practical self is taking care of all these important details, keep on speaking terms with the adventurer inside, the part of you that came up with this crazy idea of moving to Costa Rica in the first place. You'll still need a heaping portion of audacity to get yourself across the threshold of your new life. As the proverb goes, you can't leap a 20-foot chasm in two 10-foot jumps.

Immigration and Visas

Immigration policy in Costa Rica is a moving target, but the good news is that North Americans are for the most part given a warm welcome. A Nicaraguan day laborer will be treated differently from, say, a retired couple from Vermont who just invested in a seaside bed-and-breakfast. Nicaragua is to Costa Rica as Mexico is to the United States. People from the poorer country stream into the richer one, both legally and illegally, and become, for better or worse, an integral part of that nation's economy. The richer country isn't sure what to do about the situation, and often the immigrants from the poorer country are demonized and blamed for all the richer county's woes.

North American and European visitors, in contrast, have a fairly easy time of it immigration-wise; the most that a law-abiding visitor will have to deal with are bureaucratic headaches.

Those headaches, however, can get pretty fierce. In late 2006, the *Tico Times* called the agency that enforces immigration law "one of the country's most infamously inefficient bureaucracies" and noted that its policies subjected people to "astonishingly long lines and a mind-boggling lack of logic."

The agency in question is the Department of Immigration (Dirección General de Migración y Extranjería), which in turn is under the jurisdiction of the Ministry of Public Security (Ministerio de Seguridad Pública). There is also a National Immigration Council (Consejo Nacional de Migración y Extranjería), charged with review of residency petitions.

Though the processes may seem arbitrary, there are official policies in place, replete with stamps, seals, and much waiting in line. Still, even seasoned expat organizations like the ARCR (Association of Residents of Costa Rica) warn that immigration laws are hard to fathom and even harder to keep up with.

EXPAT PROFILE:
MARY ANN (RUBY) JACKSON

Born in Kentucky in the mid-20th century, Mary Ann Jackson thought her name suited her fine until one day just past the turn of the millennium. She was working at Family Court in Brooklyn, New York, and her client that day was a stately black woman in a bright yellow print native dress and head wrap. Elegant and imposing, the woman had a presence so powerful that all eyes in the room were drawn to her. When she spoke, her voice was equally impressive – a deep and rich sound that boomed through the cramped institutional rooms.

"It was [a] place where we didn't get to laugh a lot," says Mary Ann of her old job. "My boss likened it to a jurisprudence MASH unit. Sometimes it felt like the misery [had] seeped into the walls." Mary Ann had never seen a woman so fully in possession of herself and her mature beauty. It turned out the woman's name was Ruby. A jewel of a name for a jewel of a woman. Mary Ann told Ruby how much she loved her name. Ruby looked at Mary Ann for a long moment, seeming to take in Mary Ann's entire life in one glance. "It's yours," she pronounced regally. "I give it to you. It will make you smile."

Mary Ann did not take such a gift lightly. She recognized it for what it was: a chance to remake herself, to try on a new identity or circle back to one she'd lost sight of. Mary Ann had been feeling for a long time that she needed a change, something that would take her out of Brooklyn and release her from the persona that she'd settled into over the years. And so, tentatively at first and then with more confidence, she began to embrace her new name, which was all about confidence and daring. She told new friends she'd been born Mary Ann but had recently been rechristened Ruby, which felt like a part of her that had always been there but had never before been named.

The new name coincided with the working out of a new plan: to take early retirement and move abroad. She didn't want to wait until she turned 65 to get a reprieve; she knew that her new life hinged on having the courage to make big changes, and soon.

Though not born in Brooklyn, Mary Ann has a big Brooklyn personality: feisty and fearless. She's had a full life, with lots of work, travel, men, and a gaggle of nieces and nephews who adore her. She has a streak of giddy spontaneity that means she's pretty much up for anything, anytime. But she's also a practical girl who has a mania for doing her homework and plotting her course. Not one but two people – a psychic and a man who gave her a battery of psychological tests in the course of a job interview – have told her that she would have made an excellent general.

And it's the combination of those two character traits – throwing caution to the wind while making sure she knows exactly which way that wind is blowing – that makes her the perfect candidate for relocation to an exotic locale.

Costa Rica wasn't first on her list. "First I worked my way down the East Coast," she says. "Both coasts of Florida, into Louisiana – New Orleans almost had me except for the mosquitoes and heat. Texas, then Ireland, which isn't cheap anymore. I checked out Belize, but the infrastructure and medical care sucked; I have no intention of being flown to Miami for an emergency operation.

"Then a friend went to Costa Rica, and when she told me about it, bingo! It was close enough, had great medical care, decent infrastructure, lots of Americans and Canadians, cheap living."

When she got to Costa Rica she wasn't disappointed. The country was not only gorgeous but it *worked*. Mary Ann visited four times before moving down for good, exploring the Central Valley (she wanted a temperate climate) and working out logistical details, from visas to real estate possibilities. The ARCR (Association of Residents of Costa Rica) was an enormous help, says Mary Ann, as was her lawyer back in Brooklyn, who convinced her that the move was doable on a financial level. She owned an apartment building in Brooklyn – the rent from the other apartments made her mortgage, and the rent from her own apartment (along with her pension) provided the income she would need to live well in Costa Rica. A little later into her move, she sold the apartment building and is now

able to live even better than she expected, traveling at least three times a year to Europe, the United States, or more exotic locales.

Even more important than the financial details, for Mary Ann there's something special about this country, something hard to put into words.

"What's funny," she says, "is that I ran around telling everybody I was retiring to Costa Rica before I even went there. I just knew."

When Mary Ann came down for good in October 2004, she lived in a homestay in Heredia for about nine months, studying Spanish at a nearby language school. Then, with the help of a real estate agent, she rented a sprawling four-bedroom house in the verdant hills above Heredia, plunging headfirst into furnishing the new place (she loves garage sales) and bringing the garden back to life. She's still in close contact with her homestay family, making Thanksgiving dinner for them and visiting them for raucous card parties and coffee clatches.

She's got new friends, a new house, and a new country. As if that weren't enough, friends and family from the States visit regularly, she herself travels the world, and when she's home, she can barely find time to indulge her secret vices: romance novels and online mah-jongg. She's busier than she ever imaged a retired person could be. Brooklyn Family Court is far, far away, and she's finally found a place where she can be Ruby full-time.

But a few things are certain: In August 2002, the Department of Immigration issued a statement saying residency applications should be made in the applicant's country of origin rather than here in Costa Rica. (Although *pensionado* and *rentista* applications can usually still be made in Costa Rica.) And in August 2006, Immigration Law 8487 (Ley General de Migración y Extranjería Ley 8487) went into effect, though it will be years before we know just how all of the law's provisions will be interpreted.

And if policy is anything but crystal clear, enforcement (especially consistent enforcement) is even less so. Students of Costa Rican policy will find many contradictory statutes; it's often up to the individual official to play judge and jury, choosing which of the many laws he or she will enforce on any given day.

Lest you dismiss the situation as hopelessly third world, remember that many U.S. agencies—the IRS (Internal Revenue Service) comes to mind—have been shown to operate in a similarly heavy-handed and arbitrary fashion. Big government means lots of laws; some are bound to contradict others. And then, "public servants" around the world are often anything but, wielding their tiny swords with surprisingly lethal effect. When confronted with such officials, make nice. Count to 10, then grit your teeth into a smile. For the moment, they have the power and you don't. Save your rage and dreams of revenge for later, over a drink with friends. Then order another round.

But I digress. Costa Rica is making a real effort to streamline its immigration process, and everyone agrees it's high time for a change. And even with all the flux outlined above, the categories of residency are fairly straightforward and not apt to change significantly anytime soon.

One more thing you should know is that if you gain any type of residency or even citizenship in Costa Rica, your U.S. or Canadian citizenship is not affected. And there's no problem on the Costa Rican end of things, either. Since 1996 this country has recognized dual citizenship. The change in policy came about when Dr. Franklin Chang, Costa Rican–born scientist and NASA astronaut, became a U.S. citizen and was consequently stripped of his Costa Rican citizenship. There was a public outcry—the country didn't want to lose such an illustrious Tico to the United States—and in response the policy was changed.

TOURIST VISAS

No paperwork, no job, no muss, no fuss—nice work if you can get it. And it can be that easy, though recent crackdowns have put the fear of expulsion in the hearts of long-term expats who've never bothered about renewing visas or getting residency. A side note: It used to be that people from Canada,

the Costa Rica-Nicaragua border at Peñas Blancas

the United States, and Panama could enter and exit Costa Rica without a passport, though they did need some form of identification, like a driver's license. As of April 30, 2003, however, all visitors to Costa Rica must travel with valid passports.

Here's how the perpetual-tourist thing works. Visitors from Canada, the United States, and most of Europe don't need to apply for visas in their home countries but instead receive, upon arrival in Costa Rica, a stamp on their passport authorizing a 90-day stay. When that 90 days is almost up, you leave the country for at least 72 hours—maybe you've always wanted to visit the colonial city of Granada in southern Nicaragua, or snorkel at one of the Bocas del Toro islands in northern Panama. After your three-day vacation, you cross back into Costa Rica and get another 90-day stamp on your passport. This category of visa is called the B1, or tourist visa.

Some people do this for years, but it's not an ideal solution. Although not strictly illegal (you're not overstaying your visa), the practice is considered a little shady by Costa Rican officials—a way of getting around the law. What you're doing and how often is visible in full color—soon your passport will be a riot of blue, red, and purple stamps and seals that mark you as a come-and-goer. And who knows when the government will decide to crack down on this category of tourist?

If you have anything to lose in Costa Rica—a house, a business, a family—this gray-area existence is apt to make you a little bit anxious. Not to mention that leaving the country every three months gets to be tiresome and expensive. There are shady ways to skip the trip, but they are truly back-alley and indisputably illegal. A guy knows a guy who can take care of it—and suddenly your money and passport are long gone.

Even if you don't have anything to lose in Costa Rica, there are reasons to apply for residency. "I'm not sure why I was so into getting those papers," says Peggy Windle, who in 2002 took early retirement from her teaching job in Arizona and moved to Costa Rica. "I want to belong somewhere, I guess. To not be 100 percent vagabond."

If you're not planning to stay more than four months in Costa Rica, there are a few ways to legally extend your 90-day visa that don't involve a trip out of the country. You must be sure, however, to start these processes well before your visa has expired. These solutions only give you 30 additional days, are often more trouble than they're worth, and probably will not work more than once. One way is to apply at the immigration office (Migración) opposite Hospital México in the La Uruca section of San José. The office is open 8:30 A.M.–3:30 P.M. You may also be asked to obtain an affidavit, in which you swear that you have no dependents in Costa Rica, from the Justice Tribunal (Calle 17, Avenidas 6/8, tel. 506/223-7555, ext. 240 or 276, fax 506/221-2066). The results of a blood test to see whether you have AIDS or HIV may also be required. To apply for the extension you'll need three passport-sized photos, a plane ticket out of the country, and funds judged sufficient to see you through your proposed stay. This procedure also involves multiple forms, stamps, line waiting, and fees. Another possibility is to see if a travel agent or the ARCR can get you an extension. This way is usually easier but is not something you can keep doing every 30 days.

What happens if you skulk around Costa Rica with an expired 90-day visa? It depends just how expired it is. If you're a few days or weeks in arrears, you'll probably get off with some smooth talking and the payment of a fine. If you arrived in 1985 and haven't thought about visas since, you're still okay—until someone checks your passport. Then you'll most likely get a free trip home, a.k.a. deportation. If you're deported, you can't legally return to Costa Rica for 10 years.

One more thing—when you enter Costa Rica (each time), you could be asked to prove that you have sufficient funds to support yourself for the time you intend to be here. They may also ask you to show a return or onward plane or bus ticket. In practice, this rarely happens.

Types of Residency

There are countless types of residency, from refugee to diplomatic status, but for the purposes of the average North American or European, five of these will be of interest: *pensionado* (pensioner or retiree), *rentista* (loosely translated as "small investor"), *inversionista* (large investor), permanent residency, and citizenship.

PENSIONADO (PENSIONER)

Most retired people opt for this category, which requires you to prove at least US$600 a month in pension income. The income can come from a public source, like the U.S. government, or a private source, like the brokerage house that administers your IRA account. You must document that you will be receiving at least US$7,200 a year and arrange to have the checks deposited to a Costa Rican account in *colones,* not dollars. For a married couple, the spouse with less (or no) retirement income is considered a dependent, and a dependent need show no proof of income—he or she rides free on the partner's US$600. Children under 18 (or a child between 18 and 25 enrolled in university) can also be claimed as dependents and receive the same immigration status as their parents.

The downside is that two people's incomes cannot be combined to make up the required US$600 a month, though the combined income sources of one person will do the trick. If the pensioner is a little short of the US$600 a month, the balance can be made up by depositing five years' worth of the difference in a Costa Rican bank. So if your pension is US$545/month, you could make up the extra US$55 a month (for five years) by depositing US$3,300 in the bank.

Pensionados need to spend at least four months in the country a year, though the time need not be contiguous—you could spend January, February, October, and November here, for instance. You can't work as an employee, but you can own and receive income from a business.

When the Costa Rican government created the *pensionado* and *rentista* immigration categories in 1971, the idea was to attract foreign capital, and certain tax breaks were given to holders of these temporary residency visas. *Pensionados* and *rentistas* were allowed to bring in all their household goods, appliances, and one car duty-free, which with Costa Rica's high import duties was a very nice perk. But in 1992, in need of greater tax revenue, the government abolished the tax benefits associated with *pensionado* and *rentista* status. For more on what it will cost you to bring your household goods to Costa Rica, see the *What to Take* section later in this chapter.

RESIDENCY IN COSTA RICA: COMPARISON OF TYPES OF RESIDENCY

PENSIONADO (PENSIONER)

- **Requirements:** Requires proof of US$600 per month income from permanent pension source or retirement fund
- **Length of Stay:** Must remain in country at least four months per year
- **Spouse/Dependents:** Can claim spouse and dependents under 18 years of age
- **Employment:** Cannot work as an employee
- **Business Income:** Can own a company and receive income

RENTISTA (SMALL INVESTOR)

- **Requirements:** Requires proof of US$1,000 per month for at least five years, guaranteed by a banking institution, *or* a US$60,000 deposit in an approved Costa Rican bank.
- **Length of Stay:** Must remain in country at least four months per year
- **Spouse/Dependents:** Can claim spouse (add US$1,000/mo) and dependents under 18 years of age (add US$500/mo)
- **Empoyment:** Cannot work as an employee
- **Business Income:** Can own a company and receive income

INVERSIONISTA (LARGE INVESTOR)

- **Requirements:** US$200,000 in any business *or* a specified amount of investment in certain government-approved sectors
- **Length of Stay:** Must remain in country at least six months per year

RENTISTA (SMALL INVESTOR)

For those who have not yet reached retirement age but have managed to make investments that bring in regular income, the *rentista* option is an attractive one. You'll need to prove a monthly income of US$1,000 (usually a CD or annuity), guaranteed by a banking institution. Another option is to deposit US$60,000 (US$1,000 a month for five years) in a Costa Rican bank, which will authorize you to withdraw US$1,000 of your money each month. If, after two years of *rentista* status, you apply for and receive permanent residency, you can withdraw all the money out of the account.

Other details of the *rentista* visa are similar to those of a *pensionado:* You can own a business but not work as an employee; you need to be in the country for

- **Spouse/Dependents:** Cannot claim spouse and dependents under 18 years of age (must process separately)
- **Employment:** Income allowed from the project
- **Business Income:** Can own a company and receive income

REPRESENTANTE (COMPANY VISA)

- **Requirements:** Applicant must be director of a company meeting certain requirements, such as employing a minimum number of local workers as established by the labor law, with financial statements certified by a public accountant
- **Length of Stay:** Must remain in country at least six months per year
- **Spouse/Dependents:** Cannot claim spouse and dependents under 18 years of age (must process separately)
- **Employment:** Can earn an income from the company
- **Business Income:** Can own a company and receive income

PERMANENTE (PERMANENT RESIDENCY)

- **Requirements:** First-degree relative status with a Costa Rican citizen (through marriage to citizen or having a Costa Rican child) *or* may apply after three years in another residency
- **Length of Stay:** Must visit Costa Rica at least once (72 hours) a year
- **Spouse/Dependents:** Cannot claim spouse and dependents under 18 years of age (must process separately)
- **Employment:** Can work
- **Business Income:** Can own a company and receive income

DAILY LIFE

at least four noncontiguous months each year, and dependents, whether spouse or child, enjoy the same immigration status as is awarded to the applicant.

INVERSIONISTA (LARGE INVESTOR)

Although you can legally own and operate any sort of business in Costa Rica even if you only have a tourist visa, an investment of at least US$50,000 in a sector the government deems a priority will get you *inversionista* temporary resident status. Costa Rican officials have declared as priority businesses related to tourism, forestry, and low-income housing. Nonpriority reforestation projects require US$100,000 in order to qualify you for *inversionista* status, and any other business ventures call for US$200,000 or more. *Inversionistas* must stay in Costa Rica six months out of every year, though as with other categories of temporary residency, the time need not be contiguous.

For any investment, please exercise extreme caution—many people who come to Costa Rica seem to leave their common sense at home. Perhaps lulled by the tropical climate and the friendliness of the people, they trust too easily and don't do their due diligence—checking out every facet of the project before putting any money down. While living in the tropics is relatively easy, making a business profitable here is perhaps even more challenging than it would be at home.

Renewing *Rentista* or *Pensionado* Status

Expats who obtain *rentista* or *pensionado* status need to renew that status every two years. You'll have to prove that you were in Costa Rica for four months of every year. And you'll need to prove (keep those receipts!) that you've exchanged into Costa Rican currency at least US$7,200 a year (for *pensionados*) or US$12,000 a year (for *rentistas*). Remember that *pensionado* status requires a guaranteed income of US$600 a month (US$600 x 12 months = US$7,000) and that *rentista* status requires US$1,000 a month (US$1,000 x 12 months = US$12,000). Proving that you've withdrawn that money from your Costa Rican bank account and exchanged it into *colones* tells officials that you're spending the money here in Costa Rica. Officials will also do another Interpol background check to update your original one.

PERMANENTE (PERMANENT RESIDENCY)

After three years, *pensionados, rentistas,* and *inversionistas* can apply for permanent residency, which gives you most of the rights a Costa Rican citizen enjoys, save voting.

Other routes to permanent residency include marrying a Costa Rican citizen and living with him or her in Costa Rica for two years; having a child in Costa Rica; or being born in Costa Rica to non-Tico parents (of course if you're born here to Tico parents, you're automatically a citizen).

Applicants for permanent residency must demonstrate that they will make a positive contribution to the country. Benefits of permanent residency include being able to work (rather than just own a business, as is allowed under temporary residencies), reduced fares on air travel within Costa Rica, and much-reduced admission to national parks and reserves. Permanent residency also offers up the same sort of safeguards extended to citizens, such as protection against extradition (except in high-profile cases, like when drug lords or big-time financial scamsters try to hide out in the wilds of Costa Rica). As a permanent resident, you don't need to worry about remaining in the country for four months (to maintain *pensionado* or *rentista* status) or six months (to maintain *inversionista* status) out of each year. Your only obligation as a permanent resident is to visit Costa Rica at least once a year.

CITIZENSHIP

There are many paths to citizenship (also known as naturalization), none of them short. The most common route is to begin by establishing legal residency, securing *rentista, pensionado,* or *inversionista* status. After living here legally for seven years (five for citizens of Spain or other Latin American countries), you can apply for citizenship through the Office of Options and Naturalizations, a division of the Supreme Election Tribunal's Civil Registry (www.tse.go.cr, tel. 506/287-5477; Calle 15 between Avenidas 1 and 3 in San José), the same agency that records birth, deaths, marriages, divorces, and election registrations, and issues the ID cards *(cédulas)* carried by all citizens.

If you're from the United States or Canada, you don't have to give up citizenship in your home country to get citizenship in Costa Rica. You can be a citizen of both your old and new countries.

OTHER TYPES OF RESIDENCY

Other types of temporary residency usually require a sponsor and may be the way to go for:

- Anyone who renders special services to governmental, international, or educational institutions in Costa Rica.

- Highly specialized technical or professional workers granted prior authority by the Ministry of Labor. Managers and executives of multinational corporations with branches in Costa Rica often fall into this category. The company that sponsors these workers must meet certain qualifications, such as having at least 50 million *colones* in real capital investment and employing a labor force that is made up of at least 90 percent Costa Rican citizens. Companies that routinely sponsor their workers are likely to be already registered with the Department of Immigration.

- Students at public or private schools or universities recognized by the government.

- Domestic servants.

Sometimes the company that employs you, the institution you are rendering services to, or the school you attend will take care of the paperwork. Make sure that is the case, and/or contact your Costa Rican consulate or embassy for the latest on these categories of temporary residency.

The Application Process

Although in some cases it is still possible to begin the residency process from Costa Rica, it is usually preferable to begin the process in your home country, working with the nearest Costa Rican consulate (see *Resources* for a list of Costa Rican consulates in the United States and Canada). For now, *pensionado* and *rentista* status can usually be applied for from Costa Rica, but check with the ARCR to make sure that's still the case.

PAPERWORK FOR RESIDENCY

Different categories of residency have different requirements, but in general, you'll need:

1. Birth certificate
2. Marriage license if you're married (no divorce papers required)
3. Proof of income. This is the most important part of your application. The more income, the better; the government wants to be sure you have enough money to support yourself while in Costa Rica.

If you're going for *pensionado* or *rentista* status, you'll need a letter from your financial institution saying that you will be receiving at least US$600 a month (for *pensionados*) or US$1,000 a month (for *rentistas*). The financial institution must be an "internationally recognized entity," listed in Polk's International Banking Directory. If your income is from a brokerage or insurance company, you'll need to submit a copy of its annual report along with your residency application. The letter issued by your financial institution is supposed to say that your income is "permanent and irrevocable" for at least the next five years. Since it is the client who ultimately controls the investments, some financial institutions balk at using the phrase "permanent and irrevocable." The usual way around this is to have them add in their letter a line that states, "in the event the funds invested or on deposit are reduced in any manner, the bank shall notify the Costa Rican Tourism Institute," which, along with the Department of Immigration, has a say in residency issues.

For *inversionista* applications, you'll be submitting business rather than personal financial records. If you invest in an already existing business, you'll need to provide balance sheets and profit-and-loss information along with your residency application. For a new business, especially if you're hoping your enterprise will qualify as "priority" and thus allow you to invest US$50,000 rather than the usually required US$200,000, the forms and documents needed are beyond the scope of this book. A good accountant and a lawyer familiar with the Costa Rican business world will be your best resources. Starting a business in Costa Rica need not be bound up with a residency application. Many people start businesses with far less than US$50,000, and they do so while here on a 90-day tourist visa. This is perfectly legal.

4. Copies of academic or professional degrees (if you plan to practice your profession in Costa Rica)

5. Police certificate of good conduct from the last place you've lived for at least two years. The police certificate should be obtained last, as it is only good for six months and may expire while you wait for your other documentation to come through.

6. Interpol background check. This is done in Costa Rica; you'll need to provide your fingerprints. The background check usually takes about a month.

7. Authenticated copies of dependents' birth certificates (spouse and/or children) if they are to be included in the residency application. You'll also need police certificates of good conduct for dependents over 18 that you're including in your application.

8. Photos—take at least 10 facing front and 5 side views. You'll need photos at almost every step of the process.

9. You may be asked to provide proof of a doctor's exam. There are laws on the books allowing Costa Rican officials to refuse entry into the country to people with AIDS, although I've never heard of that happening.

Note: All documents must be translated into Spanish (by the office of the Costa Rican consulate), then submitted to and authenticated by the Costa Rican consulate officer in the country where the documents are issued. Having your documents authenticated by a Costa Rican consulate is not the same as having them notarized. Documents that are not "public documents" must be certified by a notary public of the state where the documents were issued. Public documents (those issued by a governmental institution) do not need to be notarized.

Authorization means that the consulate makes sure the documents are valid and belong to you; the consulate will also make sure the notary who notarized your documents is fully certified. There is, of course, a fee for each document authorized, at present about US$40 per document.

GETTING HELP

The residency process can be lengthy and frustrating. I suggest getting help. You could hire a lawyer or go through the ARCR (Association of Residents of Costa Rica—see *Resources*), which has a good reputation and has helped many an expat through the residency maze.

Moving with Children

Costa Ricans love children, and the society as a whole is more kid-friendly than the United States. Even unplanned children are cherished, and motherhood is still seen by many here as a woman's highest calling. Many family decisions—like where to live—are heavily influenced by what would be best for the children.

Ticos are indulgent parents, and kids are often given a lot of freedom, their misdeeds ignored. An interesting historical explanation of this phenomenon is offered up in *The Ticos:* "Until half a century ago, many children died very young, and parents let small children enjoy what might be a brief stay on earth. Infants and toddlers are still allowed much free rein."

If you move here with kids, you'll be in the majority—almost all Costa Rican couples have children—and you will have an edge in making friends with locals. An expat mother in San José told me that her social life consisted mostly of children's birthday parties, where the kids would go outside and play and the mothers would stay inside, gossip, and eat cake.

Schooling will of course be a concern if you're moving with kids; see the *Language and Education* chapter for information on education in Costa Rica; see *Resources* for list of public and private schools.

ENTERING AND EXITING
Non-Costa Rican Children

In an effort to foil traffic in human beings (child prostitution rings often operate internationally) and to prevent international child abduction, many governments have special rules for minors entering and exiting their countries. For children traveling with one parent, Costa Rica officially requires evidence of relationship and permission for the child's travel from the parent or legal guardian not present.

Parents must take this very seriously if they don't want to be refused entry or exit; they might miss their plane while scaring up the necessary forms and signatures. To be on the safe side, parents should carry the child's birth certificate, along with a notarized copy of a letter that says both parents agree to this particular trip.

© ERIN VAN RHEENEN

young girl in Tortuguero

For more information and for downloadable forms, visit www.familytravel forum.com.

Costa Rican Children

If your child was born in Costa Rica, or if at least one parent is a Costa Rican citizen, the child will automatically be a Costa Rican citizen. So even if your child travels on, say, a U.S. passport, if she or he qualifies as a Costa Rican citizen, in effect the child has dual citizenship and will need to comply with entry and exit requirements applicable to Costa Rican children. To exit Costa Rica, she or he will need an exit permit issued by the Costa Rican immigration office. This office may be closed for several weeks during holiday periods.

It is also imperative that if a Costa Rican–born child is visiting Costa Rica with only one parent (even if the child lives full-time in another country and his or her parents are not Costa Rican), the child must have the permission of the absent parent (signed in the presence of a Costa Rican consulate) to leave Costa Rica. Contact the Patronato Nacional de la Infancia (PANI, Costa Rica's organization to protect children's welfare) for more information (tel. 506/256-7328 or 506/257-3212; www.pani.go.cr).

The rules are complicated and inflexible, and they change often—a bad combination. Parents of kids born in Costa Rica are advised to consult with the Costa Rican embassy or consulate in the United States about entry and exit requirements *before* travel to Costa Rica. Also check the Costa Rican embassy website for more information: www.costarica-embassy.org.

Moving with Pets

Jerry Ledin arrived in San José in 1998 with six black duffel bags and Piper, his Scottish terrier. "It was crazy to think I could bring my dog along," admits Jerry. "But I never considered not bringing him." It was easier than Jerry imagined. Unlike in other countries, there is no quarantine period; Jerry could take Piper with him right from the airport. "Everything turned out just fine," he says, "and Piper adjusted faster than I did—he's converted to Catholicism and now speaks fluent Spanish."

Even if your pet is not good with languages, bringing cats and dogs into Costa Rica is a fairly simply procedure. Bringing cows, horses, and other livestock is a bit more complicated, and if you want your snake or parrot to accompany you, you'll have to jump through some hoops, especially if your scaled or feathered friend is on any endangered species list.

DOGS AND CATS

For dogs and cats and other small pets, you'll need to prove to both the airlines and Costa Rican customs officers that your animal is healthy. Schedule an exam with your local veterinarian a week or two before your departure date—the vet should fill out a health certificate stating that the animal is disease-free and has been vaccinated against distemper, hepatitis, leptospirosis, parvovirus, and rabies. The rabies vaccination is supposed to be more than 30 days but less than a year old, and it's necessary only for animals four months or older. The health certificate should then be endorsed by a Veterinary Service (VS) veterinarian, but it need not be notarized. The Costa Rican consulate says the examination for the certificate must be conducted within the two weeks prior to travel to Costa Rica, though anecdotal evidence suggests that a certificate up to 30 days old will do the trick.

Pet owners also need to get authorization from the Costa Rican Health Ministry; go through your nearest Costa Rica consulate or embassy to obtain this permission.

When you arrive in Costa Rica, the customs officer will do a visual inspection of your pet and look over the health certificate and the authorization from the Costa Rican Health Ministry. If all is in order, you're through, and you can find a pet-friendly taxi (not an easy task) and stuff your Irish wolfhound in the backseat. Some people traveling with pets report that they weren't even asked for their documents, but you can't count on encountering such relaxed attitudes yourself.

If you're missing any documents or the officer decides your pet looks ill and might transmit disease, the animal will either be temporarily released to your care (kind of like being out on bail) or (if the official decides there's a real health risk) kept in a state kennel for up to 30 days, until you work out what to do next—arrange for the necessary paperwork or contact a local vet if your animal needs care.

If you're an animal lover who arrives in Costa Rica petless, there are many cats and dogs that need adoption. See *Resources* for contact information for animal shelters.

HOLSTEINS, THOROUGHBREDS, VIPERS, AND MACAWS

Livestock will need permission from Costa Rica's Agriculture Ministry's Animal Sanitation Department to enter the country. Ask your Costa Rican consulate or embassy how to go about getting this authorization or, if you speak Spanish, call the San José office (tel. 506/253-5605). More exotic animals, like lizards, will be allowed in if they have a clean bill of health from a vet—you'll need to check what diseases might affect your particular creature to know what vaccinations will be required. If your pet is on the endangered species list, the paperwork will be more complicated (from both the Costa Rican end and from your country of origin, which may have even stricter regulations); required information may include the animal's country of origin and permission to take it out of that original country. Such regulations aim to protect against illegal traffic in endangered animals. Again, the Costa Rican consulate in your country of origin is your best source of information for up-to-date specifics.

FLYING WITH PETS

Most likely you'll bring your pet with you on the plane. Most airlines allow seeing-eye dogs in the cabin, and some allow small pets to accompany you in your seat. I know a few women who always carry their little dogs with them in big purses; sometimes the flight crew doesn't even realize the animals are along for the ride. I never asked these women what they do about letting the animals relieve themselves on long flights. Bigger animals (or all animals, on some airlines) will need to ride in the cargo hold or even on a separate cargo flight. Some airlines will not accept pets as checked baggage May 15–September 15, since the cargo hold is not air-conditioned.

Animals checked as baggage need to travel in leak-proof cages that have handles, so that baggage handlers will be able to easily lift and carry the cage. The cage should be just large enough for the animal to turn around. Vets say animals

ANGELA'S TIPS ON BRINGING PETS TO COSTA RICA

When Angela Passman came to Costa Rica in 2001, she didn't come alone. She arrived with a husband, three small children, three dogs, three cats, and two birds. But even with all that company, she felt very alone when in the first few months here everything that could go wrong did. One of her beloved dogs went missing. All of her children had to be taken to the hospital. And the house they'd rented leaked when it rained. In Costa Rica it rains a lot.

She and her family worked through all their problems – finding the dog, figuring out the medical system, arranging for non-leaking accommodations – but it was a steep learning curve. Still, eventually the Passmans fell in love with their new home, "finally understanding why it is called paradise," says Angela.

Seeing that many other people relocating to Costa Rica were in similar straits – the companies that sent them down offering very little

© ERIN VAN RHEENEN

With a little planning, it's easy to bring your pets to Costa Rica.

in the way of assistance, or newcomers underestimating the cultural differences – Angela wanted to spare others what she'd been through. She founded Guardian

should fast for six hours prior to the flight in order to reduce nausea. If the flight is longer than four hours, the animal should eat a few hours before takeoff.

The bottom line is that each airline has a different policy regarding pet transport, and those policies often change. Set aside some time before your departure to research which airlines offer the best deal for your needs.

PETS IN COSTA RICA

Most buses and taxis do not welcome animals, though they must, by law, accept seeing-eye dogs. Some hotels accept pets—check ahead of time. There are plenty of vets in Costa Rica, especially in the Central Valley area. Vets in more rural areas will probably specialize in livestock. Vets will often board pets for around US$10 a day; animals stay in cages but are supposed to be exercised daily.

DAILY LIFE

Angels, a relocation service. Her company helps with all manner of issues, from schooling to real estate, but Angela says that one of her most popular services is pet transport. Angela has helped many people bring their pets here, and she is a member of the Independent Pet and Animal Transportation Association (IPATA; www.ipata.com). Below she gives people who want to bring their pets with them from the United States to Costa Rica a few pointers.

- Even with FAA regulations, not all airlines are the same when it comes to pet travel. Our first choice when transporting a pet is Continental. In my opinion (and the IPATA agents we work with agree), Continental is very pet friendly, and they handle the transportation better than any other airline. They transport the animals from the plane to the holding terminal in air-conditioned or heated vans, so the animal is never out in extreme heat or cold.
- It is important to get a travel kennel well before you travel so that your pet can get accustomed to it before they fly.
- Never sedate your pet before they travel. The effect of tranquilizers is intensified by altitude, and sedating your pet can put it in serious danger. Your pet will settle down with the sound of the engines; they almost always handle the trip better than we do.
- The paperwork you need to bring pets into Costa Rica has been shifting in the last several years. In general you'll need proof of a rabies vaccine, which must have been administered more than 30 days and less than one year before the time of travel, along with health certificates from your vet and the USDA.

For more information on what is necessary to safely bring your pet to Costa Rica, or for other relocation help, email Angela at info@relocationcr.com or visit www.relocationcr.com. From the United States or Canada you can call her toll-free at 877/889-1131.

Pet food is easy to come by in Costa Rica, even upscale brands like Iams and Eukanuba.

Costa Rican Attitudes Toward Pets

Although Costa Ricans love their pets, they think of them differently than do most North Americans. Dogs are valued for their ability to protect people and property, and are often not let into the house. The U.S. practice of letting dogs sleep on the sofa or even the bed would be considered in Costa Rica hopelessly *cochino* (which literally means piggy and is used as a synonym for dirty).

You won't see many cats out and about in Costa Rica, maybe because the street dogs would consider them tasty morsels. Walk down any street or along any beach with your dog at your side, and a motley crew of other canines will rush out to see who dares to invade their territory. In the dog world there is a complicated pecking order that is given freer reign here than in other countries; you'd better not stand in the way as the dogs work out for themselves who's on top. Each block has its neighborhood bully dog, so if you're going to let your beagle roam free, she or he had better be street-wise. There aren't as many mangy street dogs in Costa Rica as you see in other developing countries, but they do exist, and it's best to give them a wide berth—they've had to adapt to a life of people kicking them and throwing rocks at them, so they're not likely to be too friendly.

That said, there are many good things about bringing your pet to Costa Rica. Especially if you move here with children, your dog or cat could be that living, breathing piece of home that helps its human owners adjust to their new environment. And there's nothing like a big dog—however sweet-tempered—to discourage burglars and other scoundrels. Dogs also have such keen senses of smell and direction that if you get lost in the jungle that is your new backyard, your dog will almost certainly know the way home.

LEAVING WITH PETS

Animals leaving Costa Rica require exit permits. You'll need a local vet to fill out a health certificate; often she or he will accept the original health certificate from your country of origin as proof that the animal is in good health. For a fee, the vet can take care of all the paperwork, or you could check in with the Department of Zoonosis at the Ministry of Health, located in San José (tel. 506/223-0333, ext. 331).

What is likely to be more of a hassle is getting the animal back into your country of origin, which may have stricter regulations about animals entering their territory. It's best to check out your country's regulations even before you leave for Costa Rica.

What to Take

Most people—even adventurous souls who decide to pick up and move to another country—have a lot of stuff that they've accumulated over the years. Even if you consider yourself nonmaterialistic and have made an effort to keep your possessions to a minimum, chances are that what you own is more than you could check as baggage on a flight to Costa Rica.

And this method—bringing in your possessions as checked baggage—is by far the cheapest and easiest option. As long as you can convince customs officials that everything you bring is portable, for your own personal use, and necessary for your enjoyment or for the practice of your profession while in Costa Rica, you will pay no duties (taxes on imported goods) and there will be no bureaucracy save filling out the usual customs form that flight attendants hand out just before the plane lands.

The second-easiest option is to send a small shipment as air cargo (not as luggage accompanying you on your flight)—at least some of the shipment will be taxed, and there will be forms to fill out and lines to stand in.

The third option is to ship your possessions by boat; the container will arrive at a port on either the east or west coast of Costa Rica. In terms of customs, hassles, and duties, this is the most time- and money-intensive option, but it's the way to go if you really want to bring your entire household with you: books, CDs, stereo, sofa, bed, stove, and refrigerator—even your car can go in the shipboard container.

But why lug your old life with you to a new country, especially when you have to pay so dearly for the privilege? If you've lived in one place for more than a few years, I'll bet that you've been meaning to purge your belongings—to have a garage sale or take a few trips to the Salvation Army drop-off station. It feels good to pare down, and a lot of people who move to Costa Rica do so in part because they want to simplify their lives. You can start simplifying even before you get here, by thinking carefully about what possessions you can't live without, then selling or giving away the rest. "I thought about selling all my favorite things, all the great stuff I've collected over the years, and I just couldn't do it," says Mary Ann Jackson, who moved to Costa Rica in 2004. "But I wasn't going to lug it all with me, either. So I gave it all away to friends. Now I can visit my stuff in their houses."

You may be tempted to bring your appliances, but I would advise against it. You will pay high duties on these items (sometimes more than 50 percent of the item's value), and it's easy to buy appliances here. You'll probably pay about what you'd pay in the United States, though the selection isn't as good here. The best deals are in the Pacific coast port of Golfito, near the border with Panama. There Ticos and tourists alike can buy up to US$500 in duty-free goods every six months. Many people hang around the area, selling off their buying rights to the highest bidder. Golfito is near the legendary surf spot of Pavones and close to the Osa Peninsula, home to magnificent Corcovado National Park. You could do worse than head south for a week of surfing, tapir-watching, and appliance-shopping.

Furniture is another thing that it's easy to come by in Costa Rica. In fact, many newcomers have pieces custom-made for not much more than they'd pay for ready-made items in the United States or Canada. Costa Rica is known for its gorgeous tropical hardwoods and for its tradition of woodworking. Even if you don't want to spring for a custom-made dining room table or a hand-carved headboard, there are plenty of ready-made items that show the local materials and skills to good advantage. The Central Valley town of Sarchí, for example, is known for its lovely wood-and-leather rocking chairs, which are very comfortable and will look great on your tiled front porch with volcano view.

ON THE PLANE

As discussed, bringing used goods and personal belongings with you as checked baggage is your first and best option. Some airlines allow you to pay extra and bring a little more than the usual limit. It's worth checking as much luggage as possible, as this is the only way to import your belongings without duties and customs hassles. Everything you bring must be for your own personal use (not intended for resale), be portable, and be a reasonable quantity for the duration of your stay. Most people, even those who plan to stay years, first come in on a 90-day tourist visa, so what you bring in as luggage should look like a reasonable amount of goods for that amount of time.

On the other hand, consider the case of Brenda Burnside, a former professional boxer who moved to the Pacific coast town of Nosara. When she saw the reduced circumstances of the local public school, she wanted to help. Enlisting the help of eight members of her church back home in Nevada, she offered them a free place to stay in sunny Costa Rica if they would fill their luggage with books, school supplies, and sports equipment. When Brenda lugged the precious cargo to the school, the teacher cried in gratitude—she couldn't believe such generosity. Now, a persnickety customs official at the airport could have challenged the travelers' need for so many pens, notebooks, geography textbooks, and soccer balls for a stay of just a few weeks. As luck would have it, all of the do-gooders got the green light at the airport. That's how customs decides whose bags to check at the San José airport: You push a button, and if the light comes up red, they search your bags. If it comes up green, you're on your way without even a glance inside your luggage.

What you're allowed to bring in as luggage includes:

- Clothing, jewelry, purses, umbrellas

- Medicine and medical equipment if necessary for personal use (such as a wheelchair or oxygen tank)

- Sporting equipment, including surfboards, kayaks, golf clubs, fishing poles, etc.

- One video camera, one still camera, one portable tape recorder, one portable computer, one portable telescope

- One portable television, one portable radio

- One portable typewriter, one calculator, one portable printer

- Paint and canvases

- Tools, supplies, and manual instruments pertinent to the trade of the traveler, as long as these do not constitute a complete set for an office or laboratory

- Portable musical instruments and accessories (no pianos!)

- Books, tapes, photos, CDs, if for noncommercial use

- 500 grams (1.1 pounds) tobacco, five liters (1.3 gallons) of wine or hard liquor (per adult traveler), two kilos (4.4 pounds) of candy, baby food (an amount "sufficient for your proposed stay")

- Tent and other camping gear

- Up to four hunting or marksman rifles and 500 rounds of ammunition (subject to additional regulation by the Firearms and Explosives Department of the Ministry of Security)

If you arrive at the airport with items that don't qualify as luggage, don't despair. There's a duty-free exemption of up to US$500. So if you bring, say, two portable TVs instead of one, if the second one is worth less than US$500, you're still okay. Customs will stamp your passport, and you'll need to wait six months to take advantage of that US$500 exemption again.

If the US$500 exemption isn't enough, and you get slapped with some duties, you have two choices: Pay the bill right then and there if you think the

DAILY LIFE

amount is fair, or leave the goods in question at the airport (ask for a receipt) and return the following day to argue your case (bring along someone who speaks Spanish).

AIR CARGO

You can send up to 500 pounds (227 kilograms) as air cargo. Duties for items sent air cargo differ from those of items carried into the country as luggage, though personal clothes, shoes, purses, books, hand tools, and some sports equipment will still be duty-free. Everything else will be taxed—each item has its own duty, from paintings at 15 percent to pots and pans at 54 percent of declared value. You will even be taxed on the freight charges you pay, and on any insurance, which is why some customs brokers suggest you forgo insurance.

When your shipment arrives in Costa Rica, it will be sent to a bonded customs warehouse. To pick up your shipment, you will need:

- Your passport (copy the main page and the page with your last entry into Costa Rica, proving you've entered the country within the last 90 days)

- The Air Way Bill, which the freight handler you contract will have given you

- Packing inventory that includes declared value of contents

- Then you pay the duties assessed, the Terminal Handling Fee, and the bonded warehouse fee. You can do this on your own, hire a customs broker, or bring along a calm, savvy, Spanish-speaking friend who can help you out.

- Very important: For claiming either an air cargo shipment or a surface (boat) shipment, you need to prove (by the stamp on your passport) that you have entered (or re-entered) Costa Rica within the last 90 days. If you've been here longer, your shipment will be considered a commercial one, and all hell will break loose. You'll have to pay duties on everything, even books and clothes, a health certificate will be required for used clothing, and you'll need invoices for everything shipped. And if you don't have the necessary invoices and certificates? Good luck trying to claim your stuff.

SHIPPING BY BOAT

If you have a lot you want to ship, you can pay for a quarter, half, or full ocean container, which is a steel box 40 by 8 by 8 feet. The box will be loaded onto a ship, which will eventually dock on either the Atlantic or Pacific coast of Costa Rica, depending on where it's coming from. You can fit a great deal in one of these containers—even a car—but every item needs to be numbered and inventoried, including the serial numbers of all appliances and electronic items. And you can't just dump it all in—you need to pack carefully, because it will need to withstand a lot of moving around and perhaps a lot of heat. Experienced movers recommend putting any heat-sensitive items in the middle of the load. Most people hire professional movers and so don't need to worry about packing the box themselves.

It's important that you ship only used items (more than six months old); otherwise you may end up paying duties on new items, which are much higher. The serial numbers on appliances and electronics allow customs agents to know exactly how old they are and what their average prices are.

If you choose to go it alone, you'll either meet the ship to pick up your possessions or ask that the container be trucked to a warehouse in San José. The documents needed to claim the shipment are:

- Your passport (copy of the main page and of your last entry into Costa Rica, showing you've entered the country within the last 90 days)

- Inventory list with declared value of container contents

- Original Ocean Bill of Lading

DRIVING TO COSTA RICA

If you've got some time on your hands and are good at talking your way in and out of rough spots, you might want to drive all the way from North America to Costa Rica. You could load your car or truck with all your worldly possessions, then hit the road and see what happens. You'll pass through some gorgeous country and will cross many borders, all of which will be enforcing different regulations concerning what you can and can't bring into their country. It's not for everyone, but it's not a trip you will soon forget. *¡Buen viaje, y buena suerte!*

For more information on bringing your car to Costa Rica, see the *Travel and Transportation* chapter.

HOUSING CONSIDERATIONS

You have a dream, and it goes like this: You'll quit your job, buy a dirt-cheap piece of beachfront property in Costa Rica, then build a little house with your own two hands, using driftwood and palm fronds. You've got the skills—you hammered together that tree house when you were 12, and once fixed a door that wouldn't close. In a few months you'll be spending your days surfing bathtub-warm tubes, reading all the novels you've always meant to read, or just lying in a hammock, swaying in the ocean breeze.

Or maybe your dream is more industrious: you'll take over a down-at-the-heels lodge at the foot of an active volcano. Howler monkeys will hoot you awake each morning and toucans will serenade you at dusk. With hard work you'll turn the place around, adding an upscale spa, a five-star restaurant, and stables. Soon your place will be featured in *Travel & Leisure,* tourists will flock to you, and the money will roll in.

Hold on a minute. Better yet, hold on a few good months or even years. "Things take a long time to accomplish in Costa Rica," says Brenda Burnside, a

© ERIN VAN RHEENEN

former professional boxer who now runs a health and exercise center in Nosara. "And sometimes that's a good thing." If you've done your homework—traveled the country, staying here and there a month or two and longer in the place you think you might like to call home—you'll already know that the above scenarios are about as likely as crossing a raging river in a golf cart.

You'll also know that Costa Rica has some of the most beautiful land you've ever seen, and you'll be ready to do whatever it takes to get your own private piece of it.

There are always people for whom price is no object; most of us don't belong to that select club. You *could* pay as much for property here as you would in some of the hotter U.S. markets—we're talking millions of dollars—but most people want to avoid such madness.

How do you keep costs down and still get the house of your dreams? Adaptability and patience are key. If you need to duplicate exactly how you'd live in the United States, you'll pay a high price. But if you're willing to embrace what Costa Rica has to offer rather than concentrating on what it lacks, you're off to a good start. And if you rent for a while in your area of choice, getting to know the ups and downs of the place, talking to people, and observing what properties are going for, you're more than halfway there. Some real estate agents say that property values have doubled in the past decade and are likely to double again soon. That may very well be true, in some areas and for some types of property. That doesn't mean you should snap up whatever's on offer. I've said it once and I'll say it again: *Be patient.* "It's easy to buy," cautions Chris Simmons of Remax in Tamarindo, "and not so easy to sell." Which is in itself good news, as it suggests that in Costa Rica right now, it's a buyer's market.

Another piece of good news is that regardless of your nationality or immigration status, you have basically the same property rights as native Costa Ricans. Costa Rica's solid and egalitarian property rights are a big incentive to investing here.

A COUNTRY UNDER CONSTRUCTION

As I've written elsewhere, the new national bird of Costa Rica might well be the crane—the construction crane, that is. This awkward yellow giant in often spotted in the beach communities of northern Guanacaste, on the central coast, in the suburbs of San José, and in formerly sleepy crossroads town like Liberia. The crane's call is a creaking complaint as it swings back and forth, accompanied by a cacophony of hammers, drills, and shouts of "Buy now!"

Costa Rica is a country under construction. Developers and individuals have snapped up most of the land around popular beach resorts like Jacó, Tamarindo, and Playas del Coco. Condo towers and low-rise residential complexes are popping up wherever you look. Commercial development doesn't lag behind—in Santa Ana, the upscale business park called the Forum II recently opened for business; the original model, the Forum I near Escazú, has 115,000 square meters of space and provides offices for clients such as Procter & Gamble, Hewlett Packard, and the National Stock Exchange. Along Guanacaste's Gold Coast, there are at least six major new hotels either recently completed or in the works: The Four Seasons, Marriott, Rosewood, Hilton, the Ritz, and Westin.

Malls are popping up, too. Some are modest strips on the side of a dirt road; others (like several that have opened in Liberia since 2005) are bigger enterprises, with cinemas, department stores, and dizzyingly well-stocked supermarkets.

Long-term expats have mixed feeling about the changes, depending on how close they live to the upheaval and whether or not they're profiting from it. If they live far enough out, they might like the convenience of a new place to shop and see a movie. If they're too close, they might rue the day they bought what they thought was a little retreat in a backwater town. Locals usually appreciate the new jobs and the increase in cash flow but lament the rise in prices such development can bring.

Yes, the hot spots are getting hotter, so hot that expats of modest means can't even touch them. Not to mention Costa Ricans—even middle class and professional Ticos complain that the influx of foreigners has priced them right out of much of northern coastal Guanacaste, some of the central Pacific coast, and the western suburbs of San José.

The good news is twofold. First, there's more housing stock to choose from in the areas of intense development. And two, once you start to explore the entire country—the lush back roads to Arenal, the parts of the Nicoya Peninsula not yet overrun, the San Isidro Valley, and still many lovely towns and rural areas in the Central Valley—you'll see that what at first glance seems to be a countrywide boom is still pretty much contained in a few key areas. Stray off the beaten track and you'll find pockets of the old Costa Rica.

What's Different?

In terms of buying, building, and renting in Costa Rica, most of the same rules apply as would apply in the United States and Canada. It takes perseverance and a certain measure of luck to find the place of your dreams. As elsewhere, location is everything: If everyone wants to live there, prices shoot up. The more you know about a place and the people in it, the better deal you're going to get. Would you bluster into a small town in the American Midwest and snap up the first house on offer, just because the price is half of what you'd pay in New York City? Of course not. You'd hang around for a while, get to know some real estate agents and residents. You'd learn that every spring the local meandering creek swells and jumps its banks; the houses nearby have mud marks to prove it. You'd learn that the owner of the best restaurant in town is desperate to sell because she wants to join her daughter in Santa Cruz. You'd hear about the new mall they're putting out on Highway 32, which will increase traffic fourfold on the single-lane road leading to what you'd thought was a pleasantly remote little plot of land.

In a new culture, where laws and customs are different and where you may not even speak the language, such investigations are doubly important. Some of the major differences you will encounter here are covered below.

- **Real estate agents are everywhere, none of them have to be licensed, and there is no true MLS.**

There are no requirements to be a real estate agent in Costa Rica beyond hanging out a shingle. Some of the bigger realty companies advertise that their agents are licensed in the United States or elsewhere. This may mean that the agents are more knowledgeable (at least about properties and practices in their home country), but it's unclear what that would mean if there were a problem—after all, what sort of jurisdiction would a U.S. organization have in Costa Rica? None at all. As for those with no credentials whatsoever, some of these self-styled real estate agents (many of whom are from the United States, Canada, and Europe) do a fine job. Others are incompetent at best, and downright crooked at worst.

Manuel Pinto of Carib Sur Realty in Puerto Viejo is adamant in his assessment of the situation: "There is NO ACCOUNTABILITY for bad realtors!!!" he told me in an email. He points out that a buyer must not only research the area where they want to live but also research the real estate agents in that area.

Word of mouth may be all you'll have to go on. You have to be a private eye of sorts—getting as many sides to the story as possible. Realize, too, that there's a lot of competition and backbiting, especially in small towns; you may have stepped into a family feud, or one real estate agent may badmouth another so he'll get your business. Look for real estate agents who have operated for many years in the same city or town, who have no complaints against them, and who have a good reputation in town and beyond.

In 2006 the Costa Rica government said it was cracking down on foreigners who were doing business here without the proper work permit or immigration status. The government's bark was apparently worse than its bite, however—I had a hard time finding anyone who was affected by this supposed crackdown. But it's true that many real estate agents, some here on tourist visas and so legally unable to work, would be vulnerable to such enforcement. To be on the safe side, make sure your real estate agent has the right to work in Costa Rica. Otherwise he or she might be deported in the middle of your deal.

And remember that while in the United States few people buy property without using a real estate agent, in Costa Rica, it's more common to *not* use the services of a real estate agent. Most deals here are still done without a middleman.

But if you want help, check in with the Costa Rican Real Estate Agents Chamber (CCCBR, tel. 506/283-0191, fax 506/283-0347, www.camaracbr .or.cr). Founded in 1974, the organization lobbies for mandatory licensing of real estate agents. Members must be residents of Costa Rica in good legal and professional standing, and they must take a training course in Costa Rican real estate law. Most real estate agents in Costa Rica are not members of the CCCBR, and lack of membership doesn't mean an agent is a crook. But if the agent you work with is a member, you can complain about his or her conduct to the CCCBR, and the agent may be thrown out of the organization.

The CCCBR also has a fledging multiple listing service (MLS) at www .mls-cr.com. But this isn't your home country's MLS. Since real estate agents in Costa Rica don't have any licenses to lose and since there is no effective oversight of transactions, any MLS in Costa Rica is going to be little more than some real estate agents pooling their listings. And several real estate agents I spoke with said they only had a few listings on the MLS, while they had many more on their own websites. "The majority of Costa Rican realtors do not work with exclusive listings," points out Mercedes Castro, former vice president of the CCCBR, so there is little motivation for a real estate agent to list a property on the MLS. They'd rather list it on their own website, hoping to be the one to do the deal and thus earn the commission. In addition, since many properties here are never formally "listed" anywhere, it's unclear how anyone in Costa Rica can claim a comprehensive MLS. Perhaps in the future there will be a larger, more complete list of properties, along with more effective oversight of real estate agents and their transactions. Until then, buyer beware.

· **When they hear your accent and see your face, the price will skyrocket.**

This may seem unfair, but in the larger scheme of things it makes sense—most North Americans and Europeans who come to Costa Rica have more resources than the locals. But I'm not rich, you may protest. Not by your standards, perhaps, but by Tico standards you're probably pretty flush. Which is not to say you should pay inflated prices. But you should understand and not be personally offended by sellers trying to get as much from you as they can. Is it really any different in other markets, where they won't even look at you unless you've been pre-approved for a loan, and where real estate agents start bidding wars that send costs skyrocketing 50 percent above the asking price? By the way, in Costa Rica buyers almost never bid over the asking price. Bidding substantially lower is much more common. *To avoid paying the gringo price, become a local.* Stick around for a while. Learn the language so you can bargain with the best of them. Or do what so many newcomers do: Get a trusted local to do your negotiating. When you scan real estate ads in the paper—*La Nación* is a good place to look, especially for Central Valley properties—often a price will be listed. This is a good starting point, and it makes it harder for sellers to double the price once they see they're dealing with an *extranjero*.

· **You'll need a lawyer for just about everything.**

"Costa Rica is the land of lines and seals," says writer and ex-Californian Richard Livett. He's talking about standing in line for every official document you need, and then having to get it stamped and often stamped again with all manner of official seals. Buying and selling property involves a great deal of paperwork, just as it does in the United States. Very few people want to wade through all that bureaucracy themselves, so they hire lawyers to do it for them. See the *Buying Property* section later in this chapter for more details.

The Tico House

It's hard to talk about the average Tico house, which might be anything from a condo in the city to a wooden shack on the beach. Back in the 1800s, most Tico houses were of adobe brick, formed from a mash of mud, grass, and sugarcane waste. Roof tiles were made of soft clay formed on the workman's thigh and left to dry in the sun. Doors and window frames were of one of the many tropical hardwoods found in this country. Walls were whitewashed, with a wide strip of blue at the bottom to discourage pecking chickens.

Few of these traditional houses remain, though you may see modern houses that adopt some of the traditional elements. Nowadays most Ticos live in small houses of wood or concrete block (it's hard to hang pictures or tack up postcards!). In the mid-1990s, 9 out of 10 Tico households had electricity, and 93 percent had running water (half from wells, half from government aqueducts). About 30 percent of houses were connected to sewer systems, while the rest had septic tanks or outhouses.

Tico houses can be as luxurious and well equipped as any you'd find in the world, but most in the mid- or lower price bracket will have certain characteristics that may take some getting used to if you're used to North American standards. But whether you're looking to buy or rent, many of the better deals will be Tico-style houses, so it's worth seeing if you can live happily à la Tica.

rowhouses in San José

- **Bars, bars, and more bars.**

Even in better neighborhoods, there are bars *(rajas)* on every window and usually big iron gates protecting the front of the house and parking areas. Thankfully, you don't see much of the broken-bottle-topped fences common in other Latin countries. Still, watching the sun rise each morning through barred windows takes some getting used to.

- **Noise.**

In Tico neighborhoods and towns, expect to hear roosters crowing, kids playing, music blaring, and car horns honking. "Noise pollution" is not a known concept here, and it is culturally unthinkable to demand that your neighbor tone down his or her act. The idea is that people need to live their lives, and who are you to infringe on this right? There are upsides to this situation: I've never once been asked to "Keep it down, please!"—not even by my landlord, who lives right next door.

- **Limited hot water.**

Often the only hot water to be had in a Tico house is in the shower, and it is not so much hot as *heated* water, warmed by an electric device attached just above the showerhead. Some of these devices have exposed wires bristling out and seem sure bets for causing nasty shocks or worse, but in practice they usually work well and probably save a bundle on utility costs. Many houses, especially in the hotter areas of the country, have no hot water at all. "Hot water is for wimps!" one Guanacasteco (resident of the province of Guanacaste) told me. Washing dishes, clothes, and sometimes yourself in cold water seems strange at first; you'll soon learn that there are special soaps designed to work well in cold water. And there's nothing like a cold shower to make you, well, long for a hot one.

- **No bathtubs.**

If you want to soak in hot water, you'll have to rent a room in a hotel geared to North American tastes or head to one of the country's many hot springs.

- **Telephones are a hot commodity.**

Consider yourself lucky if your house or apartment comes equipped with one, and get it in writing that the phone is part of the deal. Landlines are hard to come by—that's why so many people use cell phones, although the country is blanketed with dead spots. Some landlords ask for a separate phone deposit, not wanting to be left with an enormous long-distance bill (the phone line will almost always stay in the landlord's name).

DAILY LIFE

· **Bare floors.**

You won't find much wall-to-wall carpeting in Tico houses. Tile floors are the norm—swept, washed, and waxed each day by the homeowner or, more likely, the maid.

· **Lawns are tiny or nonexistent.**

Especially in middle-class suburbs, front yards consist of a concrete slab where you park your car. Backyards are more often patios than wide swathes of lawn. In the country you won't have a lawn, because the field or forest will come up to your door.

· **Not "up to code."**

North Americans are used to a certain level of quality when it comes to finish work and details. In Tico homes you may marvel at a piece of baseboard or molding that stops a foot short of the corner, or an electrical outlet placed too high for all but a basketball star to reach. An expat couple in La Fortuna was perplexed to find that the light bulb on their porch would be smashed each time they opened the door. Sometimes closets are nonexistent, other times they are the size of a breadbox or, even stranger, bigger than the room itself. Even in areas with many flying insects, screened windows and doors are an anomaly. When looking at a house to buy or rent, check every detail: water pressure, outlets (do they work? are there enough of them?), windows (do they open? close? lock?), electricity, door locks, toilets, shower, pipes, etc.

Renting

The best way to know if you want to live in a place is to live there, but without investing in property. North Americans are conditioned to want to own, own, own, but renting has a lot going for it. The legal period for a rental lease is three years, but as with so many other things in Costa Rica, theory and practice—what's "on the books" and what's actually done—are separated by a wide gulf. The practice here is that most leases are from six months to a year, with some landlords willing to rent month to month. Renting month to month, you could live for a few months in the expat-heavy Central Valley suburb of Escazú, then live for a while in the shadow of a highland volcano, then retreat for a season to a beachside haven on either the Caribbean or Pacific coast. (Try to strike a rental deal on the coast outside of the December–April high season; September and October are excellent

DECIPHERING THE CLASSIFIEDS

The classified ads are a good place to start your search for housing. One thing to remember: If the ad's in English, the price will almost certainly be higher. So while you may find some interesting options in the back of the excellent English-language paper the *Tico Times,* you'll find cheaper options in Spanish in newspapers like *La Nación.* Here are some terms and abbreviations that you may encounter.

¢ – the symbol for *colones* (confusingly, $ is also sometimes used)
3 dor (3 dormitorios) – 3 bedrooms
2 bñs (2 baños) – 2 bathrooms
204m2 – 204 square meters
alfom (alfombrado) – carpeted
alquileras – rentals
amplia – wide, spacious
amueb (amueblado) – furnished
apartamento – apartment
bñ (baño) – bathroom
bodega – storeroom, warehouse
casa – house
cerám (cerámica) – tile floor
coch (cochera) – garage
cocin (cocina) – kitchen
comercial – business
condominio – condominium
c/tel (con telefono) – with telephone
cta pilas (cuarto pilas) – utility room with big sink

dor, dorm (dormitorio) – bedroom
edificio – building
exc. ubic (excelente ubicación) – excellent location
finca – farm or country estate
gje (garaje) – garage
guarda – guard
jardín – garden
Lav (lavadora) – washing machine
lindo – pretty
local – office
lote – lot
lujo – luxurious
mil – 1,000 (one thousand)
millón – 1,000,000 (one million)
muy seg (muy seguro) – very secure, safe
nva (nueva) – new
parq (parqueo) – parking lot or area
peq (pequeño) – small
pisc (piscina) – swimming pool
piso – floor, as in two floors (levels)
planta baja – lower floor
playa – beach
quinta – country house
se alquila – for rent
se vende – for sale
tranquilo – peaceful
ventas – sales
vista – view
zona franca – free trade zone
zona verde – green area, perhaps a lawn

DAILY LIFE

times to negotiate.) After living in a few places, you'll know what sort of weather and ambience suits you.

Renting can be very economical or can strain your budget beyond the breaking point, depending on where and how you want to live. Rates in a recent issue of the English-language *Tico Times* ranged from US$250 per month for a two-bedroom apartment near San José to US$2,300 for a hilltop home in Escazú near the country club. In a recent issue of the Spanish-language *La Nación,* prices were lower: from under US$100 a month for a modest apartment to over US$1,000 for a larger, more luxurious home.

The above-mentioned newspapers will be invaluable to you as you search for an apartment, especially if you want to live in the Central Valley. The *Tico Times* puts most of its classified ads online (www.ticotimes.net), so you can apartment-shop even before you arrive.

Outside of the Central Valley, make contact with local English-speaking expats and see if they know of anything available. Most people I talked to found their places by word of mouth. Also try posting on one of the many Costa Rica–related message boards (see the *Resources* section), asking if anyone knows of a place to rent in your chosen area. Home-owning expats just may be looking to rent out their place so they can make a long visit home. You can also ask at language schools, which will have lists of families willing to rent out rooms (though they will give their own students priority, of course). Keep your eye out for For Rent signs, and talk to shopkeepers in the neighborhoods you've targeted.

The mechanics of renting here are much like they are in the United States. Landlords often adapt a boilerplate lease according to their own and their tenant's needs. My first apartment (in the safe and pleasant San Francisco area of San José) cost me US$200 a month, with a US$200 deposit paid in two monthly installments. The landlord was willing to make it a month-to-month lease, as long as I gave a month's notice of my departure, and we wrote that into the lease (which was in Spanish—if you don't speak Spanish, make sure you get a translation of any document). The apartment was small (but two-story), clean, and comfortable. It was furnished with a refrigerator, stove, and microwave, cable TV, a phone, table and chairs, a bed, and a desk. The landlord's wife even made sure I had sheets and towels! I paid the electricity and telephone bills, though they remained in the landlord's name. My monthly electric bill was about US$3, and I paid about US$25 for the telephone (unlimited Internet access was an additional US$20 per month, debited from my U.S. checking account).

From my apartment I could walk to two supermarkets, a bank, a few bakeries, and countless shops and restaurants. Three blocks away was a Centro Deportiva (Sports Center), where I ran around a track or watched kids play soccer. The bus stop was a five-minute walk from my apartment, with buses leaving for the city center every 20 minutes or so; the trip took 15 or 20 minutes and cost US$0.50. Sometimes I'd splurge and take a taxi into town for about US$4.50. I thought I'd discovered my own private pocket of livability, until I realized that there were two gringo families within shouting distance of my front door. For better or worse, we gringos live in every nook and cranny of this country.

If you're renting an unfurnished apartment, remember that you will probably have to supply your own appliances. In the United States an unfurnished apartment almost always comes with a stove and a refrigerator—not so in Costa Rica. So if you're looking to rent for the short term, your best option is a furnished place. If you opt for unfurnished, it's useful to make a list of what you'll need, estimate the prices, and factor that figure into your decision-making process. Setting up a house or apartment is not cheap.

It's important to check out a potential rental thoroughly. Turn on the faucets to check water pressure, see if the water drains out, and make sure the heater attached to the showerhead actually heats up the water. Check to see if there are enough electrical outlets, check the windows and doors for functioning locks, and if there's a phone, pick it up and make sure it works. Try to imagine what you'll be doing day to day and ask questions accordingly: Where's the nearest market, bus stop, bank, running track? When is garbage picked up, and do you have to pay for that service? Can the landlord tell you anything about the neighbors or the neighborhood? Is it safe to walk around after dark? Is it easy to get a taxi?

Legally, landlords are entitled to raise the rent by 15 percent each year, but of course (if you have a one-year lease), you're also entitled to then opt out of your lease. Anecdotal evidence suggests that landlords rarely raise the rent by that much, that fast. On my suburban block alone, there were two For Rent signs and one For Sale sign. The For Rent signs lasted a month or two, and I would guess that the For Sale sign is still there. Costa Rica is struggling economically, with the devaluation of the *colón,* austerity measures intended to help the repayment of foreign debts, and modest wages. With the recent influx of foreigners, many houses and apartments were built with the intention of cashing in. Right now, though, it seems that the supply exceeds the demand.

If you're thinking of being a landlord yourself, be aware that the law tends to favor renters. Lillian Iverson, who has lived in San José for almost fifty years, says it took her four years to evict her tenants, who were "very bad people." Lillian adds that the laws have changed somewhat in the past five years, and that she was finally able to get the tenants out. A property owner in Manuel Antonio says he thinks long and hard before renting out his places. "There are no zoning laws to speak of," he says. "Tenants could start a disco in your apartment if they wanted to. They could bring in ten family members and seven dogs, and it would still be hard to get them out. I rented to guy from Oklahoma who thought he was here to save Manuel Antonio [National Park] from the devil. He decided to move on, but if he hadn't, he'd probably still be in my apartment."

SHORT-TERM RENTALS

Besides a month-to-month lease, there are other options for short-term stays. The San José area has dozens of aparthotels, some of them quite luxurious. They often cost as much (if not more) than a regular hotel, but they come equipped with a kitchen and other amenities you wouldn't get in a hotel room.

But a comfortable hotel room might suit you as well as an apartment-style room. Before I found my apartment, I was thinking of staying several weeks in a midrange hotel while I looked for a longer-term place. I arrived in October, which is the low season, so many hotels were empty and quite willing to negotiate. For example, a pleasant hotel advertised at US$35 a night, close to the center of town and offering free breakfast, came down quickly to US$20 a night when I offered to pay by the week and in advance. But don't try this sort of haggling during December, January, or Easter week, when it can be hard to find a room at any price.

Another option is a homestay with a Costa Rican family. Though these are utilized most often by students in one of the many Spanish-language study programs (and often arranged through the school), you can also arrange such a stay separate from language study (and living with a Spanish-speaking family is its own sort of language study).

Buying Property

You've rented an apartment or two for a while, have explored the country, and are convinced that this is the place for you. You have an idea of where you want to live and how much you can spend. What's next? You start looking, taking it slow, secure in the knowledge that with patience and perseverance you'll be able to find (or build) the house of your dreams.

Most real estate transactions in Costa Rica are between individuals—real estate agents are a relatively new phenomenon in this country, and there is no board regulating their training or conduct. Real estate agents affiliated with local franchises of multinational agencies (like Remax and Century 21) may be slightly more accountable than unaffiliated real estate agents. A good agent can help you decide where to live, but chances are he or she will show you only the more expensive offerings. If you decide to use a real estate agent, be very clear about your budget, and make sure you understand exactly how much you're paying for the agent's services. This will not be easy—being direct is not a Costa Rican trait, and the real estate agent may arrange different deals with different clients—whatever the market will bear.

You won't have to look far for available properties.

WHERE TO LOOK

Look everywhere—in the Classifieds sections of local newspapers, on fences and trees for For Sale signs. Ask the waiter at your favorite seafood restaurant, talk with hotel owners, surfers, the woman selling fresh-squeezed orange juice on the street. As has happened in other countries, the Internet has revolutionized the real estate market in Costa Rica, allowing you to check out beachfront property as you shiver in Minneapolis. The World Wide Web is a valuable tool, but remember that mainly higher-end properties are represented there. The best deals may not even be advertised; you'll find them on the ground, talking to the owner of the *pulpería* or to other expats. The truly dedicated who read Spanish can try *La Gaceta* (www.imprenal.go.cr), the government newspaper, for notice of public land auctions, especially in more remote areas. Good deals are still out there. Spanish-speakers may also want to check out the Banco Nacional's website (www.bncr.fi.cr) to see if the bank is auctioning off any houses or lots.

RESEARCHING PROPERTY

So you've found a nice little plot of land, with or without a house on it. Your first step is to check to make sure the person selling the property actually owns it, and that there are no snags such as liens, lawsuits against the property, public road restrictions, water easements, or any other type of restriction.

WHY TO RENT BEFORE YOU BUY

Okay, so all the books on moving abroad say the same thing: rent before you buy. Live where you think you want to live to see if you really want to live there. You've heard it before, and I know that you are prepared to happily ignore this advice. Sure it's good for others, but you're impulsive, right? A free spirit. Or you have a friend who bought property on her first trip down, and she's happier than she's ever been.

Maybe so. But for every success story there are many people who tell me, "I wish I'd known..." Here are a few examples of things that, after buying property your first week here, you may wish you'd known:

- See that hill with the amazing views? Half the year, it gets winds so strong you'll have to dress like a Sherpa to have a drink on your deck.

- That charming group of expats you met your first week? Well, they don't actually live here full time. In fact, they're hardly ever here. In fact, you'll be the only full-time expat for miles.

- The guy who bought up half the land around town and carved it into tiny, expensive lots is not the only game in town – just the one with the best advertising. You'll find other, better, quieter deals to be had if you hang around long enough to get to know both expats and locals who might be selling or might know someone who is.

- The developer who touts his spread as eco-friendly wouldn't know a watershed if it burbled up in his bathtub. He's digging the septic tank too close to the water and deforesting the hillside, then planting a few "native species" saplings so he can put that in his brochure and on his website. As soon as they catch up with him, all sorts of government and environmental agencies might succeed in shutting him down.

- In the rainy season you'll become a charter member of the "bug of the week" club, as new species hatch in waves and make your house their temporary home.

So please. Rent before you buy. See if you like it here (and maybe you'll try out a variety of "here's"). Live here a while before you commit your life savings and burn your bridges back home. And you might consider that renting can be the most economical and trouble-free option, even if you plan on being here a long time.

The steps outlined below can be accomplished by a very resourceful and patient prospective buyer, although most people choose to hire a lawyer to take care of things. Both methods have their advantages: If you do it yourself, you'll learn a great deal about the country and its laws, and you'll be sure that you've really covered all the bases. On the other hand, and especially if you don't speak fluent Spanish, getting a trusted lawyer to help will save you much time and aggravation.

· Consult the National Registry.

You will find information on the property's title at the Registro Nacional (the National Registry, located in San José). In principle you are also supposed to be able to access information online at www.registronacional.go.cr, though it's not easy to get the online resource to yield what you're looking for.

Besides patience, you'll need the name and ID *(cédula)* number of the owner, along with the title number. The property section of the Registro Público is supposedly fully computerized and indexed, searchable by the owner's name or ID number or the title number, but it's best to have as much information as possible.

The title number assigned to each property is known as the *folio real.* It is a six-digit number preceded by a number indicating the province in which the property is located and followed by three additional numbers, which tell you how many people own the property. For example, a title number of 1-240871-000 means the property is in the province of San José (the "1" at the beginning of the number) and that there is only one owner of the property (the "000" at the end of the long string of numbers). Property held jointly by husband and wife will have a -001 suffix, and -002 would mean there are two separate (nonmarried) owners of the property. Condominiums have F in the title number: 1-240891-F-000. The certificate of title tells you everything about the property in question, from its dimensions to whether or not there are liens or encumbrances on it.

As with most things in Costa Rica, it's easier to research the *folio real* in person, at the San José office. It's even easier (if more pricey) to have a lawyer or other agent do it for you.

The National Registry report is the *informe registral,* and it provides the name of the title holder, boundary lines, tax appraisal, liens, mortgages, recorded easements, and anything else that would affect title.

· Get a property map.

Ask the seller to get you the latest version of the property map. Check to make sure the measurements and boundaries on the map are consistent with the property itself (take a good long walking tour of the property to make sure). If the seller has no map, you can get one at the Catastro Nacional (National Records Office), which is part of the Registro Nacional (National Registry) in San José. If no map exists, get a registered surveyor to draw up a map, and then register it at the National Registry (www.registronacional.go.cr, tel. 506/224-6668).

- **Make sure the land isn't too close to national borders.**

Only Costa Rican citizens can buy land within two kilometers (1.2 miles) of international borders.

- **Look into any zoning restrictions.**

Ask at the Ministro de Salud (Health Department) and the Instituto de Vivenda y Urbanismo (Housing and Urban Development Department) to see zoning plans that may affect your property. Consult the Dirección General Forestal (Forestry Department) for any land use restrictions. Make sure the property isn't part of a national park or reserve—the Ministro de Recursos Naturales, Energias, y Minas (Ministry of Natural Resources, Energy, and Mines) and the Servicio Nacional de Parques (National Park Service) will have this type of information. If you want to make sure they're not going to build a freeway through your land, check in with the Ministro de Obras Públicas and Transportes. Also consult your local municipality. See *Resources* for more about government agencies.

- **Certify that the seller has paid all past property taxes and assessments.**

- **Make sure any domestic employees you intend to retain have been paid off by the seller.**

Otherwise, you may be liable for any past monies due to them.

- **Check all utilities.**

Does the property have access to water, electricity, telephone lines, and waste disposal? If not, how much will it cost you to secure these services?

- **Check out your neighbors.**

Are they known cranks, water hogs, or drug runners? Ask around.

Tired yet? I never said it was going to be easy. And sure, there are a lot of people who either trust others to do the legwork for them or just slack off and forget many of the steps. You might skip some of the due diligence and be just fine. On the other hand, you might end up with a beautiful piece of land that you can't build on or even access.

RESTRICTIONS ON COASTAL PROPERTY

If you've found some beachfront property that you love and can afford, congratulations! But know that there are different rules for owning and building on this type of land. The Maritime Zoning Law says that no one can *own* the first 200 meters (219 yards) of beach frontage, at least not legally (unless you bought the land before 1977, when the law went into effect). Of those 200 meters of beach frontage, which begin at the high tide mark, you can't build on the first 50 meters (55 yards)—it's part of the *zona pública* (public zone). The next 150 meters (164 yards) inland is classified as *zona restringida* (restricted zone), which can be built on if the government chooses to grant a lease or "concession" of the property. Concessions last from 5 to 20 years and can most often be renewed without a problem, says Ryan Piercy of the ARCR.

The Maritime Zoning Law also restricts ownership of concession land. The following are not supposed to acquire concession land:

- Foreigners who have been residents of Costa Rica for fewer than five years
- Corporations with bearer shares
- Corporations based outside of Costa Rica
- Costa Rican corporations incorporated by foreigners
- Corporations with 50 percent or more ownership by foreigners.

In practice, how strictly these rules are adhered to seems to depend on where you are (How valuable is the land? Are people clamoring to use the *zona pública?*) and how much influence you wield. Tellingly, approximately 300 concessions are recorded in the Registro Nacional, but there are more than 15,000 hotel and tourist developments along the coast that somehow managed to bypass the law.

If you're a multinational corporation with money and lawyers to burn, you probably don't need to worry. For the rest of us, keeping a low profile and not stepping on anyone's toes seems to be the key to avoiding problems. Then again, law enforcement in Costa Rica comes in fits and starts, so it's prudent to operate on the straight and narrow.

If you're building on coastal property, besides getting the usual building permits, you'll need to run your plans by the Instituto Costarricense de Turismo (the Costa Rican Tourism Institute).

DAILY LIFE

TITLE TRANSFER

If everything checks out and you're ready to make the purchase, you or your agent will present the buyer with a written offer and an earnest money deposit. If you and the seller agree that you want a period of time before closing, you enter into either an Opción de Compra (Option to Buy) or Promesa Recíproca de Compra-Venta (Reciprocal Promise to Buy and Sell); both documents outline the price and time frame of purchase. At closing, the formal transfer begins.

Property is transferred from buyer to seller by executing a transfer deed (an Escritura de Traspaso, often referred to simply as an *escritura,* before a notary public. In Costa Rica notary publics must also be lawyers, and they can do a lot more than their counterparts in the United States, having extensive powers to act on behalf of the state. The transfer deed will include details of the financing of the property. The notary will then register the sale at the National Registry in San José.

You can buy property individually, jointly with other individuals, or in the name of a corporation (Sociedad Anónima, or S.A.). Lawyers and expats alike speak of the benefits of buying property in the name of an S.A. (more about forming an S.A. can be found in the *Employment* chapter). Doing so can protect the property from any liabilities the individual may incur. "Costa Rican courts in general… will not pierce through the corporation to get to the individual," explains Roger Peterson, author of *The Legal Guide to Costa Rica* (www.costaricalaw.com). What this means in layperson's terms is that if you as an individual have financial problems or claims against you, property owned through an S.A. would not be affected by those claims.

Another advantage of owning property through an S.A. is that if you sell the property, you may do so by selling the stock of the S.A. that owns the property, thereby decreasing closing costs. The property tax transfers won't apply, since the sale is of company stock rather than of property per se.

If you're a married couple, another option available to you is to declare your property an Afectación Familiar, or a homestead. Such a property cannot be mortgaged or encumbered by one spouse since it belongs to both. In effect, property designated as a homestead is shielded from the creditors of either spouse; only the joint debts of the couple can be filed against the property.

PROPERTY AND MUNICIPAL TAXES

Property taxes are very low—0.25 percent of the recorded value of the property (25 cents per $100). Recorded value is often lower than actual purchase price, bringing the property tax figure even lower. Property taxes are assessed

BORROWING MONEY TO BUY PROPERTY

Forget that 30-year mortgage with a 5.5 percent interest rate. Costa Rican banks don't offer such deals, and U.S. and Canadian banks aren't likely to lend you money to buy property abroad. Financing real estate here in Costa Rica is a very different story than financing it back home.

"Financing is the buzz word of the banks here," says Chris Simmons of Ocean Surf Realty in Tamarindo. "But their sting is not very potent. Applicants require impeccable credit and lots of patience to get a mortgage. And it's only available on a floating rate, presently about 2 percent over North American rates." Loans in *colones* carry much higher interest rates, since the local currency has historically been more volatile than the dollar.

So a mortgage from a Costa Rican bank may run you around 8 percent on a dollar loan (for which you'll need to prove income in dollars), and from 12 to 20 percent on a loan in *colones*. Loan terms also tend to be shorter here, with fewer 20- or 30-year mortgages than are available in the United States. And interest on Costa Rican loans is recalculated every few months rather than every few years, as is common in the United States. These recalculations can produce increases in your monthly payment that you weren't anticipating.

Another thing a potential borrower needs to think about is the loan-to-value ratio of mortgages here. Many Costa Rican banks offer a 70 percent ratio, which means that if the house costs US$100,000, they will lend US$70,000. Complicating this figure is the fact that banks make loans according to what the bank itself determines to be the value of the property. So if the bank decides the house you want is worth US$75,000, but the sale price is US$100,000, the bank will only loan 70 percent of the lower price, which would be US$52,500. The loan-to-value ratio on second homes is even less, around 60 percent.

Creative financing is the name of the game here, which often means all-cash deals, or big down payments and paying the rest off in a few years. A former real estate agent in Manuel Antonio outlines a typical financing situation: "Usually they'll want a 10 percent 'good faith' deposit after the first papers are signed. You'll close in 30 to 90 days, after which you'll need to come up with another 40 percent of the purchase price. Then maybe the owner will carry the remaining 50 percent for six months or a year. But don't count on it."

Slowly, banks in Costa Rica are starting to offer more and better options. Real estate agents I spoke with mentioned Banco Nacional, Banex, Banco Cuscatlan, Scotiabank, and Interfin as banks that are working to make it easier and more economical for foreigners to borrow money.

REAL ESTATE DEVELOPMENT CHECKLIST

There are a hundreds of companies and individuals building houses and condo complexes in Costa Rica. Some of them market their wares aggressively, trolling for clients by phone or email. It's difficult to keep track of all the new players in this game, and it can be hard to know how to evaluate the overabundance of offerings.

Here's a checklist to get you started in your appraisal of what's out there.

WEBSITE AND PROMOTIONAL MATERIAL

Are there real people, with real (full) names, listed on the website or in the brochures?
If not, beware. Why would a company hesitate to tell you who's in charge?

Do they give a physical address for the development?
If not, consider why they might not want you to drop by on your own.

Is a Costa Rican phone number given?
The number will have a 506 area code; you should be able to reach someone on-site if people are living or building there.

DEVELOPER'S TRACK RECORD

Is this the developer's first project?
If so, the project could work out, but the developer has no track record so you can't know for sure. If the developer has done other projects, research them to see how they turned out. If the developer has done other projects in Costa Rica, they get extra credit, because they know the ins and outs of this market and regulatory climate. Since many condos are sold in the preconstruction phase, sometimes all you'll have to go on is what the developer has done in previous developments.

How long has the company or developer been in business?
Less than two years, be wary. More than 10 years, rest easy.

FINANCING

Is financing being offered by a local bank?
If so, that's a good sign, since banks wouldn't finance a project unless they believed it to be sound. Sometimes developers will offer their own financing, which isn't a bad thing but doesn't give you that extra assurance that another company (a bank) is behind the development.

Where does the initial deposit (earnest money) go?
The best option is to your attorney's or real estate agent's account; also okay would be to a local bank or escrow service. If the money goes directly to the developer or to another individual you don't know, beware.

When can the developer use the deposit?
Best would be not until after closing; fine would be not until certain agreed-upon purchase conditions are met; not so good would be that the developer can access that deposit immediately.

DAILY LIFE

When do you need to start paying the rest of the money?

It's best to spell this out in a purchasing option, a document you draw up before giving any money. Worst-case scenario would be that you start paying immediately, with no milestones or guarantees met.

THE PLACE ITSELF

Don't assume that utilities will be provided or that the construction will be up to the standards you're accustomed to. If you don't know much about construction, you should take someone who does on a walk-through of the development. Here are some basic factors to consider.

Water

Where will your water come from? A private source/well is the best option; water from the city would be the second-best option; last is water from a rural area.

Power

Are there power lines (or underground cables) to the development? To each lot or house?

Telephones and Internet

Will landlines be provided, and if so, how many? It's not fun to have to arrange for a telephone line yourself after you've moved in. If you have a landline, you can have dial-up Internet access, but many developers will also provide DSL or cable.

Roads

How are the roads to and within the development? Concrete roads are best and easiest to maintain. Gravel and asphalt require more maintenance; who will maintain these roads in the future?

Parking

Does the house or condo come with a parking space? Is there sufficient visitor parking?

The Foundation

Does the soil slope away from the house? (It should.) It rains a lot here; how's the drainage? There should be a system to collect rainwater and divert it away from the foundation. Look for any signs of water damage around the foundation.

Walls, Ceilings, Floors

Look for cracks or bulges in ceilings, walls, and floors, which would be signs of shoddy construction or subsequent damage. Check lower corners of windows for discoloration, which could be a sign of water damage. Check for signs of recent repainting (especially in just one spot), which may signal a quick fix of a chronic problem.

Doors and Windows

Make sure doors and windows open and close easily and that they seem sturdy. Check closed doors for a close and even fit within the doorframe. How are the locks? Locks should engage fully, and doors and windows should not rattle or have a loose fit.

Electrical and Plumbing

Review the electrical fixtures and any wiring you can see. Cheap, inexpertly installed light fixtures and exposed wiring tell you that the wiring you can't see was probably done in a hurried and unprofessional manner.

Look to see how many outlets there are per room. Outlets should be grounded, with three prongs.

(continued on next page)

REAL ESTATE DEVELOPMENT CHECKLIST

(continued from previous page)

Check the master electrical panel and any subpanels. Are they neat and organized? Ideally, all breakers should be labeled.

In the kitchen, turn on all the lights and then turn on any appliances. The lights should not dim and you shouldn't blow a fuse.

In the bathroom, check for water pressure. Turn on the shower, hot water only. How long does it take for the water to heat up? Leave the shower running and then turn on the sink. Is there enough water pressure for both the shower and sink to have a decent flow?

Check the plumbing that you can see. Ideally, plumbing should be solid brass with multiple layers of chrome finish over the brass.

Where does the water in the house come from and where does the wastewater and sewage go? If the water comes from a well, what is the diameter of the water main (the supply line to the home). Ideally it should be 3/4-inch (2 centimeters) or larger. If the house is on a septic system, where is the leech field and how large is it? Use all your senses – does anything smell off, as if the sewage system isn't quite doing its job? Is there the smell of damp in the house?

Thanks to contractor Brian Van Rheenen for his tips on checking construction quality, and to the Tico Times *for some of the other tips.*

yearly (the year runs from January 1 to December 31) and are collected by the local municipal government, which also collects a general tax that covers garbage pickup, water, and sewage. The amount varies depending on where you live, but it is usually quite low.

REAL ESTATE AGENT COSTS

One of the problems with a country where anyone can be a real estate agent is that each of those middlemen can charge anything they want to on top of the purchase price. If you allow it, that is. It is imperative that you agree, in writing and up front, what the real estate agent's commission will be. There are real estate agents like Iris Maillox of Playas del Coco who were trained in North America and who follow North American guidelines—3 percent commission for the seller's agent and 3 percent for the buyer's agent. But don't count on that being the case—nail the numbers down ahead of time. Iris also cautions buyers to be aware that the more people in on the deal (the taxi driver, his brother, and their cousin the barkeep at the local watering hole), the more you'll pay on top of the purchase price, with everyone wanting their cut. Sometimes all the added commissions will double the purchase price, and the seller won't even know it!

CLOSING COSTS

Usually the buyer and seller will split closing costs, but make sure to verify that arrangement. Remember that the various fees involved are calculated according to the *registered* value (rather than the sale price) of the property. Ryan Piercy of the ARCR estimates that most people in Costa Rica register their property at 10–30 percent of what they actually paid.

Fees include a real estate transfer tax (1.5 percent), a public registry fee (0.5 percent), various stamps that cost from 10 cents to around US$30, and a notary/attorney fee of from 1 to 2 percent of the property's registered value.

If you've arranged for a mortgage in Costa Rica, there will be more fees—mortgage documents require registration fees and documentary stamps. The notary will also charge for drafting and recording the mortgage.

SQUATTERS

Imagine you buy a lot in, say, Arizona, that you hope to build a vacation or retirement on someday. While you're toiling away in California, trying to save money for just that purpose, a family sets up housekeeping on your Arizona land, plants crops, and lays legal claim to your property. Not possible, you say. And you'd be right, because in the United States, property ownership is sacrosanct. Even if you own thousands of acres, if you don't use it or even visit it, U.S. law still upholds your ownership and your right to kick intruders out.

In Costa Rica things are a little different. Early in the past century, laws were introduced to allow poor farmers to settle on land that was unoccupied or not in use and claim it for themselves. In its usual democratic fashion, Costa Rica wanted all of its citizens to have access to land. The laws sought to prevent a few wealthy and often absentee landlords from owning most of the country, while the majority worked for them as landless laborers.

Known as *precaristas,* squatters here have certain rights. If they occupy and work "abandoned" land, in three months they start to accrue property rights, and in a year they can apply for its expropriation from the "absentee landlord." Expats who buy property in Costa Rica and visit just a few times a year need to be aware of this potential problem. It's not common, but that won't be any consolation if it happens to you.

Robert Wells, a U.S. lawyer who has helped many foreigners in conflicts with squatters, said in a *Tico Times* article that landowners should file for an eviction order within the first three months of squatters occupying their land.

"As long as you can prove they've been there for three months or less, the procedure is relatively fast and painless," said Wells. "However, if you wait, the procedure is much more long and involved."

Avoiding Squatters

Before buying property, do a thorough visual inspection to make sure squatters haven't already settled in. If the seller says there's a resident caretaker, make sure that's what he or she is. Ask to see pay stubs (a caretaker will be paid; a squatter will not).

Record the property on film, and keep records of improvements made (so you can prove the property isn't "abandoned").

If you're not going to live on the property full-time, hire a caretaker. Have a written contract with him or her, and keep up-to-date with salary and Social Security payments (so the caretaker won't become a squatter).

Make sure you or someone you trust does a full inspection of the property at least every three months. Nipping this kind of thing in the bud is the way to avoid trouble.

Building a House

If you build your own home, you won't have to adjust to Tico housing styles, which may include low ceilings, no lawns, and odd ideas about finish work. In your own place, you can put the outlets where you want them, install North American–style hot water heaters and window screens, and lay down floors of tropical hardwoods. You can orient the house toward the best view (many Tico houses seem to look inward rather than outward). You can put in a lush lawn or landscape to your heart's content with native trees and

pool under construction near Lake Arenal

flowering shrubs. "You don't really have to plant things here," one gardener told me. "You just stick something in the ground, or you wait (not long) for your yard to be invaded."

In short, you *can* build the house of your dreams, for considerably less than you'd have to pay up north. But it won't be dirt cheap, and it will take a lot of sweat and patience. You will need to be scrupulous about paying your workers the minimum wage (which is far lower than it would be in the United States), plus their health benefits (see the *Employment* chapter for more details). And most people who've been through the experience say you really need to speak Spanish, to know something about construction, and to be confident you can effectively oversee workers. Those who got the house they wanted tended to be on-site as much as possible, overseeing every little detail.

BEFORE YOU BUY A LOT

Before you buy land that you intend to build on, you need to do a little research. First, make sure the lot has basic services such as water, electricity, telephone, and drainage. If it lacks any of these, get estimates for how much it will cost to install those services. Next, make sure there are no restrictions on the lot that might cause you to be denied a construction permit. Begin by checking with the Public Registry (Registro Nacional), stop in at the Permit Reception Office (see *Filing for Permits*), and consult the municipality *(municipalidad)* where the property is located.

FILING FOR PERMITS

According to Roger Petersen, author of *The Legal Guide to Costa Rica,* requests for construction permits are filed with the Permit Reception Office (Oficina Receptora de Permisos de Construcción) in San José, which is a centralized office that houses representatives from MOPT (Ministerio de Obras Públicas y Transportes—roads), INVU (Instituto Nacional de Vivienda y Urbanismo—housing), ICE (Instituto Costarricense de Electricidad—telephone), AYA (Instituto Costarricense de Acueductos y Alcantarillados—water), SNE (Servicio Nacional de Electricidad—electricity), CFIA (Colegio Federado de Ingenieros y de Arquitectos), and the Ministry of Health (Ministerio de Salud).

To apply for a building permit you'll need copies of the construction plans, the property map or plan *(plano catastrado),* the permit checklist *(hoja de comisión),* the property deed *(escritura),* the consulting contract with your architect/engineer *(contrato de consultoria),* an approval from the water company (AYA) regarding availability of water, and the electrical design plan approved by SNE. Applying for building permits for condominium projects or commercial construction requires further forms.

By law, the local municipality is responsible for ensuring that all construction complies with building regulations, so you'll also need a building permit from your municipality. There may be occasional visits to your construction site by the municipal building inspector, who must certify that the construction is proceeding according to code.

Applications for construction permits must be filed by an architect or civil engineer who is a member of the Federation of Engineers and Architects (Colegio Federado de Ingenieros y de Arquitectos; www.cfia.or.cr).

BUILDING COSTS

Building costs vary a great deal depending on materials used and salaries paid, with estimates running US$100–500 per square meter (US$9–46 per square foot), though of course you could spend even more depending on the lavishness of your tastes.

Building in remote areas is often more expensive, since you have to factor in delivery costs of materials.

LANGUAGE AND EDUCATION

Writer and humorist Dave Barry notes that "Americans who travel abroad for the first time are often shocked to discover that, despite all the progress that has been made in the last 30 years, many foreign people still speak in foreign languages."

Of course you're not like those first-timers that Barry lampoons. But even people who've visited Costa Rica many times and are serious about moving here have been known to minimize the language difference. I'd be doing you a disservice, however, if I claimed you could thrive in Costa Rica without at least some Spanish. In fact, working on your Spanish is the single most important investment you can make in adapting to Costa Rica. And you're in luck—Costa Rica has a great variety of language schools, in locations from very urban to decidedly beachy.

Sure, a lot of people in Costa Rica speak English (though not as many as you might think). ATM machines have instructions in English, and English-language TV and movies dominate the media. But before you say, "I'll learn

© ERIN VAN RHEENEN

Spanish later, maybe in a year or two," think about how you feel when some-one in your home country doesn't try to learn your language. Seems like a lack of respect, doesn't it? The same holds true here.

At the risk of stating the obvious—Costa Rica is a Spanish-speaking country, and if you're going to make this your home, you need to speak the language, if only to greet people politely and thank them for their help. Learning a new language is not easy, but Ticos applaud all genuine efforts. And language is more than just words—it carries with it an entire civilization. Deny yourself the language and you'll never get more than ankle-deep in the culture.

A strong commitment to education is one of the defining characteristics of Costa Rican culture. The 1948 decision to abolish the armed forces meant that Costa Rica could spend more on infrastructure, health care, and, perhaps most important of all for the country's future, education.

Schools for Your Children

If you have school-age children and are considering relocating to Costa Rica, schools will be a major concern and will probably determine, at least in part, where you choose to live. The Central Valley is rich in educational choices, though outlying areas have an increasing number of viable options as well.

Most expats send their kids to private school. As parents research schools, they'll want to ask whether or not the schools follow the same calendar as schools in their home country, what the primary language of instruction is, and whether the diplomas granted will allow students to apply to the colleges and universities they're interested in.

In Costa Rica there are good private schools that follow the Costa Rican model (ending at the 11th grade), others that grant U.S.-style high school di-plomas, and yet others that offer the IB, or international baccalaureate, which allows students to apply to European universities and can sometimes count toward first-year credit at a U.S. university.

This chapter describes the Costa Rican school system, both public and private, from preschool to university. For a list of private primary and sec-ondary schools in Costa Rica, please turn to the *Resources* section at the back of the book.

Schools for You

Even if you don't have kids, education will probably loom large in your life, given that you'll want to learn Spanish. For a list of Spanish-language schools, please turn to the *Resources* section at the back of the book.

Learning the Language

Spanish is the first language of the Americas, and learning it will serve any New Worlder well. Costa Rica is an excellent place to learn, with friendly people with whom to practice and a national tendency to not pronounce the *rr,* the rolling *r* that foils so many nonnative speakers.

There are as many ways to study Spanish in Costa Rica as there are students who want to learn. Sign up for a 12-week intensive course, with six hours a day of rigorous instruction, or arrange for a leisurely hour of private instruction each morning before heading for the beach. You could combine language study with volunteering or enter a specialty program geared to your profession, like courses for Spanish teachers or classes that focus on medical terminology. The biggest leaps in learning often come when you least expect them, and if you take care to mix mostly with Spanish speakers, just going about your daily business will be a crash course in the language. The best motivation for improving your skills is the genuine desire to communicate with someone who speaks only Spanish, so get out there and meet the locals.

Especially if you're a beginner, it's a good idea to sign up for a course, preferably one that meets every day for at least a few weeks. Language study benefits from daily reinforcement, and it's good to get a base of grammar and verb forms. After that, you can design your own course of study, which might include reading at least one article in the newspaper every day (dictionary at the ready), watching Spanish-language soap operas, or falling in love with someone who doesn't speak a word of English.

Most language schools are based in the capital city of San José, but there are also programs in beach towns and other tourist centers. You can find a list of schools in the *Resources section,* but note that it only scratches the surface of what is on offer. I've tried to cover some of the better-known and established places, but there are dozens more. And even if a school is listed, that doesn't mean it has my personal recommendation—call or visit the school's website to learn more details about programs offered. Competition has benefited the industry; be sure to shop around and ask about any special deals—for students, senior citizens, professionals, or off-season visitors, or for longer stays. Prices change often; make sure you obtain up-to-date prices from any schools you are considering.

STAYING WITH A HOST FAMILY

Most schools can arrange homestays for their students. This usually means a single room in a local family's home and often includes two meals a day and laundry service. The nature of the housing and the neighborhood it's located in vary considerably; some schools even offer both "standard" and "deluxe" homestays.

Homestays are a great way to get to know the people of Costa Rica. You'll get a crash course in Tico culture, or at least your host family's version of it. You'll see how family members interact, when meals are served, what they have for breakfast, how often they take out the garbage and where they take it, what they do for fun on the weekend, what they listen to on the radio, and how they treat their dog.

Wendy Tayler, who first came to Costa Rica in 1973 on an exchange program with Lewis and Clark college, liked her host family so much she became a part of it. She fell in love with her "host family brother" and married him. Their kids grew up bilingual in Costa Rica.

Even if your homestay doesn't have such dramatic consequences, staying with a family will radically improve your Spanish. Whether playing cards in the living room, waiting your turn for the bathroom, or sampling your host mother's cooking, you'll hear nothing but Spanish, Spanish, and more Spanish. If you need to ask how to get to the grocery store or let them know you'll be traveling for a few days, guess what you have to do? Tell them in Spanish. Most language learners agree that this kind of immersion is as important (if not more so) than more traditional approaches like grammar and vocabulary drills.

See *Resources* for a list of language schools, most of which can arrange homestays for you.

Education

PRIMARY AND SECONDARY EDUCATION

In Costa Rica, schooling from grades 1–11 is free, and for kids aged 6–14 (the ninth year in school) attendance is compulsory. Consequently, Costa Rica has one of the highest literacy rates—96 percent—in Latin America, second only to Cuba, and a culture that values education as one of the pillars of national life. The first two heads of state were elementary school teachers. Costa Rica is the most stable and democratic society in the region, and its emphasis on education has a lot to do with that status. On Election Day, in fact, schoolchildren participate in mock elections in their classrooms, and the results are published in the national papers. This early introduction to participatory democracy may have something to do with the fact that voter turnout in Costa Rica is traditionally high—hovering around 80 percent for the last three decades. More recently, turnout rates have started to drop, as mistrust of politicians (always a part of the national culture) increases and as people lose faith in government effectiveness.

The country's commitment to education didn't begin in 1949. In 1821, the government, newly independent from Spain, established the University of Santo Tomás, and in 1825, a law was passed requiring every municipality to found a public school. Both sexes were guaranteed equal instruction in 1847, and education became free and compulsory (for primary grades) in 1869.

Public Schools

Costa Ricans value education highly and have made sure that a good portion of the yearly national budget goes to schools. By law, 6 percent of the GDP must be set aside for education, and often many times that amount is spent. Article 78 of the 1949 constitution states that "general education" (through grade 9) is free and obligatory for all Costa Ricans; in 1992 legislators went even further, asserting that education is not only the state's obligation but a fundamental human right.

The school year is usually divided into two terms, from February through July and from August through November or December. The longest break comes between November and January and used to be associated with the coffee harvest (so kids could help), but it now is seen more as a lengthy Christmas holiday. There is usually a two- to three-week break in July as well. National standardized exams are administered during the 6th, 9th, and 11th grades; students must pass them to advance to the next level or (in the case of the exam after the 11th grade) to graduate. The above holds true for both public and private schools, as the Ministry of Education's policies apply to both types of education. Be aware, however, that the usefulness of these exams is under debate in educational circles, and some say the exam after the 6th grade may be done away with soon.

Public school begins with kindergarten and runs through what in the United States would be 11th grade. From there some students go on to local universities; the University of Costa Rica (UCR) in San José is the largest (about 30,000 students) and the most respected. Primary school (*primaria*) is kindergarten through 6th grade; secondary school (or *colegio*) consists of grades 7 through 11.

Unfortunately, public education in Costa Rica is in a time of crisis. While nearly all children attend primary school—with a growing number attending preschool—the system breaks down at the high school (*colegio*) level, where the dropout rate is growing. According to the *Tico Times,* in 2006 about one-third of the adolescent population was not in high school. And of the

UNDERSTANDING COSTA RICA'S SCHOOLS

Deciphering the Costa Rican school system can be a challenge. The following table outlines the public school system, as governed by the Ministry of Public Education (Ministerio de Educación Pública, MEP), but many private schools follow the same model and use the same terminology. Private schools geared to foreigners will usually offer a 12th year, with either a U.S.-style high school diploma and/or the IB (international baccalaureate). The cycles (*ciclos* in Spanish) are the MEP's grouping of school years; in each cycle MEP outlines what it thinks students should learn and how they should learn it. For example, in Cycle III, most schools teach physics in the 7th year, chemistry in the 8th, and biology in the 9th year. There are national exams at the ends of Cycles II, III, and IV, corresponding with the end of grades 6, 9, and 11. The last exam is the terminal exam *(bachillerato)*; students do not graduate without passing this exam. The Spanish equivalents of English terms are given in parentheses.

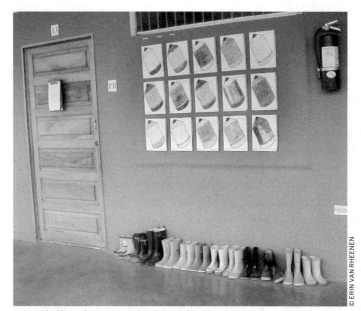

school in the rainy season: boots outside the door

© ERIN VAN RHEENEN

SECONDARY SCHOOL *(SECUNDARIA)*
OR HIGH SCHOOL *(COLEGIO)*

Grade/Year	Student Age	MEP Cycle Subdivision
11th year *(undecimo año)*	16.5	IV Cycle or Diversified Cycle
10th year *(decimo año)*	15.5	IV Cycle or Diversified Cycle
9th year *(noveno año)*	14.5	III Cycle
8th year *(octavio año)*	13.5	III Cycle
7th year *(septimo año)*	12.5	III Cycle

MEP Exam at End of Year

Terminal Exam *(bachillerato)*	IV Cycle
Ministry Exam	III Cycle

PRIMARY SCHOOL *(PRIMERIA)*

Grade/Year	Student Age	MEP Cycle Subdivision
6th grade *(sexto grado)*	11.5	II Cycle
5th grade *(quinto grado)*	10.5	II Cycle
4th grade *(cuarto grado)*	9.5	II Cycle
3rd grade *(tercer grado)*	8.5	I Cycle
2nd grade *(segundo grado)*	7.5	I Cycle
1st grade *(primer grado)*	6.5	I Cycle

MEP Exam at End of Year

Ministry Exam	II Cycle

PRESCHOOL *(PRE-ESCOLAR)*
also known as prep *(prepa)*

Grade/Year	Student Age
preparatory *(prepatoria)*	5.5
kindergarten *(kinder)*	4.5
prekinder *(prekinder)*	3.5
nursery *(maternal)*	2.5

Many thanks to Kirt Wackford for this information.

53 percent of high school students who did finish their coursework, only 66 percent passed the *examanes de bachillerato,* the national tests that students must take before getting their diploma. All the statistics add up to only about a third of all students getting their high school diploma.

In the past few decades, budget deficits have led to severe cuts in the funding of social services, and education has not been spared. Schools have had to make do with less money even as they try to educate a growing population. And while public education is technically free for students in Costa Rica, the price of supplies, uniforms, books, and other costs can be prohibitive for many poor families.

Salaries for the country's approximately 27,000 teachers were never high, and recently their pensions were reduced, causing fewer qualified people to be attracted to the field.

With public schools in crisis, private schools have rushed in to fill the gap.

Private Schools

Most expat families choose to send their children to private schools, as do many Costa Rican families who can afford to do so. Kirt Wackford, who teaches science at Saint Paul College, says it's more common here than in the United States for families of modest means to send their kids to private school. Ana, Kirt's Tica wife, comes from a family of seven. Her father was a shopkeeper and her mother a housewife, and yet they made the sacrifices that would allow all seven kids to attend good private schools. Most of them went on to public higher education at the prestigious University of Costa Rica.

The San José–area phone book lists more than 300 private elementary and secondary schools. There are Catholic schools, evangelical Christian schools, Jewish schools, German, French, and Japanese schools, and dozens of "bilingual" English/Spanish schools, with wildly varying ratios of which language is used more often. The list of private schools in the *Resources* chapter provides a good starting point.

"Private education here is top quality," another teacher told me. "From what I understand, if you compare a 9th grader here to a 9th grader in the States, the Costa Rican student will be way ahead; they could go into 10th grade in a U.S. school. If students are coming down here from the States, they'll probably have to do a bit more work to be up to speed. Spanish and science, especially, might be a challenge for them."

It's a good idea to start researching schools as soon as you know you'll be moving to Costa Rica. Ideally, both you and your children will make a scouting trip to visit campuses and talk to school administrators months in advance of your arrival. Parents agree that it's a good idea to arrive a few weeks before

TIPS FOR ASSESSING PRIVATE SCHOOLS

"First and foremost," advises a long-term expat who has taught at several San José area private schools, "parents must ask themselves what they want for their kids. They especially need to think about what sort of qualification the child will leave the school with. Tico-style private secondary schools may be very good, but they end at the 11th grade – fine if you want to go to university here in Costa Rica, insufficient if you want to go to college in the United States, Canada, or Europe. U.S.-style schools go through 12th grade, and European-style schools mostly offer the IB, the international baccalaureate, which will get the kids into European universities and can sometimes count as first-year university credit in the United States.

Another issue is language. Do you want your kid to speak mostly English, Spanish, German, or Japanese? Schools that call themselves bilingual are all over the map – make sure you know which language is emphasized."

When asked to name the top private schools in the San José area, this expat at first demurred. "It's entirely subjective – it depends what you're looking for. Some are good for science, others for humanities. And there are dozens of schools with which I'm not familiar that may well be excellent." Even so, and with apologies for lapses of memory and quirks in taste, this seasoned teacher offered up a quick list, which included the British School, the Country Day School, and Lincoln School in the top tier, and Saint Paul College, the Panamerican School, Marion Baker School, the European School, Saint Francis, and Methodist College close behind.

"There are a lot of good places here in the Central Valley," the teacher concluded. "Even the so-called 'third level' schools are high-quality institutions."

school starts, so kids can get used to a new house and area before having to adapt to a new school. Arriving too far in advance, however, may be a bad idea, since kids can begin to feel at loose ends when their days have little structure.

For a list of private schools in Costa Rica, see *Resources*.

HIGHER AND CONTINUING EDUCATION

Higher education had to wait until the 1970s to get its share of attention. The prestigious University of Costa Rica (UCR, founded in 1940) was in full swing by then, and several important public institutions joined its ranks in the '70s: the National University in Heredia, Cartago's Institute of Technology, and The State University's Distance Learning Program. The government funds public universities, and tuition is on a sliding scale, with about one in every four students paying nothing at all. At the turn of the millennium, more than 70,000 students in Costa Rica were enrolled in institutions of higher learning, with 30,000 of them at UCR.

There's a sense that students who enjoy the benefits of Costa Rican public higher education should "give back," and indeed students must complete 150 hours of public service for their bachelor's degree and 300 hours for a master's.

UCR's main campus is in the San José suburb of San Pedro; there are branch campuses in Alajuela, Cartago, Turrialba, and Puntarenas. The National University, based in Heredia, also has regional centers in Liberia and Perez Zeledon. The State University's Distance Learning Program has 32 regional centers scattered around the country. People who live far from urban centers can hear lectures on the radio or on TV, or meet once a week with professors who make the rounds of the rural outposts.

The number of private universities and colleges is growing; they may have more relaxed entrance requirements or offer programs similar to those at public institutions but at a more rapid pace and with greater flexibility in terms of when students attend classes. Some private institutions, like the tiny Universidad de Diseño (the University of Design), have excellent reputations, both nationally and internationally. Others seem to be run strictly as businesses and are dismissed as degree mills. Concerned with the declining quality of instruction at some private universities, numerous professional guilds, like the Lawyers' Guild, now require prospective members to pass an exam rather than simply present their degree.

One of the most internationally known private universities in Costa Rica is the University for Peace, an ironically well-fortified compound in the rolling hills outside of Ciudad Colón. Established by a United Nations resolution in 1980, the university serves around 100 students from dozens of countries. Many students come from the United States to work towards master's degrees in international law, human rights, peace studies, sustainable development, and gender and peace-building, to name a few concentrations.

Many public universities offer not only courses but also seminars and talks that are free and open to the general public (and are advertised in local newspapers like *La Nación*). A sampling of recent offerings at the UCR-San Pedro campus includes a talk on the history of film in Costa Rica, a discussion of Latin American literature (in English, by a U.S. professor), a panel discussion on urban development in San José, and a vulcanology seminar. In short, there's a wealth of continuing education options, especially in the San José area, with events either free or very reasonably priced. Most are in Spanish, but what a great way to improve your language skills! You can find a list of both public and private universities in the *Resources* section.

HEALTH

Costa Rica is an exceptionally healthy place, and a large number of people come here at least in part for their health. Some are suffering from stress- and work-related conditions that often clear up after a few months of this country's saner pace and salubrious environment. Others have no specific complaint but are drawn to the high-quality medical care, which is extremely cheap if, as a resident, you become part of the country's socialized medicine system, and it's still quite a bargain if you opt to go the private route. In the United States, almost 50 million people have no health insurance. A place like Costa Rica, which considers health care a fundamental human right, looks very good to refugees from societies where even basic health care seems to have become a privilege.

Costa Rica spends a lot of money to keep its people healthy, and statistics reflect this commitment. Life expectancy is high at just under 77, infant mortality low at 9.9 per 1,000 births—figures that put most other Latin American countries to shame and compare favorably with first-world nations such

as Canada and the United States. For more local comparisons, consider that Panama's infant mortality rate is 20 and Nicaragua's 29 per 1,000 live births. Life expectancy in Panama is 72, while in Nicaragua it's 70.

According to the United Nations, an impressive 98 percent of Ticos have access to health care; as recently as the 1960s, the figure was 15 percent. Ninety-two percent of people here have access to clean water; in Guatemala the figure is 62 percent, and in El Salvador only 47 percent of the population has such access.

Before You Arrive

VACCINATIONS

Epidemic diseases have mostly been wiped out in Costa Rica, and the country requires no proof of vaccination upon entry. But travelers or potential residents planning to rough it should consider vaccinations against tetanus, polio, typhoid, and infectious hepatitis. For the latest information on epidemics and vaccinations, contact the Centers for Disease Control and Prevention in Atlanta (tel. 800/311-2425, www.cdc.org).

MEDICAL RECORDS

If you have any preexisting medical problems, carry a letter from your doctor describing the condition and any prescription medications you need, including the generic name of prescribed drugs. Better yet, request your medical records before you leave home and carry them with you. Make sure any medication you bring is still in its original container, clearly labeled. You don't want customs inspectors to think you're trafficking in prescription drugs.

INTERNATIONAL MEDICAL COVERAGE

If, after reading about the health care options within Costa Rica, you decide you'd like to continue to use the health insurance you have in your home country, or if you want to look into an international policy, you have some advance work to do. Before moving to Costa Rica, learn what medical services your current health insurance will cover outside your home country. If your policy provides international coverage, be sure to carry both your insurance identity card and a claim form or two (nowadays claim forms are usually available for download from company websites). Clarify whether your insurance will come through with payment while you're in Costa Rica or if you have to save receipts and then file claims when you get home. If you know you'll be in Costa Rica for a while, it's a good idea to research the various forms of insurance that have international coverage. The best-known private clinics in San José make every effort to work with international insurers and often have a separate claims department that will tell you what your particular company covers.

Medical care in Costa Rica is very good, and it's unlikely that you'll want to be flown back home for treatment, but if you do, it'll cost a small fortune (up to US$10,000), so you might consider a policy that covers medical evacuation back to your home country.

Kaiser will cover only emergency medical care while its clients are out of the United States, and even with that, you'll need to pay out of pocket, then submit the claim when you get home. Aetna and Blue Cross/Blue Shield international policies get good marks from both customers and health care providers, but there are dozens of other companies that offer similar coverage (see the *Resources* section at the back of the book for a sampling). Do your homework, and ask the hard questions. By law, Costa Rican hospitals and clinics must accept any and all patients who need emergency care. But if your problem doesn't qualify as an emergency but still needs attending to, you'll be much better off with good health insurance.

If your current insurance has no international coverage, and you plan to be in Costa Rica for just a short time, traveler's insurance may be the way to go. Such coverage often includes health and baggage insurance, along with insurance against cancellation of a prepaid tour or flight. See *Resources.*

Veterans Health Benefits

A 2005 estimate concluded that at least 5,000 U.S. veterans live in Costa Rica, along with 10,000 to 15,000 family members of veterans. In April 2005, CIMA Hospital in San José opened an Office of Veterans' Claims and Assistance to help veterans wade through the variety of programs that cover their health needs. Other hospitals and clinics may have special help in this area as well—be sure to ask. For more information, see the sidebar *Getting Your U.S. Federal Benefits in Costa Rica* in the *Finance* chapter.

MEDICAL TOURISM

Increasingly, U.S. citizens are leaving their country to get the medical procedures they want at prices they can afford. More than 500,000 U.S. residents in 2005 traveled abroad for medical or dental treatment, according to the National Coalition on Health Care. The practice also has "spawned a cottage industry of travel agencies" willing to arrange for medical care abroad, according to the *New York Times.*

Costa Rica is one of the countries—along with Thailand, Malaysia, and

Mexico—often mentioned in articles on this new trend. Medical tourism to Costa Rica increases every year (from 2004 to 2005, the increase was 15 percent). The Spanish-language daily *La Nación* reported in 2006 that people from abroad come here for high-quality medical services that cost a lot less than in their homeland. Costa Rica's National Tourism Board (Instituto Costarricense de Turismo, ICT) reports that 95 percent of the patients come from the United States for treatments not covered by their insurance back home and that these tourists save from 50 to 70 percent off what they'd have to pay in their country.

The most sought-after procedures are dental work, face-lifts, and breast enhancement—the latter in 2006 cost approximately US$2,700 in Costa Rica and US$7,500 in the United States. One woman I spoke with said she'd had a face-lift here, recovered at a resortlike facility with trained nursing staff, and returned home as if she'd just been on vacation. "All my friends said I looked great, amazingly well-rested," she laughed. "I just told them Costa Rica tends to have that effect on people."

Types of Health Care in Costa Rica

PUBLIC HEALTH CARE: THE CAJA

More than 50 years ago, the Costa Rican government created a workers' health insurance program that has, over the years, grown to cover more than 90 percent of the population. Today a person can be insured as a worker or as part of the worker's family. Or, as a resident, you can insure yourself by paying *seguro voluntario,* or voluntary insurance. The big mama of an agency that makes this possible is the Caja Costarricense de Seguro Social, otherwise known as the Caja. Even if you self-insure, rates are reasonable, usually well below US$100 a month.

The Caja system extends to every corner of the country, although the majority of well-regarded public hospitals—including San Juan de Dios, Hospital Calderón Guardia, and Hospital México—are in San José, and outlanders routinely journey to the capital for specialized services.

Due to a general downturn in the economy that began in the 1980s, social services have suffered budget cuts, with the Caja taking its share. Though the system is overburdened, it still delivers an admirable level of care to people who could not otherwise afford it. And the Caja is expanding. In the last several years, the Central American Integration Bank (BCIF) loaned the Caja US$60 billion to modernize and expand Costa Rica's health care system. Already built or under construction are new hospitals in Heredia and Ciudad Cortéz (just north of the Osa Peninsula); new Integral Health Attention Centers (CAIS) in Siquirres, Cañas, and Puriscal; and new Basic Attention Integral Healthcare Centers (EBAIS, the smaller neighborhood clinics) scattered throughout the country. The Caja says that with the new facilities in place, it can serve 410,000 additional patients.

Still, Ticos and resident foreigners who can afford to often choose to use the Caja as a backup to private care, which they pay for out of pocket or through international or national insurance. (See the sidebar *Kafka Would Love the Caja* for more information.)

DAILY LIFE

THE INS

The Costa Rican Instituto Nacional de Seguros (INS) is the only authorized dealer in health insurance in Costa Rica, though if implementation of CAFTA (the Central American Free Trade Agreement) goes as planned, the insurance industry will be open to private competition in 2011. Currently, INS rates depend on age, sex, and physical condition. INS policies are usually more expensive than the Caja, while still cheaper than international policies. With INS insurance you can choose your own doctors and go to private clinics (which have better reputations than public hospitals), and the INS covers 70 to 80 percent of the bill.

MIXED MEDICINE

Some Ticos and resident foreigners use both public and private health care. I met a man in the waiting room at Hospital Calderón Guardia (a public hospital) who was fully covered under the Caja but had up until then paid for private care—he wasn't crazy about the Caja's bureaucracy and long waits. But now he needed an operation on his hand, and he couldn't afford to have that done by a private doctor in a private clinic. So he'd returned to the Caja fold and was trying to schedule his operation within the next decade. If he had the money for the operation, he said, he wouldn't be there.

Other people will use the Caja for routine care—minor ailments, blood tests, and medication—but turn to private care when the going gets tough. One reason for this is that the sicker you are, the harder it is to navigate all the forms in triplicate you'll need to see Caja specialists, and the more taxing will be the hours of waiting you'll endure at every turn. Another reason to go private is to engage a respected specialist who doesn't work in the Caja (though many doctors have a private practice and also work for the Caja, and they can schedule their private patients' surgeries there, thus eliminating hospital expenses but not the surgeon's fees).

KAFKA WOULD LOVE THE CAJA

If you don't have international health insurance and don't want to pay all medical expenses out of pocket, you have two alternatives.

You can arrange for coverage through the INS (Instituto Nacional de Seguros, tel. 506/223-5800, www.ins-cr.com). INS costs less than the international companies, lets you choose your own doctors, and usually pays 70 to 80 percent of doctors' visits, medication, exams, and hospitalization. Unfortunately, it won't cover you if you have a preexisting condition, and dental work, eye exams, and preventative checkups are excluded. It also refuses to cover any "illnesses or disorders related to the female reproductive organs during the first 12 months of coverage, or the birth of a baby during the first 6 months of coverage."

Or, you can sign up with the Caja Costarricense de Seguro Social (a.k.a. the Caja, tel. 506/295-2000, www.ccss.sa.cr). They'll take anyone who is a resident of Costa Rica, no matter how old, infirm, or female. Sometimes they don't even ask to see proof of residency. Once you're a part of the Caja, everything is covered – doctors' visits, prescriptions, lab tests, dental care, eye care, and hospitalization. There's no deductible. The downside is that you can't choose your own doctors and often have to wait weeks or months for an appointment. But the price is right – well under US$100 a month.

I chose the Caja. Here's what happened.

At the local police station, my papers are stamped and I'm assigned to a clinic several miles from my home. There, I wait in line to learn which line I should be waiting in. Two hours later, I find I'm at the wrong clinic. The *right* clinic is a few blocks from my house – a pleasant place where the nurses are polite and helpful, though exasperated when I don't understand their rapid-fire Spanish. The clerk issues me a Caja ID card and tells me to come back the next morning.

The next day, a doctor writes up a prescription, orders tests, and refers me to a specialist. I pick up my prescription (a few blocks away) and get my tests done (also nearby), and the following week I see a specialist who tells me I'll need to see another specialist at a hospital downtown.

Downtown, I'm directed to a drab room staffed by a clerk who takes my referral and tells me to come back the next morning between 10 and 11 A.M. to schedule an appointment. Couldn't I make the appointment now? I ask. No, comes the reply. It's 11:05 A.M.

On my way out, I catch a glimpse of a patients' room. In a small space are wedged four narrow beds; in each lies a woman dressed in a rumpled green gown. There are no partitions or curtains between the beds, and there are no televisions, flowers, pictures on the walls, or telephones.

At 10:15 the next morning, I'm back, but no one knows where the clerk is – maybe she went for coffee, someone suggests. Twenty minutes later, another clerk comes in and says she'll help us, though it isn't her job. She stamps my refer-

© ERIN VAN RHEENEN

Waits can be long at public hospitals.

ral and directs me to a window by the front door.

On my way there, I notice people staring at me and am suddenly aware that I am the only foreigner in the place. I feel guilty, making use of their already overburdened socialized medical system.

At the window, a woman says I need an *asegurado* before I can make an appointment.

"The building in back," she gestures vaguely. I wander out, and a friendly guard asks me what I'm looking for. An *asegurado*, I tell him. "Look for a pink building," he says.

I find no pink building, but then I notice some pink traces on a wall that has been painted white. Eureka!

Back at the first window, the woman smiles. "Now you're all right," she says, proud of me for not giving up. I tell her that my health situation is more serious than the referral would suggest – I've been told to exaggerate my problem so I won't have to wait months for an appointment. I get an appointment for a week later.

Next visit, after waiting two hours, I ask the nurse when my turn will come. She looks at my slip of paper and says, "We're not seeing anyone with morning appointments." I point out that when I arrived (on time) it was still morning. She shrugs – the national gesture of Costa Rica – and tells me to make another appointment for another day.

After a few months of this, I think hard about whether private care would be a better option and decide that, damn it, I'm a middle-class American with a credit card; I can buy my way out of the Caja. I'm not proud of this response, but I can't deny it, either.

Though I defected to private care for this particular complaint, I still use the Caja for more routine matters, and my private doctor employs *medicina mixta* (mixed medicine) whenever she can – if I need tests, for instance, she'll send me to a Caja lab. But I pay her for appointments, and I spend a lot of time in her waiting room. Scheduling is not a Tico strong point – everyone is told to come at 10 A.M., then wait until the doctor is available. If you don't come at 10, you lose your place in line.

Bottom line: If your Spanish is decent, if you're persistent, and if you have a fondness for labyrinths, by all means, give the Caja a try. Just bring a book along to read while you wait, maybe Kafka's *The Trial*.

If you need surgery but it's not an absolute emergency, the Caja may assign a surgery date many months from diagnosis. And while some Caja delays are unavoidable, given the system's scant resources, other delays are the result of sheer incompetence and may have lethal results. Take the case (in May 2003) in which 81 patients at San Juan de Dios Hospital in San José waited more than eight months for biopsies to ascertain whether or not they had prostate cancer. Orders for the necessary medical equipment were approved but then got lost on some bureaucrat's desk. No hospital official followed up on this incredible lapse until patients and journalists pressed for an investigation.

Such incompetence is the exception rather than the rule, and similar outrages have no doubt occurred in health facilities the world over. Still, there's no denying that public hospitals here, though the facilities are adequate and the doctors often very good, are not cheery places. Nurses are overworked, and rooms are small and often shared with three or more other patients. You'll find no telephones, TVs, or privacy in these rooms. Some public hospitals lack basic supplies, like toilet paper.

✦ PRIVATE CARE

Doctors in Costa Rica, whether they work for the Caja, in private practice, or in a combination of the two, are in general very well trained. Many have studied in the United States, Canada, or Europe. They keep up with developments in their field and often have access to the latest technology. Some doctors who work privately are associated with private clinics; others are not. Either way they can send you to private clinics for tests or operate on you there.

The best private clinics are in San José, and they are very good indeed. A note on nomenclature: A "clinic," which is sometimes the size of a large hospital, usually denotes a private institution, while a "hospital" is most often public. This is confused somewhat by the fact that smaller, neighborhood public health facilities are also often called clinics. And one of the best private clinics, CIMA, takes pains to call itself a hospital.

Prices at private clinics are often beyond the reach of the average Costa Rican, but resident foreigners—who tend to have greater financial resources and are accustomed to higher prices—find the fees refreshingly low, often half or even a third of what one would pay in the United States. Part of the reason prices are lower is that malpractice lawsuits are rare here; when damages are awarded, they're only enough to cover hospital bills and other expenses.

At private hospitals consultations start at around US$45, and overnight stays start at US$175 (not including procedures, tests, or medications).

Clínica Bíblica

Founded in 1929 by Christian missionaries from Britain, the Bíblica (as it's known) takes up more than a city block in downtown San José. A new wing opened in 2006 has nine new operating rooms and 25 new private patient rooms, with the same amenities as rooms in the old building but with the addition of flat-screen TVs and WiFi access. On the clinic's second floor you'll find a small chapel, and there's a rack of religious tracts near the front desk.

The older wing has 80 beds, 16 examining rooms, five operating rooms, and modern ultrasonography, mammography, radiology, CAT scan, and MRI equipment. The clinic's cardiology and maternity units are well known, and about 140 babies are delivered here each month.

The "old" clinic has sky-blue walls and tiled floors; each of the rooms has a private bath, cable TV, phone, safety deposit box, and electric beds. Rooms also have either a rocking chair or a recliner, along with a sofa bed so that a friend or family member can stay overnight. Other visitors are allowed from 9 A.M. to 9 P.M. Rooms in the old building cost about US$190 per night and in the new about US$250 per night.

The Bíblica works with many international insurance providers. "Almost all U.S. health care insurers work with us," says Brad Cook, the clinic's insurance and claims administrator, who was born in Costa Rica of missionary parents. "The exceptions would be Kaiser and Cigna, though Cigna International will work. Blue Cross/Blue Shield is great, but there are more than 200 others that will work just fine."

If you'll be paying out of pocket, ask for an estimate, but don't expect it to be accurate. I was quoted US$625 for a surgery that ended up costing me US$1,700, mostly because medications and surgical supplies were excluded from the estimate and ended up being the lion's share of my bill.

If you have questions about what your insurance would cover at the Bíblica, you can call or email the very helpful Brad Cook (tel. 506/221-7717 or 506/257-5252, ext. 1120, fax 506/257-7307, bcook@clinicabiblica.com).

The Bíblica is on Calle Central, between Avenidas 14 and 16 (tel. 506/522-1000, fax 506/221-0645, info@clinicabiblica.com, www.clinicabiblica.com).

Clínica Católica

Católica is a clean, rather stark clinic run by Catholic nuns. Set in the quiet suburb of Guadalupe, just north of San Pedro and the University of Costa Rica, the clinic has about 70 beds; most are in single rooms, but there are also a few shared rooms (which cost less) and several suites—large two-room spreads, with Monet prints on the walls and upholstered chairs for visitors.

Although well regarded, the Católica is not as geared toward foreign patients as CIMA and the Bíblica are. Sister Ramirez, the general director of the clinic, says at least one person per shift speaks English, and that the clinic works with INS, the national health insurance, and with many international insurance companies, including "Blue Cheese" (I think she meant Blue Cross/Blue Shield). Still, it is clear that the Católica hasn't put its energy into wooing foreigners as much as in keeping costs down (it's the cheapest of the three major clinics). "Our mission isn't a commercial one," elaborates Sister Ramirez. "We're run by a Franciscan order; our mission is one of service. If we make any profit, we immediately reinvest it in equipment and infrastructure. And unlike CIMA and even Bíblica, we don't have outside investors we have to answer to."

Sixty doctors maintain private consulting offices in the hospital's east wing, and many doctors not officially affiliated with the clinic use the facilities to treat their patients, since the clinic is known for its up-to-date equipment and quality care. Católica is affiliated with Our Lady of the Lake Regional Medical Center in Louisiana, and it has ties with Global Medical Management Inc., Group Hospitalization and Medical Services, Inc. (GHMSI; Blue Cross and Blue Shield), and is a part of the Administrative Network of Americas International Hospital Service Network.

The clinic is in San Antonio de Guadalupe, a suburb of San José (tel. 506/246-3000, fax 506/283-6171, info@clinicacatolica.com, www.hospital lacatolica.com).

Hospital CIMA

Located just off one of Costa Rica's few stretches of superhighway, CIMA is nothing if not modern. The clinic opened in early 2000, near the upscale suburb of Escazú. Rumor has it that CIMA was built to work as a hotel if it failed as a hospital, and with its marble-floored foyer, glass-bricked administrative offices, and the white tablecloths in the cafeteria, CIMA does indeed resemble a tasteful, upscale chain hotel.

Downstairs, you'll find the emergency room, the outpatient clinic, and the big guns of medical technology: a cardiac cath lab, CAT scans, sonograms, X-rays, and the only open MRI in Central America.

Upstairs, the patient rooms and nurses' stations are spotless, with watercolors of flowers and landscapes decorating the walls. Rooms feature everything that most San José private clinics offer—cable TV, phone, adjustable bed, private bath, safety deposit box, and a daybed for overnight guests—but on a grander scale. Of 58 beds, four are equipped for neonatal care, six are in the Intensive Care Unit, and six are suites (all patient rooms are private).

CIMA stands for Centro Internacional de Medicina, and there are 10 CIMA hospitals in Latin America, including facilities in Mexico and Brazil. All are owned and managed by International Hospital Corp. in Texas. CIMA is associated with Baylor University Medical Center in Dallas, which Chapa says means that CIMA "has an obligation to deliver the same standard of care as a quality U.S. hospital. We also use Baylor as an educational resource, to train medical staff. Baylor doctors will come here as well—most recently a cardiologist came down and gave a seminar for local doctors."

It's clear that the equipment here is up-to-the-minute, from the X-ray machines to the computers at the front desk. You can arrive unannounced with diagnosis in hand, speak with the admissions department about the surgery you require, and within five minutes have a written, signed estimate of how much your stay here would cost. CIMA works with all major international insurance companies, as well as with INS.

Depending on what services you require, care here will probably cost you more than it would elsewhere, though Chapa says CIMA tries to be within 5–10 percent of the prices offered at other private clinics in San José. The higher prices are relative, of course, with totals still coming in far below what you'd pay in the United States. CIMA is a favorite among resident foreigners.

CIMA is near Escazú (tel. 506/208-1000, fax 506/208-1001, cima@hospitalcima.com, www.hospitalsanjose.net).

PHARMACIES AND PRESCRIPTIONS

Pharmacies in Costa Rica (called *farmacias* or *boticas*) are on every other corner, and most are well-stocked. If you bring a prescription from outside the country, make sure it is for generic rather than brand-name medication— generic names are common to all countries, while brand names are not. And unless you're looking for antibiotics, narcotics, or psychotropic drugs, you don't even need a prescription (even many antibiotics don't require a prescription). You can tell the pharmacist what you're looking for, or, if you're not sure what you need, the pharmacist will diagnose you and suggest appropriate medication—thus saving you the price of a doctor's consultation.

A pharmacist's diagnosis is especially helpful when you're far from a doctor, but of course you shouldn't expect the pharmacist to have specialized knowledge of arcane ailments. For simple problems, however, it's a godsend that in this country pharmacists have more power than their counterparts back home. I've had skin problems, ear infections, and stomach ailments diagnosed and treated by pharmacists (in different parts of the country)—and every time,

CASH AND CARRY AT PRIVATE HEALTH CLINICS

If you're paying out of pocket for surgery at a private clinic in Costa Rica, you'll probably be negotiating the cost of your care in ways that you're not used to. Get over the feeling that health care is not something you haggle over, because here, it is – the tests, the room, even the operation are all just products. You need to be a good shopper and find the best value for your money.

Competition among the major private clinics has benefited the consumer (a.k.a. the patient), in that clinics have been driven to buy new equipment and to lower their prices to draw people in. For common operations, clinics sometimes offer package deals, like Hospital CIMA's "promotion" on cesarean sections. But don't forget to read the fine print! In the tradition of special deals worldwide, there are often some crucial components left out of the advertised price. In the case of surgical procedures, expect little things like doctors' fees and medications to be "extra."

As a side note, cesareans in the United States aren't considered elective surgery, but in Latin America, many women choose to have them. In the United States, says Alfonso Chapa, former vice president of hospital operations at CIMA, most deliveries are vaginal, while in Latin America, a greater percentage of babies are delivered by C-section. Why? I asked Chapa, who is a Texas native and has worked in hospital administration in the United States as well as in Costa Rica. One reason, he says, is that doctors get paid more for surgical procedures, so they push women to have C-sections. Another reason is that C-sections can be scheduled, so, unlike natural births, they "won't interfere with the doctor's lifestyle."

Many patients have a private doctor, who will often operate in whichever clinic the patient prefers. It's up to the patient to research the clinics and compare prices. You'll be paying a fee to your doctor (which will usually cover the assisting physician and the anesthesiologist; most doctors have teams that they like to work with). The doctors' fees are completely separate from what you pay the clinic – what you pay for at the clinic is the hospital room, the use of the operating room, and any tests or medications needed while hospitalized.

GETTING ESTIMATES FROM PRIVATE CLINICS

If your surgery is elective, you may have time to ask the various private clinics for cost estimates (*presupuesto* in Spanish) before you choose a clinic. In my experience, of the three major clinics, CIMA will come up with a written estimate very quickly; the other clinics need to be prodded, and even then they may not give it in writing.

Clinics say they are reluctant to give estimates because there are so many variables, like what sort of medication your doctor prescribes. One dose of antibiotics can cost US$25, for instance, depending on the type and the brand. Imagine if you have three doses a day for a week – that's US$500 spent on antibiotics alone.

If some clinics balk at providing written estimates, and if written estimates themselves can be off, what can a prospective patient do? If a clinic will only give you a verbal estimate, at least write it down yourself, and ask the clinic to break it down, to tell you what elements are included in the total. Then go to your doctor with all the figures and details, and ask him or her what the estimates might be leaving out. A layperson probably won't know that electrocauterization of a wound will cost around US$33, a biopsy may cost close to US$200, and a dose of generic morphine will be less than a dollar. Your doctor will know what he or she will need for surgery, what kinds of medicine he or she will be prescribing, and (hopefully) approximately how much it will all cost.

If you don't want to get into this level of nitty-gritty, you could ask the clinics and/or your doctor for the final total bill of similar operations that have been performed recently. (You'd think this would be how they'd compile estimates, but apparently it is not.) You'll need to be persistent – it seems to really throw Ticos if you ask for something that is quite possible but isn't a part of the general routine. Be friendly and respectful, but don't take no for an answer.

A few more things to remember:

- All clinics require a pre-surgery deposit, anywhere from US$1,000 to US$10,000, depending on the estimated cost of surgery. This deposit can be put on your credit card.

- You will usually have to pay your entire bill upon release from the hospital. The clinic won't mail the bill later – it wants the money before you step out (or are rolled out) the door. One of the reasons for this is that it's easy – especially for foreigners who live elsewhere – to skip the country and leave the bill behind.

- If you're in the clinic for a while, you will probably be asked to pay a little on your bill every few days. It seems ghoulish to come to someone's hospital bed and ask for money, but that's how it's done here. If your bill is more than you expected, you can usually work out a payment plan with the billing department.

- Most clinics will do their best to work with your insurance (arrange this ahead of time if you can), and most clinics accept credit cards.

the medication prescribed cleared up the problem in short order. Most pharmacists will even give injections for a small fee.

Prices are usually reasonable, but do shop around, and know that prices will be higher in heavily touristed areas. In San José, for instance, the pharmacy at Clínica Bíblica and the Fischel chain of pharmacies are known to be well-stocked but much more expensive than lesser-known shops.

ALTERNATIVE MEDICINE

Alternative medicine—such as acupuncture and homeopathy—is popular in Costa Rica, especially in the Central Valley and in touristed beach towns, where arrivals from other countries have brought with them their interest in all things holistic. You'll have no problem finding massage therapists, health-food stores, or yoga classes. The best way to find a reputable practitioner is word of mouth. Barring that, the following places are a good place to start your search.

Try the Harmony Center for Holistic Medicine in Escazú (tel. 506/288-4658, www.harmonycenters.com) or Clínica de la Paz (tel. 506/225-2620, clinicalapaz@hotmail.com), a holistic center in Los Yoses (a neighborhood in San José) with its own resident homeopaths. Ciudad Colón–based Dr. Kim (tel. 506/249-1826, www.drkimcostarica.com) gets high marks for his work in acupuncture, nutritional counseling, and allergy elimination. Casa de la Cultura Alternativa Osiris (Osiris Alternative Culture Center, tel. 506/224-5691, www.gruposiris.com) offers all sorts of activities, from vegetarian cooking classes to tai chi and astrology.

Especially on the Caribbean coast, you will hear about native healers—called bush doctors (usually of African heritage) or *sukias* (of indigenous heritage). The healers don't have websites or phones—this is one place where you definitely need a personal recommendation. But if you're in a place for a while, you'll no doubt hear stories, some of them true.

"Alternative" birthing methods—using midwives, or giving birth at home with a trusted friend or relative—used to be the norm, but over the past half century hospital births became the only way to go, with cesarean sections promoted even when a vaginal birth would have presented no hazard to mother or baby. Recently, there has been a renewed interest in midwives and natural birthing practices, although you'll have to look hard for this small but growing movement, especially because practitioners operate in a legal gray area and are not likely to advertise. In Costa Rica, one is a certified midwife only through a specialization after obstetrical nursing studies, and officially, midwives are allowed to attend births only in an emergency.

Otherwise mothers must go to the hospital. But, there are ways around these restrictions.

According to Uva Meiner, a German-born birth assistant, the handful of midwives in Costa Rica are mostly foreign-born, with a strong sense of mission. Uva herself provides extensive preparation ("spiritual, emotional, and physical") for the expectant mother, then makes house calls every day for one week postpartum and three times the following week. Some midwives use a portable birthing pool or a birthing chair, depending on the expectant mother's wishes. For more information on alternative birthing possibilities in Costa Rica, contact Uva (tel. 506/268-2127 or 506/253-8786). Uva speaks six languages, including English.

Other resources for natural birthing include www.central-american-midwives.org (website is in English), a group of midwives from many Central American countries; and Mothers in Birth (tel. 506/224-580, www.mama salnacimiento.com; website is in Spanish).

SENIOR CITIZENS

U.S. citizens need to know that Medicare does not provide coverage for hospital or medical costs outside the United States. If you've bought other coverage to supplement Medicare, that policy may pay for up to 80 percent of your care abroad, as in the absence of Medicare it becomes your primary coverage. Among other organizations, AARP offers Medicare supplement plans that include foreign medical care coverage.

Nursing Homes

Of the 155 nursing homes in Costa Rica, 26 are privately run and the rest are funded (often inadequately) by the government. More than 4,000 senior citizens (known in Spanish as *personas de la tercera edad,* or people of the third age) make use of these facilities, either residing there or coming every day for meals and activities.

There are no figures available on how many foreign-born seniors make use of Costa Rica's nursing homes, but I would guess that it's not a high number. For many seniors, the language and the culture would be barriers to feeling at home.

High life expectancy and a decline in childbearing have made people over 60 the fastest-growing segment of the Costa Rican population. In 1995, one Tico in 12 was over age 60; by 2025 the figure is expected to be one in seven. And many foreign residents who live in Costa Rica come in their later years. Under pressure from foreign lenders to make budget cuts, the Costa Rican government stopped building public-funded nursing homes in 1992. Though only a small percentage of Tico seniors live in such centers, the existing facilities barely keep up with present demand and certainly will not be sufficient in years to come.

Victoria Schwartz, who moved here from California in 2002 at the age of 52, wonders what her future holds. "What if, in 20 years, I need nursing care?" she asks. "Will I have to go back to the U.S., which by then will be a different country? People here have families—I don't. And soon, I think, Tico family will change to more closely resemble the U.S. family, in that there won't be anyone willing to care for aging relatives."

She and other expats and Ticos I spoke with think the lack of nursing homes and extended care facilities is a gap in the social services net. Some see the lack as an opportunity, especially with the growing number of English-speaking resident foreigners who might need such services. "You could pay doctors and nurses here far more than what they'd normally earn, make sure everyone speaks English, and rent or buy a great facility. You'd still be able to provide quality care for much less than it would cost in the U.S. or Canada," says Barry Wilson, who runs a company that supplies surgical gowns and drapes to private clinics.

At-Home Care

At-home care, for seniors or others in need of help, can be very reasonable here compared to how much it would cost in the United States or Canada. A registered nurse makes around US$500 a month working at a hospital, which would be a fair salary to pay an RN for a 48-hour week of at-home care. A caretaker with no official credentials would cost less.

DISABLED ACCESS

In 1996 the Costa Rican Legislature passed The Equal Opportunities Law for People with Disabilities, an ambitious directive that aimed to provide Costa Rica's more than 200,000 disabled residents equal access to work, health care, transportation, and public space. A decade later, some progress had been made: more special education programs in schools, ATMs with Braille, some curb ramps built or repaired, a few "sonorous stop signs" installed for the sight-impaired, and about 10 percent of public buses modified to accommodate wheelchairs.

But if you've ever seen an individual in a wheelchair try to negotiate San José's torn-up streets or the sandy tracks of a beach town, you'll know that the country has a long way to go. It's heartening to see friendly strangers pitch in,

"PEOPLE RUN OVER TO HELP"

Kathleen Duplantier moved to Costa Rica in 2004, after taking early retirement from her job teaching school in Louisiana. Kathleen has multiple sclerosis (MS), a disease of the central nervous system whose symptoms may include loss of balance, spasticity, and partial or total paralysis.

Kathleen uses a wheelchair, and she and her husband custom-built their home in San Ramón to accommodate her chair (see also the sidebar *Expat Profile: Stephen and Kathleen's Dream Home* in the *Central Valley and Beyond* chapter). They chose San Ramón in part because of its cool climate – hot weather tends to exacerbate the symptoms of MS.

I asked Kathleen about getting around Costa Rica in a wheelchair. She said it was a challenge but that it hadn't been much easier back home.

"I'd ask at a café or restaurant [in Louisiana] if they had a bathroom I could use. If they said no, I'd say, "Well, then do you have a mop?"

Kathleen has been impressed by how resourceful and helpful people are here in Costa Rica. "My wheelchair broke in Grecia. I had a huge number of people who came to help. One guy said, we'll take you to a bicycle shop, which was a good idea, because they have the right sort of tools there. So they carried me in my chair to the bicycle shop, brought out a little stool, and I sat there while they fixed my chair. They didn't charge me anything."

Stephen, Kathleen's husband, adds, "Wherever I'm transferring Kathleen from the car to the chair, people run over to help – the other day, it was a little old lady. They ask how they can help, and I'll say, *empuje sus nalgas* (push her bottom), and they don't mind. They know that's what it takes. Sometimes they're overly helpful and can knock her off balance."

helping people in wheelchairs up and down curbs or over rough spots. But the government's push to improve conditions is still in its infancy.

Disabled-rights activists say the problem is that the 1996 law has no teeth and is hard to enforce. There are proposals in the works that may make enforcement more of a priority and also provide incentives to private businesses that hire the disabled and who make their facilities accessible to all.

Still, the situation is definitely improving. More and more hotels, restaurants, and tour companies are making things easier for their disabled customers, especially where wheelchairs are concerned. Two popular tourist attractions—the Rainforest Aerial Tram and Poás Volcano National Park—are now wheelchair accessible, and the hope is that other attractions will follow suit.

Some places—like the Caribbean slope town of Turrialba and Belén in the Central Valley—have reportedly been moving faster than the rest of the country toward better access for all.

See *Resources* for a list of disabled-friendly tour and transportation companies.

DAILY LIFE

Health Hazards

DRINKING WATER

Water quality is, in fact, one of the biggest differences between Costa Rica and other Latin American nations. Often people don't believe it until they arrive, but it's true: You can drink the water! Something so basic has profound implications, not the least of which is that it feels like the natural world is working with rather than against you, offering up an abundant and untainted supply of the most essential of elements. Anyone who's lived in a place where they can't even wash vegetables or brush their teeth with what comes out of the tap knows what a blessing this is. Clean water also eliminates most water-borne diseases, such as cholera, typhoid fever, and dysentery. Also rare in Costa Rica are the less dangerous but still annoying intestinal upsets from tainted water so familiar to third-world travelers. The country has a few areas—such as remote parts of the Talamanca Mountains and (ironically) the upscale San José suburb of Escazú—where the drinking water is suspect. Sometimes water quality worsens with heavy rains, as debris is washed into water supplies. Ask around, and if there's any question stick with bottled water. Otherwise, turn on the tap, fill up your glass, and enjoy.

FOOD

You might get sick of all the rice and beans, but you won't get sick *from* the rice and beans. Food hygiene standards in Costa Rica are very high. Of course you'll want to take the usual precautions: Think twice about buying food from street vendors, and be careful about raw fish and shellfish (where cholera bugs like to hang out). That said, I wouldn't trade my ceviche (raw fish marinated in lime juice) for anything. I just make sure to go to established restaurants, which have a vested interest in keeping their customers healthy and happy. The usual third-world warnings—wash it, boil it, peel it, or forget it—don't really apply in Costa Rica, at least not in the Central Valley or the more developed tourist destinations. I don't have an ironclad stomach, and yet I've eaten every salad served to me here, with no ill effects whatsoever. In fact, I wish I would encounter more salads—they're not easy to come by in this starch-loving nation. Most traditional meals will boast two, three, or even four starches—usually rice, potatoes, and fried plantain, with some yucca, chayote, or a few tortillas thrown in for good measure. You may also get a dollop of cole slaw or a few slices of tomato. Making up for the lack of good salads is the astonishing variety of fruits; you'll want to try them all, from the heart-shaped *anona* to the purple-fleshed *zapote*.

SMOKING

Costa Ricans on the whole smoke more than North Americans but not as much as Europeans. Smoking is usually prohibited on buses and in some restaurants, but bars often seem to be full of smoke. Cigarettes are for sale everywhere; singles are often sold at kiosks on the street, where a lighter attached by a string is often available.

TRAFFIC

Without a doubt, the biggest threat to your safety here comes from cars and the way Ticos wield them like enormous machetes. The risk of motor vehicle–related death is generally many times higher in developing countries than in the United States (no haven of safety itself), and Costa Rica is no exception to this rule. Some observers suggest that the national character—which is one of avoiding conflict and smoothing things over at any cost—does a flip-flop when Ticos get behind the wheel, with drivers asserting every bit of the hostility they repress in other parts of their lives.

Automobile accidents are the leading cause of death here for people under the age of 50. And of the 924 violent deaths reported in Costa Rica in 2005, 41.6 percent were traffic accidents—collisions and pedestrians being run over.

Michael Kaye, owner of Costa Rica Expeditions, has a whimsical take on the situation: "Driving in Costa Rica is inspired by the ancient tradition of the bullfight. The driver who cuts you off is not insulting you. She's playing with you. The best way for you to handle this is the same as for newcomers to all games. Play; but play by local rules, don't play too intensely, and expect to lose."

Be prepared to lose that game of chicken, but take care not to lose your life. Every day the newspapers report on the previous night's wrecks and on the pedestrians who've been *aplastados* (flattened, or run over). Most of the country's roads are atrocious, and as for walking, there's a public service announcement on TV that urges pedestrians to wear white and to step off into the dirt whenever they see a car coming. No mention is made of the fact that the country could use a few more sidewalks, and that drivers should be on the lookout for "obstacles," especially in rural areas where cars share the road with horses, oxcarts, and whole families walking to weddings, baptisms, and funerals.

In Costa Rica, the car is the *patrón* and the pedestrian the *peón*. The culture here is that cars stop for nothing—not an old woman limping across the street, not a stalled car, not a group of schoolkids trying to get to class on time. In many cultures, people are taught to drive defensively. In Costa Rica,

HOW TO BE A GOOD ENVIRONMENTAL CITIZEN IN COSTA RICA

Contributed by Alexis Fournier and Sandra Shaw Homer

Its international press notwithstanding, Costa Rica is not an environmental paradise. The laws on the books are sound, but their enforcement is woeful, either for lack of resources or interinstitutional coordination. Things are improving, however, and both the influence and activism of foreign residents can help turn the tide.

Fortunately, Costa Rica's is a culture of reuse and fix it. Ticos never toss anything that might have a future use. It takes imagination to save, especially if you come from a throw-it-out culture where it's easier to buy new than get something fixed.

Recycling
Recycling is not as advanced here as in developed countries; only a few communities have programs in place. Ask at your municipal office, or consult the 4Rs Recycling Coalition (www.4rs.or.cr or 506/231-2712; website is in Spanish) for a list. Contact them also if you want to start a recycling program in your community. Most centros de acopio (collection centers, which in some cases also serve as recycling centers) handle glass, newspaper, plastic, and aluminum cans, plus some cardboard and scrap metal. A few have specially marked containers around town, and an increasing number do domestic pickup.

Many communities still have open-air dumps, and all towns of any size have garbage collection; ask at the municipality where to pay for this service. You'll want a small basurero, a metal basket on a post, so that the street dogs don't get the trash before the truck does. It's against the law to burn refuse.

Some communities are getting together to build and manage sanitary landfills, and in Puntarenas there's a new project to generate energy from trash.

California red worms are being used to generate compost commercially. These will speed up composting in your own backyard. Contact FUNDACA (Fundación para el Desarrollo del Área de Conservación Arenal-Tilarán, tel. 506/695-6550). The foundation will provide you with worms if you can come to Tilarán to pick them up.

Recycled printer paper is available from most librerías (bookstores), as are artisan paper gift items.

Travel and Transportation
Stay in "green" hotels and patronize tour operators committed to sustainable development. Check with the Rainforest Alliance (http://eco-indextourism.org/en/home, U.S. tel. 888/693-2784) or the Costa Rican Tourism's Certification in Sustainable Tourism (CST) program (www.turismo-sostenible.co.cr/EN/home.shtml) for more information on green tourism.

Public transportation in Costa Rica is excellent and cheap. With the high price of fuel, buses make sense. So does good maintenance of your vehicle to control emissions. Since annual inspections at inspection centers have been required, both emissions and gas consumption in Costa Rica have dropped. Inspection stations are all over the country and are known as RTV *(revisión técnica de vehículos)* stations. For more information, see www.rtv.co.cr (Spanish only).

Before you change the oil in your car, find a gas station or mechanic who recycles. Same goes for car batteries.

Building a House

Use recycled flame-resistant plastic roofing tiles. They look like the real thing, and they're quiet in a tropical downpour. Steel studding and drywall are available, so there is no excuse to use tropical hardwoods for framing. Use cultivated teak and gmelina for paneling, floors, and trim. Solar panels and even windmills are available for your energy needs.

Test for soil stability and underground water on your property before you locate the septic system.

Typically, rain and "gray water" share the same drains. The law now requires separate septic-type systems for water from showers, kitchens, and laundry. Responsible builders know the SETENA rules for environmentally safe construction; SETENA is the National Technical Environmental Secretariat, a part of the Ministry of the Environment and Energy. Insist these rules be observed.

Prefer Organics

Every village and many urban neighborhoods have a weekly farmers market. Look for the stands selling *organicos*. In San José, a large organic market opens on Saturday mornings. Call Oro Verde (tel. 506/236-1770) for directions in Spanish, or consult the 4Rs Recycling Coalition. Auto Mercado grocery stores sell organic produce, and BioLand dry goods, locally produced, are available countrywide. Natura Style (www.naturastyle.com) offers an online purchase and delivery service (in the Central Valley) for organic produce and health products.

Plant Trees

Costa Rica will face an energy shortage in a few short years. Every tree around a house works as an air conditioner. Trees, plus ceiling fans and good ventilation, are enough to keep you comfortable on even the hottest days.

If you want to regenerate tropical forest, some farm cooperatives sell cheap seedlings, or contact La Reserva near Lake Arenal (tel. 506/856-2977). An association in the southern zone, Women of the Osa (www.womenoftheosa.org), has written a handbook, *Living in the Jungle*, a guide to sustainable living "off the grid" in the tropics.

Alexis Fournier is a Canadian-born retiree and cofounder of the 4Rs Recycling Coalition (La Red 4Rs), an umbrella organization grouping most of what's being done about recycling in the country.

Sandra Shaw Homer has made Costa Rica her home since 1990, and she became a citizen in 2001. For several years she wrote a regular column in the Tico Times. *She has served on the Environmental Commission for the Municipality of Tilarán, and she is on the boards of both the Guanacaste Animal Welfare Foundation (tel. 506/695-8597) and Fuentes Verdes, a local community organization promoting sustainable development (its president is Ed Yurica, tel. 506/695-6717 or email at fuentes_verdes@yahoo.com).*

parents teach their kids to *walk* defensively. Ticos on foot know to treat cars as the unpredictable animals they are. Follow their lead and don't expect cars to stop just because there's a stop sign or a red light. And if you're wondering how you're ever going to cross that busy street, watch what the locals do. Shadow them; walk when they walk. And watch out for potholes—not just in the road but on the sidewalks.

If you can avoid driving at night, do so. Eighty percent of insurance claims come from nighttime accidents. In rural areas, be on the lookout for cows or dogs lying in the road, or for people who consider the bank of a highway a good place to hang out and socialize.

THE HAZARDS OF ADVENTURE TOURISM

Care to run a raging river, surf some nefarious waves, or whiz above the canopy on a zipline? It's all good fun, but be careful. Surfers should ask locals for tips and try to surf with a buddy. Riptides are common here, as are sharks, crocodiles, and, at river mouths during the rainy season, human waste and agrochemical runoff. For group activities, try to hook up with an established tour company, one that has a reputation for doing things right. There are fewer safety regulations here, and any bozo can set up a zipline or a bungee jump. Try to get a personal recommendation before stepping off into the wild blue yonder.

Costa Rican Expeditions' Michael Kaye thinks safety is adventure tourism's Achilles' heel. "A lot of accidents don't get reported," he says. "Not long ago a seven-year-old girl lost her finger—it got caught in a line. It may take fatalities to get some of these people to clean up their act."

The bottom line is that you need to go with a reputable operator. Costa Rican Expeditions, for instance, employs a safety expert to check out any canopy tour it sends clients to. "We've lost customers because we say we can't recommend any canopy tour where they're going. But in good conscience we have to have checked them out ourselves."

THE NATURAL WORLD

Threats like cars and their drivers are the most serious hazards; what comes at you from the natural world pales in comparison. Still, it's a good idea to know what kinds of creatures you'll find here and how the environment might affect you.

Bugs

In and around the Central Valley, there are surprisingly few bugs. You hardly ever see houseflies, spiders are normal-sized and lead discreet lives, and even the ants are generally small and non-biting.

In lowland and more humid areas, you'll find more quantity and variety in the insect department. Some, like the enormous Hercules beetle or the bright blue morpho butterfly, are stunning but harmless. It's the more prosaic insects like mosquitoes that do greater harm, occasionally transmitting dengue fever and, more rarely, malaria—mostly in wet, lowland areas with poor sanitation. Malaria is rare enough in Costa Rica that few doctors suggest taking chloroquine pills along on your trip. But cases have been reported, and the best prevention (against both malaria and dengue fever) is to guard against mosquito bites. Wear long sleeves and long pants, use insect repellent containing DEET, and sleep under a mosquito net. Some suggest that spraying your clothes with the insecticide permethrin will guard against dengue fever.

Africanized bees have arrived in parts of Costa Rica and are as aggressive here as they are elsewhere. Experts advise running in a zigzag pattern if they come after you, getting under a sheet, or submerging yourself in water if there's any available.

Some areas have scorpions. I heard of a woman who, when she washed her family's clothes, made sure to put them away inside out. That way, when they dressed, they'd have to turn everything right side out and thus would be automatically checking for bugs that might have hidden in the armpit of a shirt or in the leg of a pair of jeans. Despite her precautions, one day her husband found a scorpion crawling out of his sleeve. Then he noticed the seams on his shirt—it was still inside out. In scorpion areas, make sure you shake out your clothing and shoes before getting dressed in the morning. This will help with snakes, too, which love nothing better than to curl up in a warm, odoriferous boot.

Snakes

Costa Rica has more than 100 kinds of snakes, including venomous ones such as the much-feared fer-de-lance, which accounts for 80 percent of all snakebites in the country, and the yellow-bellied, black-backed sea snake, which paddles along in the Pacific Ocean with its oar-like tail. Despite the variety of snakes here, death from snakebite is rare. Most bites occur when snakes are stepped on—watch where you're going!—or if you harass or try to handle a snake. Leave snakes alone and they'll return the favor. Be especially careful in long grass, and remember that many snakes are arboreal—the tree branch you grab onto for balance just may be alive. Snakes also like to hang out in bromeliads, so be careful when looking inside these tightly wound whorls of stiff leaves and brilliant flowers. If you are bitten, move as little as possible. If the bite is to a limb, apply a tight bandage (not a tourniquet) above the bite, and release it for a minute or two every 15 minutes. Apply ice if available, and keep the bitten limb elevated while getting yourself to a hospital or clinic. Don't try that old remedy of cutting an X over the bite and sucking out the venom. Some snake venom contains anticoagulants, which will make any cut bleed like crazy.

Sun

What people come to Costa Rica for can also be their downfall. The sun can be like a molten hammer, especially around midday. Sunscreen, a wide-brimmed hat, sunglasses, and a long-sleeved, light-colored shirt may make you look like your typical gringo in the tropics, but that's a small price to pay for guarding against sunburn, skin cancer, and heatstroke. Don't forget to drink a lot of liquids, and I'm not talking beer, which goes right through you. Take it slow at first, especially in areas of high humidity. After you've been here for a while you'll adjust to your chosen area's weather. In the most sizzling areas, early mornings and late afternoons are the best times to be out and about. There's a reason hot countries invented the siesta, that midday break that gets you out of the sun and into a hammock. Do as the locals do and spend the early afternoon swaying on the front porch, a cool drink within reach.

Safety

CRIME

The good news is that Costa Rica has very little gang activity, does not suffer from political violence, and has no army, and its cops are not to be feared, as some Latin American police forces are. Violent crime here is less common than in many other places, including the United States.

But although you're probably safer anywhere in Costa Rica than in a similar-sized town or city in the United States, crime here is on the rise, especially theft. The U.S. State Department says that tourists are frequent victims of crime in Costa Rica and advises "the same level of caution that one would exercise in major cities or tourist areas throughout the world." The police here have limited capabilities and are not up to U.S. standards, especially outside of San José.

The country is trying to improve the situation. In 2006, shortly after President Arias was elected, newly appointed Public Security Minister Fernando Berrocal said he would increase the national police force by nearly 50 percent in the next four years and create a specialized tourism police to assist visitors and to help combat sex tourism. San José and the Juan Santamaría airport were his top priorities.

In late 2006, Costa Rica had about 10,000 police officers—in a country

EMERGENCY NUMBERS

911: National emergency number for all of Costa Rica
118: Fire Brigade
128: Red Cross
800/376-4266: Drug Control Police

If you have an auto accident, call the following before moving the car: **506/222-9330** or **506/222-9245** for the Transit Police (Tránsito); **800/800-8000** for the Insurance Investigator (INS).

See the Resources section for hospital and private clinic contact information throughout Costa Rica.

The Costa Rica Tourism Institute has set up a 24-hour hotline for tourists to report problems or ask advice: **800/TOURISM** (800/868-7476) or **800/TURISMO** (800/997-4766).

DAILY LIFE

of four million people, that's about one police officer per 4,000 people. For comparison purposes, check the police-to-civilian ratio in your hometown. In San Francisco in 2006, for example, there were about 2,300 officers in a city of 750,000. That's about one police officer for every 326 people.

It's no secret that there are simply too few police in Costa Rica to do an effective job. Compounding the problem is that most officers are not well trained, and, especially in areas outside of the Central Valley, police departments don't even have enough funding for a police car. In some towns the community has fund-raised to help the local police department get the basics. I've heard more than a few stories of people calling the police only to be told that if they want police service, they need to come get the officers or send a taxi.

This sort of response doesn't exactly inspire confidence, and often people with the means arrange for private security. Whether it's the men in the little kiosks you see in urban and suburban neighborhoods, the guards and dogs patrolling hotel grounds, or caretakers living in the houses of absentee owners (to prevent break-ins), this country has "an army of private security guards," according to Arturo Condo, professor and dean at INCAE business school near San José. Most experts agree that there are far more private security guards in the country than actual police.

All those bars you see on windows are there for a reason, as break-ins are on the rise and are becoming more brazen, with thieves entering the house while the occupants are at home. Gated communities are popular in large part because they offer better security. Big dogs are very popular as four-footed guards that make a lot of noise; from many accounts I've heard, dogs seem to do the trick even more than elaborate locks and bars.

When you're out and about, you need to be aware of those around you. Once you get a feel for the country and its people, you'll be able to recognize potentially dangerous situations and ease out of them gracefully. Until then, be wary. Petty theft is on the rise, especially in San José. Keep your bags close at all times, and don't be flashy with money, jewelry, or cameras. Make photocopies of important documents—passports, visas, and plane tickets—and keep the originals at home or in a hotel safe. Cars are broken into on a regular basis—don't leave anything of value in your car, and if possible, park your car in a garage or a guarded lot or make an arrangement with the man on the street who specializes in looking after people's cars. His job depends on satisfied customers, so even though we North Americans aren't accustomed to this form of makeshift security, for me and others I've talked to it has been surprisingly effective.

Costa Rica is also the land of scammers, many of whom will look like you and speak your language. Scams range from low-tech—someone spilling a drink on you and, in "helping" you clean it off, relieving you of your wallet—to more sophisticated schemes that ask for investments of tens of thousands of dollars. In late 2002, for instance, hundreds of expats and Ticos lost an estimated US$200 million when a financial entity known as Ofinter S.A. (a.k.a. "The Brothers") closed up its offices overnight and fled the country, taking investors' money with them. Clients had been lured by promises of 3.5 to 4 percent interest a month (that is, 42 to 48 percent a year), and the Brothers had indeed delivered on those promises for years, supporting many an expat in high style. But then the goose laying those golden eggs flew the coop, and investors were left in the feather-strewn mud.

There are many other such schemes still in operation—beware of investments that seem too good to be true. The maxim "If you wouldn't do it at home, don't do it here," isn't nearly strong enough, since there's less effective government oversight of financial dealings here than there is in North America or Europe.

DRUGS

The North American appetite for recreational drugs has helped make Central America a conduit for marijuana, heroin, and cocaine moving up from South America. Drug trafficking and money laundering are on the rise throughout the isthmus, including Costa Rica.

What that means to the average visitor or foreign resident is that Costa Rican police, assisted by the U.S. Drug Enforcement Agency (DEA), are on high alert. The United States and Costa Rica signed a treaty in 1998 on joint air and sea patrols to crack down on drug smuggling. The DEA's Central American headquarters, in fact, is in San José. Big guns are trained on this little republic, and anyone suspected of participating in international drug trafficking will be dealt with harshly. In 2006, some 60 foreigners were arrested in cases related to drug smuggling, a crime punishable by up to 20 years in prison.

If you tend toward addiction and have dabbled in recreational drugs, be especially careful in Costa Rica. Marijuana and cocaine (including crack) are easy to come by and a lot less expensive than they are back home. Many an expat has been brought low by the availability of cocaine, in particular. I've heard stories of gringos ending up broke and on the street.

Alcohol is another drug that expats may abuse when they move to Costa Rica. The stress of adapting to a new culture, coupled with feelings of isolation and boredom, drives many newcomers to drink. "If you have a drinking problem," advises Chris Simmons of Remax Realty in Tamarindo, "don't come to Costa Rica—it'll just get worse." Costa Ricans also like their liquor, which is no good thing but has a silver lining: There are Alcoholics Anonymous meetings in almost every neighborhood and town in the country. Some meetings are in English, but don't worry if the meeting is in Spanish and you can barely say "Hola." The camaraderie of such gatherings transcends language.

PROSTITUTION

There are tens of thousands of prostitutes in Costa Rica, and the majority operate well within the law. Yes, prostitution is legal here, and working girls are supposed to have special ID cards (*carnets de salud*) proving that they are disease-free. There are brothels in most towns and scores of them in San José, as well as bars that are known as gathering places for prostitutes and potential clients. Sixteen is the age of consent in Costa Rica, but it is illegal for young people under 18 to work as prostitutes; anyone who engages the services of an underage prostitute is at serious legal risk.

In 2000, ABC's *20/20* broadcast a report that Costa Rica was second only to Thailand in underage sex tourism. Since then, there has been increased awareness of the issue and heightened police vigilance. The Costa Rican government formed the Commission Against the Sexual Exploitation of Children, and private organizations also lend a hand in rectifying the situation, offering job training for young people who might otherwise be drawn to the "easy" money of prostitution, or providing rehab and employment opportunities for those already in the life.

DAILY LIFE

Beyond the straightforward sex-for-money world of prostitution lies a wide gray area of "arrangements." In this country, where women (as elsewhere in the world) are at an economic disadvantage, and where it is not uncommon for men to abandon their wives and children (desertion is called "the poor man's divorce"), some women actively seek out relationships with foreign men in the hopes of garnering support for themselves and their families. These women believe that most foreign men are well-off, and by Costa Rican standards, most are. Some Ticas also claim that foreign men are less likely to stray. Expat men looking for such arrangements should go in with their eyes wide open. Love *can* be found under such circumstances, but don't count on it. Think twice when a beautiful young woman claims that she truly prefers a man three times her age.

That said, marrying *por interés* (for money, or security) here is not uncommon, and it's not limited to Tica women looking for foreign sugar daddies. In terms of world history, marrying for love is a relatively recent development, and in poorer countries marriage is still seen as an economic contract as much as a romantic one. There's nothing wrong with that, as long as you don't confuse a mutually beneficial arrangement with true love.

AIDS AND OTHER STDS

Sexually transmitted diseases and the AIDS virus are less prevalent in Costa Rica than in many other nations. According to the CIA Factbooks, the HIV/AIDS Adult Prevalence Rate (which estimates the percentage of adults 15–49 living with AIDS or HIV) was .60 percent in 2003 in Costa Rica, the exact same rate as in the United States.

Even though Costa Rica has done a decent job with AIDS education, and the country's public health system cares for people living with the virus, it's still very important to be careful, especially if your plans here include casual sexual contact.

As explained, prostitution is legal, and prostitutes are supposed to be checked regularly for disease, but some prostitutes aren't registered, don't get checked, and are therefore at high risk of contracting AIDS and other STDs, and of passing them on to their clients. Even if your partner is nonprofessional, know that Costa Rican men usually prefer not to use condoms, and Costa Rican women don't tend to insist. Practice safe sex, and use condoms every time.

SAFETY NOTES FOR WOMEN

North American and European women may get a lot of attention in Costa Rica, especially if they're young and/or blonde. Some women appreciate the attention; many do not. You may hear wolf whistles, hissing, or suggestive comments as you walk down the street. If you speak fluent Spanish and are one of those lucky people who always think of the right thing to say at the right moment, by all means, attempt a witty comeback. Most of us, however, would do well to ignore unwanted attention and to walk on by with purpose and confidence.

Most guidebooks advise women to dress like the local women do, but if you did that in Costa Rica, you'd draw even more attention, since most Ticas favor skin-tight pants, plunging necklines, and high heels. If you dress conservatively, you'll get less attention, but not that much less. Costa Rican men seem to believe that North American and European women—whether in miniskirts or overalls—are easy conquests. This may have some basis in truth, as many visiting women enjoy brief beach flings or choose the optional night tour with their nature guide. There's nothing wrong with that if everyone's a consenting adult, but remember that you are in unknown waters here. Even supremely confident and experienced women probably don't know the ins and outs of dating etiquette in an unfamiliar place. For your own safety, it's best to lay low at first, taking it all in but not acting impulsively. And be sure to observe the same commonsense precautions you would in any new place: Don't walk alone in remote places, especially after dark. Grab a cab whenever you feel you've strayed into an iffy neighborhood (cabs are cheap). And don't hang out late at unfamiliar bars unless you have friends around who'll make sure you're okay.

DAILY LIFE

EMPLOYMENT

Self-starters will do well in Costa Rica. It's actually easier to establish your own business here than to get a decent job working for someone else. Compared to many other countries, which put up obstacles to foreign-owned enterprise, Costa Rica welcomes foreign investment, especially businesses that create jobs for Ticos. Tax breaks are offered to new ventures related to tourism, reforestation, and low-income housing, and specially designated free trade zones *(zonas francas)* offer further tax breaks for businesses located within their boundaries. You don't even need residency to start that rafting business, flower shop, or production plant you've always dreamed of. Since most businesses here are owned and operated by a corporation (in Costa Rica called an S.A., or Sociedad Anónima), you can even start and run a business on a tourist visa.

A few decades back, the average North American living in Costa Rica—well past midlife, living off a pension or investments—wasn't looking to work or start a business. More and more, however, those who move here are still smack in the middle of their working years. Some have been laid off; other

© ERIN VAN RHEENEN

have cashed in or dropped out. They come to Costa Rica to escape, to reassess, and to start over. If they decide to stay, most of these sojourners will, sooner or later, need to think about how they will support themselves.

You *can* support yourself here, but it will take more than picking up coconuts, sticking a straw in them, and selling them to tourists—that job is taken. And it's not a place to come to get rich quick, or to get rich at all, for that matter. Those who do best simply want to live here and do what it takes to make that happen. Lance Byron, co-owner with Adrienne Pellizzari of the ever-expanding Café Milagro in Quepos, says loving the country and its people are essential to success in business. "And when I say success," he clarifies, "I mean not only monetary, but spiritual as well. Some foreigners manage to make enough money to survive, but they're miserable," complaining about the bureaucracy and their workers to whoever will listen. Lance and other business owners emphasize that it's the newcomer who must adapt, not the other way around.

Even though you'll naturally want to turn a profit or make a decent salary, it's good to keep things in perspective. Costa Rica offers visitors the benefits of living in a nation that has made long-term investments in peace, social justice, and the environment. It abolished its army in 1948, has put aside a quarter of its territory for national parks and wildlife refuges, and continues to put money into the country's infrastructure and social services. Think of all the sacrifices this tiny nation has made to transform itself into a place where all are entitled to health care and education, where despite problems the country basically *works,* and where a disproportionate share of the world's biodiversity has been given a fighting chance at survival.

Add to all that a slower, more humane pace, and you're already enjoying a host of advantages that money can't buy. Factor these into your balance sheet, and listen to the expats who note that those interested only in money seem to do worse here than those with broader goals. Whether you choose to teach English, start a bed-and-breakfast, or run a factory, you'll do better and be happier if you want to contribute to Costa Rica rather than wring from it everything you can.

Being a contributing member of your new society and earning money are not mutually exclusive. It's not only possible to make a living here, it's often easier to start and run a business in Costa Rica than it would be in the United States or Canada. Making money hand over fist is another story.

And there's a lot to learn quickly. You're in a new environment, often using an unfamiliar language, and different labor laws apply. Legal and cultural differences come into high relief as you contract a lawyer to do the paperwork,

DAILY LIFE

DAILY LIFE

7TH STREET BOOKS: A CLEAN, WELL-LIGHTED PLACE

Need a place to find a great novel in English, a book on tropical biology, or a copy of the *International Herald Tribune?* Stop in at 7th Street Books. Located half a block off the pedestrian-only section of Avenida Central in San José, a few blocks from the landmark Teatro Nacional, the store enjoys an excellent location and sees lots of foot traffic. Expats buy their *Tico Times* here, while tourists stop by to peruse the selection of road maps and guidebooks. The store has always been a great place to meet other travelers or resident foreigners, and now there's a branch of the excellent Café Milagro right in the store, so you can sip an espresso while trying to decide between Gabriel García Márquez and Charles Bukowski. The store has been owned and operated by John McCuen and Marc Roegiers since 1995; they currently have 10 employees. Below, John answers a few questions about the business.

Can you live off the proceeds of the business?
We do pretty well, but tend to reinvest all profits in new publishing projects, so cash – as with all small business – is a perennial problem.

What's next for the business?
We've begun publishing books on the natural history of Costa Rica, and we're expanding the number of publishing projects we're working on. We're also studying opening a distribution business in another country.

What's the most satisfying thing about doing business here?
San José is small enough that one can sense the changes (however small and modest) that the business has wrought on the local scene. You also get to know your customers. In terms of employees, if you pay people fairly, you have access to lots of people who are eager to work.

The most frustrating thing?
I'm not sure the frustrating aspects are specific to Costa Rica. Small-business owners always wish they were making more money. Though foreigners doing business in Costa Rica often complain of how inefficient the business culture is here, I'd prefer to point out one positive aspect. There are fewer regulatory agencies here than in the United States; a friend who owns a fairly simple business in California must meet the requirements of 14 regulatory agencies.

If I had to mention one change in how business works in San José, a change to our detriment, it would be the change in rental laws here, which happened about seven years ago. Before, the laws were decidedly to the advantage of the renter, and in fact unfair to building owners. Basically, the renter could stay in a location forever, if he wanted to, without a corresponding lease obligation on his part to the owner. Now, I think, the rental laws are decidedly unfair to the renter. After only three years of operating your business, the building owner can send you packing.

© ERIN VAN RHEENEN

owner John McCuen at 7th Street Books

Any advice to others thinking of starting a business in Costa Rica?
Don't assume that what might work in other countries will work here.
Move here first to learn about the country. Study Spanish. These all sound
obvious enough, but when you have met someone who planned to open
a topless car wash in Costa Rica (according to his astute plan, the workers, women, would be topless, not the customers) and another who was
going to rocket the ashes of dead people to the moon, and yet another
who wanted to create a Che Guevara theme park, then you realize that
common sense is needed.

***Any other untapped business opportunities you see down here? Enter-
prises you'd start if you had the time, money, and/or expertise?***
Many people come here with the eager plan of learning how to salsa.
Apparently, it is impossible to learn, based on observations of the whirl-
ing dervish mockery that the average foreigner makes of the art of
salsa. Some of them get the steps down, but miss the groove; others
just step on their partner's feet. One might become very rich indeed
by the discovery of something in Latin dance equivalent to the Suzuki
method in violin.

Contact Information
7th Street Books
on 7th Street (Calle 7), between Avenida Central and Avenida 1 (150 meters/
164 yards south of Morazan Park)
San José
tel. 506/256-8251
fax 506/258-3302
marroca@sol.racsa.co.cr
open daily 9 A.M.-6 P.M.

hire staff to help you, and try to carve out your niche with tools you're not even sure how to use yet. It's easy to get discouraged. The successful business owners I've met all have their tales of struggle and woe, but they tell them with a comic twist rather than with bitterness. And it's a sense of humor—along with good planning, experience in the field, hard work, and just plain sticking to it—that makes a business work here (much like elsewhere in the world). It's the couple who buys a hotel though they don't know the first thing about running one, or the tourist who thinks doing business here will be like taking an extended vacation, who lose their shirts and often their affection for the country.

The Job Hunt

Costa Rica is like the United States in that it has one of the strongest economies in its geographical area, and so it attracts people who need work. If your home country is in bad economic straits, with high unemployment—think Argentina, Peru, or Nicaragua—Costa Rica looks very good to you. "It's easy to make a living here," a Peruvian living in Liberia told me. "As long as you're ready to work hard. But at least here you find something to work hard at."

For North Americans used to making a good wage or salary, however, Costa Rica is no haven. North Americans don't usually come here for job opportunities; they come because they love the country. Those who need to generate income can do so, but that income won't approach what you could make back home. Sure, the cost of living is lower here, but not that much lower. Rent is less; food is about the same. Buses and taxis are a bargain, but cars are more expensive here than back home.

You can't legally work without a work permit, and they're not easy to get. Sometimes employers will arrange for permits or give you a letter of employment so that you can hire a lawyer to apply for the permit.

Most of the jobs are in the Central Valley, the economic engine of the country. Yes, there's a lot of tourist activity on the coasts and in some inland areas like Lake Arenal. But there's also a lot of competition for those tourism-related jobs. How many wanderers stumble into cool little beach towns and decide they want to stay? Too many. These areas can only absorb so many massage therapists, surf instructors, real estate agents, and bartenders. And Ticos will always be hired before you—it's only fair. Says the owner of a large Pacific coast hotel, "Eighty percent of [foreigners] who move to Manuel Antonio seem to be looking for work. They usually don't find it, because it's very hard for businesses to hire foreigners. If it were easier, the whole tourist industry would change."

If you do get a job in a tourist town, it will probably end when high season does—in April—or even before. The few North Americans I met who had managed to land jobs in resort areas spoke of low wages, lack of shifts, and (for waiters) no tips.

The government would really rather you start your own business and provide work for others. To get an idea of how foreigners are encouraged to open businesses but discouraged from holding jobs, consider this: The most common categories of foreign residency—*rentista* and *pensionado*—allow you to be a business owner but not an employee. Understandably, Costa Rica wants to protect its own workforce.

But there are foreigners who work at salaried jobs, some even legally. What do they do, and how do they do it?

Some work for multinational corporations with branches here—those jobs are usually arranged before they get to Costa Rica. By law, these companies are allowed to fill 10 percent of their positions with foreign workers; in practice the percentage is much lower. There are many qualified Ticos to fill the positions, and they are likely to work for lower salaries.

Some foreigners work for NGOs (nongovernmental organizations). Others with specialized skills, like electricians, plumbers, or finish carpenters, get hired because there may be few people in the area (especially outside of cities) with their skills.

Probably the most common job for expats is teaching English. Victoria Schwarz, who works for two English schools in San José, says there's an explosive need for teachers.

English teachers usually make between US$4 and US$9 an hour. The bigger, more successful English schools can often give teachers enough hours a week to make a living wage, but smaller or struggling schools may only have a few slots available. Be wary of promises. A young woman I met in Monteverde had communicated by Internet with an English school there, which promised her work along with room and board. When she arrived, she found that the room was a hovel, the board not available, and she only got paid for teaching if students signed up for classes, which seemed to be a rare occurrence.

"If they don't know you," cautions Peggy Windle, who has taught at several schools in Costa Rica, "they won't give you a full-time job. They'll try you out part-time, and if they like you, maybe in four or five months they'll give you enough work to live on. Bring money."

She also advises bringing your actual physical credentials with you—diplomas, teaching certificate, et al. "They wanted my sheepskin from college!" says Peggy. "Not the transcripts, but the piece of paper that says I graduated.

ONLINE WORK

More and more Ticos are making their living working at Internet-assisted jobs, from online gambling to email customer service. Expats too can take advantage of the fact that Costa Rica is more and more wired and will no doubt take another leap forward as the telecommunications industry is transformed by CAFTA (the Central American Free Trade Agreement).

Some jobs based in your home country will travel well, and if you are lucky enough to have one, you've hit pay dirt. Any sort of independent activity that can be parlayed via Internet is a good bet. Writing, editing, transcribing, proofreading, and web design are just a few of the professions that could keep you in *gallo pinto* (beans and rice) and *guaro* (the local firewater).

With online banking and direct deposit, you don't have to worry about the check being lost in the mail. And if you're a freelancer marketing your services, no one even needs to know you're abroad. With online fax and payment services, you can ply your trade from anywhere there's an Internet hookup.

BLOGGING FOR FUN AND PROFIT

Jacqueline Massey writes a popular blog that while she was based in Costa Rica could legally earn money from gambling affiliate programs. What's an affiliate program? If you have a blog or Website, you can put ads on your site, and if people on your site click through to the advertiser's site and buy something, you get a cut. Jacqueline experimented with many affiliate programs – books, cookware, and even a place that sold bug zappers – but it was the gambling affiliates that turned out to be lucrative. Jacqueline was blogging about online poker and about gambling in general, so she attracted readers likely to click on gambling

They're very into pomp and circumstance here. I had to call my son and get him to FedEx everything down."

I asked Peggy if would-be teachers should do a lot of advance work before they arrive in Costa Rica. "You can email or call if you want," she says. "But the schools will only believe you really want a job when they see the whites of your eyes."

Annika Loughram, co-owner with Karlene Mistretta of a well-established English school, says they're always looking for qualified English teachers. The school, called Inglés sin Fronteras, caters to professional students, with teachers going on-site to give classes at the offices of multinational corporations in the San José area. Annika says that her teachers make about US$100/week, teaching four class-hours a day. Common schedules are Monday–Thursday, two hours in the morning and two in the afternoon, plus a three- or four-hour class on

ads. When a reader clicked through from her site to a casino and ended up gambling there, Jacqueline got either a straight referral fee or a small percentage of the money the casino made on that gambler.

One month, Jacqueline says, she made over US$8,000; most months brought in a few hundred dollars. When she moved back to Washington state, she had to purge the gambling affiliate ads from her blog, because online gambling is illegal in the United States.

FROM ON THE SIDE TO MAIN SQUEEZE

If you're thinking about moving to Costa Rica in a year or two and wonder how you'll make a living once you get here, think about starting an Internet business now that could eventually be your main source of income. Make sure your business idea doesn't require a good postal system (like selling items that you then have to mail out), because Costa Rica's mail system is not to be relied on.

Once the business is making enough per month that you think you could live on your income in Costa Rica (say, US$1,500 or US$2,000), you can move here, run the business online, and live well, making money at North American rates and spending it at Costa Rican rates.

The beauty of this plan is that your business is based in your home country, not in Costa Rica, so you're not coming down here and taking a job away from someone. If you start a business in Costa Rica you can own it, run it, but not be a salaried employee. And the expat owner of a business based here who "pays herself a salary" is breaking labor laws. But your online business can be located wherever your website is hosted; if you're maintaining it while in Costa Rica, you're simply managing your business from abroad.

But business and tax laws here are continually evolving, so make sure you consult a Costa Rican lawyer or accountant on the details of your business plan.

Saturday. "We ask for a commitment from teachers of at least four months," says Annika. "Otherwise it's too hard on the students, always having to get used to a new face and a new approach." Annika herself came to Costa Rica in 1996 from Marin County, California. She came with the Harvard Institute for International Development and worked with Costa Rica's Ministry of Public Education to improve English curriculum for primary grades.

Many English-speaking foreign residents also teach in bilingual primary and secondary private schools, most of which are located in or around San José. Kirt Wackford, who has a PhD in ecology, teaches science at St. Paul's College in San Rafael de Alajuela. The school emphasizes English instruction as well as other academic subjects, and Kirt teaches his classes in English. Full-time teaching earns him about US$1,000 a month before taxes.

Teachers I spoke with said they had a hard time adjusting to some aspects of the Costa Rican classroom. The biggest was noise level and a certain lack of respect for the teacher. "Kids will talk away while you're trying to give your lecture," says one teacher. "And the culture here is to just let them."

Scheduling does not seem to be a Tico strength. "When I taught at a private school," says Peggy, "I didn't have my own classroom—I always had to look for a place to teach my class. And that's not rare here. I went to a teacher-training program at UCR [the University of Costa Rica in San José], and every morning, we never knew where our class would be. If you were late, you were lost, because everyone met at a certain place on campus at 8 A.M., then we'd wander around looking for an empty classroom. If you arrived late, there was no way you'd find the rest of the class."

Self-Employment

With a stable political environment, solid infrastructure, a highly educated workforce, and no limits on foreign control of corporations, Costa Rica is a very good place for foreign residents to do business. Money flowing in and out of the country does not attract undue attention. There are no limitations on transferring capital (in whatever currency, from whatever country) earmarked for investment, and there are no restrictions on re-investment or repatriation of earnings, royalties, or capital. Costa Rica considers that it protects itself against exploitation by protecting its workforce. Labor laws are strict and well enforced. The government makes it easy for foreigners to do business here in part because it wants more jobs created for Ticos.

For a few specific kinds of enterprise there are further incentives, which include tax exemptions that can last for more than a decade. You'll need an experienced and up-to-date lawyer to tell you which of the many incentive programs you might qualify for and to guide you through applying for them.

If your company qualifies for Free Zone (export processing zone) incentives, you'll get 100 percent exemption on import duties on raw materials or components, 100 percent exemption on export taxes, and 100 percent exemption on taxes on profits for eight years (and 50 percent exemption on taxes on profits for the next four years after that).

If your company relates to tourism or reforestation, there are many other incentives to be had, and some investments even qualify you for residency. A US$50,000 investment in approved tourist or environmental enterprises qualifies you for residency, and US$150,000 in any area accomplishes the same. But many business owners don't bother with this program, as residency is not difficult to obtain through other channels.

SOCIEDAD ANÓNIMA (S.A.)

Get used to the two letters "S.A." You'll be seeing a lot of them, especially if you want to start your own business. A Sociedad Anónima (Anonymous Society) is a corporation, and in Costa Rica, everybody and their dog seems to have one. People form corporations just to buy a car, for instance. The main feature of an S.A. is limited liability. If something goes wrong, it's not you who owns the car or company or whatever; it's the corporation. Liability is limited to how much money you've put into the S.A. It works for Exxon and other multinationals; why shouldn't the average Joe or Jolene have the same protections? Here in Costa Rica, they do.

To form a Costa Rican corporation, two people appear before a notary public and execute the articles of incorporation, and they subscribe to at least one share of stock each. The incorporators needn't be citizens or even residents of Costa Rica; citizens of any nation are free to form a corporation here. An S.A. also needs a board of directors, with a minimum of three members: president, secretary, and treasurer. The two incorporators often play two of these roles, drafting a friend or relative to play the third. That third director needn't appear before the notary public if he or she sends a letter accepting the position.

Forming a Corporation (S.A.)

To form a corporation, you'll need to:

1. Execute the articles of incorporation before a notary public.
2. Publish legal notice of the corporation in Costa Rica's official newspaper, *La Gaceta*—this is to give people the chance to object to the corporation name being recorded, if, for instance, the name is already taken.
3. Register the company at the National Registry (the notary public who executes the articles of incorporation usually does this).
4. Legalize the corporation's books: A set of three accounting books—daily, main *(mayor)*, and inventory and balances—and three "legal" books—shareholders' record, shareholders' assemblies, and board of directors' meetings—are presented to the Ministerio de Hacienda for their initial authorization by the Book Legalization Department. Once legalized, these books will register all internal affairs of the company (as well as stock transfers) and are kept privately by the shareholders.

The incorporation process usually takes a few months, though I've heard of people paying extra and getting it done in a matter of weeks.

Corporation Tax

The fiscal year in Costa Rica runs from October 1 through September 30, with tax returns due by December 15. A corporation is taxed only on income earned within Costa Rica, and tax rates vary from 12 to 36 percent of

DAILY LIFE

VICTORIA SCHWARZ: TEACHING THE BODY AND MIND

From the massage table in Victoria Schwarz's Escazú apartment, you can see out the window and across most of the Central Valley. Especially during the wet season, the view is dramatic: Storm fronts move in and out, rain pours down, and lightning bolts pulse like veins across the sky.

What's happening on the massage table is equally dramatic, if more subtle. Knots release as thunder rumbles, pain washes away with the sound of rain on the roof, and the body just generally lays its burden down.

Doing massage or teaching English, her main source of income, Victoria sees herself as a sort of interpreter, whether "translating the needs of the body" or helping her students understand the complexities of the English language. And recently, she's become a student herself by attending a master's program in education at the University of Costa Rica. "I am having such a great time with this!" she tells me. "It is a lot of work, but I think everyone should go back to school in their fifties." She also points out that earning her master's here will cost her around US$5,000, while her sister's master's, obtained in the United States, ended up costing around US$28,000.

Below, Victoria talks about her dual professions and about doing business in Costa Rica.

Can you live off the proceeds of the business?
Combining massage and English teaching, I am solvent. There's an explosive need for English teachers down here. Ticos understand that from the janitor on up, they need to know English. At this point, after having taught for many years, I make almost US$9/hour teaching English. It may not sound like much, but it's pretty good for Costa Rica.

In 2002 I lived for three months in Quepos and four months in Playa Chiquita, on the Caribbean side. I loved both places, but it was very hard to make a living outside of the Central Valley. In Playa Chiquita I got hooked up with a wedding party at a hotel and did 35 massages in three days – lived off that money for months. But by the time I left Playa Chiquita, we were all bartering – no one had any cash.

When I lived in San Francisco, I would earn between US$80 and US$125 for an hour of massage. Here I charge locals US$20 an hour and people from hotels between US$35 and US$55. I like repeat customers, so I can see the progress made.

The most frustrating things about doing business here?
It's common for Ticos to just not show up for an appointment. And unless they've dealt with a lot of gringos, they don't even call to say they won't be there. I'm busy, and their slot could have been filled by one of many others. Ticos here tell me it's just something you have to get used to. I think it's about them not wanting to disappoint, or have any sort of confrontation.

Another thing is that you have to stay on top of people you hire. If

© ERIN VAN RHEENEN

you're out of sight, you're out of their minds. Sometimes it seems as if to get anything done here, you either have to do it yourself or keep pushing and pushing for someone else to do it.

The most satisfying thing?
I feel like the possibilities here are endless. Despite the problems, if you're creative and clever, you'll do well.

Any advice to people starting a business down here?
Get your friends to come down and fill their suitcases with stuff you need. I had a box mailed, which included a lot of massage oil, and it was confiscated – they thought it was food, and there are a lot of restrictions on mailing in food. Also, get your friends to bring small electronics – phones, answering machines, coffee machines. The stuff here is expensive and not very high quality. You can buy a phone for US$6 in the States.

Any untapped business opportunities you see down here? Enterprises you'd start if you had the time, money, and/or expertise?
What's needed here are good mechanics – they say that a Costa Rican mechanic is someone who's worked on a car once or twice.

But a more important gap I see is convalescent care and nursing homes. There's a saying: "It's not whether you're going to be handicapped; it's when." We will all need help. So there's a huge need here to fill that gap. More nursing homes are needed, but I'm more interested in creating communities here, maybe in a condo complex, where people will take care of each other, or pool their resources to hire the help they need.

On a more general level, I think what we gringos have to offer this country is creativity. For whatever reason, I think we're problem solvers.

net profit. Businesses will need to charge customers and then pay sales tax *(impuesto de ventas)*, also known as a value-added tax. The current rate is 13 percent, and the tax is on goods and services not deemed basic necessities. If your business imports goods, there will be those tariffs to deal with as well. Anita Myketuk of the Buena Nota in Manuel Antonio notes that a store owner needs to figure import taxes into her balance sheet. "A lot of the items in my store are imported," says Anita. "That's why, for instance, sunscreen is so expensive here. There are a couple of brands made in Costa Rica, but no one wants them, because they're not name brands—Coppertone or Hawaiian Tropic. But some things don't have import taxes or have very low taxes, like sporting gear."

Credit Card Fees for Merchants

Bookstore owner John McCuen points out that "credit card companies really stick it to merchants down here," deducting up to 7 percent from sales paid for by credit cards. In the United States, the rate is closer to 2 or 3 percent. As a shopper, I always ask if there's a discount for paying cash—sometimes the merchant will lower the price by 5 percent, since that still allows him or her to do better than giving up 7 percent to the credit card companies.

FURTHER INFORMATION

The Costa Rican–American Chamber of Commerce (AMCHAM, tel. 506/220-2200, fax 506/220-2300, www.amcham.co.cr) may be of help to businesspeople.

The Costa Rican Investment and Development Board (CINDE, tel. 506/299-2800, fax 506/299-2869, invest@cinde.org, www.cinde.or.cr) is a private, nonprofit organization, founded in 1982, that offers free advice and assistance to foreign investors trying to start businesses in Costa Rica.

CINDE also maintains offices in New York City (tel. 212/704-2004, fax 212/997-9839, cindeny@cinde.org) and in San Jose, California (tel. 408/573-6146, fax 408/988-8090, cindeca@cinde.org).

The Ministry of Economy, Industry, and Commerce (tel. 506/235-7855, fax 506/236-7192, info@tramites.go.cr, www.tramites.go.cr) has put together a booklet called *Investor's Manual: Establishing a Business Enterprise in Costa Rica,* in English and Spanish. The information is also available in CD format and on the website.

The Chamber of Representatives of Foreign Companies (CRECEX, tel. 506/253-0126, fax 506/234-2557) is an independent, nonprofit association of private companies that promotes free trade and enterprise.

Hiring Help

Education in Costa Rica is free and compulsory through ninth grade, with computers and English emphasized from an early age. So there are lots of good, qualified people here who are ready to work. But the country knows what it has, and it protects its workers with a series of regulations that you should study carefully before hiring *any* employee. Another caveat: Labor laws are constantly evolving, so please check for any new developments with your lawyer (oh yes, you'll have one, if not two or three).

LABOR LAWS

Whether you hire one person to clean your house or 30 people to sew stuffed monkeys, the same basic labor laws apply. The Labor Code of 1943 is the basis for the lengthy document now in effect, which seeks to minimize conflict between employer and employee by spelling out every detail of that relationship. These regulations are taken very seriously, workers generally know their rights, and if there is a conflict, Labor Court judges often decide in the favor of the employee.

In brief, the regulations specify that:

1. Employers must make Social Security (Caja) contributions for each employee and also deduct a percentage of the employee's pay for further contribution to the Caja.

2. Forty-eight hours is the maximum work week; hours beyond that are paid as overtime.

3. Minimum wages and salaries for most jobs and professions are set by the Caja.

4. Employers must notify the local Caja office within eight days of a hire.

5. The first 30 days of employment is a trial period; after that, employees must be given notice *(pre-aviso)* if they are to be fired, and they have the right to severance pay *(cesantia)*.

6. Employers must provide employees with paid vacations.

7. Employers are obligated to pay a Christmas bonus (called the *aguinaldo*).

8. Employers must provide for maternity leave.

9. Employers must pay employees for nine holidays off per year.

These rules are covered in more detail in the following sections.

Social Security (Caja) Contributions

The Caja Costarricense de Seguro Social (the Caja) pays for workers' health care, sick leave, and disability, but employers are expected to do their part. An employer must calculate 26 percent of a worker's gross salary and pay that amount

CAFÉ MILAGRO: A GOOD CUP OF COFFEE

Though Costa Rica is known worldwide for its *grano de oro* ("golden grain," or coffee), visitors can find it oddly difficult to get a really good cup of java here. When Lance Byron and Adrienne Pellizzari came to Costa Rica in the early 1990s, they puzzled over that riddle, then decided that they might just be the ones, at least in the Quepos/Manuel Antonio area, to solve it.

Adrienne began researching the industry. What she found was that although Costa Rica produced some of the world's finest beans, much of the best coffee was exported. She discovered that the only way to get quality beans was to become a coffee roaster herself, and that's exactly what she did, scraping up the cash to buy an old roaster that can still be seen in their Quepos roastery.

Café Milagro Coffee Roasters was born in 1994 and has since grown to include the restaurant El Patio in Quepos, Café Milagro in Manuel Antonio, and a cozy espresso bar inside San José's 7th Street Books. El Patio was called "the top place in town" in Lonely Planet's 2006 guide, and it earned the maximum three-star rating in the 2007 Frommer's. Café Milagro and the roastery itself offer bags of fragrant beans, world music CDs, and international newspapers and magazines. Adrienne and Lance also run an Internet/mail order business from which you can order everything from dark roast to a stuffed squirrel monkey.

Lance and Adrienne are very involved in their community. Lance is president of the local Chamber of Commerce, Industry, and Tourism and serves the same role in a newly formed Chamber of Tourism for the Central Pacific Coast. Adrienne is the president of a local environmental NGO, the Association for the Conservation of the Titi Monkey, while both Lance and Adrienne are association board members.

Below, Lance answers some questions about the business.

What's the most satisfying thing about doing business here?
It would have to be the sense of pride and self-confidence resulting from being successful in a foreign country, despite all the obstacles. It's a great feeling to know that you're resilient and self-reliant enough to not only live, but also operate a business, in an environment with a different language and culture.

The most frustrating thing?
There is a certain degree of discrimination toward foreigners in Costa Rica. You get the feeling you're the only one playing by the rules. It's not so bad if it's limited to paying a little extra for your dream home. But if you're trying to run a profitable business, paying a little extra for everything makes it hard to compete with the guy who has the "insider's advantage."

One example would be that although Costa Rican law states you cannot sell alcohol within a certain distance of a church or a school, recently a Tico opened a bar/restaurant that is obviously too close to both a school and a church. This business has created a considerable amount of competition for other legally established restaurants in the area. But since the established businesses are owned by foreigners and the illegal business is owned by a Tico, nothing has happened.

Any advice to others thinking of starting a business in Costa Rica?
Love it or leave it. Adrienne and I came to Costa Rica to experience the culture and improve our language skills. We stayed, not because we saw an opportunity to get rich, but because we love the country. Most new businesses fail, no matter where they are in the world, but I believe an even greater percentage of new (foreign-owned) businesses fail in Costa Rica, because the people are here for the wrong reasons.

Many people come here on a brief vacation, have a fabulous time, and decide it would be great to live here. And since you can't live on bananas and coconuts alone, the foreigner starts a business, because it will be "easy" to make a bunch of money in a country where everything, including the labor, is so "cheap."

But the foreigner finds out the vacation is over real fast and she has to work! She can't say anything but *cerveza* and *pura vida* in Spanish. Because of her inability to communicate with the locals, she generalizes that all the locals (at least the ones she meets and "interviews" at the local tavern) are untrustworthy thieves.

So now the foreigner is no longer on vacation, and is working with a bunch of "thieves" at a business that is losing money by the minute. She decides she doesn't particularly like Costa Rica. In fact, she *hates* Costa Rica and its people! But for some reason, she stays, in an apparent state of constant misery, complaining to whoever is unfortunate enough to sit on the bar stool next to her.

The moral of the story: You have to love Costa Rica. And you can't fall in love in a matter of days – that's infatuation. It's best to move to Costa Rica on a temporary basis, study the language, and live here for at least one entire year before investing a single dollar, let alone your entire life savings. If at the end of a year, you're still in love with Costa Rica, your language skills are strong enough to read and understand the labor code, and there is indeed a niche to be filled by your business plan, then go for it!

Contact Information
Café Milagro
tel. 506/777-1707
fax 506/777-2272
info@cafemilagro.com
www.cafemilagro.com

DAILY LIFE

to the Caja. Employers also need to deduct 9 percent of a worker's wages and pay that additional amount to the Caja. Example: A cashier at your bookstore earns US$400 a month. Twenty-six percent of that salary is US$104, which is the employer's contribution to the worker's Social Security. Nine percent of the salary is US$36; the employer deducts that amount from the employee's pay (leaving the worker with a salary of US$364) and pays that additional amount to the Caja.

© ERIN VAN RHEENEN

Bustling San José is the undisputed economic center of the country.

The Work Week

Forty-eight hours is the maximum workweek, 10 hours the maximum day shift (eight hours for hazardous work), and six hours the maximum for a night shift. Managers and executives can be asked to work 12-hour days. Anything exceeding these limits is overtime and must be paid at time and a half.

Minimum Wage

Almost all jobs in Costa Rica have a minimum wage, set by the National Council on Wages. In 2007, minimum wages ranged from about US$9.75 a day for unskilled laborers to US$618 a month for someone with a *licenciado* degree (roughly equivalent to a master's degree). Remember that these are minimums—to attract and retain quality workers, many employers pay more. In Spanish the list of wages is called the *Decreto de Salarios Mínimos* and can be obtained at Social Security offices or from most bookstores. See *Resources* for a web link to a detailed list at the Ministerio de Trabajo y Seguridad Social (Ministry of Work and Social Security).

If laborers here are earning about as much per day as their counterparts in the United States make per hour, what does that mean? Well, that workers here have a harder time making ends meet, and that if you want to work in Costa Rica, you won't be getting the salary you're accustomed to. It also means that as an employer your money will go further here, whether you're paying someone to build your house or keep it clean.

Domestic Servants: In 2007 the minimum wage for a domestic worker was about US$160/month, not including meals and board. The food and lodging provided to a live-in domestic is considered "in-kind" payment equivalent to 50 percent of the worker's wages, and it must be factored in when calculating severance pay or the mandatory Christmas bonuses. What that means is that if you pay a live-in gardener or maid a salary of say, US$300 a month (most people pay a good deal more than the minimum), the real total, when you calculate severance or bonus, would be US$450.

Notification of Hire

You must notify the Caja within eight days of hiring someone. This is to limit the employer's possible liability as well as to start the paperwork moving. If an employee registered with the Caja is injured on the job, the Caja pays most of the medical bills—the employer's liability is limited to four days' salary. But if the worker isn't registered with the Caja, the employer could be liable for not only the worker's medical bills but also half of his or her salary while the employee is injured or sick.

Length and Cessation of Employment

The first 30 days of employment is considered a trial period, with both employee and employer having the right to end the relationship without notice. After 30 days, unless an employee's termination is for just cause, employers must give advance notice of dismissal and are liable for severance pay. An employer can fire an employee and have no further responsibility to that worker only under very specific circumstances, outlined in Article 81 of the Labor Code. Just causes for dismissal range from deliberately damaging an employer's property to being thrown in jail. In Costa Rica, it is the employer's responsibility to document reasons for dismissal and to be ready to argue his or her case.

Pre-Termination Notice *(Pre-aviso):* If termination is not for a cause listed in the Labor Code (maybe business is slow, and there isn't enough for an employee to do), an employer must give advance notice of dismissal, and the amount of time is dependent on how long the worker has been on the job. If the worker has been with you more than three months but less than six, one week's notice is required. Employment of six months to a year requires two weeks' notice. One month's prior notice is necessary for workers who have been employed for one year or more. In lieu of notice, an employer can pay the wages that would have been earned during the notice period. Notice should be in written form or can be delivered orally in the presence of two witnesses.

Severance Pay *(Cesantia):* If an employee is terminated without just cause, he or she is entitled to severance pay. If an employee has worked more than three but fewer than six months, he or she receives seven days' wages. Employees who've worked from six months to a year get 14 days' wages. Employment of a year or more requires between 19.5 and 22 days' wages for each year, depending on the number of years worked.

What If the Employee Quits? If an employee quits for just cause (also outlined in the Labor Code), the employer has the same responsibilities that he or she would have to a worker terminated without just cause. If, however, the employee has no just cause for quitting (maybe she got a better offer elsewhere), the employer's responsibilities end with the employee's departure.

Paid Vacations

Employers must provide workers with two weeks of paid vacation for every 50 weeks worked.

Unused Vacation Pay: When a worker is terminated without just cause, unused vacation pay is due him or her. Workers get two weeks of paid vacation for every 50 weeks worked. If a worker is terminated before a year is up, he or she should be paid for one vacation day per month worked.

The Christmas Bonus (Aguinaldo)

Law mandates this "bonus," sometimes known as the 13th month of pay. Every worker who has been on the job at least a year is entitled to an extra month's wages, to be paid between December 1 and 20. If a worker is fired before December, the *aguinaldo* must be prorated and paid to the employee at the time of termination: Take the total wages paid to the worker from December 1 through November 30 and divide the amount by 12.

Remember that to calculate *aguinaldo* for live-in domestic servants, you must add 50 percent to the salary for in-kind payment in the form of room and board.

Maternity Leave

Pregnant employees are entitled to one unpaid month off before the baby is born and three half-paid months off afterwards. During those three months the employer pays full salary, half going to the worker, half to the Caja.

Paid Holidays

Employers must either provide paid time off for the following nine legal holidays or pay workers (if they agree to work) double their usual wage. Legal holidays fall on January 1 (New Year's Day), April 11 (Juan Santamaría Day), two days during Easter week (Holy Thursday and Good Friday), May 1 (International Workers Day), July 25 (Annexation of Guanacaste), September 15 (Independence Day), and December 25 (Christmas).

Unpaid legal holidays include August 2 (celebration of the country's patron saint, the Virgin of the Angels) and October 12 (Day of Cultures—formerly Columbus Day).

CULTURE CLASHES

It seems to be an international pastime to complain that you can't get good help anymore. Costa Rica's version of that game includes grumbling that Ticos lack initiative and a sense of personal responsibility. The Beisanz family writes in *The Ticos* that the "emphasis on dignity and courtesy often takes the form of saving face for others as well as oneself. Ticos rarely accept blame for mistakes and usually take care not to embarrass others, especially in public." To save face and to make the moment agreeable, Ticos will tell you whatever they think you want to hear: that your check will clear soon; that they'll be there this afternoon, for sure; or that they know which of those wires is live.

Ticos want to *quedar bien,* which means to make a good impression and to get along with others. They want to be respected as individuals and to be treated with the same consideration that they extend. Being scolded or corrected, especially in front of others, is not something a Tico will easily forgive.

Anita Myketuk, who for decades has run a successful souvenir shop in Manuel Antonio, says, "you have to charm people here in order to get them to want to help you. And never, ever yell at anyone or get nasty. North Americans are used to yelling; it's not the end of the world. Here it *is* the end of the world."

Ray Beise of Guanacaste tells how he learned to deal with the Tico tendency to nod and say yes even if they don't know what's being asked of them. "I say to my worker, 'Go over there and dig a hole.' And I leave, and come back, and he hasn't done it. Then I think, maybe there's something he didn't understand. I tell him again. 'Please, go over there and dig a hole.' And this time I ask, 'Did you understand what I said?' And he nods yes, but later I come back and he still hasn't done it. Finally—and this took a long time—I tell them what to do, and then I ask them to repeat back to me what I've just said. Usually they'll hem and haw, but then they'll say, 'okay, tell me again.'"

The culture values harmony (even if it's a superficial sort of harmony) over honesty, an approach that makes for a polite society but can be frustrating for those who prefer candor and are counting on people to keep their word.

Lateness is common, to the extent that when making plans one needs to specify *hora tica* (Tica time, which means an hour or two after the appointed time) or *hora Americana* or *hora exacta* (American time, or exact time).

Still, with all the frustrations (and there's no doubt that Ticos are frustrated with foreigners' idiosyncrasies at least as much as the other way around), almost all of the expat employers I spoke with were happy with their employees. Many think they got lucky, and they claim to have the best cook, clerk, or carpenter in all of Costa Rica. But it seems that a great many employers "got lucky," which suggests that Ticos are essentially good workers, especially if you're a good boss and make it your business to learn about cultural differences that may affect the employer-employee relationship.

In the end, it's all about people. Many foreigners move to Costa Rica because things here are on a more human scale. Personal relationships are paramount, even in the business world. Lance Byron of Café Milagro in Manuel Antonio tells of a local girl who worked in the café. "Silvia worked for us during her high school vacations, went off to college, then got a great job with Procter & Gamble International, who sent her to the United States several times as one of their prodigies. We'd see each other once in a while and she'd always tell us Café Milagro was her favorite job. Whenever Adrienne [the café's co-owner] and I would sit and dream of the day we'd export coffee, Adrienne would have an implementation panic attack and ask, 'But who's going to run it?' I'd calmly reply, 'Silvia.' Well, wouldn't you know it, after a few years in the multinational corporate world, Silvia comes back to us and says she's tired of being 'a number.' So we created the export manager position for her and she's been working on Café Milagro's export logistics."

Costa Rica is like a small town. You never know who will leave the *pueblo* only to circle back and into your life again. This kind of coziness comes as a shock to vagabonding, job- and city-switching North Americans, who may launch and then jettison a dozen different lives before they hit middle age. In Costa Rica it's a bad idea, both personally and professionally, to burn too many bridges (in Spanish it's called *quemar sus barcos,* to burn your boats). A good rule of thumb here is: Treat everyone as if you'll have to see him or her every day. It might turn out that you actually do.

Volunteering

Though many think of volunteering as giving something for nothing, seasoned volunteers see it differently. Besides the satisfaction of knowing you're helping where help is needed, volunteering often gives you a crash course in an unfamiliar subject, from the life cycle of the butterfly (if you're a guide at Monteverde's Butterfly Garden) to how to build a house (if you're helping out at Habitat for Humanity). Some organizations even provide room and board for their volunteers, though most require you to pay your own way.

Volunteering also significantly expands your social circle, often hooking you up with people whose politics and priorities are similar to yours. Sometimes volunteer positions lead to paid work within the same field, as when Robert Durkin volunteered for Habitat for Humanity and later became a paid employee, organizing the agency office in Ciudad Colón. He says at Habitat, volunteers not only pay their own way but often give financial contributions as well. "It probably started with church groups, who give of both their time and financial resources. But it seems to have also extended out to individual volunteers."

DAILY LIFE

ORGANIZATIONS

Just about every agency in Costa Rica that is working to improve society and the environment could use dedicated volunteers. If you have a special area of interest, contact organizations working in that field. See the list in the *Resources* section for ideas.

CREATING YOUR OWN OPPORTUNITIES

Though there are many ready-made volunteer positions, you may prefer to do good in your own way. It can be as simple as identifying the needs of your community and then organizing the effort to fill them. Maybe your neighborhood has no place for kids to play. What would it take to build a playground or even a community center? What kind of help could you get from local and national government, from private organizations, and from your neighbors?

In rural areas, even basic necessities like garbage pickup and a reliable water supply may be lacking. In Tortuguero, the local Woman's Association took on their Caribbean town's trash problem. "About 80,000 tourists come through here every year," says Jenny Madden of the association. "Each tourist, and every person who lives here, produces a mountain of trash—Coke cans, cigarettes, juice containers. We took on the responsibility of picking up all that trash." But they found they couldn't do it alone, and they have begun charging a small fee per house and business (much like any trash-collecting enterprise) and soliciting funds from government agencies. Their project is still a work in progress, but it shows what a small group of people can do.

Look around your town. Does the local health clinic need a vehicle so doctors and nurses can make house calls? Is the nearest preschool or library hours away? Do a lot of people drown every year at the local beach? If you're a problem solver, maybe you can help fix these things.

The best thing about getting involved, one volunteer told me, is that "it gets you to the heart of things. You're right in the middle of town life. It can be frustrating, trying to get things done, but sometimes it all comes together, and you get to help change the face of the place."

FINANCE

"Money is better than poverty," quips Woody Allen, "if only for financial reasons." Allen's smile-provoking maxim rings true wherever you are, although in Costa Rica your money will go a little further, and your financial dealings will be just different enough from what you're used to that you can't coast along on automatic pilot. There are subtle and not-so-subtle differences in how money, that universal language, is spoken here in Costa Rica. Yes, you can open a bank account, but the process won't look like it does back at your neighborhood Bank of America. Shopping, tipping, investing, and taxes will all need to be explored from a Tico vantage point.

You *can* live in Costa Rica for a lot less than what you'd be spending in the United States or Canada, but not without conscious effort. What helps is that most people who move down here want to pare down, to let go of all they've accumulated over the years. They want to own less, work and spend less, and enjoy life's simple pleasures. With this approach, it's not hard to live economically.

Cost of Living

What most people thinking of moving to Costa Rica want to know is, "Can I afford it?" Some have heard you can live like a queen on next to nothing; others say rumor has it that it's as expensive to live here as it is up north. As always, the truth lies somewhere in between. Calculating cost of living is by no means an exact science—so much depends on your personal definition of what is essential. Some can't live without everything they came to rely on in their life up north, from expensive cars to gourmet food. Those looking to create an exact replica of their U.S. life here in Costa Rica will find life very expensive indeed. Those who are more adaptable will be able to live well on a lot less. Most budget-conscious expats end up compromising—living a life that is frugal but with a few frills. They take buses but splurge on excellent restaurant meals twice a week. Or they live in a small house in a modest neighborhood but take a beach vacation every month.

"When I was married to a lawyer in San Francisco," says Victoria Schwarz, who moved here in 2002, "we had a combined income of US$450,000—and that was in 1990! I had a US$150,000 line of credit, and I used it. Sometimes I miss that life, but mostly I don't. I purposely did not transplant my U.S. life down here, as I notice many gringos do. I would say that I live better than most Ticos but far 'lower' than I lived before, in the United States. I count my pennies. If I see something I want, I wait three to five weeks, then look again, to see if that item would really enhance my life. With this technique, it's amazing how little is necessary. It's been good for me to not just go out and buy whatever I think to buy. It feels good not to consume."

What about the numbers? Again, it's hard to pin these things down, but from my observations of many foreign residents, I would say that an exceptionally frugal person could live on as little as US$500 a month. This would mean not owning a car (vehicles are very expensive here), renting a small room, eating at home, shopping at farmers markets, and thinking twice about going to the movies or ordering a double scotch. But most people, the frugal-with-frills types, will need at least US$1,200 a month to live well. These are budgets for single people—if you're a couple, add another 40 percent to the figure, though this may be an overestimate, since often two can live almost as cheaply as one. Rent is shared, food isn't that much more expensive for two, and—if you like each other—you can be your own entertainment. Dominos, anyone?

Victoria says she lives on about US$1,050 a month, with US$475 going to rent (she's got a great one-bedroom apartment in Escazú), phone and electricity at US$25, food and household miscellaneous US$300, and restaurants and entertainment claiming US$250 a month. What she'd like to add to her budget in the future is international health insurance (she thinks it'll be about US$800/year) and Internet access at home (US$15/month). She doesn't have a car and doesn't want one, but she would like to be able to travel more within Costa Rica.

Of course, there are foreign residents who spend four or five times these amounts, and more power to them—they often throw excellent parties. But the point is, if you need to live on less, you most certainly can. Some things that will drive your budget way up are: an expensive private school for your kids; luxury cars with high insurance rates; gambling habits or bad investments; child support (laws here are strict); high drug or alcohol consumption. Know thyself, and you will know thy budget.

SHOPPING

Newcomers are often surprised to see the vast U.S.-style supermarkets and up-scale malls that have sprung up all over the country, but especially in the Central Valley. The megastore of megastores, Hypermas, is like a big Target with food. You can load your cart with toaster ovens, mattresses, Häagen-Dazs ice cream, and fresh pineapple (from Costa Rica or Hawaii!), get your day's exercise just walking from one end of the store to the other, and pay with your U.S. credit or debit card. Prices are often disconcertingly similar to those in the United States, though careful shopping will yield some bargains. Soon you'll learn that the local ice cream, Dos Pinos, is quite tasty and costs a fraction of what imported brands do. Or you'll figure out that you can get cheap sheets and towels in downtown San José rather than pay Hypermas prices. But if you want everything under one roof, price be damned, these megastores are for you. There are several other grocery store chains (with branches all over the country), from the well-stocked Perimercados to the bare-bones Palí.

In terms of non-food shopping, the pedestrian-only Avenida Central

Costa Rican shopping means anything from supermarkets to street kiosks.

FARMERS MARKETS

In almost every town or neighborhood there is a weekly farmers market, offering up mounds of onions, whole hands of bananas, and row upon row of head lettuce. Quality is often better and prices lower than in supermarkets, and it's also a lot more satisfying than choosing from among plastic-wrapped cucumbers at the local supermarket. Organic produce is becoming increasingly available, even in the supermarkets. The farmers markets are social occasions, with housewives chatting with neighbors or with the vendors they've come to know. Cheese, meats, and fresh juices are often available, as are plants, from hardy daisies to delicate orchids. Arrive early in the morning for the best selection, and bring your own bags or a cart.

© ERIN VAN RHEENEN

Farmers Market in San Francisco de Dos Ríos

in downtown San José is a good place to start, as are the many malls, including Multiplaza in Escazú and Terramall on the road from San José to Cartago. There are even four PriceSmart stores (in Tibás, Heredia, Zapote, and Escazú), this country's answer to membership shopping.

Costa Rica has an interesting blend of chain stores, mom-and-pop businesses, and what economists would call "informal commercial activity." In downtown areas, you'll find rickety kiosks offering a little of everything: banana chips, fruit, single cigarettes, hair barrettes. Vendors with their wares spread on the sidewalk sell everything from mangoes to Winnie the Pooh paraphernalia (here the ever-popular bear is just Winnie-Pooh). There are roving vendors called *polacos,* after the Eastern European Jewish immigrants who arrived in the 1920s and often made their living peddling wares from house to house. Especially on weekends, ambulant vendors go up and down my suburban street: ice cream carts with their bells chiming, vegetable vendors singing out *ricos aguacates* (delicious avocados), knife grinders, and the little old man pulling his cart piled high with simple wooden furniture.

What's Available

Costa Rica is a consumer society, and most of what you'll need is available here, often in the Central Valley. Residents of outlying areas make regular shopping trips to San José.

I keep a running wish list, in part to see what is and isn't available here. Usually I find what I need. Nice clothes and shoes are easy to come by, though women will have to get used to the idea of sprayed-on attire—none of the clothes you bring down will begin to be tight enough for Tico tastes. Specific toiletries may or may not be available; I found Neutrogena skin cream but not Aveda hair conditioner. I couldn't find a pink straw cowboy hat but found a great canvas rain and sun hat. In San José's Central Market were the dried herbs a fellow in Limón had suggested I use as medicine. At a health-food store I found melatonin tablets and gel from the noxious noni fruit, said to have miraculous healing properties (the stinky fruit itself is also widely available). At Cemaco there was a good inexpensive desk lamp (made in China, US$10). I couldn't find a decent-but-cheap boombox and had visitors from the States bring one down for me. A big surprise is that in a downtown Asian supermarket I found Thai green curry paste and fish sauce. Now I can make my famous green curry chicken, which local friends—who prefer mild fare—consider closer to insecticide or jet fuel than to actual food.

Bargaining

Travelers who know the vast public markets of Mexico, Guatemala, and other developing countries may be surprised to see few such places in Costa Rica. Western-style malls are more the norm, and bargaining is a very different matter. Forget offering a quarter of the asking price, then settling in for 20 minutes of animated haggling, including the old ruse of pretending to walk away so that the merchant will call you back with a better deal.

In Costa Rica you pretty much pay the asking price. There's a little bit of room to move, but be careful and don't insult the merchant or her wares. You might ask if there's a discount for volume or, if you're in a more upscale shop that accepts credit cards, if there's a discount for paying cash. Merchants here pay up to 7 percent to credit card companies for each transaction, so they may be motivated to give you a 5 percent cash discount. For services—tours, hotels, and the like—ask if there's an off-season rate, a midweek rate, or any discounts offered senior citizens, Costa Rica residents, or ARCR members. It's best to do this with a light touch and not to insist—merchants may prefer to lose the deal than to keep haggling with someone they perceive to be difficult. And if you do negotiate a good price, be sure to get it in writing (if it applies to something in the future, like a trip or a car repair), as people here have a tendency to forget what they've promised.

TIPPING AND SALES TAX

In restaurants the bill will be 23 percent more than you expect it to be, with 13 percent added for sales tax and 10 percent for service. So you've really already paid the tip; outstanding service may warrant a little extra, but most Ticos don't leave any additional tip. The 13 percent sales tax is on all goods and services except fees to doctors, lawyers, dentists, and most other independent professionals. The sales tax on airline tickets is 5 percent. The sales tax on hotel rooms is the usual 13 percent but with an additional tourist tax of 3.9 percent, for a total of 16.9 percent.

Taxi drivers are not tipped, though you'll want to tip bell boys (about a dollar a bag), hotel maids (a dollar or two a day), and tour guides (depends on service, the length and cost of the tour, and how many people were on the tour, but a good measure is to think what you'd tip a similar person in your home country).

Banking

CURRENCY

Costa Rica's currency is called the *colón* (plural is *colones*), named for the explorer Christopher Columbus (his name in Spanish is Cristóbal Colón). Often the U.S. "cents" symbol (¢) is used to denote *colones,* but sometimes the $ is used, which can make it difficult to know if *colones* or U.S. dollars are meant. But if a car is priced at over a million, or a cup of coffee at 400, you know you're in *colón* country.

The bills you'll most often see are in denominations of 500 (orange-brown), 1,000 (red, often called a *rojo*), and 5,000 (blue, sometimes called a *tucán* for the bird on the back and in the watermark). There are also 10,000 *colón* bills, which no one seems to want to change. The bills are the same size as U.S. notes. Coins are of different sizes and come in denominations of

500, 100, 50, 25, 20, 10, and 5, though the lower denominations are slowly being taken out of circulation. The size of coins tells you little about their value: The 20-*colón* coin is bigger than the 100, for instance, and it's easy to mistake the 100 for the 500-*colón* coin, though new, bigger 500-*colón* coins are in the works. Money is sometimes called *pista* or *plata,* and loose change is *menudo.*

Counterfeits

Counterfeit bills seem to be common here, and most merchants have little light-table machines that allow them to quickly check for fakes. The low-tech method of checking a 5,000-*colón* bill (the most often counterfeited) is to hold it up to the light and look for the toucan watermark to the right of the official signatures. Other bills are also faked. Once when I was trying to pay for a bag of *pan dulce,* the bakery owner pointed out that the design on my 1,000-*colón* note was totally off-register, and so it was—the counterfeiter had been quite sloppy. I did what a Tico would do—kept the bill and paid a taxi fare with it later that night. Money is just a collective hallucination, after all—a consensus that these scraps of paper mean something. The off-register bill will be someone's change in that taxi, and it will make its way around the country much as any legitimate bill would. Maybe it's a metaphor for the world economy: If you don't look too closely, everything works just fine.

Exchange Rates and Changing Money

At the end of 2006 the Costa Rica government "floated" the *colón*—set it loose from its mooring to the U.S. dollar. Previously, inflation was slow and predictable, the *colón* losing about 10 percent against the dollar each year. The hope is that the new situation will give the Central Bank more tools to curb inflation, and that the "dollarization" of the economy will slow down. Central Bank president Francisco Gutiérrez said recently that half of Costa Rica's liquid economy was in dollars, and that the predictable devaluation of the *colón* caused people to prefer dollars.

The new system is supposed to subvert that by making things less certain. If you don't know how the *colón* will stack up against the dollar next week, the argument goes, you'll be less likely to favor the U.S. currency.

It's hard to know how this change will play out and what effect it will have on the average citizen. Experts says banks will compete with each other to offer the best exchange rates and that consumers will have to be more aware—previously the exchange rate was basically the same everywhere you went.

GETTING YOUR U.S. FEDERAL BENEFITS IN COSTA RICA

Frequently asked questions answered by the Federal Benefits Unit at the American Embassy in San José, Costa Rica.

Q: I was receiving Social Security benefits in the United States. Can I receive them in Costa Rica?
A: Yes, if you are the direct beneficiary. If you are the child, surviving spouse, or dependent, please contact the Federal Benefits Unit. At the present time, the direct beneficiary may either have checks sent to a bank in the United States and withdraw money in Costa Rica using a debit card or bank transfer, or you may have the checks sent to your address in Costa Rica. The embassy will receive the checks and have them sent registered mail to the address on file at the embassy.

Q: Is there direct deposit with Costa Rica-based banks?
A: At the present time this service is not available in Costa Rica.

Q: Can I use a U.S. mailing address to receive my Social Security checks while living in Costa Rica?
A: According to Social Security Administration regulations, you cannot use a U.S. mailing address unless you are physically present in the United States.

Q: Who handles claims for foreign medical treatment under the Veterans Administration?
A: The Denver Veterans Affairs office handles the claims. It may be reached at 303/331-7590, fax 303/331-7803. The embassy cannot process these claims. For more information, visit the Veterans Benefits and Services website at www.va.gov.

Q: I am a full-service U.S. veteran. Can I receive coverage over here for my service-connected disabilities?
A: Yes, you can be reimbursed for medical treatment, but this is limited to

However things pan out, it's smart to change money at banks or official *casas de cambio*. Don't let some guy on the street convince you that he'll give you a better rate. There's a *casa de cambio* at the San José airport where the line isn't usually very long.

GETTING CASH

The U.S. dollar is much in evidence in Costa Rica. Upon arrival, you needn't hurry to change money (forget changing money on the street—you'll get ripped off), since taxi drivers will accept dollars, as will many businesses, especially in tourist areas. Often they won't accept soiled or torn U.S. bills,

service-connected disabilities only. The Veterans Administration/Foreign Medical Program Office in Denver, Colorado, sets the protocol on how to approve claims.

Q: I am married and would like my spouse to receive survivor Social Security benefits upon my death. Can s/he?
A: Your spouse would be eligible at age 60, if s/he had been married for more than one year to you and had not remarried. Please contact the Federal Benefits Unit of the embassy for specific requirements.

Q: If I work outside of the United States, will this affect my benefits?
A: Only after age 65 may you work without your earnings affecting your pension.

Q: How soon can I apply for my retirement benefits?
A: Three months prior to your 62nd birthday.

Q: Do I need to travel to the United States to apply for Social Security benefits?
A: No, you may apply at the U.S. Embassy in San José 8-11:30 A.M. Monday–Friday and 1-3 P.M. Monday. Note: You can also apply for Social Security benefits online at www.ssa.gov.

More Resources
For more information, contact the Federal Benefits Unit at the American Embassy in Rohrmoser (San José), tel. 506/220-3050, http://sanjose.usembassy.gov/FSQSocialSecurity.htm, open 8-11:30 A.M. Monday-Friday and 1-3 P.M. Monday.
  Remember that Medicare benefits are not available outside the United States. For information about Medicare, see www.ssa.gov/mediinfo.htm and www.medicare.gov.
  Another resource is the website of the Federal Benefits and Federal Agency Services for American Citizens Abroad, at http://travel.state.gov/fed_benefits.html.

though some of the *colón* notes you'll see look as if they've been in circulation since giant sloths roamed the land.

Of course you'll eventually need to get with the program, and the easiest way to get *colones* is to withdraw them from one of many ATMs, using your U.S. or Canadian bank card. Some bank cards (like those of Wells Fargo) will only work in some Costa Rican banks (Scotiabank and Banco de San José, in this case). Check to see where yours will work. Be aware that most U.S. banks charge a fee each time you use an ATM that doesn't belong to them, and that often "currency conversion" rates are tacked on as well. It would be worth your while to get the specifics from your home

Lottery tickets are easy to come by in San José.

© ERIN VAN RHEENEN

bank before you make the move, perhaps changing to a bank with less punishing policies.

ATMs are everywhere and are usually well stocked, though sometimes (especially during the holidays) they can run out of cash. Occasionally I won't be able to get dollars but will be able to get *colones*. Sometimes the "system" is down and the machine spits my card out. Sometimes the system is down for a few days, which means I have to go inside the bank and get an advance on my credit or debit card. This can take time, and the transaction is more subject to human error.

Once I sat for an hour and a half as the clerk ran my debit card through a machine again and again and again, saying it wasn't working. Finally I left with cash in hand, only to go home and find (online) that the bank (Banco de San José) had debited my account three times the amount I had received. I spoke with the bank manager, who after an hour told me there was nothing he could do. I had to work it out with my home bank, over long-distance telephone. Now I try to do everything by ATM.

HAVING MONEY SENT TO COSTA RICA

You can have money wired money to banks here for a small fee, but it might take a while for the wire to go through. It's usually quicker (but more expensive) to have money wired through Western Union (tel. 506/283-6336 or 800/777-7777, www.westernunion.com), which operates within many Mas x Menos supermarkets, or through MoneyGram (tel. 506/295-9595 or 800/328-5678; www.moneygram.com), operating in Banex, Banco de San

José, and Farmacia Fischel. The person sending the money pays the fee; it's free to receive the funds.

BANKS AND BANK ACCOUNTS

Up until 1949 most of Costa Rica's banks were private and owned by U.S. citizens. Early efforts to nationalize banking didn't go well. In 1914 President González Flores was ousted by wealthy Ticos and U.S. oil interests for his attempt to open a state bank. But decades later, a nationalized system became part and parcel of Costa Rican identity, offering up loans on the basis of social responsibility rather than profit. National banks helped fund infrastructure, health, education, and rural development. These banks were the only ones authorized to offer checking accounts and time deposits, and the Central Bank was in charge of national monetary policy.

Despite the benefits of public banks, there were also major drawbacks. Critics complained of inefficiency, misuse of public funds, and cronyism—it was thought almost impossible to get a loan unless you knew someone high up in the bank hierarchy. National bank employees were (and are) essentially government employees, and it's nearly impossible to fire them, no matter how incompetent they might be.

The industry began to change in the early 1980s, in part because the United States Agency for International Development (USAID) threatened to halt new grants and loans to Costa Rica if the banking system didn't move toward privatization. By 1996, private banks were given the same rights as public ones—to offer checking and savings accounts, for example.

Now there are both public and private banks in Costa Rica, and neither are models of efficiency. The four public banks (Banco Nacional de Costa Rica, Banco de Costa Rica, Banco Crédito Agrícola de Cartago, and Banco Popular) at least have branches all over the country. If you live out in the sticks, it might be easier to deal with one of these entities. Also, the National Banking System guarantees deposits in government-owned banks. National banks are known to be extremely slow and bureaucratic, with checks often taking weeks to clear and wire transfers taking up to a week to register in your account. And you have to keep calling and checking—otherwise your funds may get lost in the shuffle. You can open U.S.-dollar or *colón* accounts, and the minimum for opening a checking account is usually US$500. The ARCR cautions that national banks are not a good source of capital for foreign investors or for mortgages. "The procedure can take months," it says in a booklet for members, "unless you know someone with contacts high in the bank. After waiting months it is not unusual to be turned down for any

TIPS FOR BANKING IN COSTA RICA

Opening a Bank Account

- Each of the country's approximately two dozen banks has a different process for opening an account. And just like banks back home, they offer different kinds of accounts and services, with different fees. You can also apply for credit cards. Not all banks will require them, but most savvy expats suggest getting one or two letters of recommendation from your bank(s) back home, stating that you are a customer in good standing. This will often ease the process of opening a new account.

- You can choose to do business with either a public or private bank. Public banks are generally thought to be slower and more bureaucratic, but deposits in state-owned (public) banks are guaranteed by the government, while deposits in private banks are not. On the other hand, private banks tend to have a wider array of services and choices than public banks.

- It's easier to open a savings account than a checking account. Most banks require that you be a Costa Rican resident if you want to open a checking account. You may need to show your utility bills to prove that you live here, and checking accounts usually require two letters of recommendation, either from financial institutions back home or from two account holders at the bank where you'd like to have a checking account.

- If you've formed a corporation in Costa Rica, you can often open a local corporate checking account even if you don't have residency.

- You can choose to keep your money in either *colones* or dollars. Having a dollar account protects you against *colón* devaluations.

Banking Hours and Practices

- Most banks are open 9 A.M.-4 P.M. Monday-Friday. Some branch offices have longer hours; some private banks are open Saturday mornings.

- You may wait a very long time – an hour, say – for even simple transactions. Sometimes you'll see people lined up outside of banks even before they open. Bring a good book.

- Try to avoid banking on the second and last Fridays of the month. These are paydays for many Costa Rican workers; lines might snake out the front door and down the block.

- ATMs are everywhere, though debit cards from U.S. banks won't necessarily work in all of them. My U.S. bank card, for instance, works only in the ATMs of Scotiabank and Banco de San José. (I can go inside any of the other banks and get money off that debit card from a clerk.) ATMs often let you withdraw cash in either *colones* or dollars (if you're withdrawing from a dollar account).

number of reasons." (See the sidebar *Borrowing Money to Buy Property* in the *Housing Considerations* chapter for more information on mortgages.)

Service at one of the nearly 20 private banks may be a bit less inefficient, with slightly more possibility of getting a loan or a mortgage. Fees are often higher as well. And even in private banks, it seems to be a matter of whom you know. One long-term foreign resident half-jokes, "If you want decent service in any bank, you need to woo the manager, charm the pants off the tellers, and even make friends with the guard who stands by the door. Then maybe your check will clear and you can take the manager out to a fancy lunch."

Most expats recommend keeping at least some (if not most) of your money in a bank back home and accessing it here via ATM or advances processed through real live tellers. A bank back home will allow you to pay bills online (that's just starting up with banks here) and get direct deposit of your pension or rental or investment income. As you get deeper into your life here, it will become useful to also have a local account. If you have a business, you'll definitely need one, and for residency applications, you'll need to deposit money in a local account. One of the many services provided to ARCR members is an up-to-date and detailed comparison of local banks, including minimum balance requirements, what sort of identification and references you need to open an account, and fees charged.

CREDIT CARDS

Credit cards are widely accepted, especially in upscale or tourist-oriented businesses. Visa is the most widely accepted card, with MasterCard a close second and venerable American Express a distant third. Conversion is at the official exchange rate, though merchants may tack on a surcharge to offset the 6 or 7 percent they're charged by credit card companies for each transaction. You can use your credit card to buy *colones* or dollars at a bank (there may be a minimum, often US$50). You can also get cash advances on your credit card via an ATM, provided you have arranged for a PIN. If you lose your credit card while in Costa Rica, call Visa International (tel. 506/257-4744 or 800/011-0030), MasterCard (tel. 506/257-4744 or 800/011-0184), or American Express (tel. 800/012-3211 or call collect to 336/393-1111).

Your Signature

When you use a credit or debit card in the United States, most clerks never even glance at the signature. In Costa Rica, be prepared for the clerk to carefully check your signature on the back against the one on the receipt you sign.

Here, your signature still means something, and many Ticos have worked up elaborate marks that could be hieroglyphics for all their resemblance to letters. Hard-to-copy signatures guard against fraud, as well as express the individual's personal style. North Americans, who hardly write by hand anymore, think of fraud in terms of identity theft and personal information that hackers can get off your computer, but here the signature still carries the weight of your identity.

Income Tax

COSTA RICAN TAXES

At present income tax here is paid only on income earned in Costa Rica, and taxable income is based on net income (gross income minus any expenses or deductions). Personal income tax on salaries ranges from 0 percent to 18 percent. The fiscal year runs from October 1 to September 30, with tax returns due before December 15.

Note that for many years the Costa Rican legislature has been wrestling with tax reform bills. All sorts of changes have been proposed (but not approved)—from better tax collection to a tax on "luxury housing." Expats are especially concerned about proposals that "worldwide income" be taxed—in other words, that people might have to pay tax on income earned outside of Costa Rica but spent here. Some say that without a tax treaty preventing it, this would open the way for "double taxation"—having to pay tax both where you make the money and where you spend it. It's hard to know how all this will play out, although if past attempts at "reforms" are any indication, most of the inflammatory and controversial ideas will end up being either jettisoned or toned down.

U.S. TAXES

The Internal Revenue Service (IRS) has long arms, and they're not for hugging. The United States is one of the few developed countries that tax their citizens while they live overseas. In fact, there is a small but growing number of expats all over the world who quietly give up their U.S. citizenship, in part to avoid the tax burden (including inheritance taxes) that the IRS imposes on all Americans, no matter where in the world they reside.

In 1996, the U.S. Congress passed a measure saying that anyone with a net worth of US$500,000 or more who gives up U.S. citizenship can be labeled a "tax dodger" and may be pursued by the IRS for tax evasion. The same measure requires former U.S. citizens to file U.S. tax returns for 10 years after they renounce their citizenship. There is also a law on the books forbidding

Americans who renounce their citizenship from returning to the United States. These measures were an attempt to discourage Americans living abroad from giving up their U.S. citizenship for tax purposes. It's unclear, however, to what extent the laws are enforced. Most experts say the U.S. government only goes after ex-citizens of considerable wealth.

Despite these measures, there are still a few minor tax advantages for citizens living outside of the United States.

Automatic Filing Extension

The first advantage is that the April 15 deadline is automatically extended to June 15. To qualify you must write boldly across the top of your return (which is due before June 15): *Taxpayer Living Outside The U.S.A., And Qualifies For The Automatic 2-Month Extension.* You may end up paying interest or penalties if you owe more than US$1,000. You can file your income tax return through the U.S. Embassy in San José.

Foreign Earned Income Exclusion

The second potential advantage for U.S. citizens living outside the United States is the Foreign Earned Income Exclusion. If your "tax home" has been on foreign soil for more than 330 days, you may be able to exclude from taxation up to US$80,000 of what you've earned abroad. The exclusion doesn't apply to interest, dividends, capital gains, pensions, annuities, or gambling winnings. You need special forms to apply for this exclusion, and the rules are complicated enough that you'll probably want to hire a tax professional. Even if you qualify for the exclusion, you still need to file a return. Also look into the housing exclusion or deduction—if you qualify, you could deduct almost US$12,000 in housing expenses.

Investing

There are many investment opportunities in Costa Rica—everything from pineapple processing to stocks traded on the National Stock Exchange (the *bolsa*). Costa Rica's *bolsa* (www.bnv.co.cr) was established in 1970 and offers stocks from national companies such as the *La Nación* publishing empire, coffee producer Café Britt, and Durman Esquival, seller of PVC products.

Land development is big business, with megamalls, hotel/condo spreads, and housing developments springing up all over the country. For those who don't want to go the real estate route alone, there are Real Estate Investment Trusts (REITs, or *fundos immobilarios*), companies that buy and rent out real

LAWYERS

Lawyers permeate many aspects of Costa Rican life. You'll need them for (among many other things) real estate transactions, residency permits, and forming a corporation (a Sociedad Anónima, or S.A.; see the *Employment* chapter for more information). One exasperated local jokes that you can barely get out of bed in the morning without a lawyer filing a *tramite* (the general term for legal papers).

It is imperative that you find an honest and effective lawyer, and that you nurture the relationship as you would one with your in-laws, recognizing it as a necessary evil. Personal referrals are the best way to go, though even with a highly recommended lawyer you need to be vigilant – reading over all the documents he or she will file with various agencies (errors abound) and keeping on top of dates and deadlines (because he or she might not). It's also helpful to know the basic prices for various services (ask other expats and other lawyers) to make sure you're not being overcharged.

Though the country is swarming with lawyers, ironically, Costa Rica is not a litigious society, probably because lawsuits can take seven years to come to trial, and monetary awards are limited to lost wages and hospital bills.

estate and then distribute the profits among their investors. The *Tico Times* reports that REITs have become "one of the most lucrative investments here." Most REITs require a minimum investment of US$5,000 and have been paying out 9 to 10 percent in yearly dividends.

Everything you read about investing in Costa Rica, along with every hard-luck story you hear from bilked expats, tells you to be very, very careful when parting with your hard-earned money. A lot of people seem to think, sure, lots of people get ripped off in Costa Rica, but *I'm* too sharp for that. Rest assured that the criminals out to defraud you are even sharper. It's their business to know exactly what will make you want to turn over your cash, and there are not many people trying to stop them, at least in the initial stages of the game. The investment climate here, says financial consultant Alan Weeks in one of his newsletters, is largely unregulated. "For every person who has struck it rich," he warns, "there are dozens of people left behind to tell the sad story of a lifetime's worth of savings … down the drain."

Besides the real estate scams, the teak farms that don't exist, and various and sundry swindles, there are also many financial firms offering high-yield investments that seem too good to be true.

And indeed they usually are, as the fall in recent years of two of the largest entities demonstrates. Ofinter S.A. (a.k.a. "The Brothers") offered returns of

3.5 to 4 percent interest a month (42 to 48 percent a year) and got around the regulations by claiming investors were "friends" of the man who headed the firm, Luis Enrique Villalobos. Loaning money to friends is not regulated here (nor is it in most countries). In late 2002, some of the Brothers' accounts were frozen while they were being investigated for money laundering. Shortly thereafter the company heads skipped town with an estimated US$200 million that had belonged to their many "friends." A similar thing happened to Savings Unlimited (a.k.a. "The Cubans") in early 2003.

Many of these firms' investors were foreign residents who didn't ask many questions about how they were able to earn such astronomical interest. When the rocket shook apart in midair, however, many investors blamed the Costa Rican government for their losses, sharply criticizing the loosely regulated financial environment that had allowed them to earn such impossibly high rates in the first place.

An article in *La Nación* diagnosed the problem as "an explosive mix of excessive trust, tempting high profits, and lack of regulation." Speaking of Ofinter and Savings Unlimited, former Central Bank president Eduardo Lizano said, "I do not know of traditional investments with such high returns." A *Tico Times* editorial asked, "With gray areas, who needs corruption? Costa Rica needs urgently to get clear about what's legal and what's not, and to enforce its laws."

The problem wasn't and isn't limited to the Brothers or the Cubans; almost every week you'll see headlines in the local press like "Another Financial Firm Under Scrutiny" or "Another Fraud Suspect Caught." The unregulated environment attracts a great many scamsters, many of whom are on the run from financial trouble up north or across the sea. Another headline you'll see frequently is some version of "Fraud Suspect Extradited to the U.S." Con men and women come to Costa Rica thinking they'll be able to ply their trade unfettered, and indeed they often do, sometimes for decades. With all the people getting caught, you have to wonder how many more are still doing brisk business. But some are nabbed and whisked away to Miami, Toronto, or Bartlesville, Oklahoma—wherever there's a warrant out for their arrest.

It's all mildly entertaining unless you happen to have invested with one of these snake-oil vendors. Then it's not so funny, and it could have devastating consequences if you're relying on that income for living expenses.

I don't want to scare potential investors, but I do want to stress the dangers of trusting one's savings or pension checks to suspect enterprises. Costa Rica is an extraordinary place, but basic common sense still applies here. Do your homework, ask the hard questions, and don't invest in risky ventures unless you can afford to part with that money. You've heard it before but I'm going to say it again: If you wouldn't do it at home, don't do it here.

GETTING INVESTMENT HELP

Investors thinking of putting their money into a Costa Rican enterprise should check first with the Superintendence of Financial Entities (SUGEF, tel. 506/243-4848, www.sugef.fi.cr, sugefcr@fi.cr) and the Superintendence of Securities (SUGEVAL; www.sugeval.fi.cr, correo@sugeval.fi.cr, tel. 506/243-4700). To offer investments to the public, a company must be incorporated as a Sociedad Anónima (S.A.) registered with either SUGEF or SUGEVAL (both institutions are part of Costa Rica's Central Bank). The websites of SUGEF and SUGEVAL are supposed to have current information about registered companies, including their audited financial statements and the investments they offer. SUGEF's website has much of its content translated into English; SUGEVAL has introductory information in English and is in the process of translating more of the content.

Potential investors can also look for an advisor at one of Costa Rica's 21 registered brokerage houses, which include Aldesa, Cathey, Citivalores, Inversiones Sama, Bancrecen, and Scotiavalores.

COMMUNICATIONS

Still think long-distance phone service in Costs Rica means squeezing into a wooden booth, then shouting to be heard above transcontinental static? Do you picture shredded and stained envelopes arriving six months late, by mule perhaps?

For better or worse, globalization has rendered those images as quaint as glass milk bottles. Phone service in Costa Rica is very good and is getting better and better as the state telecommunications monopoly opens up and other providers come in. Cell phone service, Internet access, and business services especially have been improving at a rapid clip. As for the public mail system, well, it's not the best, but most expats use private mail and shipping services, which rival the service you can get at home.

All in all, you can be almost as connected down here as you were in your home country. If you *want* to be, that is. Most people back home still know little enough about living in Central America that you can claim out-of-touch status even as you're shifting their email messages to your bulk folder.

© ERIN VAN RHEENEN

DAILY LIFE

Telephone Service

Costa Rica's telephone system ranks among the best in Central and South America. It's no accident that so many multinational corporations choose this country for a major branch office—they're drawn by the solid telecommunications network. The high concentration of call centers and sportsbooks (online betting agencies), with their reliance on phone lines, tells you that the system is working.

More than 80 percent of the population has easy access to telephone services. According to 2006 statistics from the CIA Factbook, there are about 1.5 million landlines in this country of four million people. According to ICE (the Instituto Costarricense de Electricidad, or ICE, pronounced EE-say; www.grupoice.com), the state utility monopoly, about the same number of people had cell phones in early 2007, with usage increasing by leaps and bounds every day. Every third person you see—on the street, waiting for the bus, drinking coffee in a café—seems to be checking in their bag to see if that's their phone ringing. Costa Rica has one of the highest numbers of phone lines per capita in Central America and even in Latin America.

Of course there are frustrations. If you don't inherit a phone line when you rent or buy a place to live, you could wait months for a line to be installed. If you're out in the sticks you might have to wait until they get around to putting up poles and stringing wires. Locals know tricks to speed up the process—like requesting a commercial line if a residential one seems slow in coming. ICE does things at its own pace, but implementation of CAFTA (the Central American Free Trade Agreement) means that parts of the telecommunications sector (broadband Internet service, cell phone service, and private data networks) are gradually opening to private competition.

In general, you can get what you need with patience and persistence. When I was having serious trouble with my line (sometimes I couldn't call out, people

COSTA RICAN PHONE NUMBERS CHANGE

Costa Rica's Instituto Costarricense de Electricidad (ICE), the government institute responsible for phone service, announced recently that in March 2008, all telephone numbers in Costa Rica will go from being 7 digits to 8. Regular phones (landlines) will have the number 2 added to the beginning of the number, while cell phone numbers will have an 8 added at the beginning.

trying to call in got cut off, or there was so much static I couldn't hear what the caller was saying), it took me several phone calls to figure out to whom I should be talking. Finally I got the right department, which sent out a repairman within the day. There was no charge for the repairman's visit.

Another surprise was that I had an answering service included in my telephone service but didn't know it. When I was online or away from home, a mechanical voice invited people to leave a message. It took months of people mumbling about how unavailable I was to figure out that something was wrong. I finally called the telephone company, and they explained how to use the system that, up to that moment, I hadn't known existed. Needless to say, my mailbox was full, and some of the messages were pretty testy.

Residential and Commercial Service

Keep in mind that options for phone service are changing rapidly as ICE loses its stranglehold on the market. As of 2007, basic residential telephone service cost about US$8/month; the basic commercial rate was US$9.50/month. Having a new line installed cost around US$90 for a residential line and US$130 for a commercial one (not to mention the long wait often required). Having an already existing line turned on costs around US$35 for residential and US$55 for commercial service.

International Rates and Internet Calling

Calling the United States or Canada can cost a small fortune from your home phone in Costa Rica, unless you have an international calling card. You can buy one before you leave home or get one here in Costa Rica (see the sidebar *Calling Cards*). Another excellent option (even cheaper than cut-rate international calling cards) comes from the rapidly evolving world of Internet phone connections. Voice-over-Internet protocol, or VOIP, is changing the way we think about phones. Already companies like www.Skype.com have loyal customers all over the world. If you have a Skype account and so does the person you're calling, your call costs nothing. Skype's claim is that you can "talk to anyone, anywhere, for free. Forever." It's pretty tempting, though I can't imagine how it guarantees the "forever" part of the pitch. VOIP works very well if you have high-speed Internet access, but even those with dial-up can use it. You just have to get used to the delays and gaps—it kind of sounds like old international phone calls, before fiber optics and other innovations made everyone sound like they were next door. You'll need a headset to plug into your computer to turn it into a "phone." Some Internet cafés have VOIP service.

CALLING CARDS

In Costa Rica, calling cards are the way to go if you need to use pay phones or someone else's phone, or if you want to call from a hotel phone without incurring the hotel's expensive per-call rates. Even if you have your own landline or cell phone, using a calling card is often cheaper than using the telephone company's plan. You can buy calling cards from supermarkets, corner stores, pharmacies, and sometimes from little kiosks on the street. There are various kinds.

The **Chip** card is available in denominations of 1,000 or 2,000 *colones* and used in the blue phone booths that accept these digital cards. Insert the card and follow the directions (in English or Spanish) on the little screen.

Colibrí 197 cards are available in denominations of 500 or 1,000 *colones*, and you can use this card from any touch-tone phone to make calls within Costa Rica only. Key in 197, then the 12-digit code on the back of the card. Then dial the number you want to reach. There's also a "CD card," which is basically a Colibrí 197 card in mini-CD form, with four minutes of music on it.

The **Viajero 199** card is available in denominations of 3,000 *colones*, US$10, and US$20. Use this card from any touch-tone phone to make either international or domestic calls. Key in 199 and you'll be able to choose between directions in English or Spanish. As with the Colibrí 197 card, you'll be asked to enter a long string of numbers, then dial the number you want to reach.

¢1000
ICE
sample
SERVICIO Colibrí 197

Costa Rican phone card

PAY PHONES

Most pay phones used to be coin-operated, and at any given time a large portion of them were out of order. The situation has improved, with booths in better repair. It's a toss-up, however, which kind of phone you'll happen upon. Some still take coins (10- and 20-*colón* coins, so you need a lot of them); others require phone cards. Your best bet is to always have a variety of calling cards (see the sidebar *Calling Cards*). If the booth is blue and has a little screen where the coin box should be, you'll need a Chip calling card, which you insert into a slot and then follow the instructions that appear on the screen. Though some pay phones have a place for you to "swipe" Colibrí cards, usually this won't work, and you'll need to punch the numbers on the back of the card into the keypad and make your call that way.

Dial 116 for an English-speaking operator and to make a collect call (called *por cobrar* in Spanish).

In little villages, there may be only one pay phone in town, usually at the *pulpería* (general store). Often you can't access the phone unless the store is open.

DIALING TO AND FROM COSTA RICA

It's easy to dial direct to most countries in the world from Costa Rica. To reach the United States, for example, you would dial 001, then the area code, and then the telephone number. If you'd rather make the long-distance call through an operator, dial 116. All the operators speak both Spanish and English.

When dialing *from* the United States to Costa Rica, the international code is 011, then you dial the country code (506), then the seven-digit telephone number.

To make a collect call from any phone, dial 09, the international access code of the country being called (these numbers are listed in Costa Rican phone books), and then the number.

Calls within Costa Rica are cheap, though even within the city of San José calls are time-charged. There's just one area code for the entire country: 506.

PAYING YOUR BILL

If you live in the city, paying your telephone bill is as easy as going to the bill-paying window at your local supermarket (you can also pay water and electric bills there). If you live in a more remote location, you'll need to find the place designated as a payment point. It won't always be an ICE office; it could very well be the local *pulpería* (corner store).

To pay your bill, however, you first need to receive it. Ask locals how and

CELL PHONE SERVICE

As elsewhere in the world, cell phone use in Costa Rica went from 0 to 60 in a matter of seconds. Not too many years ago, no one here had a cell phone. Now even grade-school students have them. Remote parts of the country that were still waiting for landlines ended up getting cellular transmission towers instead. Some Costa Ricans who never had landlines now have cell phones.

As of 2007 the only provider of cellular service in Costa Rica was ICE (pronounced *EE-say*; www.grupoice.com), the state electricity and telecommunications quasi-monopoly, but ICE allows local stores to serve as its agents, so you can buy a phone and sign up for service (if you qualify) at almost any corner cell phone store. Costa Rica's state-run telecommunications industry is in the process of opening up to private companies, and cell phone options in particular are expected to change significantly.

At this point, though, it's difficult for a nonresident foreigner to get a cell phone here. To request service, ICE asks for a national ID card, a GSM or TDMA phone (and the receipt for that phone), the original and a copy of your water, phone, or electric bill (in your name), and a US$25 deposit. Rates and plans change rapidly; check ICE's website for up-to-date information.

There are ways around the barriers. You can rent a cell phone (rates vary enormously; they're highest if you go through a luxury hotel), and there is a burgeoning gray market of Ticos renting or selling their cell phone lines to whoever will pay. It can get tricky, however. Whose name is the phone in? How do you pay the bill if it doesn't come to you? There are solutions, but they take some imagination. With the changes supposedly coming, all of these shenanigans may soon be unnecessary.

How many bars do you get in Costa Rica? Reception is generally good in the Central Valley and more problematic elsewhere. In beach and mountain communities you'll notice spots on the road where a number of cars seem to have pulled over for no reason. Look closer and you'll see that all the drivers have phones clamped to their ears – they're taking advantage of that rare spot where the signal slices through like a hot knife through butter.

when telephone bills are delivered in your area; in some cases you may need to go pick up your bill at a central delivery point. If you've inherited the line, it will be in someone else's name (it's hard to transfer the account to a different name, so many people just keep paying on an account that isn't in their name), which may complicate things further.

In ICE's eyes, not receiving a bill is no excuse for not paying it, and nonpayment of bills will, of course, lead to your phone line being shut off. The burden is on you to make sure you receive your bills and pay them on time. When in doubt, call or visit the nearest ICE office and check on your account.

BRING YOUR PHONE

If you have a favorite phone that you can't bear to part with, by all means bring it down in your luggage. The system here, down to the jacks, is the same as in the United States, and you can get cheaper, better phones in the States.

Where cell phones are concerned, you need to be more careful. ICE, for now the sole provider of cell phone service, says you need a GSM or TDMA phone here in Costa Rica. See the sidebar *Cell Phone Service* for more information.

FAXES

The RACSA office in downtown San José (Calle 1 at Avenida 5, or 1st Street at 5th Avenue, tel. 506/287-0087) will send and receive faxes and telegrams for you. You can also try post offices *(correos)*, Internet cafés, and some hotels.

Email and the Internet

INTERNET ACCESS

Costa Rica has fully embraced the digital age. Studies show one million individuals using the Internet at last count in 2005, and most government agencies have extensive websites. If you speak Spanish, these sites are an excellent introduction to how the country works. Some of the sites even have English translations. ICE has an excellent listing of Costa Rican agencies and ministries, with links to their websites (www.grupoice.com/esp/temas/herram/directorio.htm). Costa Rica's Internet code is cr.

Everyone loves to complain about ICE—the state utilities behemoth that is slowly becoming less of a monopoly—and there's a lot to complain about. Its Internet branch, RACSA (Radiográfica Costarricense S.A.), has been slow in providing higher speed Internet access, though things seem to be picking up lately. Even with improvements, many people still have to rely on dial-up service (though it's advertised as 56K, you're lucky to be getting 25K), and it's still disconcertingly common to be halfway through composing a long email when the system cuts out and you have to start all over again.

But public demand and free trade requirements are obliging RACSA to either provide better service or cooperate with companies that can. Already there are quasi-legal competitors entering the market. Wireless Internet access and voice-over-Internet protocol (VOIP) providers like Skype are just two of the sectors where gray-area business is booming and hard for state regulating agencies to track down.

If you live in or near San José, you can start things rolling at the main RACSA office downtown at Calle 1 at Avenida 5, but setting up an account can also be done quickly and painlessly at many computer stores throughout the country. Either way, they'll give you an email address and a password after you fill out a few forms. You can even pay with a debit or credit card, having them automatically deduct each month's bill from that account. Basic Internet access costs as little as US$5/month (with very limited use) but generally runs about US$15–20 a month; in 2007 RACSA was charging up to US$170/month for much faster cable modem Internet access.

INTERNET CAFÉS

There are scores of Internet cafés in the greater San José area, and you'll find a handful in tourist towns like Tamarindo, Montezuma, or Puerto Viejo. The access points in San José tend to be cheaper because there's so much competition—sometimes prices are as low as US$.50 an hour. In remote areas prices can be much higher, since often the café is the only game in town. Many hotels, even low-end backpacker hostels, now offer free Internet access, and Spanish-language schools often provide their students free access. Avoid logging on 4–6 P.M., when the entire country's circuits seem to be busiest.

Mail

EL CORREO

The national mail service can at times surprise you with its efficiency. Say you're swinging in a hammock outside your rather remote home near the beach when a man on a dirt bike roars up your gravel drive. Don't be alarmed—it's just the mailman, his pouch slung across his shoulder and his fat-tired motorcycle perfectly suited to his potholed route. It's like a modern-day Pony Express, and when he hands you an envelope with a New York postmark of just a few days back, it feels like magic.

As long as you marvel when the postal system works and don't have to rely on it, you'll be fine. Most letters arrive in a timely fashion (5–7 days from the United States; 10–15 days from Europe), but some take a lot longer, and parcels larger than a magazine-sized envelope are often held at customs until you come and pay the outrageous duties, often 100 percent of perceived value. Both receiving and sending packages can be both complicated and expensive, and safety is an issue. Theft is not uncommon—don't send valuables through the mail.

Sometimes the lack of addresses and house numbers in this country seems to stymie even experienced mail carriers. Mail sent to my San José address (which is a long recitation of turn this way and that, and look for the pink house) from across town never arrived, though bills always made their way into my *buzón* (mailbox). Many people like to pay the small fee for a post office box at their local post office. Depending on where you live, there can be a long wait to get a P.O. box.

The post office has an extensive website (www.correos.go.cr), which is in both Spanish and English, or Attempted English—we learn that P.O. boxes are available to both "phisic persons and juridic figures."

PRIVATE MAIL SERVICES

Many foreign residents swear by private mail services. You get a post office box in Miami, the U.S. city closest to Costa Rica, and from there the company couriers your letters and packages to you in Costa Rica. Plans generally have a monthly fee that covers, say, three kilos of mail a month. Excess weight is charged at various rates, mostly below US$10 per kilo.

See the *Resources* section for companies to consider.

Shipping Options

There are many ways to ship packages within Costa Rica and from Costa Rica to the United States, Canada, or Europe. It's a competitive market, with rates and services changing rapidly to meet customer needs; be sure to confirm rates and timeframes with a call or a website visit.

NATIONAL POSTAL SERVICE

The cheapest way to send packages is the *correos,* the national post office, though it only guarantees arrival time on parcels sent within Costa Rica. Go to the nearest *correos* branch, call 506/253-1901, or visit the website www.correos.go.cr, which will have the latest rates and services available. The post office provides no packing materials.

I sent three heavy book-filled boxes (approximately 15 by 12 by 10 inches) from Costa Rica to California. It cost me about US$65, a bargain compared to what I would have paid with a private shipping company. The boxes arrived in about three and a half weeks.

It's not advisable to send anything of great value or that you can't afford to lose through the *correos.* I sent my books because, well, who wants books these days?

PRIVATE SHIPPING SERVICES

Many private shipping services are available in Costa Rica, including familiar international companies like FedEx. New services come on the scene often,

and certain services may be available only in certain areas—be sure to ask locals which company they use and how they like it. No private service is perfect, but most provide an easier and more secure shipping experience than the national post office. Many companies will pick packages up from your home. Of course, you'll pay for all these perks.

There is also a host of less official shipping options, especially within Costa Rica—deals with truck drivers to bring your new furniture along with their weekly delivery of vegetables, for example, or sending a package with a bus driver whose route takes him through the little town where your friend lives.

DHL

DHL has offices in Liberia (Guanacaste), Limón, Alajuela, Ciudad Quesada, Puntarenas, and in the San José neighborhoods of Cariari, Rohrmoser, and Paseo Colón. It can get your package to other points in Central America or to Miami overnight, to the rest of the United States in one or two days, and to Canada and Europe in three days. Boxes are available at DHL offices. Rates change frequently; for more information call 506/210-3939 or go to www.la-reg.dhl.com.

FedEx

FedEx has many different ways to send packages within, from, and to Costa Rica. Its website has a lot of information on shipping internationally and on customs procedures, as well as a list of the many shipping points within Costa Rica. In terms of actual offices, Heredia has one, and in San José there's an office on Paseo Colón (tel. 800/052-1090, www.fedex.com/cr_english), 100 meters (109 yards) east of the León Cortéz statue and right next to the Iberia airlines office, open 8:30 A.M.–6 P.M. Monday–Friday.

UPS

UPS's main office is in the Pavas area of San José (tel. 506/290-2828, www
.ups.com) and has a good selection of boxes, tubes, and other packing materials. One new service is the TicoPak, which offers shipping directly from
souvenir shops in Costa Rica to homes in the United States, with special
CoffeePaks, HammockPaks, and MachetePaks to accommodate the most
frequently bought keepsakes.

Media

Freedom of the press has long been an essential feature of Costa Rican culture. It began with the founding of local papers in the early 19th century and
was formally declared a fundamental right in 1948. More recently, in 2005
Costa Rica ranked fairly high in a study of press freedom conducted by media
watchdog group Journalists Without Borders. Of 139 countries around the
world, Costa Rica ranked 35th, while the United States ranked 24th and
neighboring Nicaragua came in at 95.

Press freedom is a nebulous term, of course, and can be measured in a variety of ways. In the past, Costa Rica's three major dailies offered different
perspectives, with *La Nación* providing a more conservative outlook, while
La República and *La Prensa Libre* had left-of-center viewpoints. But now, says
Culture and Customs in Costa Rica author Chalene Helmuth, "Newspaper reporting in the three major dailies has converged into a monolithic, rightist
perspective." Press freedom is also no doubt affected by the fact that the *La
Nación* publishing empire owns three of the major papers, a couple of television stations, and countless magazines. "Most media are owned by the business
elite," writes the Biesanz family in *The Ticos*, "who are also the chief buyers
of advertising space and time."

SPANISH-LANGUAGE NEWSPAPERS

Costa Rica has at least eight major Spanish-language newspapers, one *(La
Gaceta)* belonging to the state. *La Nación* is the largest and most widely read
daily paper. *El Financiero* (owned by the *La Nación* publishing empire) is a
business weekly. *La Nación* also owns *Al Día*, known for its sports section.

As for the non-*Nación* papers, there's the daily *La República*, now mostly
devoted to business news; *El Heraldo*; and *La Prensa Libre*, the latter an afternoon paper. Then there's *Diario La Extra*, full of photos of half-naked women
and bloody bodies and home to a much-read romantic advice column, *Sen-
timientos en conflicto* (Feelings in Conflict). If you like sex, gore, and advice

on "Ten Types of Men You Should Avoid," the *Extra* is for you.

A great way to get in the spirit of Costa Rica (even if you're in the United States) and to practice your Spanish is to check out the local papers' websites. Not only will you know which government ministers have resigned and which bridges have washed out, you'll also keep up to date on daily temperatures and fluctuations in the exchange rate. Many of these sites also have background information on Costa Rica and links to other excellent sources of information. *La Nación* even has on its website (www.nacion.com) a weekly news summary in English; it comes out every Thursday. Also try www.diarioextra.com, www .prensalibre.co.cr, and www.imprenal.go.cr.

Gossip at the local *pulpería* (small general store) is one way to keep informed.

© ERIN VAN RHEENEN

ENGLISH-LANGUAGE NEWSPAPERS AND MAGAZINES

There are enough English-speaking residents of Costa Rica to support a variety of media, the most influential being the weekly *Tico Times* (tel. 506/258-1558, fax 506/233-6378, www.ticotimes.net), founded in 1956 and read front-to-back by many foreign residents. The paper has won awards for its reporting, and it covers everything from politics to tourism. It's also a great source for finding out what's happening culturally in the Central Valley, with listings for plays, benefits, and the many clubs in which foreign residents congregate—from bridge to the Association for People Who Have Had Brain Surgery.

Though it has some news coverage of the Central American region and the rest of the world (and has recently expanded its *Nica Times* insert, which covers Nicaragua), the *Tico Times* still retains a hometown feel, with news of So-and-So in Playas del Coco having their second child or opening a third bar. The advertisements reveal the preoccupations of at least some of Costa Rica's foreign community: ads for Spanish-language schools, tax lawyers, hair replacement, and plastic surgery.

Nature Air puts out *Nature Landings* (tel. 506/430-3424, www.nature landings.com), an in-flight magazine also available for free at some hotels. *Business Costa Rica* (tel. 506/220-2200, www.amcham.co.cr) is a monthly business magazine put out by the Costa Rican–American Chamber of Commerce. The bimonthly *Costa Rica Outdoors* concentrates on fishing, birding, and tourist-oriented sports. *Mesoamérica* (tel. 506/253-3195, www.mesoamericaonline.net) is produced by the Institute for Central American Studies and provides analyses of politics in all the Central American countries.

Outside of the Central Valley, you'll find lots of little regional publications. The Tamarindo area is home base for *The Howler* (tel. 506/653-0545, www.tamarindobeach.net/thehowler), a free monthly that focuses on community news and surfing reports; the bilingual *Tamarindo News* (tel. 506/828-8113, www.tamarindonews.com); and *The Flyswatter*, an irreverent newcomer that's been called "bitingly honest" (look for copies around Tamarindo). The middle and southern Nicoya Peninsula is covered by the *Península de Nicoya* (tel. 506/369-6687; www.peninsuladenicoya.com). The *Tico Trader Magazine* (tel./fax 506/643-2813, ticotrader@hotmail.com) covers the Jacó area, while *Quepolandia* (www.quepolandia.com) takes on the Quepos/Manuel Antonio region. *Caribbean Way* and *Pacific Way* (tel. 506/385-0298, www.costa ricaway.net) are regional publications with nice photography.

Many "newspapers" exist only in digital format, such as www.amcostarica .com. A web search will net you many more.

RADIO

Radio is king in Costa Rica, and you hear it everywhere you go—in homes, workplaces, buses, and taxis. Radios outnumber televisions by two to one, and there are about 130 radio stations in the country, broadcasting talk shows, sports, humor, news, and popular music from Latin America and the United States. Golden oldies and up-to-the-minute pop songs in English are surprisingly omnipresent on the airwaves here.

Ticos seem to have a high tolerance for noise, and you may be surprised when a friend keeps the radio blaring while you're trying to have a conversation. Get into a taxi and you may have to shout above an earsplitting soccer match to tell the driver where you're going. Public buses play dance music so loudly you'd think they were trying to compete with discos. Maids, housewives, and other homebound folks may keep the radio on all day for company.

Radio is a traditional link between the capital and the provinces, and a community service in many small towns. On local stations you'll hear

DAILY LIFE

RADIO STATIONS

Most stations here play a mix of local and U.S. popular music, but if you look hard you'll find alternatives. Among the English offerings is the respected **Radio for Peace** (AM 1504). **Radio Dos** (FM 99.5) and 107.5 FM mostly play music but have occasional news updates in English.

Interesting Spanish-language stations include **Radio FM 96,** which plays mostly classical music; **Radio Universidad** (870 AM and 96.7 FM), which features classical and jazz; **Radio U** (101.9 FM), with a variety of eclectic programming; **Radio Estereo Azul** (99 FM); and **Econews 95.9 FM,** which offers not only economic news but also classical and jazz music.

neighborhood news and even pleas for Juan to call María at 5 P.M. at the local pay phone.

Widespread radio ownership also makes the medium a natural for distance learning. In 1973, the newly founded Costa Rican Institute of Radio Education created *The Teacher in Your House,* a program that broadcasts primary and secondary school lessons from 12 noncommercial stations around the country. Many farmers living in isolated rural areas have taken advantage of the program, enrolling in courses that led to certificates of completion.

TELEVISION

If radio is king, then TV is most certainly queen, and a foreign queen at that. While the 20 broadcast stations here have programming mostly in Spanish, many cable channels are in English (sometimes with Spanish subtitles, sometimes without). Cable services are extremely popular, and even lower-middle-class households pay for the privilege of choosing from among dozens of channels, including ones in French, German, Italian, and Japanese. But English rules, and even the Spanish-language stations reveal the influence of English and of U.S. culture. During a long series of commercials (as in Europe, commercial breaks here are longer but less frequent), you may hear "Ya regresamos a *Six Feet Under.*" ("We will return to *Six Feet Under.*") Even if there's not an English syllable within shouting distance, the U.S. influence is often obvious, as in a local KFC commercial that has a cartoon colonel speaking Spanish with a horrendous gringo accent.

Beyond the gringo influence, there are programs and commercials from all over Latin America, especially Mexico and Argentina. I've never heard so much Argentine-inflected Spanish, with its *j* slant on the Spanish *ll*, usually pronounced *y.* Apparently the Argentine ad business is highly developed, and spots made in that country are beamed all over Latin America. But at least Argentina and Costa Rica share the preference for *vos* instead of the more common *tu* to express the informal "you."

Some Ticos worry that so much foreign influence is eroding the national character and filing away the rough edges of local lingo. Still, it's unlikely that this country will do what France has done, trying to protect its language by mandating that a certain percentage of cultural offerings, like films, must be homegrown.

Ticos watch a lot of TV, and they don't seem bothered by the flood of foreign programming. Just as the radio is left playing all day as background noise and electronic companionship, so is the TV on almost everywhere you go. In restaurants, bars, doctors' waiting rooms, and corner stores you'll see CNN en Español, *Mr. Ed* reruns dubbed in Spanish, old *Munsters* episodes, soap operas from Mexico and Venezuela, and the ubiquitous soccer games, punctuated by the announcer shouting an impossibly drawn-out "goooooaaaal!"

Network TV

Teletica (Channel 7) is the local favorite, offering news at 6 A.M., noon, and 7 P.M., as well as Monday night's popular *Siete Días* news show at 8 P.M. State-owned Channel 13 has good cultural programming, with news at 9 P.M. Channel 42's news at 7 P.M. also has news from Spain. International news can be seen on Channel 14 at noon and on Channel 16 at 6:30 P.M. Repretel, a Mexican company, owns Channels 4, 6, and 11, all of which have both international and local news.

Cable and Satellite TV Companies

Craving your CNN, BBC, or ESPN? Compare the offerings of Amnet (tel. 506/210-2929, fax 506/232-2869, www.amnet.co.cr), Cable Tica (tel. 506/210-1450, fax 506/231-7914, www.cabletica.com), and Direct TV (tel. 800/347-3288). Many plans run about US$30/month.

TRAVEL AND TRANSPORTATION

Nestled in the elbow of the isthmus connecting North and South America, Costa Rica is about as centrally located as the western hemisphere allows. Getting here is easy, and getting around is simple if not always smooth. The fabled potholed roads may slow things down a bit, but the country has cheap and efficient buses that go just about everywhere. Driving yourself around, whether as a visitor or resident, is an acquired taste, but a real feeling of accomplishment comes with negotiating Costa Rica's challenging but beautiful byways. Small planes are another viable option for getting around.

More than one million people visit Costa Rica each year, and the vast majority fly, landing at the two international airports—the largest in San José, the other in Liberia. You can also arrive by sea, either on a cruise ship or on your own boat, or come in overland. The car or bus trip from the United States takes you through five countries, all with their own laws, visa requirements, and border-crossing protocol. It's a journey not to be undertaken lightly, but you'll probably be talking about it at parties for the rest of your life.

Getting to Costa Rica

BY AIR

Costa Rica is less than three hours by air from Miami, about five hours from New York City, seven hours from Los Angeles, and 8.5 hours from Toronto. Dozens of international flights arrive daily at Juan Santamaría International Airport, half an hour northwest of San José, and in Liberia, in Guanacaste Province. Every year, carriers add more flights and more carriers get in the game. Coming from North America, you can choose from Air Canada, American Airlines, America West, Continental, Delta, LACSA (Costa Rica's airline), Mexicana, Northwest, TACA (the Central American airline), and United, not to mention charter flights that come and go as demand dictates. Charter flights seldom show up when you do web searches for the best airfare deals—call a travel agent or make direct contact with package tour companies.

Prices vary widely, but from U.S. cities fares run about US$300–700.

Direct flights to San José are available from many cities, including Atlanta, Charlotte, Chicago, Dallas/Fort Worth, Ft. Lauderdale, Houston, Miami, Newark, New York, Los Angeles, Phoenix, Toronto, and Washington, D.C. Other cities require a brief stop and sometimes a plane change, though every year it gets easier to get to San José or Liberia quickly and painlessly. From San Francisco, for instance, you can get a flight that stops briefly in San Salvador and then arrives in San José about eight hours after takeoff in California. A favorite for those able to sleep on the plane is LACSA Flight 561, which leaves San Francisco at 1:15 A.M. and arrives in San José before 10 in the morning.

Airports

Costa Rica's main airport, Juan Santamaría International Airport (arrival/departure information, tel. 506/437-2626, www.alterra.co.cr), is in Alajuela, 16 kilometers (10 miles) northwest of downtown San José. The airport recently had a major face-lift and now occupies an attractive glass-and-steel terminal with fast food options, wireless Internet access, TVs, gift shops, and a money-change counter.

After your plane arrives, you'll go through customs, pressing a button that illuminates either a green or red light. A green light means you go through without having your bags searched; a red light means you will be searched. Even with the tightening of security after 9/11, most tourists get the green light. As you exit the airport, you'll see a little booth where you can buy a taxi ticket to wherever you need to go, paying in dollars if you like. A taxi ride from the airport to downtown San José costs around US$13.

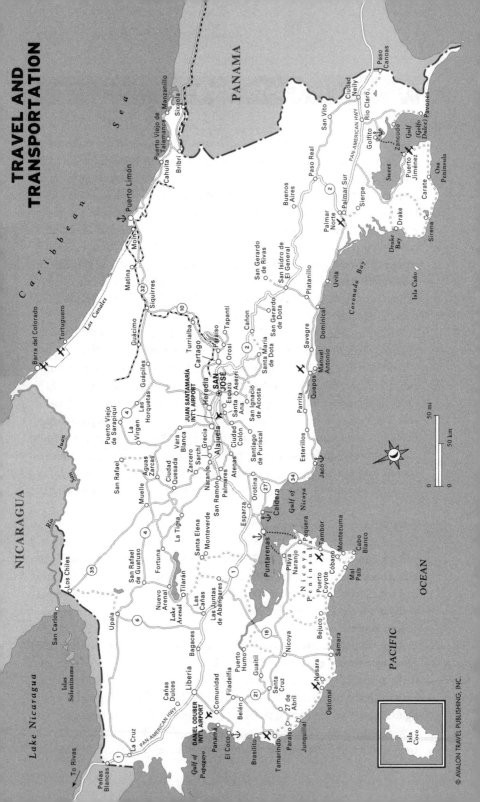

TRAVEL AND TRANSPORTATION

Juan Santamaría International Airport, just outside of San José

Getting to the airport from the San José area is a matter of hailing or calling a cab, or arranging for a shuttle (see the *Getting Around* section). Leaving by air, travelers pay a US$26 exit tax (payable in *colones*, U.S. dollars, or a combination of the two). The baggage limit (double-check with your airline) is generally 32 kilos or 70 pounds, in one or two bags whose dimensions (length plus height plus width) are not supposed to exceed 62 inches. You're also allowed a carry-on bag that weighs less than 18 kilograms (40 pounds). Airline policies on surfboards vary; call ahead.

About six kilometers (four miles) southwest of central San José in the suburb of Pavas, Tobías Bolaños Airport handles domestic flights only. For more information, see the *Getting Around* section.

Flights to Daniel Oduber International Airport (tel. 506/668-1010) in Liberia deposit you in the northern province of Guanacaste, about 40 minutes from Playas del Coco and a little over an hour from Tamarindo. For those heading for the northern Pacific coast, this flight eliminates a car or bus ride from San José, which can take four or five hours.

BY BOAT

An increasing number of cruise ships are making Costa Rica a port of call, if only for a few days or even hours. Passengers may disembark for some shopping and sightseeing, a hike, or a river-rafting jaunt. Tourism Institute statistics indicate that more than 300,000 cruise-ship passengers, coming in on about 200 large cruise vessels, docked in Costa Rica in 2004. Two-thirds of them disembarked in the Caribbean port city of Limón, the rest in the Pacific coast ports of Puntarenas, Caldera, and Golfito (relatively few). Many of these journeys originate in Miami and are part of multicountry tours that often include the Panama Canal.

Smaller boats are more flexible in where they can dock, stopping at beach towns such as Guanacaste's Playas del Coco or the Los Sueños marina in Herradura, near Jacó.

New marinas are planned for Puntarenas and Golfito.

Ports of Entry

If you're coming on your own boat, there are several official ports of entry with both customs and immigration stations. On the northern Pacific coast you have Playas del Coco (customs tel. 506/670-0216, immigration tel. 506/670-1133). The central Pacific has Puntarenas (immigration tel. 506/661-1446; nearby Caldera has the customs, tel. 506/634-4055). Quepos has only immigration, so boaters go instead to Puntarenas/Caldera. At Playa Herradura (north of Jacó) you can put in at the private Los Sueños Marina (tel. 506/643-3886 or www.lossuenosresort.com), which has its own customs and immigration, as well as a full-service fuel station and good docking facilities. The south Pacific has facilities at the old banana port city of Golfito (customs tel. 506/775-0273, immigration tel. 506/775-0423). Boaters arriving on the Caribbean coast go through customs at Puerto Limón (customs tel. 506/798-1626, immigration tel. 506/758-4466) and dock at nearby Barra del Colorado.

Commercial Ports

Costa Rica's main commercial ports are Caldera on the central Pacific coast, Golfito on the southern Pacific, and Limón and Moín on the Caribbean coast. The ships that come and go from Caldera are usually carrying agricultural products; those in Golfito are stacked with the electronics and appliances sold at the Deposito Libre (duty-free store) in that ex-banana town; Limón is now the banana port (among other things); and Moín is associated with the oil that runs in a pipeline from the Caribbean coast to the Central Valley. Puntarenas used to be a big commercial port but now only receives cruise ships.

BY LAND

Many of the people I've met who've driven overland from North America to Costa Rica seem to have done it 10 or 20 years ago, "when we were young and brave and stupid," as one traveler put it. Maybe it's the forgiving fog of memory, but most of these folks claim that despite dismal roads, corrupt and inept border officials, run-ins with police and thieves, and the inevitable mechanical breakdowns, it was a long strange trip that they wouldn't trade for anything in the world.

The most direct route from the U.S. to Costa Rica is from the Brownsville, Texas border crossing (about 2,250 miles). But these won't be highway miles—you'll be on winding mountain roads, potholed desert tracks, and occasionally making your way through sleepy one-horse towns or congested cities.

When I was a kid our family drove from California to Guatemala in our blue Ford station wagon. A hotel was a splurge, and I can still remember the smell of our old canvas army tent, mildewing in the tropical humidity. It was an amazing trip, full of sights and sounds I'll never forget. I plan to do a longer version of that same trip soon, myself at the wheel this time, seeing just how much trouble I can get into and (hopefully) out of.

More up-to-date travelers have mixed reports. Some feel that all those border crossings, bad roads, and national police forces (which love to stop foreigners) added up to a very big headache. Others say it was the trip of their lives.

Let's say you do it, taking the popular Pacific coast route through Mexico, Guatemala, El Salvador, Honduras, and Nicaragua. Driving from Nicaragua into Costa Rica, you'll cross the border at Peñas Blancas on the Pan-American Highway. Peñas Blancas is not a town; it's simply the border post, open 6 A.M.– 8 P.M. As Central American border crossings go, it's not bad at all. The website www.drivemeloco.com calls the Costa Rican border "by far the most efficient and trustworthy crossing" in the area. The Drive Me Loco site is a great resource for driving through Central America, covering all sorts of angles, including dealing with "Animals on the Road," "Carrying Arms" (Don't do it! they advise), and carrying old copies of *Playboy* to use as bargaining chips with border guards.

Your first step in crossing the border by car is to pay a few dollars to have your car fumigated: An official will spray a white liquid on the underside of your vehicle. This happens before you get to the border proper.

The Costa Rican and Nicaraguan immigration offices are four kilometers (2.5 miles) apart. Once inside Costa Rica, you'll park, go to one window for an entry stamp (a few dollars), then take your passport and car title to the Aduana window.

You'll also need to buy insurance for a minimum of one month (US$17). (Costa Rica is one of the few Central American countries where insurance is mandatory.) Officials will provide three forms: *Certificado de Entrega de Vehiculos, No Comerciales Importación Temporal; Instituto Nacional de Seguros;* and *Recibo de Dinero,* then you're on your way. There are several checkpoints just beyond the border area; show all your papers, and they'll let you pass.

Before you get to the border, make sure you have your passport and all vehicle documentation, and be prepared to stand in one line after another. There are lots of kids who will run up to you and offer to speed you through the process. Veteran border-crossers advise caution, but I've had good luck picking a kid who looks street-smart but not yet like a full-fledged criminal. These helpers will show you which line to stand in first, then hurry you to the next window, rattling off advice in Spanish that you may or may not understand. The kids expect a tip of at least a few dollars for their efforts.

I've crossed the border in a private car, by bus, and on foot (don't ask). I've sped through the border and also had to wait hours in the pouring rain. Be prepared for delays, bring an umbrella, and try not to take out your frustration on border officials, lest they return the favor. If you can help it, don't change money at the border—the freelance money changers with their bills fanned like an enormous hand of cards don't tend to offer a good exchange rate.

One big advantage of coming by car is that you can load up with all that you need to start your new life—there's no weight limit on luggage coming overland.

See *Suggested Reading* for books on driving to Costa Rica. Also check out the website of Sanborn's insurance (www.sanborninsurance.com), which specializes in overland travel from the United States through Mexico and Central America. Sanborn's has a U.S. office in MacAllen, Texas, one of the preferred border crossings for people making the drive down.

Busing the whole way is cheap, and easier than driving in terms of bureaucracy (no licenses or insurance or traffic cops to deal with). It's also harder on the body. Most Mexican and Central American buses are at least as comfortable as Greyhound buses in the United States, and some are positively deluxe, with movies, clean bathrooms, and snacks served. But some still fit the stereotype of rickety haulers of the unwashed masses and their livestock; you'll probably find yourself on one or two during your trip, maybe for that 13-hour stretch with only pork rinds to eat and no bathroom breaks. Those with delicate stomachs and weak bladders need not apply. Costa Rica–based Tica Bus has daily buses to and from San Salvador (in El Salvador), Tegucigalpa (Honduras), Guatemala City, Managua (Nicaragua), and Tapachula (Mexico).

Getting Around

BY AIR

Domestic airlines use small planes to make their short hops (20 to 60 minutes) to places like Tortuguero, Golfito, Nosara, or Tamarindo. Recently they've also been offering flights into southern Nicaragua and northern Panama, with air and hotel package deals, like three days and two nights in Granada (Nicaragua). Planes carry 4–40 passengers. Fares are always changing, but in general they're reasonable. If you're short on time these flights are a downright bargain, saving you hours in travel time and perhaps saving you the bother and expense of renting a car. Residents pay significantly lower fares.

Sansa is the domestic branch of TACA; it flies out of Juan Santamaría Airport (the terminal is over 200 meters from the international terminal, which is a long walk with luggage). I recommend Nature Air, which flies out of Tobías Bolaños Airport in the Pavas section of San José.

There are also charter companies, like Paradise Air and Aero Costa Sol; see the *Resources* section for more information on domestic air options.

BY BUS

Costa Rica has a great bus system—cheap, extensive, and often on time. You can get just about anyplace in the country for under US$15. It's also a great way to see the country without the expense or hassle of a car, and to make contact with locals, who use buses as their daily transport. Popular destinations—like Jacó, Liberia, and Limón—are served by both direct *(directo)* buses and those that stop a lot along the way (called *normal* or *corriente)*. Routes to crossroads towns like Liberia often leave every hour from early morning to late evening, while less-visited destinations may be served by just one or two buses per day. Buy tickets a day or two in advance—seats sell out fast. Popular routes are served by buses with comfortable seats and decent legroom; many resemble Greyhound buses in the United States. Urban or shorter-distance buses may be renovated U.S. school buses, with those unpadded seats that hold two small children but only one and a half adults.

In San José, there's no central bus station; instead there are many departure points throughout the city. The tourist office right next to the Gold Museum downtown has good maps that show where a variety of long- and short-distance buses leave and arrive. Most points are in decent areas, but be especially careful at the central San José bus depot known as the Coca-Cola (near Avenida 1 and Calle 16)—your bags can disappear in the time it takes to check your

DAILY LIFE

watch. Accurate bus schedules are hard to come by, but one source is John Wood's website, www.costaricabybus.com.

City Buses

Most urban routes cost less than US$.50, and passengers pay as they enter the bus. Bus drivers usually have change for small bills. When you want to get off, either pull the cable or—if there is no cable—call out *la parada, por favor* (next stop, please).

Bus stops often have shelters (essential during the rainy season) or battered signs that say the route name or number. Route numbers seem not to be much use, though: I once asked the driver parked at the Route 66 sign if that route went to my neighborhood. He looked at me quizzically—he'd never thought of his route as having a number. Buses are known for their destinations: the Desamperados bus, the bus to the university.

Shuttle Bus Companies

Fantasy Bus (tel. 506/220-2126, fax 506/220-2393, operated by Grayline Tours, www.graylinecostarica.com) and Interbus (tel. 506/283-5573, fax 506/283-7655, www.interbusonline.com or www.costaricapass.com) will take you to more than 40 destinations in air-conditioned vans. Routes leaving from San José pick up passengers at hotels and other locations throughout the city; one-way fares range US$30–40. If you want more comfort than you'd get on a regular bus, these shuttle services can be very useful, though they're not always as reliable as you'd like. Especially if you're catching one in a town outside the Central Valley, check and double-check departure times, and book ahead. Both companies also offer airport shuttle service.

BY BOAT

The Caribbean coast north of Puerto Limón is riddled with rivers and swamps, which have made it tough to build roads. This is perhaps the only noncoastal area in the country where boat travel is the daily norm, with motorized *canoas* making runs from one tiny town to the next, carrying people and freight. Boats can be hired from Moín, just north of Puerto Limón, and from Caño Blanco, among other ports.

Ferries and Launches

There are three major ferry crossings in Costa Rica, all of them carrying people and/or vehicles between Puntarenas and the southern end of the Nicoya Peninsula. Two of these—the Tambor Ferry (tel. 506/220-2034) and the Ferry

© ERIN VAN RHEENEN

Catch a boat at Caño Blanco to go up the Tortuguero canals.

Peninsular (tel. 506/641-0118)—go from Puntarenas to Paquera, and the third runs between Puntarenas and Playa Naranjo (Ferry Playa Naranjo, tel. 506/661-1069). All take about an hour. The trip is scenic, and fares are low (about US$10–15 for a car, less than a dollar for a walk-on). It's a great way to start a trip to Montezuma or Mal País. Check out www.nicoya peninsula.com/general/boat.html for ferry schedules.

There used to be a ferry across the Tempisque River in Guanacaste, but it shut down in 2003 upon completion of the Taiwan Friendship Bridge.

On the southern Pacific coast, a passenger launch goes across the Bahia Dulce, connecting Golfito and Puerto Jiménez on the Osa Peninsula (tel. 506/775-0472). The trip takes about 90 minutes. The boat leaves Puerto Jiménez every morning at 6 A.M. and leaves Golfito at 11:30 A.M.

Anywhere there's water to be crossed you can often find a guy with a boat. You may have to track him down, wait around, and pay more than you'd like for passage, but with patience and perseverance you'll get where you need to go.

BY TRAIN

For years, the train was the best way to get from the Central Valley to the Caribbean port city of Limón. In the 1970s, however, roads were improved and the train began to be utilized less. Then a 1991 earthquake destroyed miles of tracks and put an end to this scenic trip and, with it, all passenger train travel within Costa Rica. There is talk of resuming the Limón route and the old San José–Puntarenas line—time will tell.

BY CAR
Renting

Though it's expensive to rent a car here and the roads are quite a challenge, having a car in Costa Rica gives you a great deal of freedom and lets you see

THE JUNGLE TRAIN

Though trains are no longer a major mode of transport in Costa Rica, 125 years ago the Atlantic railroad was one of the key factors in transforming a tiny backwater into a prosperous nation with thriving international trade. And the railroad – through the men brought in to build it – was instrumental in fostering the Jamaican flavor that still defines this country's Caribbean coast.

The first chapters of the railroad story are dominated by coffee and then bananas.

From beans imported from Jamaica in 1808, Costa Rica became the first Central American country to grow coffee. By 1830, the highland Central Valley, with its rich volcanic soil and mild climate, had become a major coffee-producing region. Europe was growing fonder of this natural stimulant; Costa Rica's prize crop fueled many a coffeehouse debate in London, Paris, and Prague.

But the route from highland farm to European cup was long and tortuous. Beans were transported by mule (and later, when the roads were widened, by oxcart) to the Pacific coast port of Puntarenas. Boats to Europe sailed around the southernmost tip of South America, then made their way across the Atlantic.

Why not send boats from the Caribbean side of the country, canceling the need for the long detour around Cape Horn? Because the route from the Central Valley to Costa Rica's humid and sparsely settled eastern coast was all but impassable. Primitive tracks crossed raging rivers, skidded down mountainsides, and meandered through vast swamplands. Firmer ground became a stew of mud during the rainy season, which on the east coast seems to last all year long.

Merchants and officials talked incessantly of ways to improve that eastern route. But it wasn't until 1871 that the Costa Rican government set in motion a project unprecedented in scope and magnitude – a railroad from San José to the Caribbean coast port of Limón. President Tomás Guardia Gutérare awarded the contract to American Henry Meiggs. Meiggs was known as a visionary scoundrel who left many creditors in the wake of his big ideas. But he'd built 200 miles of railroad in Chile and 700 in Peru, and was a great orator, party-thrower, and wooer of government officials.

Workers were imported to do the backbreaking labor. The first wave included 400 Chinese, 600 Jamaicans, and 500 from Cape Verde Island off the African coast. Subsequent waves included Italians, Hondurans, Nicaraguans, and many more workers from Jamaica and other Caribbean nations like Barbados. Nearly two decades of work on the railroad claimed the lives of more than 4,000. Many succumbed to yellow fever, dysentery, and malaria.

Partway into the job, Meiggs bowed out and turned the reins over to his nephew, Minor Keith, who'd been managing the worker's commissary near Limón. Money was running out – for months the workers hadn't been paid. Minor Keith offered to arrange funding for the railroad's completion if the Costa Rican government would grant him a 99-year-lease on the railroad and deed him a whopping 800,000 acres of land along the rail line route. Keith planted his new land with banana trees, hoping the crop, as yet unexploited in Costa Rica, would provide much-needed revenue to complete the railroad.

It was an extraordinarily smart move. Bananas flourished and exports increased by leaps and bounds, going from 100,000 stems in 1883 to one million stems in 1890. The banana trade attracted American co-investors like the United Fruit Company (known as La Yunai in Latin America), which would come to yield such enormous influence over the so-called "banana republics" of Latin America.

Nineteen years after it began, on December 7, 1890, the 164-kilometer (102-mile) Costa Rican Railroad was inaugurated. On a bridge high above the Burrís River, tracks from the Central Valley met up with tracks from Limón, finally creating a seamless conduit for products on their way from San José to markets abroad. The trip to Europe no longer required sailing around the tip of South America and was thus shortened by three months. International trade flourished.

By 1900, bananas rivaled coffee in economic importance. The Caribbean workers who'd come to build the railroad now worked on banana plantations, and the influx of Afro-Caribbeans (mostly from Jamaica) changed the face of Costa Rica's eastern coast. Today, the port city of Limón has the highest percentage of Afro-Costa Ricans (around 40 percent); nationwide, blacks make up 2–5 percent of the general population. On Costa Rica's eastern coast, spicy Jamaican food wins out over the traditional and rather bland *casado*, and patois-inflected English is more common than Spanish.

As the Caribbean coast became less isolated and roads improved, the railroad wasn't as important as a means of getting products to port. And with the opening of the Panama Canal in 1914, goods shipped from the Pacific coast no longer had to make their way around the tip of South America.

In the early part and middle part of the 20th century, the Atlantic railroad gradually became more of a passenger train. And for several years before it shut down for good in 1991 due to earthquake damage, the railroad became known as the "Jungle Train," an eight-hour ride that cost US$2 for coach passage and about US$50 for first class. In the late 1970s, Paul Theroux took the train and wrote about it in *The Old Patagonia Express*, a travel classic that traces his journey by rail from Massachusetts to the Tierra del Fuego. He calls the route "the most scenic in Central America."

The glory days of the Atlantic railroad are gone, but the train from San José to Puntarenas still operates, carting freight and the occasional passenger.

every nook and cranny of the country. You don't have to worry about bus schedules or packing light—just load up the car and take off into the wild green yonder.

You'll probably want to rent a four-wheel drive with high clearance, unless you're sure you'll be on major roads for your entire trip. In my experience it pays to rent a medium-sized rather than the smallest four-wheel drive—you'll appreciate the extra weight when you're trying to ford a river. You can probably find a compact car for about US$300 per week, but a good four-wheel drive will cost you closer to US$400–600 per week. Sometimes you can get better deals by making reservations from the United States.

Be sure that if you're quoted a rate, the insurance you need is included in the price.

One good thing about renting a car in this country is that some companies will deliver the vehicle to your door, especially if you live far from a rental office. In Guanacaste's Playa Negra, I had a four-wheel drive delivered to the door of the rather remote place I was staying. The company sent two cars, so that the fellow driving my car would have a ride back.

No car-rental companies will allow their cars to be driven out of Costa Rica.

Rental Insurance

When you rent a car in Costa Rica you need to pay for mandatory basic insurance, which doesn't give very much coverage and usually features a high deductible. Most renters opt to buy more insurance; this expense can run up to US$20 a day and can easily double the cost of renting a car.

If you have a car insured in your home country, there's a possibility that that policy may cover you while driving another car in another country. But the probability is that it won't—call your insurance company and ask for details.

Some drivers get the basic insurance only and let their credit card cover the high deductible (often US$750–1,500!) that goes along with basic insurance. Be sure to check that your card indeed offers this benefit. And be ready for surprises—a friend thought American Express would cover him, but he found that there was a clause that said the coverage didn't hold if the driver went "off-road"—that is, on unpaved roads. Since most of the roads in Costa Rica are unpaved, he ended up having to pay a few hundred dollars to repair a small scrape.

Call your credit card company and get the lowdown on what it covers, if anything. The insurance associated with my Visa card, for instance, covered physical damage to the rented vehicle, along with vandalism and theft. It did not cover personal liability (damage to another vehicle or property), loss or theft of personal belongings, or injury to self or others. That's a lot not covered. And as with my friend's American Express card, the coverage was good only if I didn't drive "off-road."

Unless you're an insurance expert and don't mind endless claims, I would suggest getting the full coverage offered by the car-rental company.

Rental-car companies charge for the most minute scratches, so be sure to look the car over very carefully before driving off the lot. Things like rearview mirrors and tires are often not covered by insurance; you pay if they get ripped off. That's why it's so important to park the car in a safe place.

Owning

Due to high import tariffs, cars in Costa Rica are expensive. If you try to get around that by bringing in a car from outside, you'll confront another set of problems. You could import a car to use for the time on your tourist visa (three months plus a three-month extension) without paying high fees or tariffs, but after that time expires, things get complicated. Of course you have to first get the car here—which means driving it through five countries or shipping it by container. Shipping from Miami or New Orleans to Puerto Limón is the cheapest option, but it still might cost you around US$1,000, and that's before you pay any of the various taxes and fees to pick it up on this end. You can also ship from the west coast of the United States or Canada to Puerto Caldera on the west coast of Costa Rica, but that's even more expensive.

If you want to make your car a Costa Rican native after the six-month grace period has expired, the process is long and costly. You'll pay from 60 to 85 percent of the car's appraised value in duties, and then there will be lots of paperwork, stamps, and miscellaneous fees. It's often easier to buy a car down here; if it's used, get it checked out by a reputable mechanic, as you would do in the United States.

If you're driving around in your own car, be sure you have a valid driver's license, along with the originals (not copies) of the car's registration and title.

Driving

Costa Rica has about 37,000 kilometers (22,990 miles) of roads; fewer than 8,000 (4,971 miles) of them are paved. And paved is sometimes worse than unpaved—a gravel road can be well-graded and in excellent repair, while a "paved" road may be riddled with deep holes. The U.S. State Department rates roads here, and the availability of roadside assistance, as "fair to poor." I guess that's better than "poor to abysmal," but still, you need to make some adjustments when you're driving in this country.

The government is trying to improve the situation. At the end of 2006, US$170 million was set aside for the repair, reconstruction, and maintenance of the country's roads. The funds will be paid for by the fuel tax. Residents and expats hope the infusion of money will make a difference but are not holding their collective breath.

A driver in Costa Rica must be ready for anything—trucks passing on a hill, potholes big enough to do your vehicle real damage, and cops hiding behind the next palm tree. Police here have radar guns and they love to use them. Speeding tickets can be very expensive—up to US$150 if you're really making time. Pay attention to speed limit signs, even if it seems that there's no one else on the road. Speed traps are common on the most-traveled routes to tourist areas.

© ERIN VAN RHEENEN

Officials or other drivers may try to make potholes more visible.

Costa Rican drivers have developed a way of signaling to other drivers that there is trouble up ahead—they flash their lights at oncoming cars. Of course, this can also mean, "Turn off your brights!" but if someone flashes you, slow down and be on the lookout for an accident, a damaged roadway, or a police car. If you're behind someone and they flash their lights, it can mean "The road is clear for you to pass," but be aware that what Costa Rican drivers consider a safe distance to pass is a fraction of what most North American drivers deem necessary.

Wear your seat belt—it's the law. A selectively enforced law, but a law nonetheless. Motorcyclists are supposed to wear helmets.

Even as you try to drive by the book, other drivers will be throwing that same book out the window—turning across two lanes of traffic without signaling, hoisting a bottle while passing on a blind curve, or realizing that, yes, they really should have had the brakes fixed last week.

Traffic enforcement in Costa Rica is the responsibility of the Transit Police

(Tránsitos), who wear light blue shirts and dark blue pants, and drive light blue cars or motorcycles equipped with blue lights. (Regular police drive dark blue cars.) Transit cops often wave vehicles to the side of the road for inspection, asking drivers for their driver's license, vehicle registration, and insurance information. Fines are not supposed to be collected on the spot, although reports of officers attempting to collect money are common.

You can drive with a valid license from your home country for the first three months you are here, as long as you have a valid passport with an up-to-date entrance stamp.

Accidents and Breakdowns

If you have an accident or the car breaks down, try to stay with your car until the police arrive. If you're out in the middle of nowhere or in the middle of a highway, this is impractical, of course. But if it's possible to wait, do so, so as not to open yourself up to liability.

Call the Transit Police (tel. 506/222-9330 or 506/222-9245). You'll also need to call the National Insurance Institute (INS, tel. 800/800-8000). You can also call 911 and ask to be connected with whatever agency (including the Red Cross if there are injuries) you need. If you're in a rental car, call the rental agency as well. It will often send a tow truck, and it may bring you another vehicle, depending on where you are and what the problem is.

While you wait, get the names, license plate numbers, and *cédula* (ID) numbers of those involved, along with the same information for any witnesses. Make a sketch of the accident.

If you have reflective triangles, place them to warn oncoming cars. Many Costa Rican drivers improvise with piled-up leaves or branches to alert other drivers of trouble up ahead.

Stranded foreigners in nice cars, carrying expensive luggage or sports equipment, can attract the wrong sort of attention. Most people who try to assist you will be doing so out of kindness, but be wary of helpers who want to relieve you of your possessions.

When officials arrive, they may or may not speak English. They may be very concerned and helpful, or they may sullenly perform the bare minimum that their offices require. Keep your wits abut you, write everything down, and don't neglect any of the steps (like contacting the INS, which is crucial if you want to make an insurance claim of any sort).

Most accidents occur at night—do what you can to avoid driving after dark. Most roads are unmarked and unlit. Fog and torrential rains can make the way even rougher.

DAILY LIFE

DRIVING IN COSTA RICA: TIPS TO FLATTEN THE LEARNING CURVE

Contributed by Alex Murray

• Do not drive after dark in Costa Rica if you are not very familiar with your area – plan to be at your destination by 6 P.M. The days here are nearly uniform throughout the year: Dawn comes between 5 and 6 A.M. and dusk between 5 and 6 P.M. If your flight arrives late in the day or leaves early in the morning, plan on spending the night of arrival or the night before departure near the airport so you can taxi to or from your flight.

• Driving with your headlights on during daylight is not acceptable as a visibility tactic. Oncoming traffic will blink their lights at you until you turn yours off. You are disrupting an informal law of the Costa Rican roads: Lights are used here to warn oncoming drivers that you have recently passed a surprise highway patrol checkpoint and the other drivers had better slow down.

• A majority of bridges in Costa Rica are single-lane. If your end of the bridge has a Ceda el Paso sign, you must yield, permitting any oncoming vehicles to cross the bridge first.

• On windy roads drivers tend to "straighten the curves," crossing the middle line and forcing oncoming traffic to slow down or squeeze over to the right. Squeezing over to the very edge of the road on a blind curve has a further danger because it's quite possible to find yourself about to run down a bicyclist or pedestrian just around a curve on a country road. Bicyclists and pedestrians are common day or night, but lights or reflectors are uncommon, so the driver must be preternaturally vigilant and cautious. Also watch for livestock.

• Those who have trouble with parallel parking will find this

Gasoline

Both the regular and super sold at gas stations (or *bombas*) here is unleaded—the super is just a higher octane. Diesel is also available. When driving outside of main cities, get gas as often as possible. In remote areas there may be no station, or the station may be open very limited hours. In some small towns you can find a local who sells gas out of his backyard, with the kind of crazy markup that comes with being the only game in town.

Maps and Signs

As you navigate Costa Rica's roads, don't expect signs to alert you to where you need to turn off, even on major highways to popular tourist spots. And if there is a sign, sometimes it will point in the wrong direction. Coming from

skill little-needed in many Costa Rican towns. You'll probably have a choice of parking on either side of the street, including the "wrong" way on a one-way street. What's more, you can often get away with double-parking or perhaps getting just the nose of the car into a short parking space at an angle, though you won't want to leave your car in such positions for very long.

- Stop-sign protocol is liberal in Costa Rica, though often stops are required — supposedly — where stop signs are absent. The sign may have broken off, leaving a naked post, or perhaps the sign is completely faded. The infamous "California rolling stop," for which one might get ticketed in the United States, is accomplished here with guiltless panache and rarely challenged. However, in the presence of other traffic at the intersection, politeness rules.

- Recognizing one-way streets can be a problem. Usually, they are not marked. And since drivers may park in whichever direction works for them on either side of two-way streets, parked cars are sometimes a false clue. For example, in the town of Cañas on the Pan-American Highway, nearly all streets are one-way, but there are no signs. Thus, you must familiarize yourself with Cañas over time to avoid hood-to-hood impasse with someone who knows the town. Canas also is distinctive because it is the rare Costa Rican town with street signs, small metal placards high on the sides of buildings at the corners.

- For those who can handle making their own driving decisions instead of strictly adhering to signs and lines, Costa Rica is an enjoyable and even thrilling place to drive. So, relax, and enjoy the adventure. Or let a Costa Rican do your driving.

*In 2004, Alaska-born **Alex Murray** started Casa Mañana Bed and Breakfast on the Tilarán side of Lake Arenal.*

Puntarenas to San José, there's an important turn that I've gotten wrong three or four times. I keep thinking, "By now the sign most point the right way," but each time I am mistaken.

Getting around in cities and larger towns is even a bigger challenge—see the sidebar *Finding Your Way* in the *Making the Move* chapter.

As you make your way through the urban maze and along windy mountain roads or sandy coastal routes, your best bet is to consult a variety of good maps—the more the merrier, as each tends to have its own strengths. I have not found one single map that did not have errors in it, but usually the other maps in my collection set me straight. *Moon Handbook Costa Rica* author Chris Baker recommends *The Red Guide to Costa Rica* or *Costa Rica Nature Atlas-Guidebook*, which has detailed 1:200,000 maps. You can get topographical maps at the

National Geographic Institute in San José, at Avenida 20 between Calles 5 and 7; it's in the Public Works and Transport Ministry (MOPT) near Plaza Víquez (tel. 506/523-2619). Maps of the national parks are available at the Fundación Neotropical in Curridabat east of the Plaza del Sol (tel. 506/253-2130). Bookstores in San José often have good selections as well. Try 7th Street Books (tel. 506/256-8251, Calle 7 between Avenida Central and Avenida 1) or Lehmann (tel. 506/223-1212; Calle 3 between Avenida Central and Avenida 1).

Security

Whether you're driving your own car or a rental, seek out a secure place to park it overnight. Car theft is common, and the deductible on rental-car insurance policies can be as much as US$1,500. Many hotels provide secure parking, or you could seek out one of the many freelance car or neighborhood guards and take your chances giving him a few bucks to look after your vehicle.

In looking for a place to live, it's important (if you're a car owner) to find a place with a secure garage. In my middle-class neighborhood in San José, no one leaves a car on the street overnight. Never leave anything of value in a parked car.

The Fine Art of Honking

The language of the car horn in Costa Rica is a rich one that may take years to master. Ticos don't tend to "lean on their horns" like some Type A people back home, but they don't ignore them either. Only long-term residents, however, can tell the difference between the "Get out of my way!" honk and the "What a pleasure to see you, my friend, on this same stretch of road where I see you every morning and evening" honk.

There's also the "Hey baby" honk, the "I'm a taxi and I'm available" honk, and perhaps most maddening, the "I'm here! Come out of your house and say hello!" honk, which can go on for a long time, especially if no one's home.

After you've been in Costa Rica for a while, you'll start to recognize even more varieties, maybe even inventing a few of your own. After all, what occasion—no matter how humble—is not enhanced by the sounding of a car's horn?

TAXIS

In the San José area, taxis are plentiful and relatively cheap. Official taxis are red, with the taxi's ID number in a yellow triangle on the door. Taxis should have meters (called *marías*), and drivers should use them—otherwise you'll have to haggle, which is hard to do when you don't know how much the fare should be.

HOW TO TALK TO A *TAXISTA* (TAXI DRIVER)

Take me to...	*Lléveme a...*
Straight ahead	*Directo*
Stop at the corner	*Pare en la esquina*
Take a right	*A la derecha*
Take a left	*A la izquierda*
A block	*Una cuadra* or *cien metros*
Half a block	*Cincuenta metros*
North, south, east, west	*Norte, sur, este, oeste*
At the intersection	*En el cruce*
Next to	*Al lado de*
Across the street from	*Frente a*
Around the corner	*A la vuelta de la esquina*
The next street	*La proxima calle*
Are we lost?	*¿Estamos perdidos?*
Stop here	*Pare aquí*
Stop there	*Pare allí*
Wait for me	*Espéreme*
Taxi meter (in Costa Rica)	*María*
Please use the meter	*Use la maría, por favor*
How much to take me to...	*¿Cuanto cobra por llevarme a...?*
How much do I owe you?	*¿Cuanto le debo?*

DAILY LIFE

There are thousands of taxis in the San José area, and it's easy to flag one down from just about any corner, unless it's raining at rush hour. While local men tend to ride up front with the driver—perhaps to show they're just folks—foreign residents, especially single women, should probably ride in the back.

Most taxi drivers are friendly and helpful, and will sift through your broken Spanish with a smile. They know that foreigners have different ways of thinking of addresses (like street names and house numbers) and are good about helping you figure out where you need to go. You don't need to tip the drivers, though I do if they help with bags or go out of their way for me.

Besides all the official cabs tooling around the city, there are also thousands of *piratas,* pirate cabs that may be red and even have a *maría,* but which are not registered. The proof is in the ID number on the door—if a car doesn't have it, it's not an official cab. In outlying areas (like Escazú) *piratas* are the norm, and residents come to know the drivers who wait at the central square for fares. If you have the option, take an official cab. Some *piratas* aren't really taxis at all, but criminals cruising for marks. Women traveling alone should be especially wary, but everyone needs to stay alert.

Cabs waiting outside hotels or discos will often charge you several times the normal rate. Ask before getting in if there's a *maría;* if there's not, either negotiate the fare before entering the cab or look for another cab.

Taxis outside the greater San José area are a different story. They're usually high-clearance four-wheel-drive vehicles, for starters, because provincial roads are so bad. Few have meters, and they charge whatever the market will bear. You'll pay through the nose until you know the area and the usual fares from one point to the next. That said, the occasional taxi can be a good alternative if you're traveling around the country but don't want to rent a car. Using buses whenever possible, it won't break your budget to hire a taxi to take you where buses don't go.

Cabbies don't like to break large bills. They also complain that North Americans have a nasty habit of slamming car doors. Prove them wrong: be gentle.

See *Resources* for a list of taxi companies.

Renting a Taxi and Driver

When you get serious about looking for a place to live, renting a taxi and a driver by the hour or day is a good way to explore. Especially in the Central Valley, there are so many little towns down so many little roads that it helps to have a driver who knows his or her way around. Sure, you could rent a car—for about the same price as hiring a taxi for the day—but you'll spend most of your time trying to figure out where you are or how to open the gas tank.

Most taxi drivers will rent themselves and their vehicles out for about US$10 an hour or about US$70 a day. If you're going to need a car for several days, you can probably negotiate a lower rate. Hotels and travel agents can suggest reliable, English-speaking drivers, or you can ask foreign residents for their recommendations. These drivers often double as translators and cultural informants, and they might end up as friends. Buy them lunch and listen to their advice.

HITCHHIKING

Costa Rica has a good bus system, but in remote areas the bus might come only once a day. Local people routinely hitch rides, and if you have a car you may be asked for a ride or be inspired to offer one. The longer you stay in an area, the more you're likely to become part of this informal ride-sharing system.

In general ride-sharing is not dangerous, but use your own judgment. Drunks with machetes may not be a good risk, although carrying a machete in the *campo* doesn't mean you intend to use it for anything more than weed-whacking.

For women hitchers and drivers: Many guidebooks describe the ins and outs of hitching and picking up hitchers, then add a line, almost as an afterthought, urging women to not do any of this, ever. Experienced solo women travelers and women who live alone in Costa Rica know the situation is a bit more nuanced than that. There are times you need to get somewhere and there's no car or bus in sight. And if you're driving an air-conditioned car along a hot and dusty back road, it can seem criminal not to pick up women carrying babies or kids trying to make it to school in the next town.

I have hitched alone and have picked up hitchers when I was driving alone, but I am very, very careful about when and where I do this, whom I accept rides from, and whom I pick up. Sometimes I'll approach a safe-looking car full of people (at a restaurant, or stopped on the street), introduce myself, and let them know where I need to go, offering to help out with the gas. I accept rides mostly from families. I give rides to women and children and sometimes the men with them. The only time I felt even a shiver of danger was when I picked up a father and his small son; the father kept asking for money in a way that suggested that giving voluntarily might prevent the situation from escalating to the next level. I gave him a little money, then stopped to let them out. Ironically, I wasn't driving alone that time. I was with a male companion, who couldn't believe I would pick up hitchhikers.

PRIME LIVING
LOCATIONS

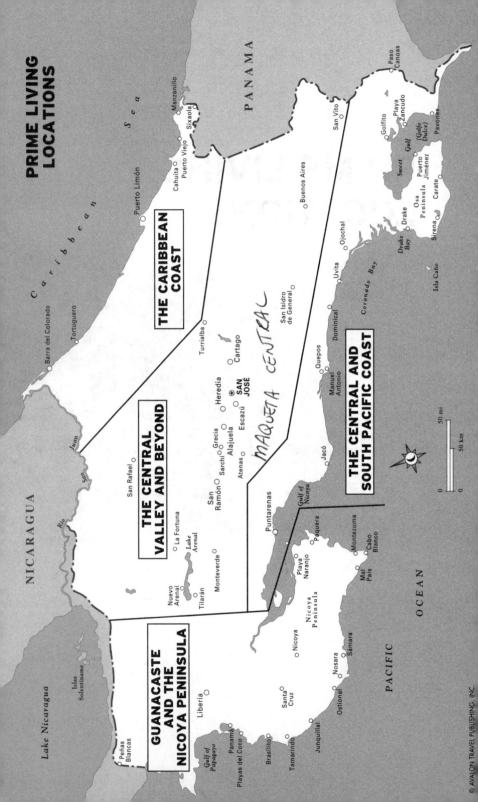

OVERVIEW

The chapters in this section describe the characteristics and appeal of the different regions of Costa Rica, also outlined in brief below. The areas profiled are by no means the only desirable ones, but they are places where a number of expatriates have decided to make their homes. For such a small country, Costa Rica has an astonishingly varied terrain. Guanacaste in late April (the end of the Costa Rican summer) will be hot and dry, its fields and rolling hills blanketed in deep yellows and browns. Just a few hours away, mountain towns like Monteverde—or La Fortuna, in the shadow of Arenal Volcano—are still wet and green. Puerto Viejo, on the Caribbean coast, will be its usual humid and rainy self, while the weather near peaks south of the Central Valley will be downright frosty.

Deciding where to live is a very personal exercise, a process of self-discovery and of getting to know your adopted country. You may love to vacation at the beach, for instance, but find that after two months there you're bored stiff. You may think you want to be far from other expats, but then realize how

© ERIN VAN RHEENEN

much you need an occasional dose of your own kind. Or the opposite may occur—you begin in an expat-heavy area and then, as your Spanish gets better and you feel more at home in the culture, decide you want to move farther afield, into a more truly Costa Rican environment. As I suggest elsewhere in this book, the best approach is to rent houses or apartments in a variety of locales, seeing which place suits you best, before settling in.

As you review the basics, like real estate prices and climate, also ask yourself how you might contribute to the towns that make it onto your shortlist. What will you do there; who will you *be* there? The owner of a thriving business that employs a dozen locals? The founder of the new town library? Or the sour-faced gringo on the hill who complains about the roads and starts drinking before breakfast? Such considerations are not solely altruistic—it's well known that to successfully relocate, a person must forge new roles and new relationships. You'll be a happier camper if you not only make friends with the locals (both Tico and expat) but also become an integral and valuable part of your adopted community.

Over- and Underdevelopment

A caveat: When you hear that a beach town in Costa Rica is "overdeveloped," take that designation with a grain of salt. It's all relative, and what for some might seem touristy will for others seem enchantingly rough around the edges.

Of greater concern is the *under*development of so many beach towns. Places whose popularity has skyrocketed in the past decade often cannot keep pace with the basic needs of visitors, not to mention residents. We're talking woefully inadequate roads, water, electricity, phone lines, garbage pickup, and sewage treatment.

But many towns are rising to the occasion, forming residents' associations to figure out what the community needs and then lobby for it, either asking the national and local governments for help or getting locals to pitch in and do it themselves. Whether it's Danish students organizing beach cleanups in Playas del Coco or hotel and restaurant owners in Tamarindo commissioning a sustainable growth plan, it's often foreign residents who spearhead such efforts. Which is only fair—it's the influx of foreigners who overtax the system and who often hope to make a living off that same influx. It makes sense that they should give something back to their adopted communities.

Not that Costa Ricans aren't deeply involved in improving their own communities. Take the recent example of a bus driver in Ciudad Neily (not far from the Panama border), fed up with the rutted roads and how long it was

RANGE OF MOTION

What it takes to make it in Costa Rica is not unlike what it takes to make it in any new environment – those who've been through the experience agree that flexibility is key. But you may not even know how inflexible you are until you try to do the cultural equivalent of touching your toes (let's not even talk about the backbends and headstands you'll be called on to perform as you adapt to your new world). In our everyday life, within our own familiar culture, we often stay within fairly narrow confines, from the route we take to work to the emotions we allow ourselves to feel. Our range of motion, both physical and otherwise, is quite limited. As we age, this becomes even more pronounced, as bodies stiffen and thoughts and feelings travel along familiar paths.

But one can consciously fight against this closing in by exercising the body and mind to increase all forms of "range of motion." And if deliberately stretching your boundaries while in your own culture is good exercise, moving to a new country and adapting to a new culture is an extreme sport. You need to train for it – to read up on the culture, to prepare yourself mentally for a period of upheaval, even to physically build up a resistance to all the new microbes that will invade your system.

Adapting to a new culture is not easy, but the rewards are immense. Increased flexibility and range of movement means you move through the world with more grace and pleasure. You will look back on your old life, your old frame of reference, and it will look small.

taking the Ministerio de Obras Públicas y Transportes (or MOPT, the agency in charge of the highway system) to fix them. He loaded his pickup with cement and sand, and spent his days off filling potholes on a 28-kilometer (17-mile) stretch of road that was especially damaged. No one paid him; he just decided to take the initiative and improve the road he had to use every day. The government's slow response to community needs has had the side effect of forcing people to be more self-sufficient. This is also why, perhaps, people who live outside the Central Valley (where all the best services are concentrated) feel more identified with their town or area than with Costa Rica as a whole.

Prices

Real estate prices in Costa Rica are as varied and volatile as they are in the rest of the world. An "average" price arrived at one week might be out of date the next. And for any price I quote, there will be people saying "But I paid much less," or "I spent a lot more." Because Costa Rica has no true multiple listing service (MLS), it's even harder to nail down average prices—you're usually going on word of mouth (or word-of-real estate agent, slightly less reliable).

Here's a little history, fodder for the ever-popular "If only I'd bought up a bunch of land way back when" laments. According to the *Tico Times,* in 1968, one *manzana* (1.75 acres or 7,000 square meters) generally went for the equivalent of about US$1,500. In 1974, the price had jumped to US$12,500. In 2006, prices were all over the map, but in hot spots like Santa Ana (near Escazú), one-*manzana* lots cost from US$105,000 to as much as US$800,000.

Of course, there were many places where prices are much lower. For instance, in late 2006 a friend bought two and a half lovely hillside acres near San Ramón for US$45,000, and beach view lots half that size in the lesser-known areas could be had for under US$50,000.

The areas most popular with expats and well-to-do Ticos will be the most expensive, both for renting and buying. The hottest spots right now are the western suburbs of San José, the central Pacific coast area around Jacó and Quepos/Manuel Antonio, and Guanacaste's Gold Coast, which runs from Playa Potrero down to a bit below Tamarindo. In some areas, like the San José suburb of Escazú, the burgeoning surfer burg of Tamarindo, or the easy-access beach town of Jacó, prices can rival those at home, with luxury condos going for as much as US$500,000 (US$2,000–4,000/month in rent), and beachfront or mountaintop spreads fetch over US$1 million (these places tend to rent by the *week,* always a bad sign if you're looking for a bargain).

At the other end of the spectrum, you hear tales of mind-boggling bargains: US$50,000 for a few acres, with a starfruit orchard, a waterfall, and a little house thrown in to sweeten the deal. As elsewhere in the world, it's a matter of supply and demand, and of location. Those amazing deals are most often way out past who knows where—you may have to build your own road or lay your own water line. But if you're looking to really get away from it all, you could live like a king on a workingman's budget.

Most people will be interested in the middle ground—nice places in nice areas, with neighbors within walking distance. It all comes down to how you define "nice." For some it means a four-bedroom, four-bath house with a pool, maid's quarters, a slope planted with mature fruit trees, and a view of the entire Central Valley. That kind of place will run US$500,000 and up in the coveted areas but might cost as little as US$175,000 in a not-so-fashionable but equally pretty location. If you're renting, the luxury places could run you thousands of dollars a month, but there are a great many pleasant two- and three-bedroom houses in the Central Valley area that go for under US$500—check the *Tico Times's* online classified ads for a small taste of what's available (www.ticotimes.net). There seem to be quite a few expats who bought houses—as vacation homes or investments—and are anxious to rent them out, especially to expats, who tend to have more money than locals. Sometimes these homes are furnished and have been built or renovated to more closely resemble North American houses—with hot water throughout instead of just in the shower, for example.

Outside of the Central Valley (and excluding Jacó/Manuel Antonio and Guanacaste's Gold Coast), prices tend to be lower. There are countless towns, nestled on the slopes of a volcano or down a sandy track on a hidden peninsula, where you can find your own little piece of paradise for under US$100,000 and often considerably less.

Manuel Pinto of Carib Sur Real Estate in Puerto Viejo says most single-family homes on popular Caribbean coast areas go for around US$140,000–200,000. Often expats will buy a small, run-down house, live in it while they build their dream home, then either tear down the original house or renovate it and make it into a guest cottage. Popular areas near Puerto Viejo include Playa Chiquitas, Playa Negra, and Punta Uva.

If you find something you like, don't rush. Settle in to that area—maybe in an economical hotel or a short-term rental apartment—and look around. Visit the real estate agents in the area, talk to hotel owners and with expats you see in cafés. Walk the streets in the early morning and at night. See how long it takes to get to the next town and what is available there. In short, do your homework, and don't be swayed by people urging you to buy right here, right now! The real estate market back home may be just as cutthroat, but it's more regulated and easier to understand. In Costa Rica, you've got to be more wary and self-reliant. There are no shortcuts to finding the right place at the right price. And in the end, the right place is more important than the right price. Just because something's a bargain doesn't mean you'll be happy there. Choose where you want to be first, then look for a good apartment to rent, a house to buy, or a lot to build on.

THE CENTRAL VALLEY AND BEYOND

Seventy percent of Costa Rica's population lives in the beautiful and fertile basin called the Valle Central. At the heart of this highland plain (1,150 meters/3,773 feet) lies the capital city of San José, the nation's undisputed political, economic, and cultural center. Here is where you'll find the museums, the theaters, the government buildings, and the University of Costa Rica, the country's largest and most important institution of higher learning. Costa Ricans from outlying areas are drawn to San José for better job opportunities, and many expats are sent here to work at branches of multinational corporations.

Temperate weather is one of the area's main draws. For those who don't

STAGES OF CULTURE SHOCK

According to many psychologists who specialize in crosscultural transitions, culture shock is a very real phenomenon, with identifiable stages.

Initial euphoria: This is the "honeymoon" feeling that usually comes with being exposed to so many new, strange, and interesting things. It doesn't really matter that the visitor can't always understand all of it, because there is so much to see and do.

Hostility: This is a feeling of rejection and alienation when real differences are experienced but not understood. People in this stage understand that things are really different, but they also can't help feeling they are also wrong. It just doesn't feel natural to them.

Gradual adjustment: With time, people begin to learn skills that make them culturally competent, like language fluency and putting cultural practices in the proper context.

Biculturalism: In this phase, visitors may not function like natives, but they fit in relatively well to the host culture. And they can move back and forth, from culture to culture, with some ease.

In the excellent *Survival Kit for Overseas Living,* L. Robert Kohls offers these wise words on the value of culture shock.

"Be ready for the lesson culture shock teaches. Culture is a survival mechanism which tells its members not only that their ways of doing things are right but also that they are superior. Culture shock stems from an in-depth encounter with another culture in which you learn that there are different ways of doing things that are neither wrong nor inferior.

"It teaches a lesson that cannot be learned by any other means: that one's culture does not possess the single right way, best way, or even uniformly better way of providing for human needs and enjoyments. Believing it does is a kind of imprisonment – from which the experience of culture shock, as painful as it may be, can liberate you."

do well with heat or humidity, the Central Valley's mild and dry climate is a godsend. It never gets very cold or very hot here—temperatures average in the mid-20s Celsius/mid-70s Fahrenheit.

Some of the most popular expat areas around San José include Escazú, where the American ambassador makes his home; nearby Santa Ana, with its lovely old stone church and upscale restaurants; Alajuela, a reasonably priced town near the international airport; and Heredia, larger and more congested but still worth a look. Farther afield you'll find Grecia, 30 minutes from San José but a world apart—it was voted "cleanest town in Latin America" and boasts an interesting sheet-metal church in its quiet main plaza; Cartago, the original capital of the country and home to Costa Rica's most stunning church; and Sarchí, a center for arts and crafts.

North of the Central Valley and over the mountains of the Cordillera Central lies the highland plain of San Carlos, home to Arenal Volcano and a series of pristine villages such as Zarcero, centered around a topiary-filled town square and part of an area cool and misty enough to grow lettuce and strawberries. Northwest of San José are the mountain towns of Santa Elena and Monteverde, the latter founded by Alabama Quakers in the 1950s and now an interesting mix of long-term expats and native Costa Ricans, many of whom have intermarried and speak both Spanish and English at home.

South of the Central Valley is the Valle de la General, an oft-overlooked zone that includes the pleasant inland towns of San Isidro de General, Buenos Aires, and San Vito, settled by Italian homesteaders and now the center of one of Costa Rica's most fertile coffee-producing areas.

GUANACASTE AND THE NICOYA PENINSULA

With Guanacaste's dependable dry season (December–April) and seemingly endless supply of beaches, it is the preferred choice for lovers of sand and surf who want to escape the rain and snow back home.

Most of the beaches are on the Nicoya Peninsula, which is 150 kilometers (93 miles) long, averages 50 kilometers (31 miles) wide, and lies almost entirely within the province of Guanacaste (the southernmost tip, where you'll find offbeat Montezuma and the surfer haven of Mal País, is part of Puntarenas Province). But provincial boundaries don't mean much here; the Nicoya Peninsula is all of a piece, though the northern part, dubbed the Gold Coast, is experiencing a building boom that is making it look a lot different from the more laid-back towns farther south.

Driving Guanacaste's potholed back roads (almost all the area's roads qualify as back roads), you'll see barbed wire looped around gnarled and crooked tree trunks, improvised fences that keep the pale, hump-backed Brahmin cattle from wandering off. In the dry season, trees blaze with bright yellow and orange blossoms made even more dramatic because they grace bare branches, before the trees leaf out. The evergreen Guanacaste tree has a full, spreading, often perfectly symmetrical crown that provides welcome shade during hot afternoons. The tree's long dark pods curl like ears, which is why the original inhabitants of the area called it *quauhnacaztli,* from the Nahuatl words *quauitl,* for tree, and *nacaztli,* for ear.

As you move toward the Pacific you'll catch glimpses of the sea through branches or across scrubby fields. Arrival at the westernmost edge of the country

294   PRIME LIVING LOCATIONS

is an inspiring experience, and Guanacaste's beaches seduce even non–beach lovers. From white-sand Playa Hermosa up north to rocky Cabo Blanco down south, there's something for everyone. Most expats in Guanacaste live (or try to live) off the tourist trade, running hotels, restaurants, Internet cafés, or real estate offices. Land prices around the most popular resorts are high, but then again, there's an entire coastline to be discovered—you needn't limit yourself to developed areas such as Tamarindo and Playas del Coco. Long-term expats warn of a lack of health care facilities and a dearth of culture—most go to Liberia or sometimes San José for more serious medical problems, and some might drive hours just to see a movie or try out a new restaurant. Still, most agree they wouldn't have it any other way—they didn't move to the beach for state-of-the-art medical care or to be able to see the new James Bond movie the day it debuts in New York.

THE CENTRAL AND SOUTH PACIFIC COAST

The grouping together of the central and south Pacific coasts makes sense geographically, but the two areas couldn't be more different in terms of ambience and density of settlement. The central Pacific coast, located between the Nicoya Peninsula to the north and the Osa Peninsula to the south, is one of the most visited and most developed parts of the country. It is anchored by the resort towns of Jacó and Quepos/Manuel Antonio, the first famous for surfing (international contests are held on Jacó's long, palm-shaded beach), the second a sportfishing mecca and home to Manuel Antonio National Park, where sloths and monkeys hang out in trees that border some of the country's prettiest white-sand beaches.

As in most areas outside of the Central Valley, expats who come to this area (and need to make a living) tend to work in the tourist trade. In fact, the majority of hotels and restaurants in Jacó and Manuel Antonio are owned and operated by non-Ticos. Industries not based on tourism include vast plantations of oil-producing African palms, which line the road from Jacó to Quepos, extending inland and often planted where bananas used to grow before that industry was destroyed by blight in the 1950s.

The central Pacific coast has a wet season and a dry season (May–November and December–April, respectively), but this area's dry season is not nearly as dry as that of Guanacaste, where virtually no rain falls. The farther south you go, the wetter it becomes. Temperatures hover around 30°C/86°F in the dry season, a little lower in the wet season.

Traveling south along the coast road from Quepos, you won't see much for about 40 kilometers (25 miles), at which point you'll hit Matapalo, a tiny beachside settlement gaining ground as a place where foreigners like to hide themselves away. A little farther along is the bigger town (all of a few hundred people) of Dominical, known for its surfing and, even more than Matapalo, increasingly popular with foreigners looking to buy property on the coast but away from big resorts. Even farther south, Uvita and Punta Dominical also have their share of foreign-owned property, but settlement is sparser and services fewer and farther between.

The southern Pacific coast is dominated by the hook-shaped Osa Peninsula and the vast, tranquil Golfo Dulce (Sweet Gulf), which borders the Osa's eastern shore. Termed Costa Rica's Amazon, this area is wetter, hotter, and more lushly verdant than the central coast. It's also wilder—less populated and less developed. Up until the early 1980s, the area had a lawless, Wild West feel, with gold prospectors making and losing fortunes daily. Old-timers say everyone carried a gun and prostitutes were paid in gold nuggets. The Osa Peninsula's Corcovado National Park was formed partly in response to mining that was destroying the country's biggest and best example of coastal rainforest. Now the park—almost 42,000 hectares (103,784 acres)—protects 139 species of mammals and 400 species of birds, including the brilliantly plumed scarlet macaw.

Bigger towns in the area include Puerto Jiménez (where a good number of expats have settled) and Golfito, a port that was United Fruit's company town until the banana producer pulled out in 1985 after a series of labor strikes. Golfito today is most famous for the Deposito Libre, a duty-free shopping compound where Ticos can buy appliances and other goods without paying the duties that can tack 50 percent onto purchase prices.

The southern Pacific coast is also known for excellent surf spots, including Pavones, home to what some call the longest wave in the world.

THE CARIBBEAN COAST

In a country where each new province seems a world apart, the Caribbean coast of Costa Rica might just qualify as another universe. Nearly all of the country's blacks, most of its Chinese, and a good part of its indigenous population can be found in the Zona Caribe, as it's known in Spanish. Though these minorities make up only a few percentage points of the total national population (Afro-Caribbeans and indigenous peoples with about 2 percent each, and the Chinese population weighing in at barely .25 percent), the fact that most live in the sparsely populated Caribbean province of Limón means that this area is the most ethnically diverse in the country.

The Caribbean coast is where the colonizing Spaniards first arrived, but it is the Jamaicans, more recent arrivals, who have had perhaps the biggest impact. They (along with people from other Caribbean islands and a number of Chinese) migrated here in the late 19th century to work on the railroad and in the banana fields, and their culture now dominates the area. What this means is that reggae overtakes salsa, spicy island-inspired concoctions offer welcome relief from bland *casados,* and a lilting Caribbean English is heard as often as Spanish.

Puerto Limón (often simply called Limón, which is also the name of the entire province) is the biggest city in the area, a bustling port that has more economic than aesthetic appeal. North of Puerto Limón, swamps and rivers dominate the area. Waterways are the zone's roads, and boats outnumber cars. In the little town of Tortuguero, at the entrance to the famed Tortuguero National Park, there are no roads. Sand paths connect the wood-frame houses built on stilts to guard against flooding, and almost everyone has a dock and a boat or two in their front yard. South of Limón there is one decent coastal road linking the beach towns of Cahuita, Puerto Viejo, and Manzanillo, where most expats tend to settle. Inland, the heavily forested Talamanca mountains are home to several large indigenous reserves, among them the Bribrí and the Talamanca.

It rains more here than in most other parts of the country, and the humidity is higher. The beaches south of Limón look like a South Seas fantasy, the water tending toward turquoise when the seas are calm, coconut palms arcing out over coral-protected coves. Limón also looks more like your stereotypical third-world country than other parts of Costa Rica—it's the poorest province, and you won't see upscale shopping malls or luxurious resorts here. What you will see are charming ramshackle villages, wildlife-rich jungles, and beautiful beaches. Fans of the area say they wouldn't trade their little piece of Limón, with its rain and its rough edges, for a dozen more developed beach towns on Costa Rica's Pacific coast. "Life is a little harder here," one expat told me, "but it's also more rewarding, somehow. It's a real place."

THE CENTRAL VALLEY AND BEYOND

It's upon returning from the humid Caribbean or the dry Pacific coast that you really start to appreciate the charms of the Central Valley, where the great majority of both Costa Ricans and expats choose to make their home. The *Tico Times* estimates that more than 100,000 foreigners live in this area—half of them English speakers—and it's not hard to see why. Drive up from Guanacaste in the dry season and you'll go from flat expanses of dry grass to a rolling panoply of every shade of green. Stands of trees alternate with deep-green patches of coffee growing up the hillside. The variety of plantlife here is astounding; you'll see pine trees next to palms, and bright yellow daisies at the foot of enormous stands of bamboo. Bougainvillea, hibiscus, and roses—yes, roses—add dashes of red, and stately trees burst with fiery orange and yellow blossoms.

But the big story is green, and to see the morning light illuminate the most delicate yellow-green all the way to the deepest emerald is to know that you're in one of the most fertile areas of a fertile country, rich in volcanic soil and irrigated by rivers, streams, and the rain that comes down in brief afternoon downpours during the green season.

© ERIN VAN RHEENEN

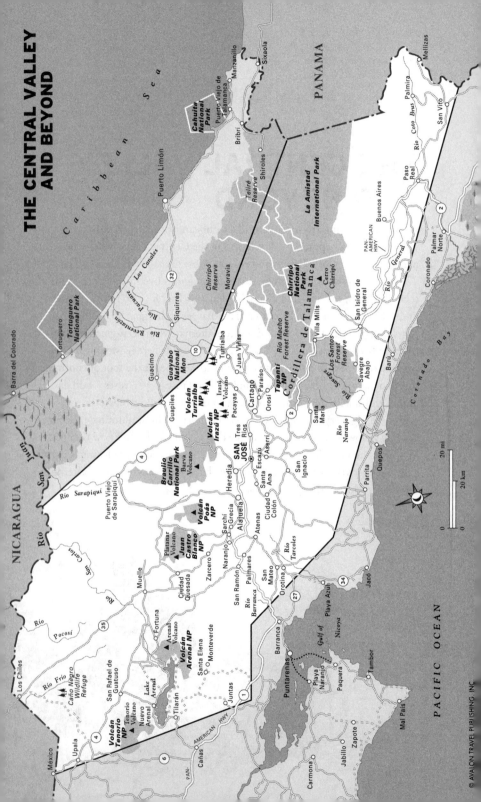

The Lay of the Land

The scenic beauty of the place owes much to the dramatic juxtaposition of imposing peaks and gentle valleys. To the north, the Central Valley is encircled by the soaring Cordillera Central, with its chain of volcanoes including the active cones of Poás and Irazú. The Cordillera Talamanca forms the area's southern perimeter. Measuring 80 kilometers (50 miles) east to west and 40 kilometers (25 miles) north to south, the plateau is actually two separate valleys, split by the Cerros de la Carpintera, which mark the continental divide. The Río Virilla drains the valley to the west, and the Río Reventazón—well-known in rafting circles—plummets down the eastern slopes of the Cordillera Central.

Elevations within the Central Valley range from 900 to 1,787 meters (2,953 to 5,863 feet), with weather at lower elevations suggesting perpetual summer. As you ascend the volcanic peaks that ring the valley, the air becomes a little cooler. Temperatures in the heart of the valley are mild year-round, averaging around 21°C (70°F). Moisture levels also weigh in at a happy medium. If you've been to a humid area, you'll find the drier air here a great relief, and if you've been in dry heat, your skin will drink greedily of the increased moisture in the air.

PRICES
San José and Environs

"Average" real estate prices in a country without a true multiple listing service are notoriously hard to come by. That said, I'll plunge into the perilous world of generalizations, starting at the high end of the market.

In white-hot spots like the San José suburb of Escazú, larger condos and single family homes go for from US$200,000 to US$450,000, with monthly rent very high for Costa Rica—from around US$1,000 to over US$3,500 a month for luxurious places. Escazú and nearby Santa Ana are still some of the most expensive places to live in the Central Valley, with Escazú a bit on the wane (there's not much room left) and Santa Ana on the rise. Foreigners and upper-middle-class Ticos come to these two areas for the high-rise condos, the full-service malls, the country clubs, and the good restaurants. Escazú's popularity means that the basic infrastructure of this one-time small town has been stretched almost to the breaking point. The narrow roads can hardly accommodate all the cars of the new residents.

La Sabana and Rohrmoser, neighborhoods near La Sabana park in east San José, were hot spots 20 years ago and still have some very nice areas (President Arias lives in this area), where spacious homes rent for over US$2,000 a month. Parts of the area have become run-down and now rent for significantly less.

downtown San José

San Pedro (in western San José, near the University of Costa Rica) and nearby Los Yoses still have affordable student-style housing for perhaps US$200–400 a month, with more luxurious places going for US$600–700. North of San Pedro is Sabanilla, a middle-class neighborhood where rentals go for US$300–500.

The middle-class areas of Zapote, San Francisco de Dos Ríos, and Curridabat offer up housing that can be as cheap as US$150 a month up to a few thousand a month for luxury condos in the better parts of Curridabat.

North of San José, the middle-class neighborhood of Tibas is affordable, with rentals going for US$200–300.

In other middle- or working-class areas (there are a lot of these), houses can cost less than US$100,000, and rent will be lower, maybe as low as US$150 to US$200 a month.

The city of Heredia, to the north of San José, is cheaper than San José's western suburbs, with condos or small houses starting from under US$100,000, with rents of US$300–500 a month. The city of Alajuela, closer to the airport, has similar prices.

Zona Norte and the Southern Inland Valleys

Prices outside the Central Valley will more closely resemble the lower end of San José-area prices, with the popular Arenal area a touch more expensive (but not nearly as expensive as San José suburbs like Escazú) and the southern inland cities of San Isidro and San Vito significantly lower.

Where to Live

SAN JOSÉ

It's not just the climate that draws people to this area. Everything is here, much of it in and around the capital city of San José—jobs, government offices, the best public hospitals and private clinics, shopping malls, restaurants, and theaters. Bill White, who in the early 1990s founded an artists' colony in Ciudad Colón, said that when he arrived he drew a circle around the national theater in downtown San José and only looked at property within a half-hour drive of the ornate building that hosts the national symphony. For a smallish city (about 350,000 inhabitants, with closer to a million people if you include the urban sprawl that extends into other cantons), San José has a lot to offer. On any given night you can choose from a dozen plays (some in English), opera, dance performances, classical and popular music, and dozens of movie screens on which you'll find some of the latest films, often premiering just a few days after their U.S. release.

While San José isn't known for its 24-hour antics, the city has a pleasant buzz. That it's the literal center of the country adds to the draw; all roads lead to San José, and residents of outlying areas come here to find what can't be found in the hinterlands. They may come for a better selection of building supplies, a hip new pair of shoes, or just to stroll down the Avenida Central, a bustling pedestrian mall great for window-shopping and people-watching. At the far end of Avenida Central is the Central Market, a jumble of stalls and smells where you'll find no Tommy Hilfiger (unless it's a knock-off) but plenty of fresh fruit, dried bunches of medicinal herbs, and whole pigs on hooks. This is the real thing, and even politicians know it. Several years ago on the TV news, then-President Abel Pacheco was shown slurping *sopa negra* (black bean soup) at one of the market's bare-bones *sodas*. Wiping soup off his chin, he told reporters he was a humble man, a man still true to his working-class roots.

People love to complain about San José—the traffic, the crime, and all those KFC franchises—but I find it an agreeable city. The excellent and very cheap public transportation puts my hometown of San Francisco to shame; you can find pretty much anything you need, from showerheads to CDs, and there are lots of opportunities to soak up culture or make some of your own. English-speaking activities are plentiful—from theater clubs to self-help groups. As for safety, you'll want to take the same kinds of precautions you would take in a similar-sized U.S. city. Violent crime is rarer here than in the United States, but petty theft is common. Awareness is the key, and the more

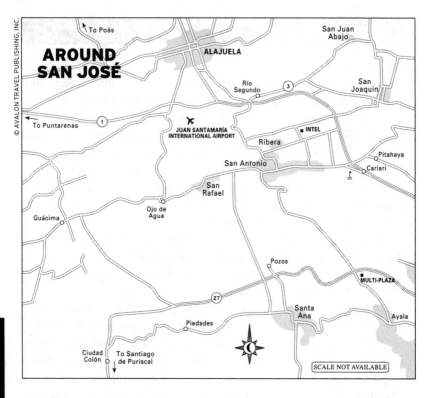

people flowing around you, the sharper you'll want to be. I probably don't need to tell you that you shouldn't take your wallet out in the middle of the Central Market and count just how many *colones* you have left. Any sort of flash is ill advised—keep your new digital camera under wraps, and leave your grandmother's sapphire pendant in the safe-deposit box. Thieves will choose another target if you look like you know where you're going. Of course, you'll have to be a good actor to pull this off; with the utter lack of street signs in San José, it's unlikely that you'll even know where you are.

Those expecting a historic jewel of a city will be disappointed. It's the rare building that is more than 100 years old, and San José boasts its fair share of remarkably ugly modern edifices. Still, the city grows on you. You find your own favorite attractions, from the guy selling fresh orange and carrot juice on the corner near the bus stop to the shady out-of-the-way park at the foot of the city's only all-metal (and all-yellow) building. It's a city of neighborhoods, and if you walk just 10 or 15 minutes from the jam-packed downtown, you'll hit quiet, spacious, often upscale neighborhoods in every direction.

The suburbs of the city and the outlying towns range from wealthy and Ameri-

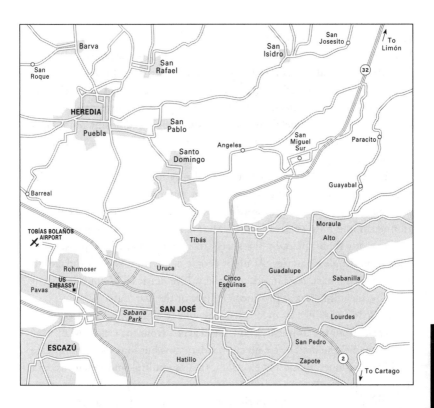

canized to working-class and *puro Tico,* but all share a truly spectacular setting, perched at the foot of, or climbing up, hills carpeted with the glossy green of coffee plants or, even higher up, towering cedar and pine. The flora here is not what newcomers expect; while there is a definite tropical undercurrent, the hills above San José look more like summertime Switzerland than the Amazon basin.

Getting to know the Central Valley can be a challenge. Just figuring out where all of the towns are will take a few months, and exploring them could take half a year of weekend jaunts. The fact that roads are so poorly signed doesn't help matters. Luckily, getting lost can have its rewards, not least of which is discovering a tidy little town halfway up the slopes of a dormant volcano, terraced fields cascading down the mountain and nurturing everything from potatoes to ornamental plants.

For each town described below, there are literally dozens of others waiting to be discovered. The places I've focused on tend to appeal to foreign residents, and there are often good reasons for their popularity. Still, I encourage those serious about living in the area (especially if you plan to buy property) to take their time in exploring the densely settled and enormously varied Central Valley.

Los Yoses and San Pedro

East of downtown, you'll find Los Yoses and San Pedro, residential neighborhoods built around cores of bustling commercial activity. Houses here range from middle-class modern to gracious old estates tucked behind lovely gardens. Los Yoses has a quiet energy during the day. Several government buildings are located on the neighborhood's western edge, and nearby restaurants serve lunch to suited-and-tied civil servants and matrons taking a break from shopping. At night, the area all but shuts down.

San Pedro is livelier, by day but especially by night. The presence of the large University of Costa Rica guarantees an abundance of bars, clubs, cheap restaurants, and funky clothing stores. When school's in session the streets around campus bustle with activity, with small businesses catering to student needs—copy shops, pizza-by-the-slice joints, and kiosks selling pens, notebooks, and single cigarettes. At night people come from all over the city to hang out at the bars, restaurants, and clubs. Live music of all kinds is easy to come by, including jazz at El Rincón de Jazz or the Jazz Café.

San Pedro was once its own town; the village church and square (just a few blocks from the university) now stand across from the Outlet Mall. Despite its name, the mall offers no cut-rate bargains but four floors of upscale clothing boutiques, music and electronics stores, multiple movie screens, and plenty of mall food.

Foreign residents who live in these areas like that they are integrated into the life of the city but also have a quiet place to close the door and regroup. In Los Yoses, the North American Cultural Center organizes conferences, film series, art exhibits, and theater. Even if you don't want to enroll as a full-time student, the University of Costa Rica is a great place to study Spanish or brush up on your art history.

Lomas de Yarco Norte

East of San Pedro, on the road to Cartago, Lomas de Yarco Norte is an up-and-coming area a few minutes from the Terramall shopping center. Because of the good roads, private schools, banks, and high-speed Internet available, some real estate agents say this area is the "new Escazú," with prices to match.

Rohrmoser and La Sabana

West of downtown, the streets get wider and green areas start to crop up with more regularity. Though not usually thought of in recreational terms, the large General Cemetery does provide a break from the surrounding hubbub, with marble mausoleums and special sections for *obreros* and *israelitas* (workers and Jews). Down the street and quite a bit livelier is La Sabana, San José's largest park, which used to be the national airport and now is one of the few places in town where you can jog without having to fight traffic. You can also play basketball, volleyball, or tennis; swim in an Olympic-sized pool; or take one of the free aerobics classes offered on weekends. On the park's northwest corner is the National Stadium; on the southeast corner is the National Gymnasium.

The park is a big draw for people who like to be in the city but within walking distance of a little piece of the country. Add to that many good restaurants and cafés, upscale strip malls, and proximity to downtown, and you've got a very desirable area.

The best known of the neighborhoods around La Sabana is Rohrmoser, northwest of the park and home to many upper- and upper-middle-class Tico families. It's also a favorite of expats, who perhaps feel at home where there seems to be a foreign embassy on every corner.

Barrios Amón, Atoya, and Aranjuez

These three contiguous neighborhoods to the immediate north of downtown are definitely not expat centers. Parts of the area are run-down, and along one stretch you'll see a fair number of streetwalkers who, if you opt for a closer look, turn out to have more than you bargained for under their miniskirts.

So why do I even mention these neighborhoods? Because they are fascinating barrios, with some of the oldest and most interesting buildings in the city. There's a feeling here you don't get in the rest of San José—namely, that the city has a history, and remnants of it are still visible if you take the time to look. Walking these streets, I have seen dozens of gorgeous old wood-frame houses that cry out for loving restoration. Hand-carved wooden latticework graces roof eaves, and the wraparound front porches remind me of grand old houses in the American South and Midwest. Architects and historians may cringe, but if pressed I'd dub these charming buildings Caribbean Gothic.

These neighborhoods are uphill from the center, which gives them a feeling of being above and beyond all the downtown bustle. The area's northern perimeter is the Torres River, which is best seen from the cliff that marks the abrupt end to Barrio Aranjuez.

Zapote, Curridabat, and San Francisco de Dos Ríos

The neighborhoods to the southeast of downtown San José are a varied lot, but in general they are pleasant middle-class areas that are drawing more and more foreign residents. Those who want to be close to the action of the city center and don't wait to pay the higher prices of upscale western suburbs like Escazú have quietly moved in, and now, especially in San Francisco de Dos Ríos, it's not uncommon to see gringos (including lots of families) going about their daily business at the supermarket or running track. There's a great kid-friendly park in San Francisco (Parque Yokohama), where the kids of foreign residents swing on the swings and mix it up with the locals on a dirt soccer field.

The Curridabat neighborhoods of Pinares and Fresa have many condos on offer, newer than those in Escazú and less expensive.

All of these neighborhoods are beginning to take off. There's a lot of recent commercial development in the area, from Multiplaza East in Curridabat to the Terramall on the highway to Cartago. Remax real estate agent Les Núñes calls it a "lead-lag situation," explaining that "commercial development leads off, and residential follows." Though this area is now on the rise, he believes the price differences among neighborhoods will remain constant. "The way it works is the west side [Escazú, Santa Ana, etc.] levels off, the east side picks up, and then the west side will take off again."

WEST OF SAN JOSÉ
Escazú

One of the oldest settlements in the country, Escazú is also one of the most up-to-date and sophisticated. This is arguably the most prestigious place to live in Costa Rica, and residents love the fact that they're only 15 minutes from San José but worlds apart in terms of atmosphere. I can't tell you how many successful lodge and hotel owners I met all over Costa Rica who told me their real home was in Escazú.

The town climbs the lower slopes of the surrounding mountains, the highest of which is 2,455 meters (8,054 feet), and the air is usually a few degrees cooler than it is in San José. Tucked amid the foothills you'll find impressive individual homes, gated condominium complexes, fine hotels with manicured grounds, and even a few affordable apartments. There's a well-regarded English-language school (the Country Day School, K–12) and not one but two country clubs. Despite the fashionable shops and restaurants, parts of Escazú still have a surprisingly rural feel. Next to a high-end furniture store you might see a couple of cows grazing in front of an adobe hut.

In proper terms, Escazú is not one but three towns, each with its own church, central plaza, and prefix (San Rafael de, San Miguel de, and San Antonio de). But as tends to happen in burgeoning areas, what were once separate areas started to bleed together, and soon it was hard to tell where one stopped and the other began. Now, the different towns function more as different neighborhoods,

© ERIN VAN RHEENEN

Escazú is known as the City of Witches, as illustrated in the town's coat of arms.

with the air growing clearer and the streets more tranquil the farther up the hill you go. San Rafael de Escazú is the lowest, close to one of the few stretches of superhighway in the country, and home to most of the modern shopping malls and services. This area's busy strip offers up the chance to drop a small fortune on an imported suit or handmade tile for your kitchen, or to sample Italian, French, or Argentine cuisine (among many other international options). Though the tenor of the place is undeniably upscale, there's still room for more down-to-earth establishments such as supermarkets, health clinics, gas stations, and, of course, a McDonald's or two.

A kilometer (0.6 mile) up the road is San Miguel de Escazú, which centuries ago began life as a crossroads between indigenous villages and later, in the 1700s, became a Spanish settlement that served the area's cattle ranchers. A few remaining cobblestone streets can be found around the village square, with its lovely red-domed church painted at its base with a strip of color to ward off witches. Despite such precautions, Escazú, traditionally known as the witch capital of the country, hasn't lost its power to captivate and enchant. Some residents seem to soak up that ability; a local *bruja* suggests that any woman who lives long enough in Escazú becomes a witch in her own right.

Still farther up the hill is San Antonio de Escazú, the most rural of the three Escazús and home to the annual Oxcart Drivers Day festival. The slopes above San Antonio are planted in coffee bushes, until even these give way to cloud forest. Just minutes from town you can be walking along a remote trail, maybe heading for the 15-meter (49-foot) iron cross on a nearby peak, with nothing but trees and the occasional dairy cow to keep you company.

Driving around the hills above town you'll see sprawling homes that combine a dizzying array of architectural styles; a starkly modern building might sprout Greek revival columns or a quasi-Victorian turret. Closer to Escazú's center(s), the municipality usually requires new construction to conform to a more traditional style.

PRIME LIVING LOCATIONS

There are a lot of gringos in Escazú, some in gated communities that allow them to leave for months and not worry about security, others more integrated into the community. Real estate prices are among the highest in the country.

Socially, there's a lot going on in Escazú, and the number of expats here ensures that you'll have plenty of potential playmates who speak your language. I'm not sure what this says about the area and its inhabitants, but if you see in the San José newspapers a notice for tai chi, meditation, or rebirthing, chances are you'll be directed to an address in Escazú. On a different note, the town also seems to be a center of charity work, with benefit dinners and book sales generating funds for local schools and clubs.

Santa Ana

Unlike Escazú, which is spread out and has many "centers," nearby Santa Ana has a village-like atmosphere with one undisputed heart: the 1870 medieval-looking stone church. Even on a Saturday night the church will be packed to its wooden rafters, worshippers dressed to the nines, throwing flirtatious glances between the call-and-response of 6 o'clock mass. It's a place to see and be seen, with young men and women dolled up as if for the disco, which is indeed where they'll probably be later in the evening.

Across the street the soccer field will be lit up, with teams of 12-year-olds playing as if the World Cup were at stake. Within a few-block radius you can find Peruvian ceviche, American steakhouse fare, or local specialties like wood-grilled chicken with fried sweet onions.

The town is famous for its ceramics, and there are at least 30 independent pottery shops in the area. An 8,000-hectare (19,768-acre) forest preserve and bird sanctuary above town ensures that Santa Ana will always be bordered by nature.

Santa Ana used to be billed as "the next Escazú," with lower prices and a more traditional Tico feel. From what I can observe, though, it's not far from Escazú in terms of real estate prices, fancy restaurants, and expat presence. Santa Ana is a little lower in elevation than Escazú, so it's a few degrees warmer.

Ciudad Colón

Eight kilometers (five miles) west of Santa Ana is Ciudad Colón, which used to be considered "way out there," laughed Bill White, who until his death in 2005 lived in Colón for more than a decade, running a hillside artists' colony on seven luxuriant hectares (17 acres). "But it's only 20 or 30 minutes from San José. Or it used to be, before the traffic got so bad."

Even so, Ciudad Colón feels far from the city. Even the weather is different—

warmer, and a touch more humid. It feels more tropical. For years everyone's been saying this place will really take off when they finish the San José–Puerta Caldera highway, an alternate route to Pacific coast resorts like Jacó. The highway will mean people living in places like Colón or nearby Santa Ana will be able to reach the beach in an hour. But in Costa Rica, you never know when and if such projects will be completed, and that suits longtime foreign residents just fine, since most came exactly because the area was a little out of the way.

Bill recalled that he paid around US$85,000 for seven hectares (17 acres) about a decade ago. He estimated that the improved property is now worth millions. That may be, but Colón is still a relative bargain when compared to other Central Valley towns like Escazú. Scan the real estate ads in the *Tico Times* or *La Nación* and you'll find that houses and apartments in and around Colón are priced consistently lower than equivalent properties in Escazú or Santa Ana. Being considered far afield can have its advantages, even if it's only a matter of a few more minutes along the road from San José.

Atenas, San Mateo, and Orotina

On the less-traveled of the two routes to the Pacific coast resort of Jacó, you'll pass through some very pleasant country, as the road gradually loses elevation and the foliage becomes slightly more tropical but the weather retains a mountain freshness. The town of Atenas (50 kilometers/31 miles from San José, population 6,500) was said by *National Geographic* magazine to have the best climate in the world. At 800 meters (2,625 feet) in elevation, it hovers between spring- and summertime temperatures and is known as an excellent orchid-growing area. Aside from weather, Atenas and nearby San Mateo (population 2,500) and Orotina (population 8,700) are clean and appealing towns, with lots of trees and some interesting old wooden houses. There's a sense of *there* there; the towns have a pleasing density that speaks of history and of gradual, organic growth. These aren't non-towns strung out along a highway, and in fact the road slows considerably as it meanders through narrow streets and past town squares. There are scattered expats here, as there are everywhere, but these towns have Costa Rican souls.

SOUTH AND EAST OF SAN JOSÉ
Cartago

Twenty kilometers (12 miles) southeast of San José lies historic Cartago, a city of 40,000 best known for sheltering in its cathedral the stone statue of La Negrita, Costa Rica's patron saint. Only 20 centimeters (eight inches) high and supposedly found amid the rocks beneath what is now the basilica,

LA NEGRITA'S GIFTS

The city of Cartago has Costa Rica's most famous church, a soaring, cupola-topped basilica to which pilgrims flock every August. And all year round, the faithful bring gifts: flowers by the truckload, piles of pencils used in exams, medals in the shape of body parts, even bridal veils. The ceaseless tribute is aimed at a diminutive stone statue the pilgrims call La Negrita.

La Negrita is the "little black woman," which sounds condescending in English but conveys nothing but affection in Spanish, for this is the nickname of the beloved Virgin of the Angels, Costa Rica's patron saint, a 20-centimeter-tall (eight-inch-tall) stone statue that inspires the yearly pilgrimage, with some of the faithful walking for days to demonstrate their faith.

The story of La Negrita goes back to 1635, when Cartago was more a scattering of crude huts than a city. One day a *mestiza* (mixed-blood woman) named Juana Pereira saw a strange light coming from between the trees of the path she took every day. Following the light to its source, she found a small black stone in the shape of the Virgin, nestled in the recess of a much bigger rock. Delighted, she took the figure home, but twice La Negrita found her way back to her place of birth. Even when Juana gave the statue to the town priest for safekeeping, La Negrita returned once again to the rock from which she had come. The Virgin's attempts to escape captivity were interpreted as a desire for a basilica of her own, built where Juana had first found her.

And so the Basílica de Nuestra Señora de Los Ángeles was constructed, and today its vaulted hardwood ceiling, stained-glass windows, and flower-painted walls host all who come to visit the shrine of La Negrita. They come steadily

La Negrita has pride of place in the Cathedral of Our Lady of the Angels, attracting pilgrims from all over the country each August 2. On the tourist circuit, Cartago is famous for Las Ruinas (the ruins), the remains of the *parroquia* (parish church) built in 1575 and damaged many times before its final destruction in the earthquake of 1910.

Earthquakes are not the only type of natural disaster Cartago has had to endure. The town is only a few kilometers from the steep slopes of Irazú Volcano. In 1723, the volcano erupted, destroying the city, which at the time was little more than a collection of adobe huts and a single church. Since then, Irazú seems content to burble and boil and periodically shower Cartago with a fine layer of volcanic ash.

Cartago is one of the oldest Spanish settlements in the Central Valley; it was the nation's capital until shortly after the 1823 civil war. Central America had just declared its independence from Spain, and the subsequent battle in the Central Valley was over whether to join with other former Spanish colonies

all year long but arrive in the hundreds of thousands for the Día de la Virgen de Los Ángeles, a national holiday on August 2, when the pious make the old story new again. The story has some unexpected twists. For instance, in recent times, late April and early May have seen spikes in the national birth rate. It seems that the pilgrimage is one of the few times "good girls" are allowed to stay out all night, and the religious revelry can turn carnal. If you walk the 22 kilometers (14 miles) from San José to Cartago the night of August 1, you'll see pilgrims with flowers in one hand and a beer in the other.

Even back in 1782, the party sometimes got out of hand. That year, a priest ordered the statue moved from the basilica to a local church called El Carmen, so that La Negrita wouldn't have to witness how her day had been taken over by drunken carousing. Partying now takes a back seat to devotion, but the tradition of moving the statue to El Carmen has endured, and from August 3 to September 7, La Negrita takes a post-party vacation in the parish church.

Now what about those offerings? The pencils, the charms, and the wedding veils? They're fervent thank-yous for miracles performed. For prayers answered, exams aced, bodies made whole again, and husbands delivered to the altar. And what becomes of those countless tokens of gratitude, too much by half to fit into a church, even one as large as the basilica?

The flowers are used to decorate the church. The non-rusting medals are put in glass cases in a side chapel, while the lower-quality ones are kept in some unspecified back room. And the bridal veils are cut up to make veils for poor girls about to undergo their first communion. Call it the recycling of miracles, short work for La Negrita.

PRIME LIVING LOCATIONS

in a federation or to declare Costa Rica its own independent republic. The cities of San José and Alajuela favored independence; Heredia and Cartago wanted to be part of the larger federation. Those seeking independence won the day, and Cartago lost its capital-city status to San José.

The city's loss may have also been its gain, in that urban growth here hasn't been as helter-skelter as it's been in San José. Cartago feels a lot more traditional and reserved than the current capital. This tidy, bustling town has not attracted as many foreign residents as places like Escazú and Santa Ana. But that may change, as Cartago seems a very livable place indeed and is not yet so "hot" that property values are rising daily.

Turrialba

About 40 kilometers (25 miles) east of Cartago and 65 kilometers (40 miles) from San José lies the small but bustling town of Turrialba. Not yet a magnet for foreign residents, the town is pleasant, and the surrounding cane fields, coffee farms, and dense forest are quite beautiful. The drive from San José, up to Cartago and then down to Turrialba, reveals new shades and textures of green at every turn, with mist drifting down from the higher ridges. You'd never pick this town out as the place where Rawlings manufactures the baseballs used in Major League games in the United States, but it is.

Twenty kilometers (12 miles) north of Turrialba is Costa Rica's best-known archaeological site, Guayabo National Monument, where you can study the workmanship of a 3,000-year-old cobblestoned street or watch water rush through an equally ancient aqueduct system that still functions today.

Walk around Turrialba and you'll see some gringos, the majority of whom are here to run the Reventazón and Paquare Rivers and one or two of whom actually live here. As San José continues to sprawl, places like Turrialba, not far from the capital but far enough to avoid its fumes and grit, will become more and more attractive for relocators.

NORTH AND NORTHWEST OF SAN JOSÉ
Heredia

Founded in 1706 at the foot of Barva Volcano, Heredia is home to the National University, whose student body (the second-largest in Costa Rica) injects into the town a good measure of youthful energy. There are also several Spanish-language schools in this city of 22,000, and these students—mostly from Canada and the United States—add to the cosmopolitan feel of the place.

The *Tico Times* calls Heredia "arguably the Central Valley's most charming urban center," and there's no denying that the town's tree-shaded central park is a first-rate place to people-watch and listen to free live music on the weekends. The nearby Cathedral of the Immaculate Conception was built in 1797 and has managed to withstand several earthquakes since then. Another historic building, El Fortín, is a lesson in how not to build a fortress. Alfredo González Flores, president of Costa Rica from 1914 to 1917, designed the gun slits on the circular tower so that they easily allowed bullets in but made it nearly impossible for soldiers to shoot out.

Local expats do better at defending the charms of their adopted city. "It feels cozy," says a woman who's lived here for years. "But you can still run all the errands you need to run—the bank's down the block, and the Central Market is one of the best places for fruit and vegetables in all of Costa Rica."

With its understated charm and its proximity (just 11 kilometers/6.8 miles) to San José, Heredia has attracted its share of expats, though many tend to settle in and around nearby small towns—Santa Barbara is set in the heart of coffee country, while San Joaquín de las Flores is known for its upscale residences and lively Easter week processions. Santo Domingo de Heredia, a quiet, bougainvillea-draped town, is an easy 20-minute bus ride from downtown San José. A gleaming white and silver basilica presides over the soccer field and the weekly farmers market. Just outside town is Casa Zen (www .casazen.org), founded in 1975 and, as far as I know, the only Zen Buddhist community in the country. Casa Zen has ties to Zen centers in Vermont and Toronto.

Heredia is slightly higher in elevation than San José, so it's a little cooler and greener all year long; towns farther up the slopes of the volcano are even cooler.

Alajuela

The City of Mangoes is often called a mini San José, but it's warmer than the capital in both senses of the word. The temperature is consistently higher, and though Alajuela is a bustling city of 50,000, the plaza at the heart of the city makes it feel more like a small town. Shaded by enormous mango trees (hence the city's nickname), the Parque Central is where it all happens. Local teenagers cruise, money changers trade *colones* for dollars, and the town's substantial population of North American retirees comes here to trade information about available apartments, where to find a good masseuse, or the current price of a round-trip ticket home. The talk slows when professional musicians file into the park's bandstand and begin to tune up for a program of classical or popular music.

Every April 11, the Parque Central is the center of a raucous party celebrating Juan Santamaría, Alajuela's native son and Costa Rica's beloved national hero. Also known as El Erizo (The Hedgehog) for his bristly hair, Santamaría set fire to the invading enemy's barracks after a ragtag army chased them out of Costa Rica and over the Nicaraguan border. The enemy happened to be William Walker, a pint-sized Nashville native drunk on Manifest Destiny. Dreaming of a Central America firmly under U.S. control, Walker and his band of mercenaries invaded Nicaragua in 1855, then turned their sights on Costa Rica. Santamaría, who died in that final battle, became a symbol of Costa Rica's capacity to oust foreign invaders. Even so, everyone—regardless of nationality or secret desire to rule the world—is welcome at the town-wide fiesta celebrating the Hedgehog's bravery.

On Saturdays, there's an excellent farmers market. During the rest of the week, there's no shortage of supermarkets and *pulperías,* the corner stores where you can find at least one of everything.

PRIME LIVING LOCATIONS

Grecia

Aside from the oddly columned structure at the turnoff to this town, Grecia feels about as Greek as a scarlet macaw. In the 1820s, shortly after Costa Rica won its independence, the towns of Grecia (Greece) and Atenas (Athens) were named to honor the Greek struggle for independence from Turkey. However it came by its name, Grecia is a pretty little place, just 30 minutes from San José's international airport, small enough to be safe and friendly and large enough to have a critical mass of expats and some decent services. The road into town winds past coffee *fincas* and fields of sugar cane, which looks like enormous clumps of grass topped with pale yellow tassels. Every bend in the road reveals stunning views of gently sloping valleys and steep volcanic peaks.

At the center of town is, of course, the church, in this case made of an unlikely material: metal. Constructed of steel plates imported from Belgium in 1897, the church is prettier than it sounds, with stained-glass windows and an attractive tiled floor. Streets around the church and town square are wide and pleasant. Locals like to remind you that the town was voted "cleanest town in Latin America" not once but several times, and indeed Grecia does have a tidy and prosperous feel. Expats (along with everyone else in town) congregate in the palm-shaded main square or shop for fresh fruit and vegetables at the nearby Central Market. If you need a little excitement, you can always visit a must-see attraction just east of town: El Mundo de los Serpientes has a living collection of 300 snakes from around the world, including some of Costa Rica's most beautiful and deadly.

Sarchí

A few kilometers northwest of Grecia is the crafts center of Sarchí. Famous for the brightly painted oxcarts that are one of Costa Rica's most visible examples of folk art, the town is now on the tourist map, with crafts emporiums offering everything from miniature oxcarts to handmade wooden furniture. In fact, Sarchí rockers—simple but attractive chairs combining hardwood and leather—have become famous, with the added advantage of being collapsible and thus easy to transport.

The main street, which connects Sarchí Sur (population 4,000) with Sarchí Norte (population 6,500), is lined with somewhat tacky tourist shops (avoid the area on weekends during high season, when tour buses clog the road). Beyond this unpromising introduction, however, the town is quite charming. Whitewashed buildings and the bridge into town are painted with the intricate geometric designs originally found on oxcarts—the colorful patterns remind me of Pennsylvania Dutch motifs found on barns in that state, but amped up a notch or two until they hit tropical exuberance. Equally festive is Sarchí Norte's church: birthday-cake pink with bright turquoise trim. Inside are vaulted hardwood ceilings and striking carvings made by local artisans. The town's setting can't be beat—it's surrounded by hills blanketed in coffee and sugar cane, and has spectacular views of higher peaks farther off.

There's not yet a large expat contingent in Sarchí, but the town is definitely worth a look, being fairly close to San José and only a few minutes from better shopping and services in Grecia.

San Ramón

About an hour west of San José on the highway to Puntarenas, San Ramón is beginning to attract a few expats but is still undiscovered by the masses. The small city (or large town) has an interesting history. In 1870 a local priest published a satire of those who couldn't find the time for church. The book's fame drew other writers and San Ramón became known as the City of Poets, well as the City of Presidents; former heads of state José Figueres Ferrer and Rodrigo Carazo were born here.

Nowadays, the José Figueres Ferrer Cultural Center organizes weekly events, from art exhibits to readings, and the nearby San Ramón Museum offers up an interesting re-creation of a traditional *campesino* home.

Four miles north of San Ramón, on the road to La Tigra, a small group of expats congregates around tiny Ángeles Norte, taking advantage of the area's mild climate, rolling green hills, and quiet, rural feel.

Zarcero

Tucked in the folds of the mountains you cross to get from the Central Valley to the Zona Norte, Zarcero is dominated by a pretty church and a plaza filled with shrubbery cut into fanciful shapes, from bears to cartoon characters. The town is clean and the air cool enough so that strawberries and lettuce thrive, planted in neat rows just outside the

topiary in Zarcero's main plaza

EXPAT PROFILE:
STEPHEN AND KATHLEEN'S DREAM HOME

Originally from Louisiana, Stephen and Kathleen Duplantier moved to Costa Rica in early November 2004. Stephen made documentary films about Cajun food and music and taught at Southwestern Louisiana State University. Kathleen taught grade school, taking early retirement when she contracted multiple sclerosis (MS). (Read more about Kathleen's experience as a disabled expat in the sidebar *People Run Over to Help* in the *Health* chapter.)

A month after they arrived, they bought a hectare (about 2.5 acres) outside of San Ramón for US$45,000 from a local farmer. Next door, a developer was taking hectare lots, dividing them into six or seven pieces, then selling each of those tiny lots for US$30,000. Stephen and Kathleen found their land through a friend, a gringo who'd been in the area for 20 years. They hired a local architect, Carlos Reyes of San Ramón, with whom Stephen worked closely to design the house. It took about 14 months to build the house, which is 2,250 square feet.

Stephen warms to the subject of designing and building the house. "This was my bible," he says, handing me *A Pattern Language*, by architect and builder Christopher Alexander. Paging through, I see that this well-illustrated tome covers everything from city planning to the proper height of windowsills, each solution a "pattern."

"Take the window," says Stephen. "The pattern expressed here is the idea that in a place with a beautiful view – and we certainly have a beautiful view – it's a mistake to put in a picture window. It becomes like a painting on the wall; you never look at it. With small panes, it's like having hundreds of small views rather than one large view. It keeps things interesting."

How about costs, I ask, looking around at this spacious three-bedroom house with high ceilings and a deck from which to enjoy the view. It is clear that every detail, from the wood of the window seat to the tile in the kitchen, has been meticulously planned and lovingly realized.

"We sold our house in Abita Springs (Louisiana) for US$200,000," says Stephen. "With that money we bought the land here, built the house, bought a car for about US$8,000, and lived for 18 months – which probably cost around US$1,500 a month. So I guess the house probably cost around US$120,000 to build."

High Security and Wheelchair Accessibility

This was not an on-the-cheap building job. Take the front door, for example. Almost eight centimeters (three inches) thick and 130 centimeters (51 inches) wide (all doorways are wide to allow easy access for Kathleen in her wheelchair), the slab of mountain almendro is so heavy they needed to make special hinges, flame-shaped pieces of iron now bolted to the wood. When they couldn't find a lock strong enough to hold the door, they special-ordered one from an Italian company that makes bank vaults.

Security became very important to Stephen and Kathleen after they were robbed a few months after arriving in Costa Rica. They were in a rental house, building their dream home, when the thieves "pretty much just walked right in – anyone could have in that house." They were asleep in the house when burglars entered, taking everything, though fortunately many of their prized possessions were at that moment somewhere on the high seas between Miami and the port of Limón. But all of their computer equipment – including all the backup disks – was taken.

"We had an instant and massive case of digital Alzheimer's," laughs Stephen. "It wiped the slate clean. It was kind of like cutting the final cords with the past. The up side of the robbery was that we thought, 'Now we know what kind of house to build. It's going to be a fortress.'"

Of Alcoves and Finger Puppets

But oh, what a lovely fortress it is. It's the kind of place where each new room, each new alcove (there are three window seats) calls for you to settle in for a good read, a nice nap, or just to contemplate the beauty and birdsong surrounding you.

Stephen is showing me the capacious window seat they call the Drifters Alcove, named for the James Michener book, one of a small collection of travel classics on a shelf above this inviting space. Stephen and Kathleen met Michener in 1969 in Pamplona, Spain.

Three sides of the alcove hold nothing but views; a heavy curtain can be pulled across the front to make it like a couchette in a train. Kathleen tells me it doubles as their guest room, but to me it's like a grown-up version of the forts kids make with chairs and blankets.

Another guideline from *A Pattern Language* says that you should decorate a house with things that are important to you. "Kind of obvious," admits Stephen, "but it's surprising how many people hire decorators, who then lug in all sorts of objects that have nothing to do with the people who live in the house."

Stephen and Kathleen haven't made that mistake. All the objects in their house conspire to tell the story of their lives. In the study, for instance, are framed certificates, awards for innovative teaching that Kathleen earned during her long and inspired career. There are also more puppets and photos of performances – Kathleen was part of a folkloric puppet theater that performed everything from Cajun tales to Choctaw myths. And there's a framed letter of censure from the Saint Tammany Parish School Board.

"Please," the letter admonishes in fading typescript, "do not make finger puppets from personal hygiene products."

"When I taught puppet-making to kids," explains Kathleen, "I'd bring in any materials I could find. I'd been using these little cardboard tubes, the perfect size. One year, they found out where the tubes came from [they were tampon applicators]. The nuns got kind of mad."

Kathleen went right on using the materials she wanted, however unorthodox. And in building a new life, Kathleen and Stephen bring to the project their usual imagination and irreverence. Their next project is to build the area's first wheelchair-accessible butterfly house. Not a house, they assure me, for wheelchair-bound butterflies but one that Kathleen can roll up to and see the multicolored flutterings of Costa Rica's most famous nonhuman residents.

town limits. Farming in general is good here, and there's a fair amount of wealth that displays itself in well-kept homes and farms.

Zarcero, though cute as a bug's ear, is not the only town of its kind. All across Costa Rica you will find the kinds of places you'd never expect to find in this country. Costa Rica enchants in part because it so often surprises. The fun is in wandering far enough afield (and opening your eyes wide enough) to be amazed and delighted by what you find.

ZONA NORTE

There are several routes north over the peaks of the Cordillera Central, but all offer spectacular views and a glimpse of a Costa Rica the casual tourist rarely sees. Narrow roads rise up out of the Central Valley, winding past mountain towns and highland farms before dropping down to a fertile plain that extends all the way north to the Nicaraguan border.

Comprising the Llanura (Plain) de San Carlos and the Llanura de Guatuso, this 40,000-square-kilometer (15,444-square-mile) area has been called the breadbasket of the nation, though rice bowl would be more accurate. Ticos eat rice with every meal (including breakfast), and most of the rice consumed in Costa Rica is grown here in the Zona Norte (Northern Zone). Three great rivers and their countless tributaries irrigate the region, flooding during heavy rains and creating the swampy conditions ideal for rice cultivation.

I've heard the area described as a tropical Tuscany or a steamier Oregon. Boulder-strewn streams alternate with lush farmland. You pass fields of knee-high pineapple plants, a single fruit at the center of each burst of blade-like leaves, and papayas growing on small trees, all the fruit hanging from the central stalk. Bean fields give way to rice paddies and banana groves.

Rising up out of this lush plain like a whale breaching the ocean's surface, Arenal Volcano is one of the most dramatic sights in the country. If you can see it, that is. Arenal is so often shrouded in clouds that some tourists wonder if the steep-sloped gem really exists or is just a clever figment of a tour agency's imagination. (One local guide reports that a tourist asked if they turned on the volcano at night.)

Whether or not you see it, you can always hear the volcano, grumbling deep in its fiery throat and just generally making sure you never forget that although it slept through the colonial times and most of the modern era, when it woke in 1968 its eruptions wiped out two towns. Not quite as furious now, it still coughs up smoke and truck-sized cinders daily, and on clear nights you can see red-hot rocks bouncing down the mountain. There's nothing like soaking in the hot springs at the foot of the volcano, a light cool rain pocking the water, secure in the knowledge that if Arenal blows again like it did in '68, you'll have about nine minutes to get out of the danger zone.

Around Arenal there are two seasons: wet and really wet. Theoretically, there's supposed to be less rain February through April, but locals rarely go out without a rain hat or umbrella. During the really wet season, they don't go out without heavy-duty slickers or ponchos. When it rains here, it pours, and it's part of local hospitality to offer you dry clothes if you arrive soaked.

Joy Rothke, a writer from California who lived several years in La Fortuna, says that the humid climate gave her a new appreciation for the clever survival strategies of mold, which takes hold in unlikely places, like books, jewelry, or even bills in a wallet.

There aren't many expats in the area yet, at least not when compared to the throngs in the Central Valley and along parts of the Pacific coast. Joy could tell me the names and histories of each of the handful of foreign residents living in and around La Fortuna. To thrive here requires integrating into the local community, which isn't always easy. "The locals [Costa Ricans] are friendly," says Joy's husband Bill, "but it's like you move to Maine from Wyoming, and two generations later, you're still the family from Wyoming. You can be accepted here, but you'll never be a Tico. You will forever be an outsider." This isn't something peculiar to the Zona Norte—I heard the same sentiments echoed all over the country, but in smaller towns with fewer expats, that truth may be felt more keenly.

La Fortuna

A town built in the shadow of Arenal Volcano, La Fortuna has, in the past few years, become something of a tourist hub. More than a dozen tour agencies line the main street, as do souvenir shops, whose most appealing wares come from Guatemala, Panama, and Indonesia (Costa Rica isn't known for its crafts). At the center of this town is not the usual soccer field (that's down the street, near the high school) but a plaza dominated by a basketball court, the backboards neon-orange advertisements for a rent-a-car company. Taxis line up along one side of the plaza; local buses stop along another. The inevitable Catholic church is unremarkable save for the view of the volcano as you look up from the main steps: The white cross on the church's roof is like a tattoo on Arenal's huge green shoulder.

Visitors on their way to Caño Negro Wildlife Preserve, windsurfers heading for Lake Arenal, or those who come to catch a glimpse of the volcano all pass through and often stay in Fortuna. To accommodate the influx, everybody and their dog seems to be building small hotels or tourist *cabinas,* some of which are little more than huts in someone's backyard. There's a lot of construction going on in town, and the place seems quite prosperous given that two decades ago it was hardly a bump in the road. Real estate is still reasonable (especially when compared to other parts of the country), but Fortuna is changing so rapidly that it's hard to predict how long that will last.

Most, but not all, business opportunities revolve around the tourist trade. Foreign residents run a variety of enterprises, including an adventure-tour agency, an Internet café, a massage parlor, various restaurants and hotels, and at least one art gallery.

There are some very pretty places to live just outside of town, especially near the river on the road to La Catarata, the local waterfall.

Nuevo Arenal

Though it's often called simply Arenal, the *nuevo* (new) in this town's official name reminds us that the old town is at the bottom of lovely and pristine Lake Arenal, a 32-kilometer (20-mile) reservoir created in 1973 when the Costa Rican Institute of Electricity (ICE) built a dam at the eastern end of the valley. ICE also erected wind turbines along the new lake's southwestern shore, taking advantage of the stiff winds (30–80 kph, 19–50 mph) that blow almost constantly and make Lake Arenal one of the world's best windsurfing spots.

Thankfully, Nuevo Arenal is more protected and is a pleasant, prosperous-looking town built on the lake's upsloping shore. Perhaps because it was a planned community, it looks more spacious and less haphazard than most Tico towns, though some newer construction seems to be slumping along in usual Costa Rican fashion.

One guidebook says this town of 2,500 has "nothing of tourist interest," but what draws tourists is not always what draws new residents. Though residents hope the area will never be as popular (or as expensive) as some of the Pacific coast beaches, it is nevertheless experiencing its own boom, with real estate prices rising and more people arriving all the time. Views of the lake from town are stunning, and the weather is temperate. Lakefront property is not subject to the same restrictions as beachfront property; if you find your Eden on Arenal's shores, you can own it outright rather than having to lease it from the state.

The town itself consists of a few dozen houses scattered in the folds of hills, the main street offering up a handful of businesses: a hardware store, a place to buy cowboy hats and saddles, a few restaurants and several bars, and a real estate office or two. Off the main street there's a well-established German bakery called Tom's Pan, where expats can linger over big German lunches or take home delicious bread and pastries. The land around town has quietly been changing hands over the past decade or two—from Tico to German, Swiss, Italian, U.S., Canadian, and other nationalities. But Nuevo Arenal still feels like a small Tico town, where people leave their doors open and keep their front yards neat and blooming.

Tilarán

Although it's only a few dozen kilometers from Nuevo Arenal to Tilarán, the unpredictable state of the highway means the trip could take anywhere from 30 minutes to well over an hour. Sometimes you'll fly along on what appears to be well-maintained blacktop, but don't be fooled—around the next bend may be a lacework of potholes or a mudslide blocking the way. Take your time and enjoy the view. The road skirts the north end of lovely Lake Arenal and is the site of an increasing number of hotels, lodges, and private homes. Five kilometers (three miles) after the road heads west, away from lake, it arrives in Tilarán, a pretty highland town with a population of around 22,000, including a number of expats. At 550 meters (1,804 feet) above sea level, Tilarán is high enough to have pine trees as well as palms in the town square, and the temperate climate, springlike and drier than Arenal, is a big draw.

Tilarán sits atop a hill, with the land sloping away to the west, down to the Guanacaste flats, and climbing a little more to the east, up to gorgeous Lake Arenal. The streets are wide and immaculate, and the soaring church tower is flanked by two tall monkey-puzzle trees. Last time I was in town, traffic slowed to let an iguana cross the street from the churchyard to the main plaza. In the shadow of the church is the town's vocational center, complete with horse and cattle stalls—ranching is one of the area's main sources of income and employment. From the main street, you can see Arenal Volcano in the distance, looking too small to do the damage it did during its last big eruption in 1968.

Not as many foreigners have chosen to settle in Tilarán as in Nuevo Arenal (the lake is a big draw), and the town feels like a Tico version of a Norman Rockwell painting. As in Nuevo Arenal, there are few bars on windows, and people leave their front doors open to the street. On weekends you'll see people working in their neat gardens or washing their cars out in front of well-maintained homes. Kids playing hopscotch on the sidewalk smile as you walk by; the older folk sit in rocking chairs on bougainvillea-draped tiled front porches.

There's an alternate route to Tilarán that spares you the Lake Arenal road. From San José you drive toward the Pacific coast, then go north for an hour or so on the Pan-American Highway. At Cañas you bear east on Highway 142, which winds through very pleasant rolling hills reminiscent of the Sierra Nevada foothills in northern California, except for the big volcanic boulders strewn among the grazing cattle. Golden grasses wave in the wind, stately trees spread their shade, and creeks run in the clefts of the hills.

Monteverde

In 1951 a small group of Quakers left Fairhope, Alabama, to settle on 1,214 fertile hectares (3,000 acres) high in Costa Rica's Cordillera de Tilarán. Of the fewer than 50 emigrants, five had just been released from prison for refusing to register for the draft. The judge had told them that they should obey the law of the land or leave the country, and after their release, the latter is exactly what they did. They chose Costa Rica because it had recently abolished its army, and had done away with the death penalty years earlier. Besides draft resisters, the group also included farmers, teachers, and a retired rural mail carrier.

It's hard to imagine that in the 1950s there was still an opportunity to be a pioneer, but at that time many parts of Costa Rica were still inaccessible or very sparsely settled (some parts still are today). The Quakers needed horses and oxcarts to convey their belongings to their new home; the roads were so bad that not even Jeeps could make the journey.

The land they purchased was at 1,400 meters (4,593 feet) and straddled both the Guacimal River and the continental divide. Plantlife was riotous and varied, a mix of tropical, subtropical, and, with the mist drifting in from the Atlantic side of the mountain, cloud forest as well. Wilford Guindon, one of the original settlers, spoke of the land's "drippy tropical tangle"; that tangle supported (and still supports) a great variety of wildlife. The more than 400 species of birds include 30 species of hummingbirds and the resplendent quetzal, a little-seen bird that draws naturalists to Monteverde.

Upon arrival, the settlers cleared land for crops and dairy cows, built houses and barns and roads, and founded a creamery that nowadays produces some of the best cheese in the country. Half a century after their arrival, the area is also one of the best-known tourist destinations in Costa Rica, in large part because of the private Monteverde Cloud Forest Reserve, one of the best wildlife reserves in the New World tropics.

Monteverde and nearby Santa Elena are still influenced by Los Cuaqueros (the Quakers), but the settlers have intermarried with local Costa Rican families, and now the two communities have formed a hybrid, with many a bilingual household and customs that include traditional Tico fiestas,

Quaker meetings, and the weekly Scrabble games instituted by some of the original settlers.

Over the years, many non-Quaker expats have joined the community, and modern-day Monteverde (which now numbers around 2,400) is an appealing mix of scientists, artists, retired folk, and dairy farmers. Wendy Rockwell, granddaughter of one of the original settlers, was born in Monteverde but went back to the United States to go to high school and college. She brought her California-born husband back to her birthplace, where they now run Chunches (a Costa Rican word for "stuff"), a kind of enlightened general store/launderette in the heart of Santa Elena. At Chunches you'll find everything from books on midwifery to a decent cappuccino, which you can sip as you wait for your clothes to dry.

Speaking of dry, Monteverde isn't. Like the area around Arenal, Monteverde (which means Green Mountain) is perpetually green. How does it stay so green? Rain, more rain, and then a little more rain. Locals learn not to wait for the skies to clear before getting on with their business. A little rain never hurt anyone, and a lot of rain—well, you'll probably live through that too. If you like perpetually clear skies and dry heat, by all means visit Monteverde, but don't plan to stick around.

It seems to me that settling here would appeal to a very special type of person—someone who is moved by the unusual history of the place and willing to participate in its multifaceted present. Residents here are aware and involved, especially in regards to environmental issues. Echoing Quaker practice, community decisions are made by consensus. One expat (who lives elsewhere in Costa Rica) called it a mini-Berkeley, after the city in California known for its progressive politics. But you won't find half as many butterflies in Berkeley, nor will you be able to walk through old-growth forest, marveling at how one tree can support so much life, from sinuous vines to blossoming bromeliads. Monteverde is like that tree: A surprising variety of species have found a home here.

SOUTHERN INLAND VALLEYS
San Isidro de General
Besides being the only stretch of the Pan-American Highway not called Highway 1, Highway 2 south of San José will put even the most confident driver to the test. One hundred kilometers (62 miles) from the capital, the road reaches the 3,500-meter (11,483-foot) peak at Cerro de la Muerte (Hill of Death), then plunges dizzyingly down. Landslides often block the way, potholes proliferate with each heavy rain, and dense fog adds spice to the brew. Big trucks

and diesel-spewing buses often hold up long lines of cars, with drivers waiting their turn to hazard passing on the winding road. But it's a stunning drive, especially when the mist clears to reveal jaw-dropping views.

What you'll see below, if the weather cooperates, is the Valle de El General, a 100-kilometer-long (62-mile-long) depression between the Talamanca range and the Fila Costeña. At about 700 meters (2,297 feet) in elevation, the valley is balmier than the Central Valley but not as hot as either coast. At the north end lies San Isidro de General, the regional capital and a natural stopping-off point for those looking to hike up nearby Cerro Chirripó (at 3,819 meters/12,530 feet, the highest peak in Central America south of Guatemala), raft the Ríos Chirripó and General, or continue on to Dominical and other Pacific beaches. It's also a bustling agricultural market town of around 35,000 people, the center of a fertile zone where pineapples are the major crop.

After the drama of the journey, the town itself may underwhelm, though it's a pleasant enough place. Laid out in a grid, the town is centered on the plaza at Calle Central and Avenida 0, with a concrete church at one end and an astonishing number of taxis lined up on three sides of the square. San Isidro de General is a young town—founded in 1897, but built mostly after World War II—and there's a palpable sense of commerce rather than history here.

The non-Ticos you'll see around town—those who aren't on their way to climb a mountain, run a river, or surf the beach break at Dominical—most likely don't live in the town proper but have made their stand near the beach or in the hills around San Isidro. They come to town to do their shopping, wait in line at the bank, or make use of the hospital, the biggest one for miles. Expats who live in or near the beach town of Dominical, for instance, regularly make the 40-minute drive up Highway 243 for San Isidro's better variety and lower prices, whether they're stocking up on food or shopping for building materials.

Guidebooks often describe San Isidro (also called Perez Zeledon, after the name of the district) as without interest or charm, but those who come here often find themselves developing an affection for this very Tico town. There's an excellent *polideportivo* (sports complex) at the edge of town, with a gym, a running track, and lush grounds for hiking or picnicking. And there's a good variety of restaurants, bars, and cafés. Sample the real Mexican food at Taquería México Lindo, or have an espresso at the Strapless Kafe, where Betty Boop, Jackie O, and Princess Di dolls peer out of locked glass cabinets. You'll almost certainly run into other expats—from North America, Europe, and South America—taking a break from their errand-running. Most foreign residents are appalled by the new McDonald's on the main highway, but local Ticos aren't averse to heading for the golden arches.

Though the coast is a definite expat magnet, there are those who have settled along the waterfall-rich stretch of road (Highway 243) from Dominical to San Isidro, in little mist-shrouded towns like Platanillo and Tinamastes. Some settle in the hills around San Isidro itself, like Ed Bernhardt, founder of the New Dawn Center (www.newdawncenter.org), an organic farm and education center 15 kilometers (nine miles) northwest of San Isidro. Two decades ago, Ed left the United States and settled here, choosing the area because it was far from what he saw as the Los Angelization of Costa Rica's Central Valley. The land was cheap, the people friendly, and, as a child of the turbulent 1960s in the United States, Ed wanted to settle in a country dedicated to peace. "The Ticos don't have the scars we carry," says Ed, "growing up with war."

Ed married a Tica, and the couple's two sons, now young adults, were born on the farm. "They were like nymphs, running around naked. Then they got socialized, and now they're Ticos." One of his sons attended "the first environmental high school in Costa Rica," founded by former neighbor Alexander Skutch (who died in 2004 at 99), coauthor of the classic *Birds of Costa Rica*. Ed himself contributes a weekly gardening column to the *Tico Times* and is the author of the highly detailed and useful *Costa Rican Organic Home Gardening Guide*.

Ed "goes into town" (San Isidro) a few times a week. The farm has no phone, no email, and no papaya or pineapple, though they do well with mangoes and avocados. "Each microclimate supports different crops," says Ed, just as each nook and cranny of Costa Rica sustains different varieties of expats. But Ed worries about how fast San Isidro is growing. "Did you see the McDonald's? That's a death knell if I ever heard one. Maybe it's time to move up to San Vito."

San Vito

Heading south from San Isidro, Highway 2 leaves the Valle de El General and enters the Valle de Coto Brus. The road is surprisingly good, at least until Paso Real, where those heading for San Vito leave the Pan-American Highway and take winding and scenic Route 237 up to the prosperous regional capital. This is coffee country, with glossy-leafed bushes marching up steep mountains and blanketing gentle slopes. Views of the valley below are spectacular.

Until the 1950s, the area was all but inaccessible, and indigenous peoples (the Guaymi and Boruca, among other groups) made up more than half of the area's population. The Pan-American Highway finally cut through to nearby

Buenos Aires in 1961, and by then nonindigenous Costa Ricans had begun
to outnumber the original inhabitants.

Non-Ticos also had a hand in changing the face of the area. In 1949, an
Italian named Vito Sansonetti visited the remote valley and was so drawn to
the fertile and heavily forested frontier that he set in motion what was essentially an Italian colonization of the area. Scores of war-stricken families, most
from the south of Italy, saw in the plan the opportunity for a fresh start. The
Costa Rican government helped to finance a proposal in which 250 families,
20 percent of them Ticos, would settle in what became San Vito. The plan
became reality in the early 1950s, and in San Vito today, though most of the
Italian settlers have married into Tico families or returned to Italy, there are
still traces of their influence, from blue and green eyes to the excellent pasta
at places like Liliana's Restaurant, just uphill from the tiny central park.

Early townspeople made good use of the area's temperate climate, planting the bushes that would make the valley the country's largest coffee-
producing region.

One of the town's draws is its climate—warm days and nights cool enough
for a real blanket. Stands of pine alternate with tall tropical hardwoods draped
with vines and orchids. The abundance of budget hotels in town might lead
you to believe that this is a tourist center, but don't be fooled—these rooms
fill up with Ticos, most of them traveling on business. Besides the Italian
colony, other stray foreign residents have made their way here, but they are
the exception to the rule and usually arrive for a very specific purpose. Their
stories demonstrate how far hard work and a consuming passion can take you,
and also how recently this area has been "settled," though indigenous peoples
had been scattered across the zone for centuries.

Darryl Cole-Christensen, for example, came with his family from the United
States in the 1950s to carve a farm and a life out of what was nearly impen-
etrable rainforest. In his book, *A Place in the Rain Forest: Settling the Costa
Rican Frontier,* he tells of how the roads, when they existed, were too much
for Jeeps and, during the rainiest parts of the year, even impassable to horses.
In his book he takes a thoughtful look at the frontier mentality that allowed
settlers to "tame" the land but which resulted in the destruction of vast tracts
of tropical forest.

"The frontier was generally seen at this time in two ways," writes Cole-
Christensen. "There was the land, and there was the forest. On the land homes
could be raised, communities would rise," and crops could be planted. The
forest, on the other hand, "was the great obstacle and antagonist to overcome."
Settlers were hardworking and resourceful folk. They saw a fertile land and

believed the abundance would shine forth even after they'd cut down the forest and planted crops. What they eventually realized, explains Cole-Christensen, is that the fertility of the rainforest lies in its canopy rather than in the soil. But the farmers prevailed, using their newfound knowledge to raise crops and a community on the land. Cole-Christensen still lives in the area, and his farm, Finca Loma Linda, has been given over to research of tropical sustainable farming methods.

The rich flora of the area also drew Robert and Catherine Wilson, who first came in 1959 and shortly thereafter bought a ridgetop farm that had been denuded by years of cattle grazing. The couple had run a tropical plant nursery in Florida, and they wanted to see what marvels they might be able to raise and sell in the lush environment just above San Vito. When they realized that their location was too remote to be the base for a successful tropical plant business, they allied themselves with the Organization for Tropical Studies (OTS, a worldwide consortium of 66 universities and research stations, six of them in Costa Rica). The Wilson Botanical Garden was born. Now part of the Las Cruces Biological Station, today the garden welcomes mostly students and scientists, though bird-watching and plant-loving tourists have begun to discover this 283-hectare (700-acre) gem, which boasts 5,100 species of plants, 330 species of birds, and dozens of mammal species, including 37 kinds of bats.

Catherine Wilson died in 1984, Robert in 1989. The Wilsons loved their adopted land so passionately that they wanted to be buried here, on the reserve itself. Friends who tried to honor their wishes ran into problems, however. By Costa Rican law, bodies can only be buried in a cemetery. After much bureaucratic wrangling, a solution was found: A tiny piece of the reserve was declared a cemetery. "A very selective cemetery," says resident biologist Rodolfo Quiros. "Just two people are buried there"—the two expats who dedicated more than half their lives to turning a cattle pasture into a remarkable garden and reserve.

GUANACASTE AND THE NICOYA PENINSULA

In its early years, Guanacaste was independent from the rest of Costa Rica, and to this day the area retains its own flavor quite distinct from the rest of the country. First its own province, then a part of Nicaragua, Guanacaste didn't officially became part of Costa Rica until 1858. Home of the *sabanero* (cowboy), this area is the country's Wild West—where a maverick spirit combines with the interdependence necessary in a frontier society—and also its Gold Coast, with 70 percent of the nation's beach resort infrastructure. Local residents consider themselves Guanacastecos first and Ticos second. In fact, the Guanacasteco heritage is so strong that it has seeped into the national character, with the spreading guanacaste tree the Costa Rican national tree and the local *punto guanacasteco* celebrated as the national dance.

Even the weather here is at odds with the rest of the country, much to the visitor's delight. They say the sun shines brighter here, and it most definitely shines longer. From mid-November through April, the area receives almost no rain, a boon to those from northern climes used to seemingly

© ERIN VAN RHEENEN

endless rain, sleet, and snow during the North American winter (which is Costa Rica's "summer," or dry season). Newcomers can't believe their luck, but even so, by May everyone is ready for the rain that transforms the yellow-and-brown landscape back into a riot of lush green. Chris Simmons, originally from Vancouver but now in the beach town of Tamarindo for the past decade, says, "Everyone remembers the first day of rain—last year it was May 18. By the end of April, you're thinking, It's got to come. People who can't wait shoot up to Arenal for a couple of days," where the two seasons are wet and really wet.

The Lay of the Land

The second-largest province (about 10,000 square kilometers/3,861 square miles), Guanacaste has the fewest inhabitants (around 265,000) of all seven provinces. The heart of Guanacaste is a sparsely populated plain that extends northward to Nicaragua. To the east rise two mountain ranges, the Cordillera de Guanacaste and the Cordillera de Tilarán, and to the north loom several volcanoes, many of which are protected in national parks. The largest towns are small by North American standards: Liberia, the provincial capital and the largest town in the area, has all of 40,000 residents. The Liberia airport began to receive commercial flights in 2002, and more and more flights are added each year. This development is transforming not only Liberia (some locals predict it will be "the next San José") but the nearby Guanacaste beaches as well, some of which, like Playas del Coco, are only 30 or 40 minutes from Liberia by car. Another change in accessibility came in 2003 with the long-awaited completion of the Taiwan Friendship Bridge across the Tempisque River, which separates the 130-kilometer-long (81-mile-long) Nicoya Peninsula from the mainland. Previously there was a slow ferry that could only carry 40 cars at a time, and waits were up to two hours. Now you can whiz across the bridge, cutting hours off the trip from San José to midpeninsula beach towns such as Tamarindo, Nosara, or Sámara.

On the Nicoya Peninsula, the most bustling towns are inland, strung out along Highway 21, which runs from Liberia through Filadelfia, Santa Cruz, and Nicoya, Costa Rica's oldest colonial city and the place beach dwellers go to do their shopping if they're not up for the trip to the capital. From the inland cities, a web of roads—some paved, most not—extends to remote beaches and coastal towns so laid back that each day seems to last a week. These are the kinds of places where the local grocery store lets everyone run a tab, and where you run into the same people seven times a day.

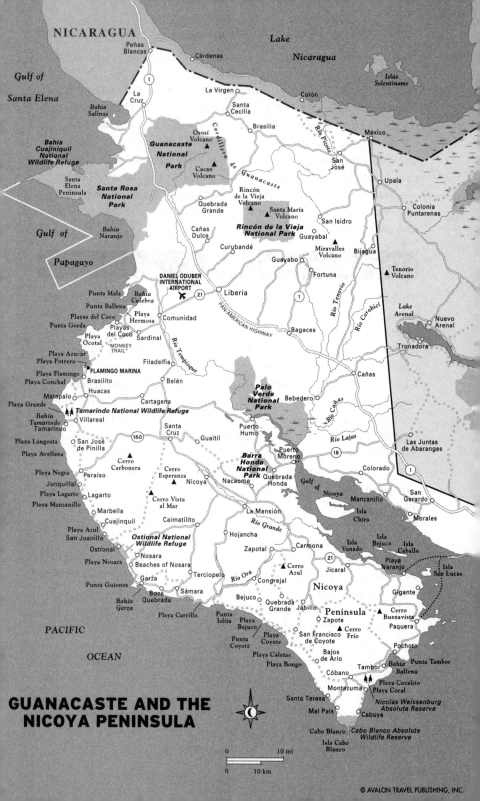

Most newcomers to Guanacaste choose to live on or near the beach, where ocean breezes alleviate the dry-season heat. The Nicoya Peninsula—most of which lies within the province of Guanacaste—is where you'll find most of the coveted beachfront property, with more ground cleared every day for new development. There are towns where you'll be hard-pressed to find many locals. Many hotels, restaurants, and real estate agencies are owned by foreigners, among them Germans, Americans, Canadians, Italians, Swiss, and French. There are also growing numbers of immigrants from other Latin American countries such as Argentina, Colombia, Peru, and Nicaragua, drawn to Costa Rica's peaceful and stable environment and looking to escape their home country's economic, political, or military strife. "It used to be," a Peruvian told me about his home of Lima, the capital city, "they'd kill you on your way to work. Now they kill you on your way to *look* for work. Here it's *tranquilo,* and you can find a job without much problem."

Every year, a local tells me, the number of foreigners who come to live (rather than just visit) increases. It takes some of them years to build their houses—they go back to the States to work, then come down and build another room. But there are also those, with more resources and more time, who build fantasy houses overlooking the Pacific or who invest in already-built homes or condos, many in gated communities with golf courses, stables, and their own supply of water and electricity. Some of the country's biggest developments are located in northern Guanacaste, like the Club Med–style Playa Melía Conchal (just north of Tamarindo). In 2003, a large and luxurious resort complex opened along the Gulf of Papagayo, anchored by a Four Seasons hotel and offering up lots and pricey housing options for those who want to own a piece of that coast.

It's an odd combination of rapid development—the building trade is booming, employing many grateful locals—and underdevelopment, with rutted dirt roads leading to million-dollar spreads. Infrastructure can be a problem, with overextended municipalities unable to fix the roads or improve electrical, water, and waste-removal systems. Often developers or homeowners shoulder what in other countries would be the state's burden, paying for new roads, stringing electrical wires, and arranging for secure water supplies and waste removal. During the dry season, water can become a real problem, especially with elaborately landscaped grounds and sprawling golf courses sucking up so much of the precious fluid.

In terms of prices, real estate agents and contractors say that building costs here are higher because so much of the material must be trucked in, often via

REVIVAL OF A PRE-COLUMBIAN PAST

Perched on a wooden stool in his open-air studio, Jesús Villareal slips moistened fingers around the rim of a bowl revolving on a potter's wheel. To his right is what looks like an enormous wooden mortar and pestle, in which Jesús's wife, Susan Chavaria, pounds earth to the fine powder required for the best clay. The earth comes from the low hills above town, from spots locals have been digging for thousands of years. And just as their Chorotega ancestors did, Jesús and Susan will polish the pottery with jadelike stones said to come from nearby archaeological sites.

Although it might seem that Jesús and Susan are part of a long and unbroken tradition of indigenous pottery-making, in fact the tradition had all but died out when recently is began to be revived.

Jesús puts aside the still-wet bowl and turns to a row of kiln-fired vases. He dips brushes into little jars of glaze arrayed on the table before him. Earlier Jesús and Susan carefully ground powders made of earth or dried plants, adding water to create the earth-toned colorings that make their pieces come alive. Behind Jesús is the beehive-shaped kiln in which the family fires the pieces that line the shelves of the gift store at the other end of the studio.

Working in the tradition of their Chorotega ancestors, Jesús and Susan also consult a heavily illustrated academic reference work, *Costa Rica Precolumbina* (Pre-Columbian Costa Rica), by Luis Ferrero. The book is as treasured and battered as an old family bible. It's been in the family for about 20 years, Jesús says, and he often models his own work after the ancient examples of Chorotega pottery pictured in the book. Such are the ironies of ancient traditions lost and found.

Jesús, Susan, and their family are among a handful of clans that make up the village of Guatíl, the epicenter of a renaissance in Chorotega ceramics that draws tourists and locals interested in the area's pre-Columbian past and its indigenous present. Often presided over by matriarchs who have been working with clay since they were girls and who learned their craft from mothers and grandmothers, the families of Guatíl are hoping that reviving the work of their matrilineal tribal ancestors will prove not only spiritually satisfying but also economically viable. Pottery is the only "industry" in this

some truly atrocious roads. In Playa Negra, south of Tamarindo, I watched as a truck sent to repair some enormous potholes (which the rains had turned into muddy lagoons) became stuck in one of the very holes it had hoped to fix. A tractor had to come and pull it out.

From the Gulf of Papagayo down to funky Montezuma at the southern tip of the peninsula, Guanacaste and the Nicoya Peninsula feature stunning beaches and beach towns that range from party central to places so remote they verge on inaccessible.

© ERIN VAN RHEENEN

Jesús Villareal with the book that helps him revive ancient Chorotega pottery designs

with some of the artists and to look at their different takes on Chorotega themes: figures that are half-animal, half-human or ones that have exaggerated genitalia in celebration of fertility; plates, bowls, and vases enlivened with the traditional geometric or botanical patterns in black, ocher, and red. Also take time to head down the road to San Vicente, another small town known for its pottery.

Costa Rica has not traditionally been seen as a place to encounter Central America's indigenous heritage. It doesn't have the majestic ruins of high-profile pre-Columbian empires like the Aztec, the Maya, or the Inca. And its modern-day indigenous population is small in comparison to those in countries like Mexico and Guatemala. But pre-Columbian Costa Rica was in an interesting position in that it was a crossroad of sorts. Objects and traditions from as far north as Mexico and as far south as Ecuador and Peru found their way to Costa Rica. The Gran Nicoya, located in what today is Guanacaste and the Nicoya Peninsula, was most influenced by Mesoamerican cultures from the north like the Maya, Aztec, and Olmec. From these and other cultures came traditions and pottery styles now being revived in towns like Guatíl.

tiny town on the Nicoya Peninsula (12 kilometers east of Santa Cruz). The town is arrayed around a soccer field and consists of a church, a small general store, and a dozen or so spreads that do triple duty as studios, shops, and family homes.

Roll into town and you won't have to ask where the pottery is – pottery is all there is here. Unless you coincide with a small tourist van you may be the only visitor around. Take time to talk

PRICES

Guanacaste's Gold Coast, which runs from above Playa Potrero to just south of Tamarindo, is one of the priciest areas in the country. New construction is mostly aimed at foreigners with comfortable incomes; condos and new homes go for from US$200,000 to over US$1 million. Aside from the dizzying prices at places like the Four Seasons resort complex north of Coco, Tamarindo has the dubious distinction of being the highest priced town on this high-priced stretch of coast.

There's a lot of construction going on in places like Playas del Coco, Playa Ocotal, and Liberia, too. Some of it, like the many projects under the direction of the Mapache Group (www.grupomapache.com), are more moderately priced, with studio-style condos going for around US$60,000 and a two-bedroom duplex for less than US$200,000.

Farther south, on stretches of coast that are harder to get to and so remain sparsely settled, you can still find better prices for lots and houses. If you're willing to live inland you can find *much* better deals.

How much better? It depends on luck, timing, and (most of all) persistence. As I say elsewhere, there's no substitute for on-the-ground research. The more you know the better deal you'll get.

Where to Live

PLAYAS DEL COCO TO TAMARINDO

The concave sweep of coastline south of Santa Elena and north of the Nicoya Peninsula is dominated by the Golfo de Papagayo, an enormous gulf that holds within its waters smaller and more protected bays and coves, like the nearly enclosed Bahia Culebra, or Snake Bay.

More than half of the gulf's stunning coastline and nearly all of the scrubby interior of the Santa Elena Peninsula is protected in Santa Rosa National Park, home to oft-deserted Playa Naranjo and a dramatic outcropping just offshore called Witch's Rock, mythic in surfing circles. The route to this remote wave-riders' mecca is either by boat or overland on one of the worst roads in the country.

The formation of the park had a few high-profile twists and turns. Several decades ago, Anastasio Somoza, former ruler of Nicaragua, owned the Hacienda Murciélago (Bat Ranch) on the Santa Elena peninsula. In 1979 the Costa Rican government decided it didn't want to host an ousted dictator, and furthermore that the flora and fauna of this remote area needed protection from encroaching development. Hacienda Murciélago was seized and became part of Santa Rosa National Park. Another addition to the park came in the form of the once-secret Santa Elena airstrip, used by Oliver North and his Contra buddies in their fight to undermine Nicaragua's Sandinista government in the 1980s. Oscar Arias (in his first presidency, and in the role of Central American peacemaker) shut down the strip in 1986. Surfers still refer to a nearby landmark as Ollie's Point.

More accessible (and ownable) land begins around Nacasolo, at the northern headland of Snake Bay. But even that area is fairly remote; most people choose to live in the Playas del Coco area, which includes (from north to

DO YOU REALLY WANT TO LIVE ON THE BEACH?

We're talking Guanacaste (the northern Pacific coast) here, but most of the concerns apply to any Costa Rican beach community.

1. Weather is a big issue – it's much hotter and drier on the coast than in the Central Valley.

2. Doing business here is good, though it's not easy. It's competitive, and it ain't pretty. You need the same things to succeed here in business that you'd need to succeed anywhere: hard work and the ability to overcome obstacles. But here what's more important is a big dose of patience.

3. Consider your social life – do you want to get involved, volunteer, do activities? If not, you'll be pretty isolated and won't have much to do.

4. Rent first, for a year.

5. If you're a perfectionist and can't roll with the punches, don't even think about moving here.

– *Thanks to Chris Simmons of Remax Real Estate in Tamarindo.*

PRIME LIVING LOCATIONS

south) Playas Panama, Hermosa, Coco, and Ocotal. A perfect semicircle of gray sand, **Playa Panama** is so protected that there are hardly any waves breaking on its quiet shores.

Playa Hermosa is one of the most beautiful beaches in this area, and the number of visitors it receives reflects that. Condos and hotels climb the hill north of town. Boogie boards and kayaks lie in multicolored stacks on the beach, ready to be rented. Roving vendors sell coconuts (for the refreshing milk) and souvenirs; you don't see that on the other beaches in the region, except maybe Coco during the highest season. The water is cool enough to be refreshing on a hot day but warm enough to stay in for hours without feeling chilled. Waves break close to shore; out beyond the breakers you can still stand. Swells lift you off your feet and deposit you gently back down on the white-sand bottom.

Although there's just one beach, **Playas del Coco** is always expressed in the plural. The name also applies to the lively strip of a town that runs a few kilometers from the beach inland, where you'll find not only good seafood restaurants and fun dive bars, but also real-life services like banks, hardware stores, and supermarkets. On the hills above **Playa Ocotal,** just south of

EXPAT PROFILE:
WEDDING PLANNERS IN LALA LAND

When Stephen Denton and Anahi Contreras married in 1998, they had a simple ceremony. Sure, it was in Costa Rica, but there were no tiki torches on the beach, no barefoot wedding party wearing orchid leis, no vows timed to coincide with the setting of the tropical sun.

Neither dreamed that a few years later they'd be helping other couples pull off their fantasy beachside weddings. Anahi is the Tamarindo coordinator for Tropical Occasions, founded by Aimee Monihan, one of the first independent destination wedding planners in Costa Rica. And Stephen, who has done everything from run a dive shop to manage property, pitches in as occasional officiator (he's a Reverend in the Universal Life Church) and sometimes DJs for the parties afterward.

Their entry into the wedding business came about serendipitously – which is not to say Stephen and Anahi aren't focused and ambitious. They are. Stephen has a master's in business administration from the University of Costa Rica; Anahi has a BA in political science from George Washington University and a master's in ecotourism from CATIE (a tropical agriculture school and research center here in Costa Rica). Both are bilingual and bicultural, if not multilingual and pan-cultural.

The daughter of a diplomat, Anahi was born in Paraguay and lived in (among other counties) Belgium, Japan, Brazil, and El Salvador. She speaks Spanish, English, Portuguese, and French.

Stephen was born in Michigan, moved to California as a young child, then to Costa Rica with his family in 1975. He went to high school here, headed back to the United States for college, then returned to Costa Rica.

Once Stephen and Anahi linked forces, they lived in Montreal for a few years, which they loved but which also taught them, Stephen says, "the value of connections – of knowing people in the place you're trying to start a career, a business, or even just a social life." And they missed Latin America. They decided they wanted to go back to working in the hospitality industry. They considered several options, including relocating to Costa Rica's humid Caribbean coast, which in the end they thought would be a harder place than the Pacific coast to make a living, and which Stephen voted against because he has "a problem with mold and damp – "I really don't like slipping under damp sheets at night, or having mold grow in my shoes."

Meanwhile, they'd told family and friends in Costa Rica that they were looking for work at a hotel or B&B. And here's where the beauty of connections comes in. Stephen's older brother Fred was good friends with Aimee's husband. Aimee (who Anahi later would go to work for as a wedding planner) is a friend of Barry and Suzy. Barry and Suzy needed someone to manage their Tamarindo B&B, Villa Alegre. So Stephen took the job of manager, and he and Anahi moved to Tamarindo, which is, lucky for Stephen, one of the drier places in Costa Rica. And it's a boomtown with a lot of opportunity for creative and hardworking people.

"In a place like Tamarindo,"

says Stephen, "there's so much growth, so much opportunity. If you have the staying power to survive the first year, you'll probably do okay. The first year is the hardest. There's so much to figure out, down to where you pay your electric bill. Do you go out to that little house in Villa Real, or do you pay it online and then fax a copy to the electric company in Santa Cruz? Once you get all that rolling, you start to know more and more people, and things start happening for you."

"The challenge of living in Tamarindo," Anahi adds, "is that it's so expensive. As a local, you have to pick and choose when and where you want to go out. As for cooking at home, you have to remember that the produce truck only comes Wednesdays and Thursdays, and will be here from 6 A.M. to noon. If you miss that, you won't have the lettuce for your salad."

The town (and in fact the entire country) demands resourcefulness, and that trait serves Anahi well in her work as a wedding planner. She tells me that most couples want to get married on the beach at sunset, which means the entire day must be planned with military precision around the tide tables and the exact moment the sun drops below the water.

"There's a website where you plug in the date and where you are," Anahi tells me, "and it gives you the exact time of sunset for that day. " "The ceremony needs to be finished just as the sun is hitting the horizon," Stephen adds. "That's when you have the beautiful golden light for photos." Tides can be a problem. "The last wedding I officiated at," says Stephen, "the waves were washing up over my feet. But of course everyone was barefoot – we knew the tides would come in and everyone had left their shoes up the beach."

People choose to get married in Costa Rica for the romance of it, of course, but there are also practical sides to destination weddings. They're usually cheaper, for one thing. For what a couple would pay for just the wedding up north, they can have the wedding here, plus a trip to Costa Rica and perhaps that trip for a few close relatives and friends.

Another reason for having a destination wedding is to limit the guest list. "A couple I'm working with right now," says Anahi, "had more than 100 people they felt they needed to invite. But they didn't really want all those people to come. Having a wedding in a foreign country can be a diplomatic way of reducing your guest list. Usually only those closest to you will attend."

"But once in a while, that backfires," Stephen points out, "and everyone shows."

"That's what happened with this couple," says Anahi, "People hear they have an excuse to go to Costa Rica, and suddenly more people are RSVPing than the hosts expected."

Any final words of wisdom for people thinking of not just getting married here but actually making a new life?

"Learn Spanish," says Anahi.

"Make sure you're realistic about what you plan on doing and what your life will be like here," advises Stephen. "It's not like being on vacation. Don't live completely in Lala Land when you're planning your move. I mean, partial Lala is fine. Partial Lala is Costa Rica."

PRIME LIVING LOCATIONS

Playas del Coco, million-dollar vacation homes and more modest condos overlook the secluded gray-sand beach. Many of the properties available here lie within gated communities, a security plus for owners who only make it down a month or two every year.

Playas Flamingo, Brasilito, and **Potrero** lie just north of Tamarindo, with radiant Playa Flamingo serving as the central community and boasting the prettiest beach—Christopher P. Baker, in his *Moon Handbooks Costa Rica,* calls it one of the most magnificent beaches in the country. Some say nearby Playa Brasilito has been compromised by the Melía Conchal Resort, which bulldozed a lot of the funkiness out of the place. Still, a sizable community of expats has settled here and in nearby Playa Potrero. A few years ago the prestigious Country Day School of Escazú opened a branch just outside Potrero, making the area more attractive to expats with school-age children.

Ironically, the Country Day School building was constructed by Melía Conchal; it was meant to be a small shopping center. Country Day School converted the shops to classrooms and added a gymnasium and a swimming pool. The school goes from pre-kindergarten through 12th grade. Most students are children of expats, but a few are local Ticos, some on full scholarship. Yearly fees amount to some US$25,000 for boarding students and US$7,000 for day students, unthinkable sums for most Ticos and prohibitive for many expats as well. But outside the Central Valley, good private schools are few and far between, and some expats would no more send their kids to a Costa Rican public school than they would trust their health to the Caja, the government-sponsored health care system. Other expats choose to partake of Costa Rica's extensive social services and have good things to say about the school and health care systems, considered some of the best in Latin America.

TAMARINDO TO OSTIONAL

Someone should print up T-shirts that say "I survived Tamarindo." This is the new Wild West, its outlaws not only the druggy thieves drawn to any tourist hot spot but also the wheeling and dealing developers intent on making a killing off this town's painfully loud and fast boom.

The former fishing village has good bones—great weather, a lovely span of white-sand beach, and an international cast of characters. But the flesh hanging off those bones is getting so heavy it's a wonder the carcass is still upright.

It's like many towns that develop too fast—the infrastructure, such as it is, just can't keep pace with the influx of new residents and the increasing number of visitors. Imagine sushi restaurants, surf shops, and art galleries with first-world prices strung along a couple of decidedly third-world roads, dusty in dry season and a stew of mud when it rains. Drivers slow to a crawl as they try to get around the huge trucks bearing building materials for the next condo project.

The town has come a long way, fast, from its origins as a funky little community where a few in-the-know surfers carved their names on empty waves. The development in this town is staggering, and the prices are some of the highest in the country.

Longtime residents, both Tico and expat, are trying to help the town through its growing pains. Many of the local hotels and restaurants are owned and run by Italian, German, Dutch, Swiss, Canadian, and American expats, to name just a few of the nationalities represented in this multicultural burg. Some of those business owners came together in 1993 to form the Asociación Pro-Mejoras de Tamarindo (Association for the Betterment of Tamarindo), "dedicated to satisfying the needs of tourists without compromising the environment and rich biodiversity of the area."

It's no secret that without tourism and wealthy foreigners looking to buy vacation homes, towns like Tamarindo would most likely dry up and blow away. But it's also clear that people visit for the beauty of the natural environment, which must be preserved while the town's basic needs are seen to. The association organizes and lobbies to keep the streets in decent repair, protect sources of potable water, and make sure there's a waste-management system in place.

Italian expat Simona Filippini, who with her sister founded the hotel/dance studio/community center Arco Iris, says it's gratifying to work at this sort of grassroots level. Though there are frustrations, she feels like these sorts of citizen groups can have more impact here in Costa Rica "where things aren't so fixed, and where there's more room to move." The association puts out a bilingual newsletter, *Noticias de Tamarindo/Tamarindo News,* whose masthead quotes Molly Ivins: "Where there is greed there is no vision," and then adds its own motto: "Don't let individual short-term gain prevent us from doing what's best for the future of our community."

Despite the increasingly gritty feel of the town, people who come to visit often want to stay, and this small town has a disproportionate number of real estate agencies to help them in that pursuit. You've got Remax, run by Canadians; Hidden Coast, with Dutch and Argentine agents; and numerous agencies run by escapees from the United States.

South of Tamarindo is one of the older developments in the area, a sprawling gated community called **Hacienda Pinilla.** Billing itself as "an exclusive resort community," the development spreads across more than 1,821 hectares

PRIME LIVING LOCATIONS

(4,500 acres) of a former cattle ranch and stretches along 5.5 kilometers (3.5 miles) of coastline. Pat Pattillo of Pattillo Construction, an Atlanta-based developer, bought the land in the early 1980s but only recently began transforming it into an upscale complex geared to wealthy North Americans who want to relocate or buy vacation homes.

Pattillo had to start from scratch, building roads; putting in phone, electrical, and sewage systems; and planting tens of thousands of trees in an effort to bring back to life vast tracts of land denuded by cattle grazing.

Farther south, **Playa Junquillal, Playa Avellana,** and **Playa Negra,** which used to draw only surfers willing to rough it, are having their own building boomlets, as Tamarindo pushes its own envelope. But it's still true that the expats you meet on this stretch of coast are likely to be fiercely independent men (and rarely, women) with a mission. Take Ray Beise, a former Minnesotan crackling with energy and ideas. Just up the road from Paraíso and a few kilometers inland from Playa Negra, Ray has created Pura Jungla, 100 hectares (250 acres) of ecologically sound development containing 32 building sites of about 0.8 hectare (two acres) each (much of the land will be left undeveloped).

"What you're looking at right now," Ray told me, as we stood in lush woodlands, listening to birds try to outdo each other in song, "was a cattle pasture. There were no animals, no trees, no iguanas, no bugs, no spiders, no cockroaches—nothing. It was burnt, dried-up cattle pasture. What we had here 15 years ago you couldn't even call earth—the land was hard as concrete. A herd of buffalo could walk across it and you'd never know they'd been there—it was so hard they wouldn't even leave a mark. Now it's soft. In the wet season you'll sink up to your ankles. We've done all kinds of work in soil building, soil regeneration. Water is the key to the regenerative process. If you have water, a lot of the regenerative process will happen on its own. All of these little *quebradas* (creeks) that are dry now, would have run, 100 years ago, all year long. We're trying to work with the land so that the water stays, doesn't just run off, taking all the soil nutrients with it."

Residents must agree to leave about a third of their land undeveloped, ensuring that living in Pura Jungla will continue to be like "living inside a national park," and guarding against the building of monster houses that push against lot boundaries. Two homes have already been built, and five more are on the drawing board. The house I saw was like a luxury tree house, built on stilts and floored with tropical hardwood; it had sweeping views of the ocean from its upper levels.

South of the Playa Negra area you'll find small fishing villages like **San**

Juanillo, or slightly bigger Tico towns like **Ostional,** whose beach is known for its *arrivadas,* great invasions of egg-laying Ridley turtles.

Between Ostional and Nosara runs the Río Montaña, often impassable during the rainy season. I had to hire a big tractor (called a *chapulín,* or grasshopper) to pull me across. It was either that or backtrack all the way to Playa Negra and then head inland for the better roads. The trip back would have added three or four hours to my journey; the *chapulín* cost me about five dollars.

NOSARA, SÁMARA, AND PLAYA CARRILLO

Nosara is a quiet place that grows on you. Guidebooks say there's not much to do here, and in terms of sights, they're right. What people do is stick around and soak up the good vibes. The Nosara Yoga Institute up on the hill casts a benevolent eye over the community, and the town attracts residents whose idea of heaven is to perfect their headstand, amble along one of the three absolutely pristine beaches, or paddle out to surf when the waves are big. Mornings, locals meet at Café de Paris for good coffee and even better blueberry muffins.

The town has two main parts: **Bocas de Nosara,** five kilometers (three miles) inland and a typical Tico small town, clustered around the soccer field; and **Beaches of Nosara,** closer to the beach and home to a large foreign community, made up mostly of American and Canadian expats who live in houses tucked among lush trees and flowers.

Although Nosara is blessed with stunning natural beauty, it isn't by accident that the area has avoided some of the worst pitfalls of seaside tourist towns. Residents are active in keeping their town low-key, and the Nosara Civic Association leads the way. The association began back in 1962, when Allan Hutchison bought 121 hectares (300 acres) in Nosara, built roads, put in electrical wires, and drilled wells to create one of the only private water systems in the country. He sold off parcels within this area and charged residents a monthly fee for the water and services.

"Water is the key," says Linda Cox, former manager of the association. "If you have good water, everything else is gravy." But Costa Rica is known for its potable water, and the association is about more than a steady supply of water. It also works to improve trash pickup, sends out crews to maintain the roads when the municipality can't afford to, and perhaps most important, works doggedly to see that development doesn't spin out of control.

The association influences development within and outside its boundaries. The fact that few structures in Beaches of Nosara are over two stories is no accident. Builders aren't following municipal zoning laws but rather are

EXPAT PROFILE: BRENDA BURNSIDE

I stumbled across a boxing gym in the jungle entirely by accident. The place I'd wanted to spend the night in the Pacific beach town of Nosara had closed, but the ex-manager said I might try Brenda next door – sometimes she rented out *cabinas*. I should look for the little path just past the stone that's painted bright blue.

And there the path was, littered with tiny purple blossoms and wending its way across a stream and to an unlocked gate. Brenda? I called out. Dogs started to bark, and soon a woman with short-cropped blonde hair appeared. She had tiger-stripe tattoos up and down her bare arms and legs.

It was Brenda Burnside, former professional boxer and owner of the shady domain she calls the Enchanted Forest. And the tattoos? She was called the Tigress, she told me. There'd even been a film made about her, called *A Tiger by Her Stripes.*

The heart of this tigress's domain is an open-air gym, with a high thatched roof from which bats swoop out during late-afternoon training sessions, feasting on mosquitoes. There's also a lovely domed-ceiling sauna made of fragrant cedar wood that she fires up after classes, an outdoor kitchen, and a scattering of one-room cabins.

As birds squawked and fire ants nipped at my ankles, I wondered: What had brought this woman to a quiet town on a pristine stretch of Costa Rican coastline?

A dream, as it turned out. Her first visit, in 1999, coincided with one of the largest *arrivadas* in years. An *arrivada* is when sea tur-

tles arrive on the beaches by the hundreds, scrambling up the sand to lay their eggs. Brenda had never seen anything like it, and she went to sleep that night with images of the vast army still in her head.

She dreamed of a turtle diving into a hole made not of air nor water but of something in between. She followed the turtle in and there encountered a sea of eyes – the slanted eyes of this area's Brahmin cattle, the round dark eyes of the local howler monkeys, and the ancient eyes of Ridley turtles – all looking at her and beckoning.

Brenda woke up feeling that she was needed here in some way, and that she had to find a way to live here. On the remaining days of her vacation, she looked into real estate and learned that a nearby piece of land was available. It had been for sale for 18 years, the real estate agent told her. Nobody wanted it. The price was about US$30,000.

First she used the land as a campground, but she knew that although she'd retired from pro boxing in 2000, she didn't want to entirely give it up.

When she first arrived, she'd done exhibition matches during halftime at bullfights. The guys were impressed; they couldn't believe a woman could fight. Someone said she should give lessons to the kids in Nosara, which is what she started doing. The kids loved her classes. First it was 7 people, then 20, then 40. But Brenda had trouble with her feet and the cement floor at the local community center where she'd give the classes.

She started building a wood-

© ERIN VAN RHEENEN

Brenda Burnside, ex-professional boxer, keeps in shape in her "jungle gym."

floored gym on her land, tearing the floor out twice to get it to her liking. The resulting space is beautiful and well equipped, though Brenda jokes that it's her Flintstone gym – along with the regulation heavy bags are sand-filled inner tubes, and some of her weights are Coke bottles filled with sand. But people come, and more will come when school's out in December. The boys love it, but she wants especially to encourage the girls. Brenda's dream was to be an Olympic athlete, and though she was good at many things – fencing got her closest, she thinks – she never quite made it. Women's boxing will soon be an Olympic sport, and Brenda would love to see a girl from Costa Rica make it to the Olympic ring.

By 2007, the Enchanted Forest had a boxing ring with room for 100 spectators (Brenda calls it her stadium), along with a restaurant. Brenda gives boxing lessons and arranges exhibition matches, popular with both locals and tourists. She also sometimes rents out her enchanted premises for private gatherings.

Her time here hasn't been without challenges, but she loves living in Costa Rica. "In the States you always have to be doing something. Here, you can be productive but still live day to day. It's hard to describe. In a way it's much easier here."

But still, she cautions, you need to be smart about it. Her advice to someone coming down? "Bring lots of money. Come down and check out the different places. Do you like the city, the mountains, the ocean? Then learn about the place you like. If you live near the ocean, for instance, anything electrical doesn't last very long. This is my eighth coffeepot since December, and it's going. That's almost a coffee pot a month. It's the salt and humidity. You got to keep those things dry, and nothing's dry here. Everything goes here. Zip! It's gone. You got to have a room that has a dehumidifier. I've got a little box that I built, with two light bulbs in it. I keep my computer and DVDs in there."

"Look around," she continues. "Ask questions. But in the end, you need to follow your dream. If the turtles tell you to stay, you stay."

PRIME LIVING LOCATIONS

Sámara has a protected bay perfect for swimming or learning to surf.

adhering to guidelines set by the association, which will fight in the courts any development it considers antithetical to the understated ambience of the area. One of its biggest fights was against Marbella Corporation, which wanted to build a high-rise hotel on the beach. That battle raged for 18 years, and the association recently won. "But there will be more," predicts Linda Cox. "It's a never-ending battle." A few kilometers south, in the more traditionally Tico town of **Garza,** prices are a bit lower.

About 15 kilometers (nine miles) south of Garza, the next town of any size is **Sámara,** as unlike Nosara as *guaro* (the local firewater) is different from chardonnay. Fans of Nosara are likely to turn up their noses at Sámara's party atmosphere and beachfront development, but both places have their charms. It's interesting to note that recently the powerful National Tourism Board (Instituto Costarricense de Turismo) developed a plan that sets aside certain areas for high-density tourism—large hotels and beachfront development—and designates other areas as low-density. Perhaps building on how things are already shaping up, Nosara was designated low-density and Sámara high-density. This means that developers in Sámara will face far fewer hurdles than those wanting to build in Nosara, and that the already large difference in character of these two beachside communities is likely to be accentuated in years to come.

But before you start to picture Sámara as some sort of evil anti-Nosara, picture this: a beautiful half-moon of a protected bay, with palm trees and vines acting as a green fringe to the gray-sand beach. It's a great place for learning to surf, as the waves never get too big and you can stand in chest-deep water waiting for the perfect one to come your way. There are hotels and restaurants built right on the beach, it's true, but so far they're low-rise and casual, open-air bars with sand floors or small *cabinas* partially hidden by beachside vegetation. Consider, too, that the center of the community is *puro Tico,* the usual town built around a soccer field; the town hasn't yet bifurcated into separate areas for Ticos and expats. The place is very popular with Tico tourists, which suggests that Sámara is the Costa Rican idea of what a beach resort should be. Ticos like the feel of Sámara, and after all, it's their country.

A few miles south of Sámara is **Playa Carrillo,** a gorgeous pink-sand beach protected by an offshore coral reef. Yachts anchor at the south end of the bay, and hotels and residential communities are being built along this quiet stretch of coast, which boasts its own airstrip. Investors have long felt that Carrillo has enormous potential, and with the new bridge over the Río Tempisque (at the upper end of the Nicoya Peninsula), access to all of Nicoya is easier and faster than before.

South of Carrillo, the road gets really, really bad and is often impassable during the wet season. A string of stunning beaches goes all the way down to Cabo Blanco, the southernmost tip of the Nicoya Peninsula. The area is sparsely populated and requires some gumption to visit; you need even more to live there.

MONTEZUMA

The approach to Montezuma is dramatic—you wind down a gravel road, catching glimpses of nothing but blue, blue ocean, all the while wondering if there's really a town down there. Turn a sharp corner and there it is—a charming little place tucked into the folds of overgrown hills. Low buildings line the narrow main street, with hibiscus, palm, and acacia crowding in and making the way even narrower. Tourists arrive in rented four-wheel drives, and a few times a day the bus from the Paquera ferry squeezes through and deposits its load of surfers, backpackers, and people like Lauren, a middle-aged pipe fitter from Alberta who comes down a few months every year to swim, read, and relax.

This is a very good place to relax. The influx of mostly young North Americans and Europeans has made Montezuma a cool little "alternative" spot, with excellent vegetarian food at the American-run Sano Banano and the German-run Bakery Café, a bookstore (the Librería Topsy) where you'll find "wicked good books" to buy, trade, or rent, and a couple of bars that pump out dance music deep into the tropical night. On one visit I watched as a film crew trailed the finalists for Tica Linda, a national beauty contest, through the streets and down to the beach. The entire town, always slow-paced, ground to an absolute halt as young beauties tottered along in high heels, draped in strategically placed strands of jute. Local surfers were recruited to stand in as atmospheric background. No doubt the town was chosen as much for its funky vibe as for its natural beauty, but the point is, the place has cachet.

The coastline here is convoluted, jutting out into the sea and doubling back on itself. Walk a few hundred meters and you're out of town; walk 10 minutes and you'll find beaches where you'll have the place to yourself except for the occasional pelican, iguana, or troop of monkeys. The jungle rushes right up to the edge of the beach, where brown sand alternates with volcanic rock and pulverized pink and white shells. Rivers and streams cascade over boulders and empty out into deserted coves.

The alternative feel of the area has roots that go back at least to the 1950s, with the arrival of two Europeans who would transform the landscape of the place or, more accurately, work hard to make sure that the land they loved so passionately would still be there for future generations to enjoy. Olaf Wessberg of Sweden and Karen Morgenson of Denmark had a dream of escaping the Scandinavian winters and of growing organic fruit in tropical America. They tried California, Guatemala, and Mexico, and visited many parts of Costa Rica before they found their niche in Montezuma, where they moved in 1955. They spent their time raising 30 varieties of fruit and getting to know and love the diverse flora and fauna of their adopted home. Journalist Bill Wienberg knew the couple and described them as strict vegetarians who "had a reverence for nature that bordered on the mystical, taking great joy in the company of monkeys and coatimundis."

In the late 1950s, the couple watched in horror as more and more squatters moved into the area, clearing land for crops and then selling out to lumber companies and cattle ranches. Afraid that soon the land would be beyond repair, Wessberg wrote an appeal for donations so that he might buy up property around Montezuma and thus protect it from destruction. His call was heeded, with contributions coming from the British World League Against Vivisection, the Sierra Club, and the Philadelphia Conservation League, among many other organizations and individuals. Wessberg and Morgenson bought a big parcel of land to the south, on the headland between Cabuya and Mal País, which in 1965 became Cabo Blanco, Costa Rica's first nature reserve. The reserve protects one of the last large tracts of mixed evergreen and deciduous moist tropical forest in the area and is home to rare and threatened species such as currasow, crested guan, brocket deer, and jaguarundi.

Montezuma is a good place to visit, but what about living here? Out of gas? You're out of luck. Stove blew up and you need a new one? Get used to cooking over an open fire. In terms of stores, you've got one grocery store and that's it. And try not to get sick or slip on the rocks at the waterfall south of town (like I did), because there's no doctor, no clinic, not even a pharmacy.

If you want to eat, drink, lounge, get a tattoo, or buy handmade jewelry, Montezuma is the place. You need anything halfway practical, you go to **Cóbano,** 20 minutes inland. If you don't have a car and the bus isn't coming for hours, well, you can try to find a taxi, or you can start walking, hoping someone will take pity on you and give you a ride.

To the north of Montezuma is **Playa Tambor,** a gray-sand stretch of beach chosen by Spain's Barcelo company as the site of a massive oceanfront development. This all-inclusive resort, which was the first of its kind in Costa Rica, has everything from a golf course to a 350-seat theater to a helicopter landing pad. Barcelo is said to have destroyed wildlife habitats and drained wetlands to build the sprawling complex. Nevertheless, the Costa Rican government not only gave it the green light but also agreed to pave the road to the hotel, to add a new ferry to bring visitors from Puntarenas on the mainland, and to house construction workers who would later be employed by the resort. If the choice is between protecting the environment (enforcing already existing laws) and promoting tourism, Costa Rica seems to choose the latter.

MAL PAÍS AREA

Southwest of Montezuma, on the Pacific ocean side of the Nicoya Peninsula, **Mal País** and **Santa Teresa** are more remote than Montezuma but still draw their share of expats, especially those who appreciate the great surfing on both beaches. From the inland town of Cóbano the (mostly unpaved) road leads southwest to Carmen. Go left at the crossroads and you'll find Mal País; go right and you'll hit Santa Teresa. Keep heading north (the road gets progressively worse) and you'll come to Manzanillo; those in search of remote living and real estate deals head to this Tico town and venture even farther north. Keep going up the coast, and if the road is passable, you'll eventually reach **Bongo, Caletas,** and **Punto Coyote,** tiny towns more often accessed from the north or from inland.

The coastline here is beautiful and dramatic, rock outcroppings alternating with long stretches of white sand, and dense foliage covering the hills sloping down to the shore. Carmen and Santa Teresa especially are expanding rapidly and consist of hotels, restaurants, and new homes strung along the main road, which is unpaved and runs parallel to the beach. Rutted lanes veer off the

PRIME LIVING LOCATIONS

main road and head for the beach, where due to the pounding waves you'll find more surfers than swimmers.

There's a building boomlet going on in this area, so you'll see big trucks, lots of rebar and cement, and crowds of Nicaraguan workers here to do the heavy lifting.

Despite the changes, the area still has a laid-back feel. During low season (May through November), you can walk on the endless-seeming beach and see almost no one.

THE CENTRAL AND SOUTH PACIFIC COAST

Speaking in generalities, the farther south you go along Costa Rica's Pacific coast, the less developed the area and the more tropical the climate. For the purposes of this book, the central Pacific coast is from Jacó to Palmar Norte, and the south Pacific coast starts where the Osa Peninsula pushes out from the mainland and ends at the Panamanian border.

The central Pacific wins the accessibility contest without even breaking a sweat. From the Central Valley, where the majority of expats and Costa Ricans make their home, central Pacific beach towns like Jacó and Quepos are the most convenient vacation spots in the country. And it goes both ways, of course—residents of these areas can easily shoot up to San José for a shopping excursion or a visit to a well-regarded specialist, or to meet a friend's incoming flight. Roads in the area are relatively well-maintained, so travel time from San José to Jacó is under two hours, with Quepos another forty minutes down the road. After Quepos, things get a little trickier, and they become downright dicey near the Osa Peninsula.

© HOUMAN PIRDAVARI

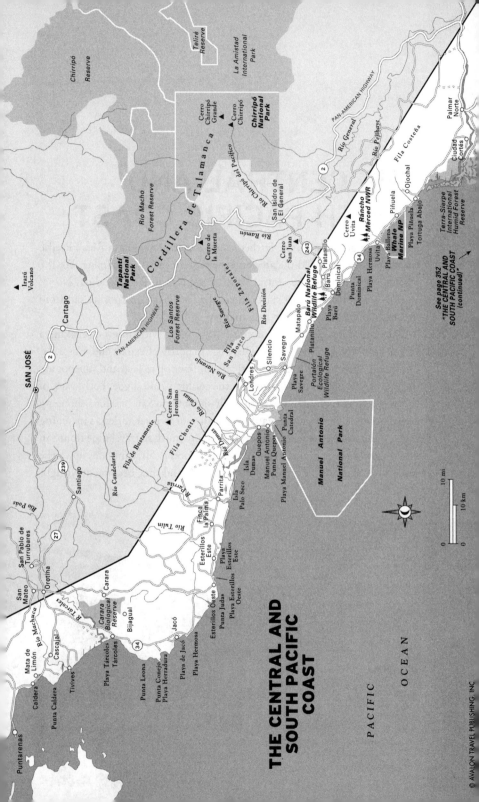

THE CENTRAL AND SOUTH PACIFIC COAST

See page 352 "THE CENTRAL AND SOUTH PACIFIC COAST (continued)"

© AVALON TRAVEL PUBLISHING, INC.

The Lay of the Land

Geographically, the central Pacific consists of a narrow coastal strip backed by steep and heavily wooded mountains. This juxtaposition makes for some very dramatic beaches, where the jungle pushes right up to the sand and where monkeys and sloths join your afternoon tanning session. The climate offers up two fairly distinct seasons—wet (or green) being May–November, and dry running December–April. Those who consider Guanacaste (in the north) too dry and the southern zone too humid feel that the central Pacific coast is, like something out of a fairy tale, just right. Towns like Quepos and Jacó, along with national parks such as Manuel Antonio and Carera, are blessed with a happy medium of rainfall and sunshine. While the summer sees considerably less rain than the winter here, even in dry season you will see a riot of green cascading down the hills to the sea.

The south Pacific coast's seasons correspond roughly to those of the central Pacific coast, but the dry season here isn't all that dry. Locals are prepared for rain at any time of year, as the area receives 4–8 meters (157–315 inches) per year. But the wet season definitely lives up to its name, and May through November is when legendary surf spots like Pavones (with its kilometer-long left-breaking wave) really go off. Thunderstorms are not uncommon late in the year; Caño Island, off the Osa Peninsula, has the dubious distinction of being struck by lightning more often than any other place in Central America.

Puntarenas (and nearby Caldera) are the Pacific coast's most important ports.

PRIME LIVING LOCATIONS

© ERIN VAN RHEENEN

In stark contrast to the central Pacific's straight and narrow coast, the southern coast is positively convulsive, disrupted by swamps and estuaries near the Valle de Diquis, thrust out into the ocean at the Osa Peninsula, and deeply indented at the Golfo Dulce. As the crow flies, the central and southern coasts are roughly equivalent in length, but tracing the shoreline convolutions of the southern zone would probably take two to three times longer, if there were roads that allowed you to do so.

But even with all the time in the world and a hardy four-wheel drive, you couldn't drive the whole of the coastline. A road traces the eastern perimeter of the heavily wooded Osa Peninsula, but it stops at Carate. On most maps there's a dotted line running along the Osa's west coast; map keys call it a "track," passable in dry season. It may be passable, but you'll be passing on foot, because this "track" is most often a path, wide enough for one person when it isn't petering out into the bush. On the narrow Burica Peninsula, which Costa Rica shares with Panama, the road ends almost before the land begins its jut into the Pacific.

The lack of roads means that the towns you *can* get to feel like outposts, islands of civilization amid vast tracts of wilderness. Darryl Cole-Christensen, in his book *A Place in the Rain Forest,* writes of pioneering in the Coto Brus Valley in the late 1950s. The forest was their adversary, he says. Gloomy and dangerous, home to venomous snakes, jaguars, and wild pigs, it was something that had to be fought and cleared as settlers carved out a place for themselves, their livestock, and their crops. Nowadays there has been much clear-cutting of trees and destruction of animal habitat (even on so-called protected land), here as elsewhere in the country. But the southern zone still feels wild, a place that even now provokes primordial fear and wonder.

The area has a very interesting pre-Columbian history—the indigenous people here were influenced by South American tribes, while indigenous peoples elsewhere in Costa Rica had ties to more northerly civilizations. Like the Inca of Peru, the tribes in southern Costa Rica created gold ornaments using lost-wax technique; many are in the shapes of local animals such as crocodiles and jaguars. They also created perfectly round stone spheres, some weighing up to 16 tons. These mysterious spheres have generated many theories as to their origin—Erich von Daniken, in his *Chariots of the Gods,* claimed that they were projectiles shot from starships. Others suggest that the spheres were shaped by hydraulic pressure, tumbled with other rocks at the base of thunderous waterfalls.

Recent history is just as colorful. Gold fever hit in the 1970s, concentrated in what was to become Corcovado National Park. Puerto Jiménez was a rowdy

SAN LUCAS ISLAND: FROM PENITENTIARY TO WILDLIFE RESERVE

For 116 years it was a place of anguish. In the early years felons were never without their leg irons, and escape was all but impossible from this notorious penitentiary just a few nautical miles from Costa Rica's mainland. Isla San Lucas was a place where men became less than human, crammed into dank underground cells, scratching their pain into the thick prison walls. You can still see the graffiti; one sketch, a woman in a crimson bikini, is said to have been drawn in blood.

But now Costa Rica is counting on tourists wanting to visit the island that, two decades after the prison finally shut down in 1989, has become the country's newest wildlife reserve.

For despite San Lucas's painful past, it is still a relatively unspoiled tropical island, one of a dozen in the Gulf of Nicoya, which separates Costa Rica's mainland from the Nicoya Peninsula. From the deck of the ferry connecting the two, travelers catch a glimpse of overgrown San Lucas with its lovely and deserted beaches.

San Lucas is geographical if not spiritual kin to nearby Tortuga Island, a day-tripping destination where people come by boat to snorkel, lounge, and play volleyball on the white-sand beach. But Costa Rica has bigger plans for San Lucas. The country wants to look to the island's future without forgetting its past.

For 10 years after the prison closed, the island's fate hung in the balance, as the municipal government of Puntarenas, a short boat ride from the island, and Costa Rica's Environment Ministry (MINAE) fought over jurisdiction. The municipality wanted to raze the remaining prison buildings and erect a megaresort, with hotels, marina, golf course, and airstrip. MINAE wanted to preserve the prison ruins, study the island's seven pre-Columbian archaeological sites, and declare the 472-hectare (almost two square miles) island a wildlife reserve, open to day visits from tourists. Costa Rica's Supreme Court had to make the call, and to the relief of many, it decided on the latter option.

In 2005 San Lucas became the newest addition to a park system that is the envy of the Americas, with more than 25 percent of the country's territories protected in parks and reserves. MINAE, working with other government agencies and with private organizations, is training locals to be the custodians and guides of the new reserve.

THE ISLAND OF LONELY MEN

Opened in 1873, San Lucas was modeled on the British penal system of that era, which favored the natural isolation of island penitentiaries. The best-known example of this approach was Australia, to which the British sent criminals whose offenses were "very grave." Before San Lucas became a prison island, Costa Rica set up a penitentiary on Isla de Coco, at that time 36 hours by boat off the mainland and now a destination for scuba divers who go for the schooling hammerhead sharks. Predictably, Coco proved too remote to effectively oversee, and they shut that prison down and built the prison on San Lucas, a short boat trip from Puntarenas.

The most famous of the island's former inhabitants has to be prisoner number 1713, otherwise known as José León Sánchez. In 1950 he went to San Lucas an illiterate felon. Paroled in 1969, he emerged a writer who would receive international acclaim and who in 1999 would finally be absolved of the crime he always maintained he never committed.

The best known of his 27 books is a novel based on his experiences on San Lucas, *La Isla do los Hombres Solos*, or *The Island of Lonely Men* (the English version, *God Was Looking the Other Way*, is out of print).

Born in 1930 in Cucaracho del Río Cuarto, a settlement of 700 Huetar people near the Nicaraguan border, León Sánchez's original name was Ocelotl (a Nahuatl word meaning jaguar), but a Catholic priest named Sanchez, who baptized the whole town, decided to name all the converts after himself.

León's supposed crime was one of the most highly publicized of its time. One account says that at the age of 19, after consulting with the Toroc (the wise man or shaman) of his town, he was compelled to reclaim the gold and jewels from the country's most opulent church, the Cartago basilica, as the rightful property of the indigenous people of Costa Rica. Other accounts deny he had anything to do with the foiled robbery, during which a church guard was killed.

One thing is certain: León was accused of stealing the jewels of La Negrita, the beloved patron saint of Costa Rica. Hundreds of thousands of pilgrims make the trek every August to her shrine at the basilica in Cartago. If any crime was designed to outrage the entire country, this insult to its patron saint was it.

After two days of torture, León confessed to the crime. The press dubbed him the "Monster of the Basilica," he was excommunicated from the Catholic Church, and he was forced to argue his own case because no lawyer would represent him.

At San Lucas, prisoner 1713 logged 19 years of confinement, 2 escapes (he was recaptured on the mainland), and 17 attempted escapes. He also learned to read and write in jail, and he self-published his first books there, putting together a primitive press from instructions in an old *Popular Mechanics*.

After he was paroled in 1969, his home in Heredia became another sort of island; he emerged mostly to travel abroad, where he was better known and appreciated than in his own country. He continued, however, to maintain his innocence and to work to get his case reconsidered. In 1999, Costa Rica's Supreme Court declared Leon "absolved of all responsibility" for the crime for which he served 19 years and which made him a pariah in his own country for half a century.

I imagine that León, a tireless advocate of prison reform, appreciates how the island that took a big bite out of his life is being transformed: the prison shut down, the land allowed to return to its natural state, but no one permitted to forget the horror endured on the island of lonely men.

PRIME LIVING LOCATIONS

boomtown, with *oreros* trading nuggets for booze and prostitutes. Longtime locals tell of wild times, with everyone packing a gun and fortunes being made and lost every day. Even a young José Figueres (president from 1994 to 1998) succumbed to the fever and tried his hand at panning for gold. The miners' destructive methods—chopping down the rainforest, dynamiting riverbeds—prompted outrage and led, finally, to the creation of Corcovado National Park in the mid-1980s.

ACCESS

If you're looking to relocate or buy a vacation home along the Pacific coast, geography and climate may be less important than accessibility. As elsewhere in Costa Rica, the question here is not, Is it beautiful? but, Can you get there? The days may be gone when you needed a horse and several days to reach what are now decent-sized towns, but you still need to consider how hard it will be for you to get home. Of course, if you never leave home—even if you dwell deep in the jungle—you won't have any trouble. But chances are, the more remote the area, the more likely you'll need to go—often!—somewhere else. Whether you need a stack of plywood, a big bag of rice, or emergency medical care, what are the roads like that will get you there? Most North Americans can't imagine planning their day (or life) according to the state of nearby roads, but that's the reality in the more remote areas of Costa Rica. And the "wild south" most surely qualifies as remote. For example, driving from San José to Puerto Jiménez (on the Osa Peninsula) is a full-day affair, more if rains have washed out the road or made rivers impassable.

Or let's say you want to live on land that borders the magnificent Corcovado National Park. The easiest entry point would be at Carate, a "town" that consists of an airstrip and a general store that charges an arm and a leg for a can of Coke. The road there from Puerto Jiménez isn't too bad, though of course it's not paved and there are a few rivers to cross. But with a four-wheel drive and a few hours, you can get there. If your car breaks down, you can hope your timing is right to catch the once-a-day "shuttle"—riders sit in the back of a truck and hold on for dear life.

PRICES

The places to look for real estate deals are the towns you've never heard of: little villages not far from bigger name-brand destinations, or bends in the road that catch your eye with their leafy rural charm. Start in a bigger town in an area that appeals to you, then see what you find within a short drive.

The most expensive areas to buy property on this stretch of coast are Jacó, an hour or two from the international airport and in the throes of condo-fi-cation, and the region around Manuel Antonio National Park, about an hour south of Jacó. Prices in these areas rival those of Guanacaste's Gold Coast, with luxury beachside homes going for US$1 million and more modest properties going for a few hundred thousand. Lots and inland homes go for less.

Some of the heat of those markets is seeping southward; Dominical, for example, is now quite popular.

You will find lower prices as you go farther south, although some remote areas (like the span of coast between Puerto Jiménez and Cabo Matopalo on the Osa Peninsula) have become hot spots of a different sort. They aren't being developed in the ways that more northerly stretches of coast are, but wealthy individuals (like actor Woody Harrelson) have bought up large tracts of land, keeping them relatively pristine but also making it less likely that you'll stumble upon your own little piece of affordable paradise there.

As always, it's about doing your homework and being persistent. Great deals don't generally fall into people's laps; you have to go looking for them.

Where to Live

CENTRAL PACIFIC COAST TOWNS
Jacó
Jacó is a beach town turned boomtown. There are hundreds of new condos and homes for sale and hundreds more being built. Ease of access is part of the place's charm. You can land at the international airport near San José and be at the beach in less than two hours.

As in many beach towns, the layout is basically one long strip, parallel to the long beach, with few building over two stories high. There are the usual open-air bars and restaurants, souvenir shops, budget *cabinas,* and some larger chain hotels (like Best Western) outside the town proper. And everywhere you look, there are new buildings going up—both commercial and residential.

There are also the businesses that make a place not just visitable but livable: banks, medical clinics, hardware stores, and car repair shops. Other beach towns force you to go elsewhere if your needs go beyond food, alcohol, or a new bikini.

Javier Barquero, manager of Best Western Jacó, describes how the town has changed in the last few years. "Now there's more construction, more invest-ment, more opportunity. Better services. Lots of nice places to go out for a drink or have dinner. But there's also been an increase in drugs and prostitu-tion." Javier, himself from San José, sees Jacó as a town of people who've come

EXPAT PROFILE: SHIFI SURF SHOTS

The sun is going down over Playa Hermosa, just south of Jacó on Costa Rica's Pacific coast. Most of the surfers are out of the water by now, and a good number of them are clustered around a girl with braces and a laptop, sitting at a beachside table at Las Olas restaurant. Sinewy guys with bare chests and dripping hair vie for position, crowding in and peering over the girl's shoulder. They're looking at her laptop screen, where image after image layers up in brilliant color – the dense blue-green of the water, the softer blue of the sky, and the ragged white fringe of a breaking wave.

All the photos are basically the same – a surfer on a wave – but the guys are rapt. They're looking for the subtle differences in the photos: the size and shape of the wave; whether the surfer is going right or left; whether his stance denotes experience or kookdom. But most of all, they're looking for themselves.

The girl with the laptop is Shifi Ettinger. She's in her late twenties (she got braces late), she's a surf photographer, and she's made a business out of people wanting a snapshot of themselves at the crucial moment: The moment when they feel most alive. The moment when there's nothing in their head but getting in sync with a piece of

Shifi shoots more than waves.

the ocean about to release all its pent up energy in one final throw and curl.

She'll copy the shots she took this afternoon onto CDs for surfers who want a souvenir of their time at this beach, on this day, on these particular waves. Shifi throws in some nature shots of Costa Rica and sells the CDs for US$25 a pop. For the guys who are seeing themselves on a wave for the first time, it's a bargain. "It's like, Hey! I can surf," one of her customers down from Florida confesses. "I mean I

from elsewhere. "There are lots of Canadians here," he says. "Some Americans, some Italians. The foreigners don't mix so much with the Ticos; sometimes they don't even mix with other foreigners."

Betty, from Argentina, would probably agree, but wouldn't see it as a problem. A stylish and affable woman in her forties, Betty runs a popular juice stand on the main drag. Often other Argentines, including the owner of the Argentine-style Tango Grill down the street, are perched on the juice bar's

thought I could, but now I'm sure. I've got proof."

If she had stayed in her native Israel, Shifi tells me, she'd be photographing weddings. So how did she escape that fate? When she was an 18-year-old in Rishon LeZion (Israel), she saw someone's home movie of surfers in Pavones (on the southern Pacific coast, down near Panama). "I was fascinated by the wave," she says. "I knew I had to go." She and her boyfriend traveled through Central America in 2000, and they stopped in Pavones.

"The swell made me stay. We were camping, and we said, 'This is crazy, but let's give this place two weeks and see what happens.'" They found property in those two weeks, and soon after they opened La Manta, a restaurant with Israeli food and a huge white wall that Shifi used to screen the videos she was shooting of each day's waves. The restaurant filled up with surfers wanting to see if they'd made it into Shifi's movies that day. She was also taking stills and selling them, and all was sand and sun and digital fun until she and her boyfriend broke up.

On the rebound, Shifi returned to Israel but knew within a week that she had to go back to Costa Rica – aside from the beauty of the place, there was also more opportunity here for her as a photographer. There weren't many people in Costa Rica even attempting to do what Shifi did – being out there on the beach every day, aiming her impossibly long lenses, shooting wave after wave after wave.

She circled back to Costa Rica, this time *sola*, and this time settling in the Jacó/Playa Hermosa area, much easier to get to than Pavones and thus offering many more potential customers. She works hard, taking her craft seriously. Nothing excites her more than seeing her photography skills getting better each day. Her photographs also appear in magazines, and last I spoke with her there were a couple of shows in the works. After she's done for the day Shifi often goes in the water herself, not with a surfboard but with fins and a body board. She says it's more *pura vida* that way.

Everyone in town knows her. She tools around in her black Jeep with Shifi Surf Shots stenciled on the side. When she walks into the Tabacón, the waiters smile and greet her, and the surfers who were playing pool or hanging at the bar approach her table like she's a movie star, only better, because she is witness to *their* artistry – Shifi gets it down in blue and green and gold and sells it back to them for a reasonable fee.

Shifi can be reached at shifisurf @hotmail.com.

stools, sipping her concoctions. "It's my little colony," she says. She and her family arrived a few years ago, and she's very happy with Jacó. "It's a real town," she says. "Actually, it feels more like a neighborhood." She says she would prefer to live outside of town, up in the mountains where it's quieter and cooler, but her teenaged kids would always need to be driven somewhere. "Here," she says, "it's flat and you can bicycle everywhere. That's what my kids do. They're always flying by on their bikes. I just wave."

Among the better-known beaches close to Jacó, **Playa Herradura** (7 kilometers/4.3 miles north) is the site of Los Sueños, a Marriott megaresort and residential complex with hundreds of condos and its own marina (www. lossuenosresort.com). There are also tennis courts and a championship golf course. If you want to see what Playa Herradura looks like without the bother of traveling, rent the movie *1492*, starring Gérard Depardieu as Christopher Columbus—the beach is featured in many scenes. Local indigenous peoples were recruited to play the indigenous people Columbus encountered; they were paid US$15 a day, with women who bared their chests getting three times that rate. The 10 weeks of filming was said to contribute US$8 million to the local economy. Ten kilometers (six miles) north of Playa Herradura is Punta Leona, where vacationers from the Central Valley and abroad own condos in a gated community.

Just south of Jacó is **Playa Hermosa,** a 10-kilometer (six-mile) stretch of gray-brown sand battered by the kind of waves surfers love. It's become a favorite among those who want something more laid-back than Jacó, and many of the businesses serving tourists are owned and operated by expats. The bartender at a local club told me he came here in 2000 to surf and now has a Tica wife and a young daughter. "It's easier to be a good father down here," says this South Carolina native. "The people are so nice, and the society is less materialistic. There's free medical care, and then you've got an extended family that helps out. Sometimes it's too much," he admits. "Seems like there's a baby shower or birthday party every other day. But there's much less stress down here."

He loves Playa Hermosa, but he and his family live in Jacó because there are more services there—health clinics, supermarkets, and the like. "Jacó has some problems, for sure," he says. "But if you don't run in those circles, they don't much affect you. And my neighborhood's great—I leave my bike out, unlocked, no problem."

But the problems in Jacó are starting to spill over into nearby areas, and locals report that now there's more petty theft in Playa Hermosa and nearby beaches. Development has also arrived, and on the gravel road between Playa Hermosa and the next beach south there are housing developments going up, sporting Spanish-style stucco homes on narrow lots that go for about half a million dollars each. Check out www.hermosa paradise.com and www.hermosapalms.com for examples of what's on offer. Oh, and don't be confused when you find Playa Hermosa after Playa Hermosa all over Costa Rica—it means Pretty Beach, and there are a lot of those in this country.

Quepos and Manuel Antonio

Quepos sits sandwiched between a tranquil harbor dotted with fishing boats and the steep, wooded slope southeast of town. Incoming and outgoing traffic take turns across the narrow bridge into town. Locals walk by with fishing poles over their shoulders or pedal along on bicycles, often with a cell phone scrunched between shoulder and ear. A pleasant grid of streets lined with low buildings, Quepos was once a banana town; the United Fruit Company built a compound south of town in the 1930s and drew workers from other parts of the country. In the 1950s, disease blighted the banana trees, and they were replaced by oil-producing African palms.

Nowadays, Quepos does triple duty as a major sportfishing destination, a working Tico town where you can buy a stove or some new shoes, and the gateway to the most-visited tourist site in the country, Manuel Antonio National Park. Budget travelers often opt to stay in Quepos, but the more upscale tourist facilities are strung along the seven-kilometer (four-mile) road that winds through jungly hills from Quepos to the park entrance. There is also a small cluster of hotels, bars, and restaurants at the Manuel Antonio end of the road, all within walking distance of the park.

Property here is some of the most expensive in all of Costa Rica. But fans of the area feel like they have it all: swimmable white-sand beaches, a gem of a national park where monkey and sloth sightings are all but guaranteed, lush tropical foliage, and enough tourist infrastructure to ensure good roads and services.

Many real estate offices in town will be glad to help you look for the place of your dreams. It's important to have the inside scoop on the area, and a good agent can provide just that. A local told me about a squatters' town on the road from Quepos to Manuel Antonio (which is lined with luxury hotels and pricey restaurants; not the kind of place you'd imagine a shantytown). Apparently, one of the biggest properties in the area was owned by a drug dealer who didn't come around much. This absentee ownership attracted squatters, who built small houses and planted crops, thereby laying claim to the land. Eventually, some of squatters sold "their" land to other locals, who then sold to foreigners. "Buying property here," the local told me, "you really need someone who knows the area and its history, to make sure you know what you're getting yourself into." Just because land was once squatted on doesn't necessarily mean that there would be a problem if you bought it—the property could very well have a clear title, and everything would be ducky. But then again, the property might exist in some legal no-man's land that would allow you to buy it (or at least pay for it) without actually owning it.

EXPAT PROFILE: ANITA MYKETUK

Anita Myketuk has lived in the Pacific coast town of Manuel Antonio for more than 30 years, running the Buena Nota gift shop for a good part for that time.

"We arrived in 1974, and there was nothing here – no electricity or running water or telephones in Manuel Antonio. Quepos was a small fishing village; there was no tourist trade, just one hotel and a couple of *pensiones* that mostly the truckers and delivery people would use. The roads were bad. We camped – had a Volkswagen. It was really primitive. Vegetables would come twice a week on the back of a truck. There were no supermarkets. After a year and a half we brought our cat down, and you couldn't get cat food, not even in San José. Now there's everything here. Even the little *pulpería* up the road has cat food.

"It was always expensive here. It's never been cheap. We came here, walked to the end of the beach, and said, 'This is paradise. I bet we can pick up some property for next to nothing.' But it was never like that. Everything was expensive, even in the '70s. We bought some property up on the hill for US$20,000; we could have bought a place in Marin County [California] for the same price.

"Don [Anita's husband, who passed away a few years ago] was diabetic, and he was losing his eyesight. Our place had a great view. We bought it with the idea that he wanted to see the most beautiful view in the little time he had left to see. But he went back to the States and had various procedures – laser surgery – and he never lost his eyesight!

"We were really excited when we bought it; we'd never owned property before. But if people are going to come down here, I'd definitely emphasize: Come down here for at least a year, not as a tourist, before you even consider buying anything. People say to me, But we've been coming here for nine years! And they build or buy something, and then they're stuck, and find out they don't like it. Because the bureaucracy is really bad, or they're retiring, which is stressful even in the States, and then they come here and it's worse. And they don't know any Costa Ricans, so nothing works for them. You do much better here if you know a few people who can help you, give you a few contacts.

"But I love it here. And as compli-

Many of the hotels, bars, and restaurants in the Manuel Antonio area are owned by Americans, Canadians, Argentines, Italians, and other nonnatives, and there is a strong gay (male) presence, with many establishments gay-owned or at least gay-friendly. "We are an open-minded place" boasts a sign in English that hangs in the doorway of an open-air bar right off Manuel Antonio beach. Businesses cater primarily to tourists, and as such there are many non-Tico items on offer, like the excellent iced lattes and toasted bagels with cream cheese at the two branches of Café Milagro.

Getting work (as opposed to running your own business) is not easy. A hotel

cated as it is, you really shouldn't worry about it – it's really not that stressful if you don't take it to heart. It's nice because there's a lot here now: a supermarket, some good restaurants, other foreigners. It's fine to think you can go out and live in a very primitive place, like we did when we first came, but it's not that easy. I like being able to go get my mail, to go to a coffee shop and chat with other people, or to have some live music if I want to go out at night. And we have good cable here – we can watch CBS and NBC movies every day if we want to.

"Anything besides general medical care, I go to San José. Bigger purchase items I usually go to San José, though now there are two stores in Quepos that have big electrical appliances, even refrigerators. Even furniture you can get here now. You don't have to go out of Quepos much anymore. What we're really lacking here is a library and a university. A lot of people wouldn't think that is important, but for me it is.

"We have transport service that will bring things out from San José. They come almost every day, and the cost of them delivering a big box is only a couple of dollars. They deliver right to my door – they brought all these tiles, and the furniture. You don't have to get a moving van. Most parts of Costa Rica have similar services that are very reasonable.

"We lived here for quite a few years before we bought the property. It's not for everyone. Some people love it; some people adapt really well. Couples sometimes have a hard time. One likes it better than the other, one adapts better, learns the language faster. Makes friends easier. I've seen couples break up. Also, weird things happen – men go off with young girls and women go off with young guys. It's real common here. There are three or four women that came down with nice men, nice families, and then took off with some young construction worker. I think maybe the young Ticos want to be with a wealthier gringo, and they'll do whatever they can to make it happen. I can't imagine they'd have a lot in common.

"All of Costa Rica is like a small town. Even in San José, I run into people all the time who know me. I went into a little hole-in-the-wall liquor store in Heredia, and the guy there said, "Oh, you're Anita from the Buena Nota." I thought I'd never seen this guy before in my life. He said, 'I used to live in Quepos 20 years ago, and I remember you.'"

owner told me, "Very wealthy people do come here to hang out, but 80 percent of the people who move here seem to be looking for work. They usually don't find it, because businesses can't legally hire foreigners."

I talked with two Canadian sisters who had managed to land waitressing jobs but quit after a few months. "They hardly gave us any shifts, and the wage was less than two dollars an hour. People here don't tip, and the tourists pick up that custom when they see how much of their bill is tax and 'service.' Somehow we didn't see much of that service charge. It was like charity work, except the customers were really demanding."

Dominical

About 45 kilometers (28 miles) south of Quepos, or an hour from the inland city of San Isidro de General, lies Dominical. The town is a low-key "resort," a latticework of potholed dirt roads framed by the Barú River to the north, the Tinamaste mountains to the east, and a four-kilometer (2.5-mile) gray-sand beach to the west. The beach's booming waves are heaven for good surfers, but not so great for swimmers. Each year many people succumb to the punishing waves and dangerous riptides; the town recently organized a force of lifeguards at the residents' own expense. The coastline around Dominical is gorgeous, and the forest that comes down to the sea is riddled with rivers and spectacular waterfalls.

Most resident *extranjeros* live outside of Dominical proper; the foreigners you'll see in town are mostly young backpackers and surfers. They stay in low-budget beachside *cabinas,* check their email at Internet cafés, and eat pizza at San Clemente Bar & Grill, where the ceiling is paneled with broken surfboards. Dominical is known as a board-breaking beach, and if you donate your busted board to the existing collection, you get a free beer and a taco. One wit wrote on the remaining half of his board: "This wave was at least 2 feet tall!"

The town has the same ragged patchwork of rapid development and underdevelopment as many a burgeoning tourist town. There are at least four real estate offices, but no full-time health clinic (more on this later). There are plenty of bars, restaurants, and minimarts, but fewer useful businesses like supermarkets and hardware stores. Residents are trying, however, to retain the town's laid-back charm even as they try to accommodate new arrivals. A *centro commercial* in the middle town, for example, is not an ugly strip mall but a cluster of pleasant low buildings connected by raised wooden walkways wending their way through a tropical garden. The center has an Internet café, some tour agencies, and a small health food store where they sell homemade yogurt, herbal potions in bottles with hand-lettered labels in English, and brownies so good you'll want to buy up all they have.

Though Dominical is much more wired than communities just a half-hour south—there's high-speed Internet access and plenty of working pay phones—the place still feels like a bit of an outpost. A citizens' committee tries to keep the town's bare-bones health clinic supplied with basic first-aid supplies, but the clinic is often locked; you ask around and get someone to open it up, then dress your own wound. A doctor visits the clinic once a month. For anything serious, people go to the small emergency room in Platanillo, 13 kilometers (eight miles) east of Dominical, or drive an hour over the hill to the hospital in San Isidro de General. Those living south of Dominical may head south to Palmar Norte's medical facilities. For nonemergency medical care, residents often drive the four hours to San José.

Dominical's quickly improving roads are one reason the area is developing so fast. Dominical sits at the intersection of Highway 243, coming down the mountain from San Isidro, and the coastal highway, gravel to the north and newly paved to the south. It won't be long before the entire coast highway is paved, providing easier access to coastal areas that right now still feel a little remote. Just how long that will be is a subject of much debate, especially among developers and real estate speculators, who want to get in early but not so early that they have to wait decades for a return on their investment. Most established expats would prefer that the roads remain a challenge, keeping development and large-scale tourism to a minimum.

A few kilometers south of Dominical is Punta Dominical, a beautiful high rock outcropping with views down the cliffs to crashing surf below. Some lucky few (almost all foreigners) have built houses to take advantage of this setting. Not far from the rocky point is Playa Dominicalito, reef-protected and providing good mooring and decent swimming. From the mouth of nearby Higuerón (also called Morete) River to Point Piñuela to the south, Ballena (Whale) Marine National Park protects 45 terrestrial hectares (110 acres) and 2,175 marine hectares (5,375 acres), including the largest coral reef on the Pacific coast of Central America.

Uvita and Ojochal

Uvita is a small community 16 kilometers (10 miles) south of Dominical, on a newly paved road that in some places is already reverting back to its pot-holed splendor. Before you get to Uvita, there's a bridge where big chunks of concrete have fallen into the river below, with ocean breezes blowing through the remaining metal grid. Considering how long the area had to wait for the road to be paved, the bridge might fall into the river altogether before repair crews arrive.

But right now the bridge is serviceable, and it brings you to Uvita, a pleasant town of both Ticos and expats, which has so far managed to avoid being overwhelmed by the low-budget travelers that flock to Dominical.

Ojochal, 20 kilometers (12 miles) south of Uvita, is a tiny town offering unexpectedly good food, in large part due to the resident community of French Canadians, some of whom saw ads in their hometown papers and bought lots sight-unseen, with the guarantee of their money back if they didn't like the place. They liked it, they told their friends, and now there's a little piece of Québec here on Costa Rica's Pacific coast. The French aren't bad cooks, something even Canada couldn't change. The talent seems to have also survived Costa Rica (not known for its cuisine), and one of the joys of being in the area is deciding whether to stop for filet mignon at the truly exceptional Exo-Tica, crepes at Chez Elle, or croissants from the French Bakery past Ojochal's soccer field. If French food isn't to your liking, defect to the Dutch and their former colonies, sampling the international cuisine at Villas Gaia or the amazing Indonesian rice platter at Balcón de Uvita, up a gravel track that begs for four-wheel drive but rewards with amazing views.

Strung along the highway from Dominical to past Ojochal are a number of nice hotels, frequented by Europeans and North Americans who've heard about the area's international community and low-key vibe. Though there's a lot to do here—bird-watching, snorkeling, kayaking in the ocean, or hiking to waterfalls—it takes some effort to find out where to go and what to do. This is true in spite of the fact that the area is one of the most well-signed I've seen in this country. Uniform signs—blue, with icons for food and lodging reminiscent of those on U.S. highways—suggest a community-wide effort aimed at attracting tourists, though Ojochal still seems more geared to residents than tourists. Speaking of residents, they aren't all French Canadians. There are also French-from-France (one of whom opined that French Canadians were "so American"), Belgians, Dutch, Italians, British, non-French Canadians, people from the United States, and of course, Ticos.

Ojochal also appears to be blessed with an abundance of enterprising residents who cooperate on projects to improve the community. In 2003, after several robberies in the area, residents asked the Ministry of Public Safety if they could have some police stationed in their town. If you build a station, replied the ministry, we'll provide six officers. Project coordinators gathered contributions from people throughout town, then organized the construction of a spiffy new station—all in four months! The Minister of Public Safety himself attended the inauguration of the new building, no doubt to get a look at the folks who in a few months had accomplished what in other Costa Rican communities might take years.

SOUTHERN PACIFIC COAST TOWNS
The Osa Peninsula

National Geographic magazine calls the Osa Peninsula "the most biologically intense place on earth." This is Costa Rica's Amazon, a tropical rainforest where tall trees drip vines and lianas, macaws screech, and most of the country's remaining 250 jaguars prowl. The numbers are staggering: 42,000 hectares

© ERIN VAN RHEENEN

Corcovado tent camp, near Carate

(103,784 acres) of land (a good part of the peninsula) are protected in Corcovado National Park, which supports 13 distinct habitats and on which six meters (236 inches) of rain falls annually. Five hundred kinds of trees thrive here, as do hundred of species of birds, mammals, and reptiles. Crocodiles lurk in marshy areas, sea turtles lay eggs on deserted beaches, and tapirs pick their way shyly through the trees.

The peninsula juts 50 kilometers (31 miles) out into the Pacific, sheltering the Golfo Dulce to the south, whose warm, calm waters draw humpback whales, three kinds of dolphins, and all manner of sport fish. On the northern side of the peninsula, beautiful and isolated Drake Bay is usually reached by boat from the riverside settlement of Sierpe; there's hardly a town to be seen on the 90-minute trip, and the river is lined with huge stands of stilt-rooted mangroves.

Though the Osa has had its share of environmental problems, including invasive gold mining, slash-and-burn farming, and the poaching of endangered wildlife, the area's relative inaccessibility has saved it from large-scale exploitation. Visitors need to make an investment of time and effort to sample the peninsula's delights, and prospective residents should have that extra measure of patience and resourcefulness that makes living in the outback an adventure rather than a hardship.

That said, it's getting easier to get to the Osa, at least during dry season. Small planes fly from San José to Puerto Jiménez every day, and charters land at Carate and other makeshift airstrips on demand. Until rain makes it impassable, there's a decent dirt road from Rincón on the south side of the

MAMA CHI

On September 22, 1962, in the northern Panamanian province of Chiriquí, a young Ngäbe woman was called on by a mysterious couple. The two turned out to be none other than the Virgin Mary and her son, Jesus Christ. The visitors told the young woman that the Ngäbe should cultivate the land – even that dominated by banana companies – and worship the divine in ceremonies blending traditional Ngäbe beliefs, Catholic doctrine, and even elements of evangelical Protestantism. The resulting religion is called Mama Chi, and it has adherents not only in Panama but also across the border in southern Costa Rica.

peninsula to Drake Bay on the north. You can travel by bus from San José to Puerto Jiménez (a 10-hour trip), but driving your own car (four-wheel drive recommended) will make the trip quicker and more comfortable.

Puerto Jiménez

With a population of around 7,500, Puerto Jiménez is the largest town on the Osa Peninsula. Visitors to Corcovado National Park most often come through PJ, as local expats call it, and there is a handful of hotels, restaurants, bars, and Internet cafés to serve them. There's also a bank, a post office, an emergency health clinic, a tourist information center, and a library (supported by donations), and the town's airstrip, rising up out of bird- and crocodile-rich wetlands, is actually paved!

Flying into town is much easier than driving, and you're just as likely to hear the drone of a light plane as the revving of a car engine. It wasn't long ago that the road into the area was even worse than the potholed tracks drivers now endure; until recently boats were the main method of transport. Still crucial to the area, vessels both big and small find excellent moorage in the deep and calm Golfo Dulce.

The town's history is a colorful one, with tales centering on the gold rush of the 1980s, when Puerto Jiménez (to hear locals tell it) was a modern-day Wild West, with blood feuds, horses tied up outside saloons in which gunfights raged, and prostitutes with hearts of gold (or at least pockets full of gold nuggets).

Things are quieter these days, and many of the area's foreign residents like it that way. Those wanting even more peace than town life can offer settle deep in the jungle or along the spectacular coastline between Puerto Jiménez and Carate, where the road ends and you must walk into Corcovado. Beaches are tucked away between rock outcroppings, and at Cabo Matapalo, on the southeast tip of the peninsula, waves get big enough to draw surfers. Matapalo also draws foreign residents, some of whom operate luxury hotels, and some of whom, like actor and activist Woody Harrelson, keep to themselves, though he and other foreign landowners have been instrumental in attempts to preserve the area's flora and fauna.

Golfito

Golfito is located on a small gulf within the larger Golfo Dulce, and this double dose of protection from the ocean swell means that waves breaking on the town's shore never get more than knee-high. Would that Golfito had similar protection from economic storms. The town started life as a banana port when, in 1938, the Boston-based United Fruit Company (now called Chiquita) moved its operations from the Caribbean to the Pacific, fleeing banana blight and labor strikes. During the 1950s, 90 percent of Costa Rica's banana exports were shipped from Golfito, and the banana company was the major employer in the area. But just as it abandoned the Caribbean side of the country, United Fruit pulled out of Golfito in 1985, leaving the land around town pumped full of pesticides that made it hard to grow anything else here.

Since the departure of United Fruit, the Costa Rican government has tried to promote other businesses to shore up the area's depressed economy. The major effort is the Deposito Libre, a duty-free shopping compound opened in 1990 that looks like a prison but draws Ticos from all over the country, especially at Christmastime. They're looking to avoid the high import tariffs on everything from refrigerators to perfume, and Golfito's lodgings are mostly geared to the tourists who must wait 24 hours before being able to shop.

The face of Golfito may change quite a bit, however, if a US$350 million marina and resort project proceeds as planned and opens in 2008 or 2009. But right now, when non-shopping tourists and sport fishers come through town, they usually hire a boat to get out on the water or are quickly on their way to beach towns like Playa Zancudo and Pavones to the south. December–May is sailfish season, June–September is good for marlin, and May–September you're likely to find snook.

Golfito isn't much of a tourist attraction in and of itself, though it's interesting to hang out at the town's dock, watching rough-and-tumble locals unload headless marlin, or notice that in the old section of town (the *pueblo civil*), rickety houses hang out over the water, and every other business seems to be a bar.

Two kilometers (1.2 miles) south is another part of town that looks like it's in a different country. The Zona Americana was built by United Fruit to house its higher-ups. Generously proportioned wooden homes were built on stilts to combat the damp and catch the breeze. Spacious lawns and gardens give the area a luxuriant feel that has endured even as many of the buildings fall into ruin.

The town's foundering economy means that there are some great real estate deals to be had, while the area's slightly rough vibe seems to have attracted some rather shady characters. There's the sense that half the expats here are on the lam. Hang out at the Latitude 8 bar, a tiny place with a view of the water, and see who's drinking bourbon shots at 4 in the afternoon, or order an espresso at the bunker-like Coconut Café and watch the town, locals and expats alike, parade by.

Golfito is a seven- or eight-hour bus ride from San José, and it's an hour or two drive to Pavones or Playa Zancudo. There's a daily (except Sunday) passenger-only ferry between Golfito and Puerto Jiménez. You can also hire water taxis to take you to Playa Zancudo or Pavones.

Playa Zancudo

Playa Zancudo isn't far from Golfito, at least as the crow flies or the water taxi skims. If you drive, however, you'll negotiate a 45-kilometer (28-mile) unpaved route that includes crossing the Río Coto on a two-car ferry that stops operating at 9 P.M.

This seriously laid-back town is strung out along a sandy spit of land between the Río Coto Estuary and the waters of the Golfo Dulce. It's a lovely place where you can buckle down to the serious task of doing very little. In fact, if you need a lot of stimulation, Playa Zancudo is probably not for you. It has that end-of-the-road feel that can either charm the pants off you or drive you nuts. If you end up staying, no doubt you'll have days when it does both.

Some of the town's foreign residents run hotels or restaurants, and that keeps them busy, at least during high season (December–April). Debbie Walsh of Oasis on the Beach says she looks forward to low season, when she can catch up on repairs and spend more time with her five dogs, 18 horses, and three parrots. She visited the area six years ago, drawn by the promise of seeing parrots in the wild. No strangers to the colorful birds, she and her then-husband ran an exotic-pet shop in Boston. When she came to Playa Zancudo, says Debbie, something clicked, and she stayed.

Oasis at the Beach's open-air restaurant is very popular, a good place to catch a glimpse of the local expats, who come here to enjoy drinks at sunset and to sample treats like wood-oven pizza. Snatches of overheard conversation reveal expat concerns: the need to drive seven hours to San José to buy some things for the house or to pick a friend up from the airport; the need to get away, especially in the very rainy months of September and October; the frustrations of having the power go out or the phone lines on the blink. But there's a general good cheer as well, and a celebration of being in a beautiful spot, pretty much left to one's own devices. The beach here is the focus of many a lazy day. It stretches six lovely kilometers (four miles), is bordered by tall coconut palms, and offers good swimming at the south end and decent surfing further north. Fisherfolk will be in heaven, as some of the best fishing in the area can be had close by. In fact, there's a yearly sportfishing competition, based at Roy's Zancudo Lodge, that draws a surprising number of musicians, including, in recent years, Taj Mahal and former members of the Allman Brothers Band.

The fact that Zancudo is hemmed in by an estuary on one side and the sea on the other has sparked some questions about property ownership in the area. Maritime zone law stipulates that no one can actually own land until 200 meters (219 yards) up from high tide line, and lately the municipality has been questioning the right of foreigners to lease property in this zone. If you're looking to buy here, be sure to get the up-to-the-minute news by talking to as many foreign residents as possible.

Pavones

At least as small as Playa Zancudo, Pavones has more of a center, even if that center consists of a scruffy soccer field around which the town's few businesses are clustered. There's the open-air cantina, a few humble *pulperías* and casual restaurants, a variety of low-budget *cabinas,* and, in the emotional if not geographic center of town, a surf shop.

For make no mistake, Pavones is a surf town. The famous left-breaking wave is the reason people come, it's the reason a select few stay, and it's the reason nonsurfers whine, "There's nothing to do here." It's why most of the town's visitors are young and male, with biceps hard from paddling and skin an international brown, making it hard to say whether the guy in the long shorts is Israeli, French, Argentine, Floridian, or Tico. These fellows are also why Pavones has a different tourist season than most other towns in Costa Rica. The usual high season is dry season, December–April, but surfers know that the rainy months (May–October) are when the waves in Pavones really go off.

Even the nightlife, such as it is, revolves around surfing. Guys gather at the cantina to hoist a Pilsen or seven, going into the kind of excruciating detail about the day's waves that only fellow fanatics can appreciate. You'll also see them propped before the big screen at the thatch-roofed Manta Club, looking for themselves in video footage of the day's action or watching reruns of *Endless Summer.*

Did I mention that Pavones and its environs are absolutely gorgeous? Sometimes the surf vibe is so strong you forget that even civilians can appreciate how the rainforested hills slide down to meet sandy beaches or how the rocky tide pools burst with life. Especially to the south of town, the coastline is pristine and often deserted. In contrast to surf spots like Tamarindo and Puerto Viejo, Pavones is harder to get to, which means that only the dedicated make it here, and the town has not yet mushroomed into a more general tourist destination, with the attendant bars and Internet cafés. Electricity didn't arrive in Pavones until the mid-1990s, and private phone lines are still hard to come by. Cell phone use is on the rise, but the technology is primitive; you'll see people scurrying around to find the best spot to catch a signal, yelling into their headsets, "Can you hear me now!?"

Most people give up and wait to use the one public phone at Doña Dora's open-air *soda,* where you can also get a delicious fish *casado.* While waiting your turn for the coveted phone line you'll notice that half the town is there with you, and chances are good that someone lounging nearby can tell you which *cabinas* have fans, who can take you fishing, who's driving to Golfito that afternoon, or where to paddle out when the river mouth is spewing mud and detritus. As in many small towns, but especially technology-challenged ones, word of mouth is the way almost everything is communicated.

Property ownership issues are complicated by the area's recent history. After United Fruit pulled out in 1985, foreigners bought up big stretches of coastline. Even financial fugitive Robert Vesco owned land here for a while, as did many others whose sources of income would not bear much scrutiny. In 1988, Danny Fowlie, who'd bought up a fair amount of land around Pavones, was convicted of drug trafficking and put in jail in the United States. His enterprising lawyer sold Fowlie's land to other gringos, and to himself, but the Costa Rican government wanted the land for itself (by rights it can expropriate the land of convicted felons). Squatters also tried, with some success, to claim the property.

In 1992, a showdown between squatters and those who had bought pieces of Fowlie's land ended in one man (a Tico guard hired to protect gringo-owned land) being killed. In 1997, a 79-year-old U.S cattle breeder got into an altercation with a squatter, and they shot each other. Or, to hear the gossip, the squatter's boss shot the old man, then shot the squatter and put the gun in his hand. Whatever the truth of the matter, prospective buyers should be careful, making sure that land being offered them has a clean title and actually belongs to the supposed seller. Locals insist that Pavones now welcomes foreign investment and residence, but there's still a feeling of caution here.

Foreign residents joke that they haven't had to shoot anyone for a few months, and that Pavones is perhaps the most dysfunctional town in the country. No doubt the jokes are based in truth; how much truth is up to the intrepid relocater to find out.

THE CARIBBEAN COAST

As the toucan flies, the Caribbean coast is significantly closer to the capital city of San José than fabled Pacific coast beaches like Tamarindo and Montezuma. Puerto Viejo, the east-coast version of those offbeat surfer havens, is an easy four-hour bus ride from San José. The provincial capital of Puerto Limón, a bustling port and the only real city in the area, can be reached in half that time. The entire coastline, from Nicaragua to Panama, is only 160 kilometers (almost 100 miles) long, while the more convoluted west coast measures 480 kilometers (about 300 miles). Still, Limón—the province that encompasses the entire east coast of Costa Rica and the mountains that back it up—seems much more remote and exotic than the west coast.

The differences are apparent to even the casual observer. The Zona Caribe is more racially mixed than the rest of Costa Rica, with blacks and Chinese descended from the men who came to build the railroad, and indigenous peoples whose ancestors were here when Columbus arrived. The area also looks

© ERIN VAN RHEENEN

and feels more like the Caribbean islands, with picture postcard beaches and more humidity and evident poverty than elsewhere in the country.

North Americans who move here are often drawn to the natural beauty of the place, and also to its slightly rougher edge. There are still very few condo projects or mega-malls on the coast, and the people who love it here hope it stays that way.

The Lay of the Land

Transportation—or lack thereof—is a good way to begin to understand the Zona Caribe. Until the late 1970s, travel to this coast meant taking a slow train from San José to Puerto Limón, and travel around the area itself, especially in the north, was by motorized dugout canoe or via the slow *African Queen*–style boats that still bring mail and supplies to outlying areas.

In 1979, the road from Puerto Limón south (which takes you to Cahuita, Puerto Viejo, and Manzanillo) was improved and became passable most of the time, though heavy rains often washed out bridges and stretches of pavement. The 1991 earthquake destroyed the railroad, but by then the coastal strip south of Puerto Limón was fairly well-served by Highway 36, which was paved (sort of) to the town of Puerto Viejo. More recently, the pavement has been extended south to Manzanillo, a small village located within the Gandoca-Manzanillo National Wildlife Refuge—a reserve that doesn't get half the visitors of the more popular protected areas, but where you can see twice as much wildlife, including rare tucuxi dolphins and an alarming variety of pit vipers.

It wasn't until 1986 that Puerto Viejo (the most touristed town on the coast) got 24-hour electricity; Manzanillo and Tortuguero had to wait until 1988. Private phone lines arrived in Puerto Viejo in October 1996, and now some businesses and individuals have email accounts. In Manzanillo, it was just a few years ago that private phone lines became available (government offices had phones, and there were a few public pay phones in town). Now the government-run utility company is building antennae for cell phones in the area. If there are no major snags (always a long shot in Costa Rica), all who can afford a cell phone will be reachable, which is a huge change from fighting over the few private landlines the government deigned to make available. Puerto Viejo got its first bank (the Banco de Costa Rica) in early 2005. Before that locals and tourists had to travel to Puerto Limón to do their banking.

Nowadays you can fly by light plane from San José to Tortuguero, in the north, and to many points south—most flights last no more than 30 minutes. North of Limón, there are still very few roads; canals dug in the 1960s to link

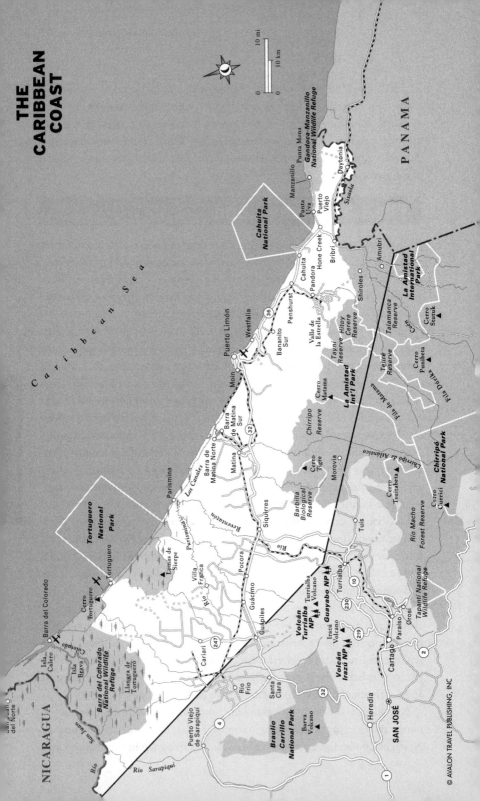

THE CARIBBEAN COAST

© AVALON TRAVEL PUBLISHING, INC

up lagoons and meandering rivers now connect remote villages and lead tourists to Tortuguero National Park, where huge numbers of sea turtles arrive to lay their eggs, usually close to the very spot where they themselves hatched.

The area's historical isolation meant that the Zona Caribe was pretty much left to its own devices. Often ignored by the government, Limón province was the poor stepchild in terms of infrastructure, education, and health services (it still is, to some extent). A third of Limón's population is Afro-Caribbean, and blacks in Costa Rica didn't even have full citizenship until 1949; there were also restrictions on where they could travel and live within their own country. Indigenous peoples, like the Bribrí and the Talamanca, also had a hard time of it historically, though nowadays they are a much more organized and vocal minority that has done much work to preserve their culture and lands.

Remoteness and cultural diversity have deep roots in the Zona Caribe. Columbus landed here in 1502, on his fourth and final journey to the New World, but he didn't stay long. Cortéz came and went 22 years later. The conquistadors hoped they'd find gold, but they were for the most part disappointed—there were no gleaming, gold-encrusted cities in Costa Rica, like those found up north in Mexico or down south in Peru. There was no real reason for the Spaniards to stick around; the coast was left to its own devices and became a refuge for rumrunners, gun traders, and mostly British pirates, who between raids would retreat to the swampy interior or hide out along stretches of wild coastline. They traded and sometimes intermarried with indigenous tribes who farmed and fished the sea and rivers. Among the tribes were the Votos, who had female chiefs; most of the tribes here were, and are, matrilineal, meaning tribe membership comes through one's mother.

To this day, the Caribbean coast retains its reputation as a smuggler's haven; nowadays the area is, unfortunately, an important transshipment point for drugs on their way from South to North America. Florentino Grenald, a guide who specializes in hikes through the Gandoca-Manzanillo Wildlife Refuge, showed me a pristine and deserted white-sand beach that he called Cocaine Beach. A few years back hundreds of kilos were dumped here when smugglers had boat trouble; locals soon discovered the cache, generously giving the water-tight bricks better hiding places in their own homes.

Isolation from the rest of the country and neglect from Costa Rica's centralized government may have had its benefits for the Zona Caribe. The natural world fared a bit better on this coast, though banana companies razed large tracts of forest and then pumped toxic insecticides into the ecosystem. Still, more of Limón province is protected than any of the other six provinces in the country. Almost half the Caribbean coastline is sheltered in reserves. The

PRIME LIVING LOCATIONS

isolation also meant that the culture—already quite different from the rest of Costa Rica—retained its individuality. Substandard health care facilities may have helped to preserve some of the folk healing and herbal remedies that came from indigenous cultures and from Africa, via West Indian immigrants. Knowledge and use of medicinal plants is common, and nontraditional healers do a brisk business in their communities, with many expats numbered among their patients. Their specialties are various and they go by many names—midwives, bush doctors, shamans, and *sukias,* to name a few. Many work hand-in-hand with more western approaches, referring people to nearby clinics if they believe that type of intervention is in the patient's best interest.

This coast has always been sparsely settled and less developed than settlements in the interior of the country and on the west coast. In 1882, the Costa Rican government offered land grants here to encourage migration. Around the same time, the railroad was being built, and workers came from as far away as Italy and China, though most came from the Caribbean islands. Of these, the majority came from Jamaica, and that culture's influence is still strongly felt here, in the English patois spoken, the spicy coconut curries served with jerk chicken, and the oversupply of Bob Marley music—hang out in a few bars and you'll reach your lifetime Marley limit in under a week.

"Don't worry about a thing," could be the area's mantra. Don't worry about the rain—the biggest *aguaceros* (downpours) usually come at night, and overcast days provide welcome relief from the dazzling sun. Don't worry if you don't have money for dinner—just pull some red snapper out of the ocean and pick from a dozen varieties of fruit growing year-round on trees that, if they aren't yours, don't seem to be watched over too closely either. And don't worry that if you have serious health problems, you'll need to go to the hospital in Limón or—if it's an emergency—that you'll most likely be airlifted to better facilities in the Central Valley.

Despite the rough spots, things move along at an easy rhythm, with a little syncopation to liven up the proceedings. The Caribbean coast is full of surprises, from lacquer-red poison dart frogs jumping out from under leaves to the prevalence of an English that confounds even more than Spanish, because you think you should understand it but don't. The people here constitute a heady brew of Afro-Caribbean, Chinese, indigenous, mestizo, European, and North American. The animal life is even more varied. I almost ended up in the Tortuguero River after my hydro-bike collided with an enormous creature that turned out to be one of the few remaining manatees in the area. Probably as startled as I was, the half-ton beast batted its fleshy tail against the boat's pontoons, then thrashed away upriver.

Such wonders are everyday fare in the Zona Caribe, and life is slow enough here to savor them.

The climate, too, is phenomenal, though whether it will inspire awe or lament depends on your constitution. The coast south of Puerto Limón (often called the Talamanca coast) averages a prodigious 2.4 meters (95 inches) of rain a year, with the wettest months being December, January, July, and August. Drier times may be had in September and October, as well as from the second half of February through April. But those in the know say there's no real dry season, just a few months where it doesn't rain quite as much. Still, it's unusual to go more than a day or two without a glimpse of sun and blue skies. Often it rains at night or for a brief spell in the morning and is clear the rest of the day.

North of Limón, the drier seasons are longer, but when the rain comes down, it really comes down. July, the wettest month, averages almost a meter (39 inches) of rain in just 31 days.

Temperatures stay the same year-round, with lows around 21–23°C (the low 70s, Fahrenheit) and the highs in the 28–30°C (80–85°F) range. Humidity can be high, but cooling breezes help to alleviate the stickiness. The sun is very strong, especially around midday, when it's best to seek out some shade lest you end up looking like the Sunburned Tourist tree, red and peeling.

PRICES

Land and home prices (and rents) on this coast are significantly more reasonable than those you'll find on the Pacific coast or in popular Central Valley locations. Local real estate agents say that the two most popular towns for expats, Cahuita and Puerto Viejo, have plenty of one-family homes from US$100,000 to US$200,000.

Where to Live

TORTUGUERO

A remote hamlet reachable only by boat or light plane, Tortuguero has drawn just a handful of permanent foreign residents. Every year, though, tens of thousands of tourists pour into nearby Tortuguero National Park, hoping to catch a glimpse of the tens of thousands of sea turtles that each year flipper their way up the beach, dig a hole in the sand, and lay their flexible-skinned eggs. Most visitors bypass the ramshackle town and spend their money in all-inclusive lodges along the river, though resident groups in the town of Tortuguero are working to change the situation.

PUNTA MONA

In 1997, Stephen Brooks, a Grateful Deadhead from Florida, bought 35 hectares (86 acres) of land on a remote peninsula called Punta Mona (Monkey Point). There were no roads leading to his new property; getting there meant (and still means) a 30-minute boat ride or a few hours tramping through the rainforest. The only neighbor within miles was an old man named Padí, who taught Stephen a great deal about the area and lived in a little house a few hundred feet from the open-air kitchen and dormitories of what has become Costa Rica's best-known organic farm.

In a few short but busy years, Stephen, known locally and with affection as the *gringo loco,* transformed this isolated plot of land into a living demonstration of permaculture, a term that at its most basic means working with, rather than against, nature. In practice here at Punta Mona, permaculture means everything from experimenting with organic black pepper, ginger, and vanilla to recycling human waste to create the methane gas that fuels the kitchen stove. Thatch-roofed *cabinas* are scattered amid lush gardens and provide a place to hang the hammocks in which visitors and residents sleep. When not helping out on the farm, farm denizens enjoy the yoga center, strum guitars, and beat drums, or pick up one of the many books lying around, from the *Popul Vuh* to *The Lord of the Rings.*

More an educational center than a working farm, Punta Mona draws a constant stream of students, travelers, and fellow *locos* who stay for a few days, a week, or a year, soaking up knowledge and inspiration. One recent visitor, David Becerra of Spain, wants to go home and start a European version of Punta Mona. That's just the kind of response Stephen Brooks hopes to provoke in visitors: His project serves as a handful of seeds, some of which will germinate here in Costa Rican soil, others that will find their way halfway across the world.

For more information about the Punta Mona Center for Sustainable Living and Education, check the website at http://puntamona.org.

Perched on a sandy spit of land between the oft-rough sea and a calm lagoon, the town can be walked end to end in minutes. You'll see wooden houses built on stilts, their corrugated tin roofs blazing in the tropical sun. Most houses are painted various shades of weather-beaten blue, with doors and shutters flung open to take advantage of the cooling breezes. There are narrow paths through the village, but most homes are oriented to the river or lagoon, the way residences elsewhere are oriented to the road. Brightly painted dugout canoes are pulled up onto the muddy bank or bob gently in the water. Herons and egrets lurk at the river's edge, keeping a sharp eye out for fish or the shrimp that congregate around the floating water hyacinth. Iguanas sun themselves on the branches of vine-draped trees.

Tortuguero's church

© ERIN VAN RHEENEN

It's a lazy, out-of-the-way place, a town you're either born to or are drawn to because of the nature that surrounds it. Volunteers come to work with the respected Caribbean Conservation Corporation, founded by biologist Archie Carr in the 1950s to help preserve and study sea turtles. The few nonnatives who settle here tend to be involved in conservation or work as nature guides. Daryl Loth, a Canadian transplant who now works as an independent guide, arrived in 1994 to manage a biological station run by a Canadian nonprofit institute. He married a local girl and settled down in a riverside home that he recently expanded to include four pleasant, airy rooms that he rents to tourists. Daryl points out that Tortuguero has its own time zone. "When it's 9 A.M. in New York City," he says, "in Tortuguero it's 1973."

Some are attracted to just that town-that-time-forgot feel. Jenny Madden, for instance, had reached the end of her rope running a successful catering business in San José. She and her four children built the business up and they were doing very well, but the stress was literally making her sick. Her hands were the first to go, and soon she couldn't even make a fist. She felt tired all the time. Knowing she had to make a life change, she sold her business and moved to Tortuguero, but she couldn't quite give up the habit of feeding people. She and her oldest son run La Casona, an eclectic restaurant offering up welcome alternatives to the ubiquitous rice and beans.

Jenny (who despite her Anglo name is *pura Tica*) is president of the local Women's Association, which has taken on the unglamorous but essential problem of trash collection. She's also the secretary of the Development Association, whose current project is to build a public dock in town to encourage tourists to disembark. She's a busy woman, and as I spoke with her about the community, she was teaching her son, Andres (who studied law), to make banana pancakes. The next day she was leaving for San José, and Andres would be in charge of La Casona during her absence. "He's great with pasta and fish, but somehow never learned pancakes. If I know he can make them, I'll breathe easier in San José." She's heading back to the capital only until her daughter gives birth; then she hopes to bring the young family back to Tortuguero, a place that's good, she's found, for what ails you. Here she has recovered strength in her hands and her energy level has soared. She credits the smell of the ocean, the slow pace, and the songs of the birds.

Tortuguero gets my vote as one of the most unusual places in the country. It wouldn't be easy to relocate here—everything, including advanced health care and higher education, is at least a few hours' boat ride away. On the other hand, the town is located within spitting distance of one of Costa Rica's most-visited national parks, and there's talk of a road that would cut a swath through the swampy jungle and end just across the river from this car-less village. Residents are actively trying to attract more tourists, and if they succeed, drowsy, aquatic Tortuguero is bound to morph into a very different kind of beast.

PUERTO LIMÓN

This down-at-the-heels port city bristles with energy, and it's where expats and locals living in more tranquil towns come to shop or visit the doctor. Terri Newton of Cahuita says Limón, a city of around 60,000, has several good private doctors and dentists. It's also where the biggest hospital in the province is located—if you're part of the Caja, the national health care system, this is where you'd come if you needed more than the basic care provided at the small clinics scattered throughout Limón province.

The rest of Costa Rica doesn't have much affection for Puerto Limón, citing crime statistics and calling it Piedropolis (Crack City). But there's no denying Limón's vitality. It's the economic engine of the area, and the streets have a definite buzz you won't find elsewhere in the province. Five kilometers (three miles) west is the sister port of Moín, where crude oil arrives for processing and boats are piled high with bananas bound for Europe and North America. Trucks loaded with freight barrel through Moín and Puerto Limón night and day, and many of the rough-and-tumble waterfront bars are open 24 hours. A major earthquake in 1991 mangled the wrought-iron balconies and toppled the open-air arcades that gave the city its ragged tropical charm, though there's been much rebuilding since then. The Limóneses walking the street are of every race, with lots of interesting blends that will have you trying to tease out the ancestry of a particularly arresting face.

But all in all Limón is not a place that inspires one to dream about buying a little house and settling down, and you'll want to hang on to your purse when you make the inevitable visit. The city's one indisputable claim to fame is that it explodes every October in Carnaval, with fireworks, dancing in the streets, and bands from all over the Caribbean and Latin America. Christopher P. Baker, author of *Moon Handbooks Costa Rica,* says the raucous festival is like the plague: You either flee or succumb. The same might be said for the city itself.

CAHUITA

A few years ago, *La Nación,* the country's largest newspaper, called Cahuita "the best beach on the Atlantic coast." It should have used the plural, because Cahuita has a parade of delectable beaches, from black-sand Playa Negra to the 14 kilometers (nine miles) of palm-shaded white sand within Cahuita National Park. Some of these beaches have earned high marks within the country's two rating systems: blue flags for cleanliness (only 27 beaches in all of Costa Rica have earned this flag, three of them in the Cahuita area) and the only "Double A" awarded to a Caribbean coast beach. Lush jungle flanks these pristine stretches of sand, the tangle of foliage so dense in places that 75 meters (82 yards) in from the beach you can't hear the surf. Offshore coral reefs create protected coves excellent for swimming and snorkeling.

The land around the coast tends to be swampy and prone to flooding. In fact, much of the area in and around town was not so long ago under water; brush aside a few centimeters of topsoil a few hundred meters from the beach and you'll hit coral. Here and there coral outcroppings rise up out of the fertile loam, which supports all manner of flowering plants and trees, including jackfruit, ornamental ginger, carambola (starfruit), and varieties of citrus and palm.

Long-term expat Paul Vigneault thinks Cahuita has an ideal climate. "It's either surfing weather—a little rough—or snorkeling weather," when the sea is aquamarine and pacific. When Paul arrived more than 15 years ago, "there was a lobster under every rock, and just one restaurant in town, a lady who had two tables in her living room." Cahuita is still a modest village, with an unpaved main street leading to the entrance to Cahuita National Park. It's one of the few parks in the country so accessible to nearby towns, and it's also one of Costa Rica's loveliest preserves. A jungle trail parallels the beach, where green flags tell you when it's safe to swim and red flags advise you to stay out of the surf. Monkeys cavort in the trees and crabs scuttle across your path.

Nowadays the lobsters may have been overfished, but the restaurant situation has definitely improved; now there are a dozen places to eat, from traditional

EXPAT PROFILE: ALAINE BERG

The last winter Alaine Berg spent in her native North Dakota was the coldest on record. Fleeing the snow, she moved to Houston in 1995 to work for the Earth Foundation, "the only environmental job in that big polluted city," she says. But Houston wasn't far enough south for her tastes, and in 2001, she headed to Puerto Viejo on Costa Rica's Caribbean coast. Why Costa Rica, and why the less-visited eastern coast? Alaine had studied Latin American culture at North Dakota State, and Noble, her "husband figure," as she puts it, had a long-standing connection to Puerto Viejo, having visited his father there every summer since 1975. So on their one-year anniversary, Alaine and Noble moved to "Old Harbor" – Puerto Viejo.

Almost immediately, both became involved with ATEC (Asociación Talamanqueña de Ecoturismo y Conservación, or Talamanca Association of Ecotourism and Conservation; the southern Caribbean coast area is also called Talamanca). ATEC's office in Puerto Viejo is also a bookstore, Internet café, and a place to arrange for eco- and community-friendly tours to nearby national parks and indigenous reserves.

I asked Alaine about ATEC and about her life in Puerto Viejo.

Tell me about your involvement with ATEC.

Noble's dad, Mel Baker, was one of ATEC's founders. He wanted to retire from running the show. For a couple of years he looked for someone to run the office but could find no locals with the right skills who'd do the job for so little money. The position was one 3/4-time job for US$400 a month. That 3/4-time job would mean a 36-hour week as the work week in Costa Rica is 48 hours. But the job can be a 170-hour work week when things get going.

Noble and I interviewed for the position over beers at a local restaurant and were both hired to fill the one position, for the one salary. Noble is the computer geek – running the Internet café part of the office – and I guess my title is project manager. A local woman, Ivette Grenald, is office director, so I work mainly in environmental education. For instance, last year another local lady (Susana Schik) and I had a grant through ReciCaribe, the Association for Recycling in Talamanca. We invited 12 schools and community groups into the recycling center in Patiño, gave presentations on the three Rs and responsible consumerism.

Right now my main projects are with ReciCaribe (working to get another grant to expand the recycling center and do another push of environmental education) and ADELA (the Action for the Fight against Petroleum, www.grupoadela.org). With ADELA we're trying to put a positive slant on the organization. Rather than keep on saying No! – No to petroleum exploitation, No to pollution – we're trying to say Yes. Yes to job growth in Talamanca. Yes to a bio-fuel project called Klean Air Fuel, a technology developed by a Costa Rican that uses leftovers from the banana plantations to produce a clean bio-fuel.

With the Talamanca Institute (www.talamancainstitute.com), ATEC is designing courses for visiting students in sustainable development, migratory bird monitoring, sea turtle conservation, and even one in Comparative Religion.

Do you travel much, or get back to the United States?
Noble and I go back to Texas for three months every spring to help with his mother's project, Eve's Garden Organic B & B and Ecology Resource Center (www.evesgarden.org). It's in the high desert, so we can dry out for while [the Caribbean coast gets a lot of rain and tends to be humid]. Without a little break from here, I wouldn't appreciate it nearly as much.

What do you like best about Costa Rica?
I love Talamanca. It's *tranquilo* [peaceful] and green. With the national park, the wildlife refuge, the indigenous reserves, and the private reserves, 82 percent of Talamanca is protected! And Talamanca has the most cultural diversity in all of Costa Rica. People here are real. For example, I come back from vacation and they tell me I'm fat, or when I vex the women I work with, they tell me. I love my work here and the people who work so hard together to protect this place.

What do you like least about Costa Rica?
I don't like so much change so fast. Yes, I'm a stranger here too, but I lived here for years before I thought about buying land, and I still haven't bought land. One of the reasons ATEC formed was to help local people survive with all of this foreign investment coming in. Foreign investment has changed things dramatically and rapidly for the people here.

Foreigners come in and expect gringo-landia. They fall in love with the *tranquilo* attitude, the amazing forests, and the uncontaminated sea. They end up getting pissed about how slow things go, or get frustrated with the *mañana* attitude. They fall into the corruption, they try to do things the quick way, use the wrong type of lumber in building, for example, make un-smart choices, get thieved, get fined, and get angry and leave a big chunk of land that they were in love with all destroyed. I'm trying to get over my "holier than thou"-ness. But people need to just come and rent for a while, get to know things, and to learn that there is no paradise on earth.

Any advice for people thinking of moving to Costa Rica?
- Rent first.
- Hire locals and pay fair wages – better than fair even. Support local business.
- Examine your intentions for wanting to invest here. If you've got an idealized image, rethink it, or you'll get disappointed.
- Learn about the area, the language, customs, history – it shows respect.
- Cultural sensitivity! English is not the national language.
- If you want to come here and make it just like home – just stay home.

Cahuita's Playa Negra

Afro-Caribbean fare to pizza and pasta. The school situation has also improved, with a K–12 private school that counts among its 100 students both expat and local kids. Parents formed the Escuela Complementaria de Cahuita (see *Resources*) because they felt frustrated by the local public school. "It would be pouring rain," says Swiss-born Brigitte Abegglen, who runs Cabinas Brigitte and has a young daughter, "and kids would walk half an hour or more to school, arriving tired and soaked to the skin. Then they'd be told to go home—the teacher hadn't shown up, or there was a staff meeting that took precedence over classes."

Basic health care is available at a small clinic in town and a larger one in nearby Hone Creek; for more serious matters, residents travel to Puerto Limón or San José. Some residents head for the Talamanca mountains to one of many famed indigenous *curanderos* (curers) or seek out Afro-Caribbean bush doctors versed in herbal and folk remedies. One long-time expat "did the whole deal—made the trip, spent the night being eaten by bugs, then stood in line with the other supplicants." When her turn came, she told the *curandero* she wanted to quit smoking. "He gave me a potion, which I drank. Then I traded my lighter for a cigarette."

Just seven or eight years ago, Cahuita was the prime tourist spot on the Caribbean coast, but now Puerto Viejo has taken over that role. Why that shift occurred is an interesting question that locals like to debate. Some say it's just the fickle nature of tourism, where a town is a hot destination one year and cold as ice in the tropics the next. It could be the Salsa Brava, Puerto Viejo's fabled wave, which draws surfers from around the world.

Cahuita is still a popular destination, if not quite as hot as a decade ago. And the decline in visitors may be a boon for potential residents, in terms of lower land prices and a quieter, more livable environment. "People always have time for each other," notes Slavko "Topo" Topolovsek of Cahuita's Magellan Inn. "You drop by, and people are glad to see you. No calling ahead here." Growth in Cahuita tends to be slow but steady, continues Topo, who also sells real estate. His town is prettier and safer than Puerto Viejo, he says, echoing what I heard all over town. Locals are constantly invoking Puerto Viejo as Cahuita's debased twin, where discos rock on into the night, drugs are plentiful, and real estate is overpriced. Interestingly, no one in Puerto Viejo had much to say about Cahuita, good or bad. Opinions are mixed as to which town, in the final analysis, will be better off.

More than a dozen countries are represented among the area's foreign residents, with the majority being from Switzerland, the United States, Germany, Canada, and Italy.

PUERTO VIEJO AND VICINITY

Puerto Viejo is the hip, slightly seedy cousin who earns enough money and has enough fun to make the rest of the family resent her terribly. It's a tumbledown place on a melancholy coast that has somehow managed to become a staple of international alternative travel. The place definitely has its charms. It's hard to beat drinking a cold beer while digging your toes into warm sand, watching expert surfers cut across the face of belligerent waves. You may have heard of the Salsa Brava—a hard, fast, dangerous wave that draws riders from near and far—but did you know you could languish in a beachside bar and still see all the action? When the surf dies down, you get to watch the newcomers choose the wrong route in, picking their way around shelves of razor-sharp coral. Buy them a beer if they arrive really cut up.

Driving the town's paved main street, you'll need to slow for bike and foot traffic—people pedaling by on beat-up beach cruisers or ambling from lunch to hammock or from coffee to Internet café. Not everyone here is tattooed and 22, though sometimes it seems that way. On closer examination, you'll see that even some of the surf gods look like they've been around long enough to remember Jimmy Carter's beer-swilling brother Billy, who, come to think of it, would probably feel right at home in Puerto Viejo. If you head south out of town, you'll pass Playa Cocles and Punta Uva, areas that have high concentrations of long-term North American and European expats. "They're all old hippies out there," a townie told me. "Good people." Nobody would hazard a guess as to how many foreign residents there were in the area, but locals lament that more and more land seems to end up in foreign hands. Richard Cunningham, born in Puerto Viejo and owner of Momchies Bakery, estimates that 75 percent of the town is now foreign-owned. "They flash a lot of money, and people are people—they take it." I asked him if he too was looking to sell out. His reply: "What're you offering?"

The influx began in 1991, when a newly paved coastal road made Puerto Viejo easily accessible from San José. Locals began selling off their land to newcomers, in part because many considered their farms worthless, since their principal crop, cacao, had recently been destroyed by the *Monilia* fungus.

Foreigners are still coming. Many tourists arrive and know from day one that they want to stay. Some go back home, make a little money, and return to build a beachside home or start a business. Others never leave, and eke out a living any way they can—I met a young man from Portland, Oregon, who seemed to be the waiter for half the restaurants in town.

Speaking of food, it's very good here. Where many tourists come, businesses spring up to cater to their every whim. So there's sushi as well as rondon (or rundown), a spicy fish stew with Afro-Caribbean roots, and Thai curry as well as rice and beans. Several places serve respectable coffee, and one (Café Rico) serves an espresso that will knock your flip-flops off. Nightlife is there if you want it, but the vibe is gentle—lots of reggae and its companion herb. Bambu Bar has reggae nights twice a week, and it's fun to watch the motley crew on the dance floor, most of them with eyes closed, swaying to their own beat. The jerkier dancers may have gotten into the coke, which is available and cheap enough to make it a problem. Says a *norteamericano* who's been here five years: "People come down here; they don't come for the drugs. But then they get a bump at a party, and they say, 'This stuff costs how much?' And oh, they're locked. Some of them never come back." Most foreign residents, however, are too busy with their businesses, their projects, or just trying to get their house built to have time for such hard-edged diversions.

For example, a decade ago Lindy and Peter Kring bought an abandoned cacao farm and transformed it into Finca la Isla Botanical Garden. "We've had our successes and failures," they explain in their brochure. "In many respects as a commercial farm, it is very inefficient. We tend to get carried away with collecting and experimenting. However, as boutique black pepper growers and nursery-landscapers we have been able to support ourselves."

Some expats help out with a local grassroots organization called ATEC (Asociación Talamanqueña de Ecoturismo y Conservación, or Talamanca

Association of Ecotourism and Conservation). ATEC's office on the main street is Puerto Viejo's unofficial community center and tourist information bureau. Born in 1990 out of a concern that increasing tourism was benefiting outside investors but leaving native Puerto Viejans high and dry, ATEC has trained locals to be guides and is creating a small-loan program to help locals finance hotels, restaurants, and other small businesses. It also arranges trips to the nearby Kèköldi Indigenous Reserve, where Cabécar and Bribrí people live and work.

Other newcomers want to make a positive impact on the community but choose to go it alone. German-born Carlston "Ken" Teimann founded a company, Surayöum, which also offers tours to the KéköLdi Reserve, along with seminars on sustainable agriculture and the Bribrí way of life. Ken married Yuri, a Bribrí woman, and the two are proud parents of Surayöum, the daughter after which their company is named. "It means 'the sacred land where all Bribrí clans were created,'" explains Ken. "Bribrí's not an easy language—it's tonal. It took me a year to be able to pronounce my own daughter's name."

At Ken's 40-hectare (99-acre) farm, he planted 400 fruit trees and built a conference center and dormitory in the traditional open-air Bribrí style. He believes that we must pay attention to nature and how indigenous peoples have coexisted peacefully with the natural world of which we are all a part. "Somewhere most of the world took a wrong turn. We can learn a lot from indigenous people as to how to get back on track."

Most residents agree that allowing offshore drilling is not the right track, and locals and expats recently joined forces to drive Harkin Energy, which wanted to construct eight drilling platforms, out of town. The fight still rages on, and time will tell where the path Puerto Viejo is following will lead it. But there's no denying that things are changing here, and fast. The 13 kilometers (eight miles) between Puerto Viejo and Manzanillo and nearby Gandoca-Manzanillo Reserve used to be bad enough to make people think twice about living out that way. Now it's all paved, and some fear that soon that stretch of highway will be as developed as the road between Quepos and Manuel Antonio National Park on the west coast, with dozens of upscale hotels, restaurants, and residences. On the other hand, points out one expat, "the way roads are paved in this country, it'll be full of potholes again in six months. They lay on such a thin layer of asphalt they might as well just paint the dust black. But maybe that's not such a bad thing. We don't want to be too accessible."

PRIME LIVING LOCATIONS

RESOURCES

© ERIN VAN RHEENEN

Embassies and Consulates

For general information, visit the Costa Rican embassy website (www.costarica-embassy.org) or the Costa Rican Ministry of Culture and Foreign Relations website (www.rree.go.cr).

COSTA RICAN EMBASSIES AND CONSULATES IN THE UNITED STATES

COSTA RICAN EMBASSY
2112 S St. NW
Washington, DC 20008
tel. 202/328-6628
after-hours emergencies: tel. 202/215-4178
fax 202/265-4795
consulate@costarica-embassy.org
Jurisdiction: all U.S. states, particularly District of Columbia, Delaware, Maryland, North Carolina, South Carolina, Virginia, and West Virginia

ATLANTA
Consulate General
1870 The Exchange, Ste. 100
Atlanta, GA 30339
tel. 770/951-7025
after-hours emergencies: tel. 770/797-7700
fax 770/951-7073
consulate_ga@costarica-embassy.org
Jurisdiction: Georgia, North Carolina, South Carolina

BOSTON
Honorary Consulate
175 McClellan Hwy.
East Boston, MA 02128
tel. 617/561-2444
fax 617/561-2461
consulate_bos@costarica-embassy.org
Jurisdiction: Massachusetts (temporarily closed as of 2007; contact the Costa Rican Consulate General in New York)

CHICAGO
Consulate General
203 N. Wabash Ave., Ste. 1312
Chicago, IL 60601
tel. 312/263-2772
after-hours emergencies: tel. 312/399-3997
fax 312/263-5807
crcchi@aol.com
Jurisdiction: Illinois, Indiana, Iowa, Michigan, Minnesota, Missouri, North Dakota, Ohio, South Dakota, Wisconsin

DALLAS
Honorary Consulate
7777 Forest Ln., Ste. C-204
Dallas, TX 75230
tel. 972/566-2871
fax 972/566-7943
Attention to the public: by appointment only
Jurisdiction: Dallas

DENVER
Honorary Consulate
3356 S. Xenia St.
Denver, CO 80231-4542
tel. 303/696-8211
fax 303/696-1110
cronsul@mmsn.com
Jurisdiction: Colorado

HOUSTON
Consulate General
3000 Wilcrest, Ste. 112
Houston, TX 77042
tel. 713/266-0484
after-hours emergencies: tel. 281/597-1194
fax 713/266-1527
consulatecr@sbcglobal.net
Jurisdiction: Colorado, Kansas, Nebraska, New Mexico, Oklahoma, Texas

LOS ANGELES
Consulate General
1605 W. Olympic Blvd., Ste. 400
Los Angeles, CA 90015
tel. 213/380-7915 or 213/380-6031
fax 213/380-5639
costaricaconsulatela@hotmail.com
Jurisdiction: Alaska, Arizona, Hawaii, Nevada, Southern California, Utah

MIAMI
Consulate General
1101 Brickell Ave., Ste. 704-S
Miami, FL 33131

tel. 305/871-7487 or 305/871-7485
after-hours emergencies: tel. 305/331-0636
fax 305/871-0860
consulate_mia@costarica-embassy.org
Jurisdiction: Florida

NEW ORLEANS
Consulate General
World Trade Center Bldg.
2 Canal St., Ste. 2334
New Orleans, LA 70130
tel. 504/581-6800
after-hours emergencies: tel. 504/256-2027
fax 504/581-6850
consulcrno@aol.com
Jurisdiction: Alabama, Arkansas, Kentucky, Louisiana, Mississippi, Tennessee. (Temporarily closed as of 2007; residents of Arkansas, Louisiana, and Mississippi, contact the Consulate General in Houston; residents of Kentucky, Tennessee, and Alabama, contact the Consulate General in Atlanta.)

NEW YORK
Consulate General
225 W. 34th St.
Penn Plaza Building, Ste. 1203
New York, NY 10122
tel. 212/509-3066 or 509-3067
fax 212/509-3068
costaricaconsul@yahoo.com
Jurisdiction: Connecticut, Maine, Massachusetts, New Hampshire, New Jersey, New York, Pennsylvania, Rhode Island, Vermont

PUERTO RICO
Consulate General
1413 Avenida Fernández Junco, Ste. 2-D
San Juan, Puerto Rico 00909
tel. 787/723-6227
fax 787/723-6226
consulate_pr@costarica-embassy.org
Jurisdiction: Puerto Rico

SAN FRANCISCO
Honorary Consulate
P.O. Box 7643
Fremont, CA 94537
tel. 510/790-0785 (9 A.M.-noon only)
after-hours emergencies (beeper): 800/790-8561
fax 510/792-5249
consulsfo@hotmail.com

Jurisdiction: Idaho, Montana, Northern California, Oregon, Washington, Wyoming

SCOTTSDALE
Gainey Ranch Financial Center, Ste. 200
7373 E. Double Tree Ranch Rd.
Scottsdale, AZ 85258
tel. 480/951-2264
fax 602/365-4435
burkeap@aol.com
Jurisdiction: Phoenix

ST. PAUL
Honorary Consulate
2424 Territorial Rd.
St. Paul, MN 55114
tel. 651/645-4103
fax 651/645-4684
cr-consulate@2424group.com
Jurisdiction: Minnesota (temporarily closed as of 2007; contact the Costa Rican Consulate General in Chicago)

TUCSON
Honorary Consulate
3567 E. Sunrise Dr., Ste. 235
Tucson, AZ 85718
tel. 520/529-7068
fax 520/577-6781
CostaRica@missiontrust.com
Jurisdiction: Arizona

COSTA RICAN EMBASSIES AND CONSULATES IN CANADA

ALBERTA
Consulate
P.O. Box 21117
Edmonton, AB T6R 2V4
tel. 780/438-7878
fax 780/435-8313
costaricaconsul@shaw.ca

MONTRÉAL
Consulate
1425 René Levexque West, Ste. 602
Montréal, QC H3G 1T7
tel. 514/393-1057
fax 514/393-1624
costarica@bellnet.ca

OTTAWA
Embassy
325 Dalhouise St., Ste. 407
Ottawa, ON, K1N 7G2
tel. 613/299-4609
fax 613/562-2582
embcria@travel-net.com

TORONTO
Consulate
164 Avenue Rd.
Toronto, ON M5R 2H9
tel. 416/961-6773 or 961-6771
fax 416/961-6771

VANCOUVER
Consulate
205-1401 Lonsdale Ave.
North Vancouver, BC V79 2H9
tel. 604/983-2152
fax 604/983-2178
consulado@sprint.ca or arreaga@axionet.com

COSTA RICAN EMBASSIES AND CONSULATES IN THE UNITED KINGDOM

LONDON
Consulate
Flat 1, 14 Lancaster Gate
London W2 3LH, England
tel. 207/706-8844
fax 207/262-9982
costaricanembassy@btconnect.com

WINDSOR
Consulate
3 Church St.
Windsor SL4 IPE, England
tel. 175/386-4652
fax 175/386-4652
patrilig@hotmail.com

Foreign Embassies in Costa Rica

U.S. EMBASSY
Calle 120, Avenida 0, Pavas
San José, Costa Rica
Hours: 8 A.M.–4:30 P.M.
tel. 506/519-2000
after-hours emergency tel. 506/519-2280,
506/519-2279, or 506/220-3127
fax 506/220-2305 or 506/232-7944
http://usembassy.or.cr
local mail address:
Apartado 920-1200 Pavas
San José, Costa Rica
U.S. mail address:
U.S. Embassy San José
APO AA 34020

CANADIAN EMBASSY
Officentro Executivo La Sabana, Sabana Sur
Edificio 5, Piso 3
San José, Costa Rica
sjcra@international.gc.ca

http://geo.international.gc.ca/latin-america/
sanjose
mailing address:
Apartado Postal 351-1077
Centro Colón
San José, Costa Rica
tel. 506/242-4400
fax 506/242-4410

BRITISH EMBASSY
Paseo Colón, between Calles 38 and 40, in the
Edificio Centro Colón, 11th floor
tel. 506/258-2025
after-hours emergency tel. 506/225-4049
(leave message)
fax 506/233-9938
britemb@racsa.co.cr
www.fco.gov.uk
mailing address:
Apartado 815, Edificio Centro Colón,
Piso 11, San José 1007, Costa Rica

Government Organizations

For an excellent list of government agencies, newspapers, radio and TV stations, banks, universities, political parties, and more, see www.grupoice.com/esp/temas/herram/directorio.htm.

ASSOCIATION OF AMERICAN CHAMBERS OF COMMERCE IN LATIN AMERICA
AACCLA
www.aaccla.org

BANCO CENTRAL DE COSTA RICA
Central Bank of Costa Rica
www.bccr.fi.cr

CAJA COSTARRICENSE DE SEGURO SOCIAL
tel. 506/295-2000
www.ccss.sa.cr
Costa Rica's Social Security ministry, which (among the many services it provides) ensures that most of the country's inhabitants can receive medical care at public hospitals

CÁMARA DE INDUSTRIAS DE COSTA RICA
Chamber of Industries
www.cicr.com

CÁMARA DE LA CONSTRUCCIÓN
Chamber of Construction
www.construccion.co.cr

CÁMARA NACIONAL DE TURISMO (CANATUR)
Costa Rica National Chamber of Tourism
www.costarica.tourism.co.cr

COMPAÑÍA NACIONAL DE FUERZA Y LUZ, S.A.
National Power Company
www.cnfl.go.cr

DIRECCIÓN GENERAL DE ADUANAS, MINISTERIO DE HACIENDA
Costa Rican Customs Office
www.impuestos.go.cr

DIRECCIÓN GENERAL DE MIGRACIÓN Y EXTRANJERÍA
Costa Rica Department of Immigration
www.migracion.go.cr

INSTITUTO COSTARRICENSE DE ACUEDUCTOS Y ALCANTARILLADOS (AYA)
National Institute of Aqueducts and Sewage
www.aya.go.cr

INSTITUTO COSTARRICENSE DE ELECTRICIDAD (ICE)
National Electricity Institute
www.ice.go.cr
Telecommunications, cell phones, phone lines

INSTITUTO NACIONAL DE SEGUROS (INS)
National Insurance Institute
www.ins.go.cr

INSTITUTO NACIONAL DE ESTADISTICA Y CENSOS (INEC)
Census Bureau
www.inec.go.cr

INSTITUTO DE VIVENDA Y URBANISMO
Housing and Urban Development Department
www.invu.go.cr

MINISTERIO DE AGRICULTURA Y GANADERÍA
Ministry of Agriculture
www.mag.go.cr

MINISTERIO DE CIENCIA Y TECNOLOGÍA
Ministry of Science and Technology
www.micit.go.cr

MINISTERIO DE EDUCACIÓN PÚBLICA
Public Education Ministry
www.mep.go.cr

MINISTERIO DE HACIENDA
Finance Ministry
www.hacienda.go.cr

MINISTERIO DEL AMBIENTE Y ENERGÍA (MINAE)
Ministry of the Environment and Energy
www.minae.go.cr

RACSA
Radiográfica Costarricense

www.racsa.co.cr
Telecommunications, Internet

SISTEMA NACIONAL DE AREAS DE CONSERVACIÓN
National Park System
www.sinaccr.net

Environmental Organizations

CARIBBEAN CONSERVATION CORPORATION
www.cccturtle.org

EARTHWATCH
www.earthwatch.org

GUANACASTE CONSERVATION AREAS
www.acguanacaste.ac.cr

MONTEVERDE CONSERVATION LEAGUE
www.monteverdeinfo.com/monteverde_conservation_league.htm

NATIONAL PARKS OF COSTA RICA
http://centralamerica.com/cr/parks/

NATURE CONSERVANCY
www.tnc.or

ORGANIZATION OF TROPICAL STUDIES
www.ots.ac.cr or www.ots.duke.edu

SISTEMA NACIONAL DE AREAS DE CONSERVACIÓN
National Park System
www.sinaccr.net

TROPICAL RIVER FOUNDATION
www.riostro.com

People and Culture

ARTS

THE JULIA AND DAVID WHITE ARTS COLONY
tel. 506/249-1414
www.forjuliaanddavid.org
Ex–Los Angeleno Bill White started this lovely retreat after both of his children tragically died. Both were artistically inclined, and Bill decided he would create a gorgeous, peaceful place where artists could come and do nothing but pursue their work. At any given time there are two writers, two visual artists, and two composers lucky enough to be in residence at this lush spread half an hour outside San José in Ciudad Colón.

MUSEUMS IN SAN JOSÉ

MUSEO DE ARTE COSTARRICENSE (COSTA RICAN ART MUSEUM)
east end of Sabana Park
tel. 506/222-7175
www.cr/arte/musearte/ musearte.htm

MUSEO DE ARTE Y DISEÑO CONTEMPORÁNEO (ART AND DESIGN MUSEUM)
in the old prison building (Antigua Fanal) on Avenida 3 between Avenidas 13 and 15
tel. 506/257-7202
www.madc.ac.cr

MUSEO DE INSECTOS (INSECT MUSEUM)

on the UCR campus (San Pedro), in the Music Building
tel. 506/207-5318

MUSEO DE JADE (JADE MUSEUM)

on the 11th floor of the INS Building, between Avenidas 5 and 7, and Calles 11 and 13
tel. 506/223-5800
www.cr/arte/jade/musejade.htm

MUSEO DE LOS NIÑOS (CHILDREN'S MUSEUM)

Avenida Central, at Calle 17
tel. 506/258-4929

MUSEO DE ORO (GOLD MUSEUM)

Plaza de la Cultura, Calle 5 at Avenida 2
tel. 506/243-4202
www.museosdelbancocentral.org/eng/gold/index.htm

MUSEO NACIONAL (NATIONAL MUSEUM)

Calle 17 at Avenida 2
tel. 506/257-1433
www.cr/arte/museonac/ museonac.htm

THEATERS IN SAN JOSÉ

TEATRO MELICO SALAZAR (MELICO SALAZAR THEATER)

on Avenida 2, diagonal from the cathedral
tel. 506/221-4952
www.teatromelicosalazar.go.cr/

TEATRO NACIONAL (NATIONAL THEATER)

Plaza de la Cultura, Calle 5 at Avenida 2
tel. 506/221-1329
www.guiascostarica.com/teatro.htm

CULTURAL CENTERS IN SAN JOSÉ

ALLIANCE FRANÇAISE

Avenida 7 at Calle 5, 200 meters (219 yd.) west of the INS building
tel. 506/222-2283
fax 506/233-5819
alcultfr@sol.racsa.co.cr
www.alianzafr.ac.cr

CASA ITALIA

200 meters (219 yd.) south of KFC in Barrio La California
tel. 506/224-6049

JEWISH COMMUNITY INFORMATION

www.centroisraelita.com/centro_israelita_informacion_visitantes_eng.htm
This web page also has broader info about the Jewish community in San José.

MEXICAN CULTURAL CENTER

250 meters (273 yd.) south of Subaru dealership in Los Yoses
tel. 506/283-2333

NORTH AMERICAN CULTURAL CENTER

100 meters (109 yd.) north of the Automercado Los Yoses, in Barrio Dent, San José
tel. 506/207-7500
fax 506/224-1480
mercadeo@cccncr.com
www.cccncr.com

SPANISH CULTURAL CENTER

next to the Farolito in Barrio Escalante
tel. 506/257-2919
ccultucr@racas.co.cr

GAY CULTURE

UNO@DIEZ

Calle 3 and Avenida 7 in San José
tel. 506/258-4561
www.1en10.com
GLBT information center

THE SEXUAL DIVERSITY CULTURAL CENTER OF COSTA RICA

tel. 800/247-2227
www.cipacdh.org
This center provides counseling and support groups for gay, lesbian, and transgendered persons. It's also involved in the June Gay Pride festivities and World AIDS Day each December 1.

THE AGUA BUENA HUMAN RIGHTS ASSOCIATION

tel. 506/234-2411
www.aguabuena.org
AIDS activism

GENTE 10
www.gente10.com
Gay magazine and website

WWW.GAYCOSTARICA.COM
Search this website for gay-owned and gay-friendly lodging, restaurants, or tour agencies; it also has news and personal ads.

MUJER Y MUJER
www.mujerymujer.com
Website dedicated to Costa Rica's lesbian community

GLOBAL GAYZ
www.globalgayz.com
International site covering a variety of countries, including Costa Rica

Making the Move

VISAS

VISA/ENTRY REQUIREMENTS
www.costarica-embassy.org

U.S. STATE DEPARTMENT
http://travel.state.gov/passport_ services.html

DIRECCIÓN GENERAL DE MIGRACIÓN Y EXTRANJERÍA (COSTA RICA DEPARTMENT OF IMMIGRATION)
www.migracion.go.cr

COSTA RICAN MINISTRY OF FOREIGN RELATIONS
www.rree.go.cr
This department administers all the Costa Rican embassies and consular offices abroad.

RELOCATION TOURS AND ASSISTANCE

ASSOCIATION OF RESIDENTS OF COSTA RICA (ARCR)
tel. 506/221-2053
fax 506/255-0061
www.casacanada.net/arcr
Membership organization that offers valuable help in relocating to and thriving in Costa Rica

BOOMERS IN COSTA RICA RELOCATION TOURS
tel. 506/350-7647
www.boomersincostarica.com

Andrew Mastrandonas, cofounder of Angel Valley Bed and Breakfast in San Ramón, leads a relocation tour company that focuses on the Central Valley.

GUARDIAN ANGELS
tel. 506/832-2450
U.S./Canada toll-free tel. 877/889-1131
info@relocationcr.com
www.relocationcr.com
Angela Passman founded Guardian Angels to help with corporate and family relocation to Costa Rica. As a mother and pet lover, she's also great with pet transport and helping to find schools for your kids.

LIVE IN COSTA RICA TOURS
tel. 506/222-1090
crbooks@racsa.co.cr
www.liveincostarica.com
Author Christopher Howard offers relocation/retirement tours around the Central Valley, to the mid-Pacific coast, and to Guanacaste.

RETIRE IN COSTA RICA ON SOCIAL SECURITY TOURS
tel. 506/888-4543 or 506/417-1041
U.S./Canada toll-free tel. 877/779-9503
george@costaricaretireonss.com
www.costaricaretireonss.com
George Lundquist runs this relocation tour company.

LEGAL HELP

WWW.COSTARICALAW.COM
Indispensable site covering all things

legal in Costa Rica—from residency petitions to property rights. Roger Petersen, the creator of the site, was born in Costa Rica of a Tica mother and U.S. father. He went to college and worked in the United States before returning to his beloved home in Costa Rica. He's also written a book, *The Legal Guide to Costa Rica,* available for sale on his site.

PET TRANSPORT

See also *Guardian Angels* under *Relocation Tours and Assistance.*

IPATA
tel. 903/769-2267
fax 903/769-2867
inquiries@ipata.com
www.ipata.com
A Texas-based international trade association of animal handlers, pet moving providers, kennel operators, and veterinarians

PET ADOPTION IN COSTA RICA

There are many local organizations in addition to the ones listed here—ask around in your town.

ASOCIACIÓN HUMANITARIA PARA LA PROTECCIÓN DE ANIMALES (AHPPA)
tel. 506/267-7158
fax 506/267- 6374
refugio@infoweb.co.cr
www.animalsheltercostarica.com
The "humane society" of Costa Rica, founded in 1992 and based in the city of Heredia. It rescues strays, then vaccinates, deworms, and neuters the animals before putting them up for adoption. The website says that about 80 dogs and 50 cats are adopted out per month.

ASOCIACIÓN NACIONAL PROTECTORA DE ANIMALES (ANPA)
tel. 506/255-3757 or 506/233-0779
info@adoptame.org
www.adoptame.org
Founded in 1980, this organization aims to educate people about animal cruelty

and to help rescue and neuter abandoned animals, then make them available for adoption.

REFUGIO DE ANIMALES (ANIMAL REFUGE)
tel. 506/267-7158
In San José.

COSTA RICAN TOURISM OFFICES

There are four official offices of the Instituto Costarricense de Turismo (ICT): Peñas Blancas (at the border with Nicaragua, open 8 A.M.–8 P.M.); Paso Canoas (at the Panama border, open 6 A.M.–10 A.M.); at the Juan Santamaría Airport (near San José, open Mon.–Fri. 9 A.M.–5 P.M.); and in downtown San José (open Mon.–Fri. 9 A.M.–1 P.M. and 2–5 P.M.).

The San José office is right behind the Teatro Central, in the Plaza de la Cultura, Calle 5, Avenida Central y Segunda. You could call (tel. 506/222-1090), but it's better to go in person, since the staff rarely answers the phone. Or try the website, www.visitcostarica.com.

Apart from the official tourist offices, cities and towns bristle with signs advertising "Tourist Information." Mostly these are private agencies trying to sell specific tours, but the people there are usually friendly and will give you information even if you don't want to go on their tour.

UNITED STATES
Costa Rica Tourist Office
1100 Brickell Ave., Ste. 801
Miami, FL 33131
tel. 800/343-6332

CANADA
Costa Rica Tourist Office
135 York St., Ste. 208
Ottawa, ON K1N 5T4
tel. 613/562-2855

UNITED KINGDOM
Costa Rica Tourist Office
14 Lancaster Gate
London W2 3LH
tel. 0171/706-8844
fax 0171/706-8655

Primary and Secondary Schools

SAN JOSÉ AREA

AMERICAN INTERNATIONAL SCHOOL OF COSTA RICA (FORMERLY THE COSTA RICA ACADEMY)
Ciudad Cariari
mailing address:
Interlink 249, P.O. Box 02-5635
Miami, FL 33102
tel. 506/293-2567
fax 506/239-0625
ais@aiscr.com or neli@aiscr.com
www.aiscr.com
Founded in 1970, AIS offers pre-K through grade 12, with a U.S.-style curriculum. The school year comprises two semesters, from mid-August to mid-December and from mid-January to mid-June. Classes are in English, and Advanced Placement (AP) programs are available. The total student body numbers around 200, there are 40 or so teachers, and class size averages about 15 students. The school is accredited by the Southern Association of Colleges and Schools.

ANGLO-AMERICAN SCHOOL
Centro Educativa Angloamericano
Concepción de Tres Ríos (near Cartago)
tel. 506/279-2626
fax 506/279-7894
aaschool@angloamericano.ed.cr
www.angloamericano.ed.cr
This school was founded in 1949, grades encompass pre-K through high school, and classes are in mostly Spanish with some English. Day care is also available.

BLUE VALLEY SCHOOL
Escazú
tel. 506/215-2203 or 2204
fax 506/215-2205
bvschool@racsa.co.cr
www.bluevalley.ed.cr
Founded in 1989, this school has around 600 students from pre-K through high school and about 70 teachers. Instruction is in English, and both U.S.-style high school diplomas and the IB (international baccalaureate) are available.

BRITISH SCHOOL
Escuela o Colegio Britannica
Pavas
tel. 506/220-0719
fax 506/220 0131 or 232-7833
britsch@racsa.co.cr
www.infoweb.co.cr/britsch
Grades are K-12, with around 850 students total; 85 percent of the students are Costa Rican, with 23 different nationalities represented. Classes are taught mostly in English. The school offers National or IB (international baccalaureate) curricula. It's ECIS (European Council of International Schools) accredited. Runs on a Costa Rican school year schedule.

CALASANZ SCHOOL
Colegio Calasanz
San Pedro
tel. 506/283-4730
fax 506/283-1890
colegio@colegiocalasanz.com
www.colegiocalasanz.com
Founded in 1961, this Catholic school has instruction in Spanish for grades K-11.

COUNTRY DAY SCHOOL
Escazú
tel. 506/289-0919
fax 506/228-2076
trent@cds.ed.cr
www.cds.ed.cr
Founded in 1963 and modeled after prep schools in the United States, CDS is one of the most prestigious schools in Costa Rica, and also has a branch in Guanacaste. Pre-K through 12, with classes in English and extras such as outdoor education, arts, and college counseling.

EUROPEAN SCHOOL
Colegio Europeo
San Pablo de Heredia
tel. 506/261-0717
fax 506/263-5793
info@europeanschool.com
www.europeanschool.com

Founded in 1989 by Anne Aronson, mother of five, the European School goes from pre-K through high school and has about 350 students from 20 countries. Key to the school's philosophy is the concept of integrated teaching, in which "a central theme unifies and interrelates academic work in literature, history, geography, and art."

The school offers the IB (international baccalaureate), and the school year runs from late July through late June, with short vacations every 9–10 weeks.

FRENCH SCHOOL
Liceo Franco-Costarricense or Lycée Franco-Costaricien
Concepción de Tres Ríos
tel. 506/273-6373
fax 506/273-3380
http://franco.ed.cr
Pre-K through high school, about 800 students, with classes taught in French, English, and Spanish

HUMBOLDT SCHOOL
Colegio Humboldt
Pavas
tel. 506/232-1455
fax 506/232-0093
humboldt@humboldt.ed.cr
www.humboldt.ed.cr
K-12 classes taught in German, English, and Spanish; around 750 students

INTERNATIONAL CHRISTIAN SCHOOL
Heredia
tel. 506/241-1445
fax 506/241-4944
cscr@icscr.net
www.icscr.net
U.S. missionary William Tabor founded this school to promote "academic excellence and the active lordship of Jesus Christ in all respects of life." Pre-K through 12th grade; around 600 students. Operates on U.S. academic calendar; language of primary instruction is English. There's also a smaller branch in Liberia.

LINCOLN SCHOOL
Santo Domingo de Heredia
tel. 506/247-0800
fax 506/247-0900
www.lincoln.ed.cr
Offering classes from pre-K through 12th grade, Lincoln is one of the larger private schools in the San José area, with around 1,200 students and a faculty of 120. It offers either a U.S.-style college-prep curriculum or the IB (international baccalaureate). Lincoln is considered a prestigious place to send your kid—it's where "the kids of big Costa Rica politicians go," according to one source.

MARIAN BAKER SCHOOL
San Ramón de Tres Ríos
tel. 506/273-3426
fax 506/273-4609
mbschool@racsa.co.cr
www.marianbakerschool.com
Pre-K through 12th grade; around 200 students. Operates on the U.S. academic calendar; instruction is in English.

METHODIST COLLEGE
Colegio Metodista
San Pedro and Sabanilla
tel. 506/280-1220
administracion@metodista.ed.cr
www.metodista.ed.cr
Founded in 1921, this bilingual Christian school serves students from pre-K through grade 12.

MONTERREY COLLEGE
Colegio Monterrey
San Pedro
tel. 506/224-0833
fax 506/244-3386
asculmon@ice.co.cr
www.colegiomonterrey.ed.cr
A Christian school with bilingual education for pre-K through 11th grade

PANAMERICAN SCHOOL
Colegio Panamericana
San Antonio de Belen
tel. 506/298-5700
fax 506/293-7392
cpcrsa@racsa.co.cr
Pre-K through 12th grade; 700 students

SAINT ANTHONY SCHOOL
Moravia

tel. 506/235-1017
fax 506/235-2325
santhony@racsa.co.cr
Pre-K through 6th grade; 500 students

SAINT CECILIA BILINGUAL COLLEGE

San Francisco de Heredia
tel. 506/237-7733
fax 506/237-4557
colsupcr@racsa.co.cr
Pre-K through 11th grade; 680 students

SAINT CLARE EDUCATIVE SYSTEM

Sistema Educativo Saint Clare
San Vincente, Moravia
tel. 506/235-7244
fax 506/235-7271
Grades 7–11; 650 students

SAINT FRANCIS COLLEGE

Moravia
tel. 506/297-1704 or 506/240-8277
sfc@stfrancis.ed.cr
www.stfrancis.ed.cr
K through 11th grade; over 1,200 students

SAINT GREGORY SCHOOL

Tres Ríos
tel. 506/279-4444
fax 506/279-9727
info@sgs.ed.cr
www.sgs.ed.cr
Pre-K through 11th grade; 350 students; instruction mostly in Spanish

SAINT MARY'S SCHOOL

Guachipelín de Escazú
tel. 506/215-2135 or 506/228-2003
fax 506/215-2132
cosama@racsa.co.cr
Pre-K through 6th grade; instruction in English and Spanish

SAINT MONICA'S SCHOOL

Escuela Santa Mónica
Guadalupe
tel. 506/235-4119 or 506/228-0349
fax 506/240-2172
Pre-K through 6th grade; instruction in English and Spanish

SAINT PAUL COLLEGE

Colegio Saint Paul
San Rafael de Alajuela
tel. 506/438-1661
fax 506/438-2120
hsstpaul@racsa.co.cr and infocol@saintpaul.ed.cr
www.saintpaul.ed.cr
Pre-K through 11th grade, bilingual English-Spanish; the majority of the approximately 1,200 students are Costa Rican. "The idea behind this school is to offer a quality bilingual education to national students," says a teacher here.

SAINT PETER'S SCHOOL

Curridabat
tel./fax 506/272-2045 or 506/302-2100
Pre-K through 11th grade

SAN JUDAS TADEO BILINGUAL SCHOOL

Colegio Bilingue San Judas Tadeo
Barrio Don Bosco
tel. 506/257-8778
fax 506/233-3973
Pre-K through 12th grade

UNITED WORLD COLLEGE (UWC)

tel. 506/282-5609
fax 506/282-1540
admisiones@uwccr.com
www.uwccr.com
In March 2007 UWC Costa Rica opened in Santa Ana (a suburb of San José) with 118 students from 64 countries, including, of course, many students from Costa Rica. UWC is a two-year college prep program for 16- to 18-year-olds who want to earn an International Baccalaureate (IB) degree. Part of a world-wide network of 11 such colleges, UWC Costa Rica is the first bilingual school (English-Spanish) in the group and is the only one affiliated with SOS Children's Villages International, which provide housing and education to poor students. Prospective students from 130 countries apply to the UWC program; if accepted, they are able to choose which UWC campus they would like to attend. Besides the campus in Costa Rica, there are schools in Singapore, Swaziland, Italy, and New Mexico, to name just a few. UWC also provides scholarships to help cover the $15,500 yearly tuition.

WEIZMAN INSTITUTE
Instituto Dr. Jaim Weizman
Mata Redonda
tel. 506/231-5566 or 506/231-5705
fax 506/220-1127
weizman@amnet.co.cr
Pre-K through 11th grade

Turrialba

CENTRO EDUCATIVA JORGE DEBRAVO
Turrialba
tel. 506/556-0411 or 506/556-1516
fax 506/556-1516

ESCUELA INTERNATIONAL CATIE
Turrialba
tel. 506/556-7942
fax 506/556-1533
School associated with CATIE (Centro Agronómico Tropical de Investigación y Enseñanza/Center for Tropical Agriculture Investigation and Learning), one of the top tropical research stations in the world. Turrialba is about 65 kilometers (40 miles) from San José.

MONTEVERDE

CREATIVE EDUCATION CENTER
Centro de Educación Creativa
Monteverde, Puntarenas
tel. 506/645-5161
tel./fax 506/645-5480
www.cloudforestschool.org
Bilingual school serving about 220 students in grades K through 11

MONTEVERDE FRIENDS SCHOOL (MFS)
Monteverde, Puntarenas
tel./fax 506/645-5302
mfschool@racsa.co.cr
www.mfschool.org
MFS was founded 50 years ago by a group of Quakers who settled in the Monteverde region. It now has about 100 students and 14 full-time staff, and a curriculum that meets both Costa Rican and U.S. college prep standards. Pre-K through 12th grade.

GUANACASTE AND THE NICOYA PENINSULA

ACADEMIA TEOCALI
Liberia, Guanacaste
tel. 506/384-3093
fax 506/666-0273
academiateocali@ice.co.cr
Founded in 1982; pre-K through 11th grade

COCO BEACH SCHOOL
Playas del Coco, Guanacaste
tel. 506/670-0378
tedshirl@racsa.co.cr
In 2006 Coco Beach School rose from the ashes, literally, of the Institute for Bilingual Schooling, after a fire destroyed most of the school, including 7,000 books in the library. The current school is under the direction of Canadian expat Shirley Bergeron, in partnership with Mapache Realty (one of the most powerful companies in the area), who is helping the school build a better-equipped new campus that will accommodate a larger student body. Pre-K through 6th grade; about 70 students, 10 teachers.

COUNTRY DAY SCHOOL OF GUANACASTE
Playa Brasilito, Guanacaste
tel. 506/654-5042
fax 506/654-5044
infocdsg@cds.ed.cr
www.cdsgte.com
Billed as "a serious school at the beach," this is a branch of the well-known institution based in Escazú. CDS Guanacaste offers classes in English from pre-K through 12th grade, and boarding for students in grades 8–12. About half of the students are children of U.S. or Canadian expats, with the other half from Costa Rica, other Latin American nations, and Europe. There's a nice campus, with gym, pool, playing fields, library, and computer lab.

INSTITUTO PEDAGÓGICO EUPI
Guanacaste
tel. 506/686-6561
fax 506/686-4884

INTERNATIONAL CHRISTIAN SCHOOL/CIUDAD BLANCA SCHOOL
Liberia
tel. 506/665-0007
fax 506/665-4311
www.icscr.net
Ciudad Blanca School became in 2004 a branch of Heredia's International Christian School. About 300 students (K–11) from 17 different countries are instructed in Spanish, with some classes taught in English. They operate on the Costa Rican calendar (February to mid-December, with a three-week break in June and July).

PINILLA ACADEMY
Playa Avellanas, near Tamarindo
A work-in-progress, Pinilla Academy hopes to open its primary school in late 2007 or early 2008 and to be a fully functioning K–12 prep school by 2011. Its aim is to offer both the IB (international baccalaureate) and U.S.-style high school diplomas. The school is located between the main entrance of Hacienda Pinilla and Avellanas Beach.

THE CENTRAL AND SOUTH PACIFIC COAST

PRIVATE SCHOOL OF QUEPOS
Escuela Privada de Quepos
Quepos, Puntarenas
tel. 506/777-2211
fax 506/777-0164

The Caribbean Coast

CENTRO EDUCATIVA CARIBE
Limón
tel. 506/798-0307
fax 506/798-1152

ESCUELA COMPLEMENTARIA DE CAHUITA
Cahuita, Limón Province
tel. 506/755-0075
Founded in 1994, this school teaches an international student body of approximately 100, from pre-K through high school.

Higher and Continuing Education

PUBLIC UNIVERSITIES

INSTITUTE OF TECHNOLOGY
Instituto de Tecnología de Costa Rica
tel. 506/552-5333
www.itcr.ac.cr
The campus is in Cartago.

THE NATIONAL UNIVERSITY
Universidad Nacional
tel. 506/277-3317
fax 506/277-3225
www.una.ac.cr
Based in Heredia, the National University also has regional centers in Liberia and Perez Zeledon.

THE STATE UNIVERSITY'S DISTANCE LEARNING PROGRAM
Universidad Estatal a Distancia
tel. 506/253-2121
www.uned.ac.cr

The main campus is in San José, with 32 regional centers scattered around the country.

UNIVERSITY OF COSTA RICA
Universidad de Costa Rica
tel. 506/207-5535
www.ucr.ac.cr
Main campus in San José; branch campuses in Alajuela, Cartago, Turrialba, and Puntarenas

Private Universities and Other Educational Facilities

CATIE (CENTRO AGRONÓMICO TROPICAL DE INVESTIGACIÓN Y ENSEÑANZA)
Turrialba
tel. 506/558-2000

fax. 506/558-2060
communicacion@catie.ac.cr
www.catie.ac.cr

The Tropical Agricultural Research and Higher Education Center was founded in 1942 by what would become the Organization of American States (OAS). This multifaceted institute offers master's and doctorate degrees in areas such as integrated watershed management and tropical agroforestry.

EARTH (ESCUELA DE AGRICULTURA DE LA REGIÓN TROPICAL HÚMEDA)

Guácimo de Limón
tel. 506/713-0000
fax 506/713-0001
jzaglul@earth.ac.cr (rector Jose Zaglul)
www.earth.ac.cr

Since 1990, EARTH University in Costa Rica has been educating students to "shape the direction of environmental protection and development in Latin America and the entire global community as a whole." It offers a *"licenciatura"* (a degree midway between a bachelor's and master's) in agricultural sciences, among other degrees and concentrations.

INCAE (INSTITUTO CENTROAMERICANO DE ADMINISTRACIÓN DE EMPRESA)

Alajuela
tel. 506/433-9908 or 506/433-9961

fax 506/433-9983 or 506/433-9989
costarica@incae.edu
www.incae.ac.cr

Associated with Harvard Business School, this business school just outside of San José would be a good choice for someone looking to specialize in Latin American markets. It offers master's programs in "areas critical for Latin American development" as well as executive training programs and seminars.

OTS (ORGANIZATION FOR TROPICAL STUDIES)

San Pedro, San José
tel. 506/524-0607
fax 506/524-0608
www.ots.ac.cr
cro@ots.ac.cr

Graduate studies for real scientists and short *"biocursos"* all over Latin America for us scientist wannabes. Study sharks off Cocos Island or glaciers in Patagonia.

UNIVERSITY FOR PEACE

tel. 506/205-9000
fax 506/249-1929
info@upeace.org
www.upeace.org

Near Ciudad Colón, this United Nations–affiliated school serves a small, international student body as they work toward master's and doctorate degrees in everything from sustainable development to peace-building.

Spanish-Language Schools

The schools listed below are just a sampling of the many operating in Costa Rica, and their rates and schedules changes frequently. Check their websites for current pricing and programs.

ACADEMIA DE IDIOMAS ESCAZÚ

Escazú, a suburb of San José
tel. 506/228-7736
escazu@amerisol.net
www.amerisol.com/costarica/edu/escazu

Small classes (about four people) use the total immersion method; most programs have four hours of classes a day, five days a week.

ACADEMIA TICA

locations in San Isidro de Coronado, a town 10 kilometers (6.2 miles) northeast of San José, and also in the beach town of Jacó
tel. 506/229-0013
actica@racsa.co.cr
www.academiatica.com

Academia Tica offers two- to four-week programs. Most meet every weekday morning 8 A.M.–noon, with starting dates throughout the year. It also has specialized programs that include internships or volunteering, and there's a "parent and child" program. Homestays can be arranged.

BERLITZ LANGUAGE CENTER
Centro de Idiomas Berlitz
San Pedro tel. 506/253-9191
downtown San José tel. 506/248-0725
Sabana Norte tel. 506/291-4327
Santa Ana tel. 506/204-7555
Liberia tel. 506/665-5544
berlitzinfo@berlitzedu.net
www.berlitzedu.net

Berlitz has four locations in the San José area (San Pedro, downtown, Sabana Norte, and in the Forum building in Santa Ana) and one location in Guanacaste (Liberia).

CENTRO DE IDIOMAS DEL PACÍFICO
Quepos/Manuel Antonio
service@costaricareisen.com
www.costaricareisen.com/info/schulen/cipacifico/indexeng.htm

CENTRO LINGÜÍSTICO CONVERSA
downtown San José and in the nearby town of Santa Ana
Costa Rica tel. 506/221-7649
U.S. tel. 888/669-1664
U.S./Canada toll-free tel. 800/354-5036
fax 506/233-2418
info@conversa.net
www.conversa.net

Founded in 1975, the Centro offers small classes; choose intensive (four hours per day) or super-intensive (5.5 hours per day). College credit is available through Miami-Dade Community College (Florida) and Truman State University (Missouri).

CENTRO PANAMERICANO DE IDIOMAS (CPI)
Costa Rica tel. 506/265-6306
U.S. tel. 877/373-3116
Canada tel. 888/864-3133
fax 506/265-6866
info@cpi-edu.com
www.cpi-edu.com

CPI has three campuses—in Heredia (near San José), in the mountain town of Monteverde, and near the Pacific coast beach of Playa Flamingo. Programs are from one to four weeks, and they include specialized courses like Spanish for medical workers and Spanish for social workers.

CITY PLAYA
Jacó (Pacific coast)
tel. 506/643-2123
fax 506/643-2122
citima@racsa.co.cr
www.cityplaya.com

COSTA RICAN LANGUAGE ACADEMY
Barrio Dent, San José
tel. 506/280-1685
U.S. toll-free tel. 866/230-6361
fax 506/280-2548
spanish@crla.co.cr
www.spanishandmore.com

Courses are offered year-round, and class schedules are flexible. You can choose to study 3–6 hours a day, in small classes or one-on-one with an instructor.

COSTA RICAN SPANISH INSTITUTE (COSI)
San José tel. 506/234-1001
U.S. toll-free tel. 800/771-5184
fax 506/253-2117
office@cosi.co.cr
www.cosi.co.cr

COSI offers classes in San José and near Manuel Antonio National Park on the Pacific coast.

ESCUELA D'AMORE
Manuel Antonio
tel./fax 506/777-1143
U.S. tel. 800/261-3203
info@escueladamore.com
www.escueladamore.com

FORESTER INSTITUTE
Los Yoses, San José
tel. 506/225-3155
U.S. tel. 305/767-1663
fax 506/225-9236
forester@racsa.co.cr
Skype user name: foresterinstituto
www.fores.com

Founded in 1979, this school offers one-to four-week programs, with many extras like dance classes and excursions. The institute has hosted many foreign universities' study abroad programs.

HORIZONTES DE MONTEZUMA
tel. 506/642-0534
collina@racsa.co.cr
www.horizontes-montezuma.com
Hotel and language school near the beach in Montezuma

ICADS: INSTITUTE FOR CENTRAL AMERICAN DEVELOPMENT STUDIES
Curridabat, San José
tel. 506/225-0508
fax 506/234-1337
info@icads.org
www.icadscr.com
Offering "study programs for progressive minds," ICADS allows you to earn college credit while learning Spanish and interning in the areas of public health, wildlife conservation, and women's issues.

ILISA LANGUAGE INSTITUTE
San Pedro neighborhood of San José (it also has a campus in Panama City)
tel. 506/280-0700
U.S. tel. 800/454-7248
fax 506/225-4665
www.ilisa.com
Billing itself as a "school for professionals" that "does not cater to backpackers," ILISA offers a variety of programs, including small group classes 8 a.m.–noon Monday–Friday. Special programs for professionals—from nurses to teachers—are also on offer.

INSTITUTE FOR CENTRAL AMERICAN STUDIES
Sabanilla, San José
tel. 506/253-3195
fax 506/234-7682
OurSchool@mesoamericaonline.net
www.mesoamericaonline.net
This organization puts out a monthly English-language newsletter covering Central American politics and also offers language study and internships.

INSTITUTO BRITANICO
tel. 506/225-0256
fax 506/253-1894
info@institutobritanico.co.cr
www.institutobritanico.co.cr
With two locations in San José (Los Yoses and Paseo Colón), this school offers everything from two weeks of general Spanish (40 hours a week) to a week (15 hours of instruction) of "Spanish Express," a crash course in basic Spanish, as well as corporate training and programs for teachers.

INSTITUTO UNIVERSAL DE IDIOMAS
Moravia, San José
tel. 506/223-9662
fax 506/223-9917
spanish@universal-edu.com
www.universal-edu.com
Intensive instruction, small classes. It also offers business Spanish, medical Spanish, Spanish for teachers, and volunteer programs.

INTENSA: INTENSIVE LEARNING PROGRAMS
tel. 506/281-1818
U.S. tel. 866/277-1352
toll-free in U.S. and Canada: 866/277-1352
fax 506/253-4337
info@intensa.com
www.intensa.com
With three campuses in the Central Valley (San Pedro, Alajuela, and Escazú), INTENSA offers programs that last from one to four weeks. College credit is also available.

INTERCULTURA
Heredia, north of San José, and in Sámara Beach
tel. 506/260-8480
tel./fax 506/656-0127
toll-free in U.S.: 866/363-5421
info@interculturacostarica.com
www.interculturacostarica.com
Intercultura has campuses just outside of San José (in Heredia) and in the Pacific coast beach town of Sámara. Programs range from one to four weeks and provide four hours of daily instruction. Volunteer programs, cultural enrichment extras.

IPEE SPANISH LANGUAGE SCHOOL: INSTITUTO PROFESIONAL DE ESPAÑOL PARA EXTRANJEROS

Curridabat, San José
tel. 506/283-7731
U.S. tel. 813/643-0416
fax 506/225-7860
ipee@gate.net
www.ipee.com

Intensive one- to eight-week courses. There are specialty programs for Spanish teachers, to learn Spanish medical terminology, or to study Latin American literature.

LANGUAGE AND INTERNATIONAL RELATIONS INSTITUTE (ILERI)

tel. 506/289-4396
tel./fax 506/228-1687
info@ilerispanishschool.com
www.ilerispanishschool.com

In Escazú, a suburb of San José (it also has campuses in Panama City and Bocas del Toro, Panama). The school can arrange volunteering positions around the country after a student has studied Spanish.

LAS OSAS MAYOR Y MENOR LANGUAGE CENTER

Puerto Jiménez, on the Osa Peninsula
tel. 506/815- 8919
fax 506/735-5045
www.lasosas.org
cocoterotico@yahoo.com or lasosas@lasosas
.org

The very friendly master nature guide Oscar Cortes Alfaro presides over this center, where you can arrange language study with an emphasis on nature (Puerto Jiménez is close to the spectacular Corcovado National Park); homestays also available.

NEW DAWN CENTER

near San Isidro de General
thenewdawncenter@yahoo.com
www.thenewdawncenter.info

Spanish classes are offered at this organic farm, along with seminars on natural health care and tropical medicinal plants. Accommodations and meals available at the farmhouse. The center was founded and is run by Ed Bernhardt, naturalist and author of classics such as *The Costa Rican Organic Home Gardening Guide*.

REY DE NOSARA

tel. 506/682-0215
fax 506/682-4057
reydenosara@ice.co.cr
www.reydenosara.itgo.com

Group and private lessons in Nosara Beach, Guanacaste

SPANISH ABROAD, INC.

based in Phoenix, Arizona
tel. 602/778-6791
U.S./Canada toll-free tel. 888/722-7623
fax 602/840-1545
info@spanishabroad.com
www.spanishabroad.com

A clearinghouse for many programs in the Spanish-speaking world, it links up with schools in many parts of Costa Rica.

UCR'S SPANISH AS A FOREIGN LANGUAGE PROGRAM

San Pedro, San José
tel. 506/207-5634
fax 506/207-5089
espaucr@le.ucr.ac.cr
http://cariari.ucr.ac.cr/filo/ingles.htm

UCR (University of Costa Rica), the largest and most prestigious university in Costa Rica, has a "Spanish as a foreign language" program that also gives participants access to a community of more than 30,000 students. Language students (who need not be enrolled in the larger university) are issued student cards, which allow them to use campus libraries and sports facilities. One-month intensive courses are offered most months of the year—classes meet four hours a day, Monday through Friday, and cost around US$600 for the month. Two-month classes on Latin American literature, advanced Spanish conversation, and advanced Spanish literature are also available. Homestays can be arranged.

WAYRA INSTITUTO DE ESPAÑOL

Playa Tamarindo, Guanacaste
tel./fax 506/653-0359
info@spanish-wayra.co.cr
www.spanish-wayra.co.cr

A school in the popular beach town of Tamarindo that offers small group classes and private lessons. Class and homestay rates go down the longer you stay.

Health

GENERAL HEALTH INFORMATION

THE CENTERS FOR DISEASE CONTROL
traveler's health hotline: tel. 877/394-8747
www.cdc.gov/travel
This Atlanta, Georgia, institution is an invaluable resource for the health issues you may confront when traveling or living in countries all over the world.

TRAVEL HEALTH ONLINE
www.tripprep.com
Vaccination requirements and health issues in more than 200 countries

THE WORLD HEALTH ORGANIZATION
www.who.int/ith
The Geneva, Switzerland–based WHO has a special section devoted to travelers' health on its website.

EMERGENCIES AND REPORTING CRIME
Dial 911 in an emergency.

Crimes discovered after the fact should be reported to the nearest Organization of Judicial Investigation (OIJ) Office. The OIJ is the equivalent of the FBI but is under the authority of the judicial branch of the Costa Rican government. The OIJ is responsible for investigating major crimes. Call 506/222-1365 or 506/221-5337.

If you have a traffic accident, leave the vehicles where they are, and call both the Tránsito (Transit Police, tel. 506/222-9330 or 506/222-9245) and the Insurance Investigator (800/800-8000). Both of these officials will come, eventually, to the accident scene upon notification and file their reports. Only after they do so can you legally move your vehicle.

HOSPITALS AND CLINICS
For a Red Cross ambulance, dial 128 or 911, or call 506/221-5818.

Public Hospitals in San José
BLANCO CERVANTES
tel. 506/257-8122

BURN UNIT
tel. 506/257-0180

CHILDREN'S HOSPITAL
tel. 506/222-0122

HOSPITAL CALDERÓN GUARDIA
tel. 506/257-7299

HOSPITAL MÉXICO
tel. 506/232-6122

POISON CENTER
tel. 506/223-1028

SAN JUAN DE DIOS
tel. 506/257-6282

WOMEN'S HOSPITAL
tel. 506/257-9111

Private Clinics/Hospitals in San José
CLÍNICA BÍBLICA
on Calle Central, between Avenidas 14 and 16
Apartado 1307-1000
San José
tel. 506/257-0466 (emergency number) or
506/522-1000
fax 506/221-0645
info@clinicabiblica.com
www.clinicabiblica.com

CLÍNICA CATÓLICA
in San Antonio de Guadalupe, a suburb of San José
tel. 506/246-3000
fax 506/283-6171
info@clinicacatolica.com
www.hospitallacatolica.com

CLÍNICA SANTA RITA
tel. 506/221-6433

HOSPITAL CIMA
in Escazú
tel. 506/208-1144 (emergency number)
tel. 506/208-1000
fax 506/208-1001
cima@hospitalcima.com
www.hospitalsanjose.net

Hospitals/Clinics in Alajuela

SAN RAFAEL
tel. 506/441-5011

VALVERDE VEGA
tel. 506/445-5388

SAN FRANCISCO DE ASÍS
tel. 506/444-5045

UPALA
tel. 506/447-0181

LOS CHILES
tel. 506/447-1045

MONTE SINAÍ, CIUDAD QUESADA
tel. 506/460-1080

SAN CARLOS
tel. 506/460-1176 or 506/460-0553

CCSS (CAJA) CLINICS IN SAN CARLOS
tel. 506/479-9142 (La Fortuna)
tel. 506/473-3089 (Pital)
tel. 506/477-7075 (Santa Rosa)
tel. 506/472-2044 (Venecia)

Hospitals/Clinics in Puntarenas

MONSEÑOR SANABRIA
tel. 506/663-0033

MAX TERÁN
tel. 506/777-0922

GOLFITO
tel. 506/775-0011

CIUDAD NEILY
tel. 506/783-4111

SAN VITO DE COTO BRUS
tel. 506/773-3103

CIUDAD CORTÉS
tel. 506/788-8197

Hospitals/Clinics in Guanacaste

ENRIQUE BALTODANO
tel. 506/666-0011

ANEXIÓN DE NICOYA
tel. 506/685-5066

Hospitals/Clinics in Limón

TONY FACIO
tel. 506/758-2222

GUÁPILES
tel. 506/710-6801

Hospitals/Clinics in Heredia

SAN VICENTE DE PAUL
tel. 506/237-5944

Hospitals/Clinics in Cartago

MAX PERALTA
tel. 506/550-1999

CHACÓN PAUT
tel. 506/279-9192

WÍLLIAM ALLEN
tel. 506/556-4343

NATURAL CHILDBIRTH

CENTRAL-AMERICAN-MIDWIVES
www.central-american-midwives.org
Website created by a group of midwives
from many Central American countries

MOTHERS IN BIRTH
tel. 506/224-580
www.mamasalnacimiento.com

UVA MEINER
tel. 506/268-2127 or 506/253-8786
German-born birth assistant who speaks
six languages, including English

DISABILITY ACCESS

THE ASSOCIATION OF COSTA RICAN SPECIAL TAXIS
tel. 506/296-6443 or 506/396-8986
This association has a fleet of 40 vans equipped for wheelchair travel.

THE COSTA RICAN DEAF TRAVEL CORPORATION
tel. 506/289-4812
fax 506/289-3894
These guides are deaf or hearing-impaired and are certified in U.S. and international sign language.

INTERNATIONAL INSTITUTE OF CREATIVE DEVELOPMENT
tel. 506/771-7482
mchabot@consult-IIDC.com
www.empowermentaccess.com
Canadian Monica Cabot and staff design tours for travelers with disabilities.

SERENDIPITY ADVENTURES
Costa Rica tel. 506/558-1000
U.S./Canada tel. 977/507-1358
www.serendipityadventures.com
Specializes in active tours; has experience customizing trips for disabled travelers

THE SOCIETY FOR ACCESSIBLE TRAVEL AND HOSPITALITY (SATH)
tel. 212/447-7284
fax 212/725-8253
sathtravel@aol.com
www.sath.org
New York-based nonprofit trying to "raise awareness of the needs of all travelers with disabilities, remove physical and attitudinal barriers to free access and expand travel opportunities in the United States and abroad."

VAYA CON SILLA DE RUEDAS (GO WITH A WHEELCHAIR)
tel. 506/454-2810 or 506/391-5045
www.gowithwheelchairs.com
This company has air-conditioned vans with up to three wheelchair stations; it also arranges tours.

ENVIRONMENTAL CONCERNS

CERTIFICATION IN SUSTAINABLE TOURISM (CST)
www.turismo-sostenible.co.cr/EN/home.shtml
The Costa Rican Tourism Institute's program to recognize hotels and tour operators that work toward sustainable development.

THE 4RS RECYCLING COALITION
tel. 506/231-2712
www.4rs.or.cr
Find out about recycling programs in different parts of Costa Rica.

THE RAINFOREST ALLIANCE
http://eco-indextourism.org/en/home
Among many other resources, this group has information on sustainable tourism and lists operators whom it believes to be "green."

HEALTH INSURANCE IN COSTA RICA
The government has a monopoly on all forms of insurance, and since 1924 there has been only one provider: the National Insurance Institute. But even monopolies need help sometimes, so the INS allows private agents to help you arrange for INS-provided insurance. The INS website lists many agents, including English-speaking Garrett and Associates, listed here. Other organizations that can help arrange health insurance in Costa Rica are American Legion Post 10 and the Association of Residents of Costa Rica (ARCR).

CAJA COSTARRICENSE DE SEGURO SOCIAL
tel. 506/295-2000
www.ccss.sa.cr
Costa Rica's Social Security ministry, which (among the many services it provides) ensures that most of the country's inhabitants can receive medical care at public hospitals

GARRETT AND ASSOCIATES
Apartado 5478-1000, San José, Costa Rica
tel. 506/233-2455
fax 506/222-0007
garrins@sol.racsa.co.cr
www.segurosgarrett.com

**INSTITUTO NACIONAL
DE SEGUROS (INS)**
National Insurance Institute
tel. 506/223-5800
www.ins-cr.com

INTERNATIONAL HEALTH INSURANCE

Most U.S. health insurance companies—like Blue Cross and Aetna—have international policies available.

INTERNATIONAL MEDICAL GROUP
www.imglobal.com

INSURANCE BROKERS

You can buy insurance through these companies; their websites can help you compare prices among insurance providers.

GLOBAL INSURANCE NET
www.globalinsurancenet.com

**INSURANCE CONSULTANTS
INTERNATIONAL**
www.globalhealthinsurance.com

INSURANCE TO GO
www.insurancetogo.com

MEDIBROKER
www.medibroker.com

TRAVEL INSURANCE PROVIDERS IN NORTH AMERICA

Some of these companies also provide longer-term international health insurance.

AMERICAN EXPRESS
tel. 800/234-0375
www.americanexpress.com

MULTINATIONAL UNDERWRITERS
tel. 317/262-2132 or 800/605-2282
fax 317/212-2140
www.mnui.com

TRAVELERS
tel. 203/277-0111 or 800/243-3174
www.travelers.com

TRAVELGUARD INTERNATIONAL
tel. 715/345-0505 or 877/216-4885
www.travelguard.com

WALLACH AND COMPANY
tel. 703/687-3166 or 800/237-6615
www.wallach.com

BEAUTY

MED AND DAY SPA
Country Plaza, Escazú
tel. 506/288-0059, 506/288-2980, or 506/288-0115
Expat Elaine Chalmers runs this salon and spa in Escazú, where I got the best haircut I've had in Costa Rica.

Employment

CÁMARA DE EXPORTADORES DE COSTA RICA (CADEXCO)
Chamber of Exporters of Costa Rica
www.cadexco.net

CÁMARA DE INDUSTRIAS DE COSTA RICA
Chamber of Industries
tel. 506/202-5600
fax 506/234-6163
www.cicr.com

CENTRO PARA LA PROMOCIÓN DE EXPORTACIONES E INVERSIONES (PROCOMER)
Export and Investment Promotion Center
www.procomer.com

COLEGIO DE ABOGADOS (LAWYERS' GUILD)
tel. 506/202-3600
fax 506/224-0314
www.abogados.or.cr

COSTA RICAN-AMERICAN CHAMBER OF COMMERCE (AMCHAM)
tel. 506/220-2200
fax 506/220-2300
www.amcham.co.cr

COSTA RICAN INVESTMENT AND DEVELOPMENT BOARD (CINDE)
tel. 506/201-2800
fax 506/201-2869
U.S. toll-free tel. 866/577-4783
www.cinde.or.cr

MINISTERIO DE TRABAJO Y SEGURIDAD SOCIAL
Ministry of Work and Social Security
www.ministrabajo.go.cr/Macros/Salario/Salarios%20Minimos.htm
A detailed list of minimum salaries in Costa Rica, in Spanish and using *colones* as the currency

Volunteer Organizations

ANAI ASSOCIATION
tel. 506/224-3570
fax 506/253-7524
www.anaicr.org
Work in bird conservation and to protect leatherback turtles on the Caribbean coast

APREFLOFAS
tel. 506/240-6087
fax 506/236-3210
www.preserveplanet.org
Work mostly in wildlife protection

ASVO (ASSOCIATION OF VOLUNTEERS WORKING IN PROTECTED AREAS)
tel. 506/258-4430
fax 506/233-4989
www.asvocr.com
Basic Spanish and one-month commitment are required for work in national-park maintenance and turtle conservation.

CARIBBEAN CONSERVATION CORPORATION
tel. 506/297-5510 or 506/709-8091
fax 506/297-6576
www.cccturtle.org
Protect leatherback and green turtles on the Caribbean coast.

CRUZ ROJA (RED CROSS)
tel. 506/233-7033
www.cruzroja.or.cr

DAMAS VOLUNTARIOS DE ESCAZÚ
tel. 506/228-0279
fax 506/288-0235
cguerra@racsa.co.cr
Help out in day care/nutrition center for young kids.

DOLPHIN FOUNDATION OF COSTA RICA
tel. 506/847-3131
fax 506/786-7366
www.divinedolphin.com
Work with marine mammals in the Drake Bay area.

ECOTEACH
tel. 800/626-8992
www.ecoteach.com
Matches U.S. student volunteers with humanitarian and ecological organizations

FINCA LA FLOR
tel. 506/534-8003
www.la-flor-de-paraiso.org
Environmental education, including organic farming and medicinal plants

FUNDACIÓN PANIAMOR
tel. 506/234-2993
fax 506/234-2956
www.paniamor.or.cr
You'll need good Spanish to work with this agency dedicated to preventing domestic abuse.

HABITAT FOR HUMANITY
tel. 506/296-3436
fax 506/232-3430
www.habitatcostarica.org
The Costa Rican branch of this international organization needs help building simple houses and in its office.

HUMANITARIAN FOUNDATION
tel. 506/390-4192 or 506/282-6358
gynstrom@racsa.co.cr
Provides programs for at-risk Ticos

MCKEE PROJECT
fax 506/239-6045
www.mckeeproject.org
Needs vets and support workers to help spay and neuter street cats and dogs

MONTEVERDE BUTTERFLY GARDEN
tel./fax 506/645-5512

wolfej@racsa.co.cr
Tour guides and groundsworkers are needed.

NATIONAL PARKS OF COSTA RICA
within Costa Rica, dial 192
Needs help with park maintenance

PEACE CORPS
www.peacecorps.gov

SALVATION ARMY
tel. 506/223-4864
fax 506/223-0250
ejercito@racsa.co.cr
Rehab programs for alcoholics; shelters for abused women and children

SARAPIQUÍ CONSERVATION LEARNING CENTER
tel. 506/766-6482
fax 506/766-6011
www.learningcentercostarica.org
Teach English and computer skills to locals; good Spanish and a six-month commitment preferred.

TROPICAL ADVENTURES
tel. 800/832-9419
www.tropicaladventures.com
Founder Scott Pralinsky arranges volunteer, homestay, and language-learning opportunities, mostly on the Caribbean coast and in the Central Valley.

VECINOS
tel./fax 506/227-3868
vecinos@racsa.co.cr
Programs for at-risk kids.

VIDA
Association of Volunteers in Research and Environmental Development
tel. 506/221-8367
fax 506/223-5485
www.vida.org
Matches volunteers with humanitarian and ecological organizations

Finance

SUGEF (SUPERINTENDENCE OF FINANCIAL ENTITIES)
tel. 506/243-4848
www.sugef.fi.cr

SUGEVAL (SUPERINTENDENCE OF SECURITIES)
tel. 506/243-4700
correo@sugeval.fi.cr
www.sugeval.fi.cr

Check out SUGEF and SUGEVAL for financial information about companies registered in Costa Rica. Both are part of Costa Rica's Central Bank; SUGEF's website has much of its content translated into English; SUGEVAL has introductory information in English and is in the process of translating more of the content.

Communications

The area code for all of Costa Rica is 506. There are no city codes, and telephone numbers have seven digits (as they do in the United States).

PHONE AND INTERNET SERVICE

RACSA (RADIOGRÁFICA COSTARICENNSE)
in San José at Avenida 5 and Calle 1
tel. 506/287-0087
www.racsa.co.cr

PRIVATE MAIL SERVICES

AAA EXPRESS MAIL
tel. 506/233-4993
fax 506/221-5056

AEROPOST OR AEROCASILLAS
tel. 506/208-4848
servicesjo@aerocasillas.com
www.aeropost.com

DAILY MAIL
tel. 506/233-4993
fax 506/221-5046

STAR BOX
P.O. Box 405-1000
San José
tel. 506/257-3443
fax 506/233-5624

TRANS-EXPRESS "INTERLINK"
P.O. Box 02-5635
Miami, FL 33102
tel. 506/296-3973 or 506/296-3974
fax 506/232-3979

Travel and Transportation

DANIEL ODUBER INTERNATIONAL AIRPORT
tel. 506/668-1010
Located in Liberia, Guanacaste, an hour from northern Guanacaste beaches

JUAN SANTAMARÍA INTERNATIONAL AIRPORT (SJO)
tel. 506/437-2626
www.alterra.co.cr
Has international and domestic terminals and is just north of San José

TOBÍAS BOLAÑOS AIRPORT
For smaller domestic and charter flights; located in Pavas, a bit closer to San José than the larger international airport

AIRLINES THAT FLY WITHIN COSTA RICA

AERO BELL
tel. 506/290-0000
www.aerobell.com
aerobell@racsa.co.cr

AERO COASTAL SOL
tel. 506/440-1444
fax 506/441-2671
flyacs@racsa.co.cr

HELICÓPTEROS TURÍSTICOS TROPICALES
tel. 506/296-0460

NATURE AIR
U.S./Canada toll-free tel. 800/235-9272
Costa Rica tel. 506/299-6000
info@natureair.com
www.natureair.com
The preferred domestic carrier for many travelers and expats, Nature Air flies its small planes out of Tobías Bolaños Airport all over Costa Rica and also to Granada, Nicaragua, and Bocas del Toro in Panama. Baggage limit is 14 kilograms (30 pounds); surfboards under two meters (six feet, eight inches) are allowed but cost $15 extra to transport.

PARADISE AIR
tel. 506/231-0938
fax 506/296-1429
U.S. toll-free tel. 877/412-0877
www.flywithparadise.com

PITTS AVIATION
tel. 506/296-3600

SANSA AIRLINES
tel. 506/221-9414 or 506/255-2176
fax 506/255-2176
www.flysansa.com
Costa Rica's domestic airline; part of TACA, the Central American airline.

FERRY SERVICE

FERRY FROM PUNTARENAS TO PAQUERA AND NARANJO
www.nicoyapeninsula.com/general/boat.html

BUS COMPANIES
For more bus information, check out www.costaricabybus.com.

FANTASY BUS
tel. 506/220-2126
fax 506/220-2393
www.graylinecostarica.com
Shuttle vans

INTERBUS
tel. 506/283-5573
fax 506/283-7655
www.costaricapass.com
Shuttle vans

TICA BUS
tel. 506/221-8954
fax 506/223-8158
www.ticabus.com
Big buses

TAXIS

ALFARO
San José
tel. 506/221-8466

COOPEGUARIA
San José
tel. 506/227-9300

COOPETICO
San José
tel. 506/235-9966 or 506/224-7979

TAXI 5 ESTRELLAS
San José
tel. 506/228-3159

They also rent vans and drivers by the hour and day.

UNIDOS AIRPORT TAXI
San José
tel. 506/221-6865

RADIO TAXI LIBERIA
Liberia
tel. 506/666-0574

Housing Considerations

COSTA RICAN REAL ESTATE AGENTS CHAMBER
tel. 506/283-0191
fax 506/283-0347
www.camaracbr.or.cr
Professional association of real estate agents that lobbies for mandatory licensing of real estate agents; it has begun a fledging multiple listing service (MLS).

THE CHAMBER'S MULTIPLE LISTING SERVICE (MLS)
www.mls-cr.com
Not your home country's MLS, this online resource is in its infancy and is at this point of limited value. Even real estate agents who belong to the chamber say they have far more listings on their own sites than on this MLS. For more discussion of Costa Rica's MLS, see the *Housing Considerations* chapter.

COSTA RICA GLOBAL ASSOCIATION OF REALTORS (CRGAR)
www.costaricare.net

Like the chamber, CRGAR promotes professionalism among real estate agents, brings buyers and seller together, and has its own nascent MLS.
tel. 506/653-1320

REGISTRO NACIONAL
506/202-0800
www.registronacional.go.cr
The National Registry (also sometimes called the Public Registry), located in San José, is where all properties in Costa Rica are listed, along with information such as the name of the title holder, boundary lines, tax appraisal, liens, mortgages, recorded easements, and anything else that would affect title.

STEWART TITLE
tel. 506/258-5600
fax 506/221-5320
www.stewarttitlelatinamerica.com
Provides title searches and title guarantees

Prime Living Locations

THE CENTRAL VALLEY AND BEYOND

Regional Information
MONTEVERDE
www.monteverdeinfo.com

SARAPIQUI
www.sarapiquirainforest.com

Real Estate Agents
HOT TROPICS
Santa Ana
tel. 506/203-7700 or 506/203-7704
cell 506/884-1264
fax 506/203-7701
U.S./Canada toll-free tel. 800/407-3903
www.hot-tropics.com
Harvey Haber, author of the first editions of the *Insight Guide to Costa Rica*, arrived here in 1989. He now works in real estate and is a refreshingly honest guide to what you'll find here in his adopted country. Also check out his newsletter and blog.

REMAX LIDER
San José area, especially Escazú
tel. 506/228-0767
cell 506/391-5088
fax 506/228-1145
andresz@racsa.co.cr
www.remaxlider.com
Andrés Zamora, manager

TOUCAN REALTY
Lake Arenal area
tel. 506/369-8408 or 506/695-5819
www.toucanrealty.com
Gerry Aust and Sarah Murrillo

GUANACASTE AND THE NICOYA PENINSULA

Regional Information
Northern Guanacaste Coast
www.beachtimes.com

TAMARINDO
www.tamarindo.com
www.tamarindonews.com
www.tamarindobeach.net

NOSARA
www.nosara.com

SOUTHERN NICOYA PENINSULA
www.nicoyapeninsula.com
www.peninsuladenicoya.com

Real Estate Agents
BRATTON BROYLES AND ASSOCIATES
Tamarindo area
tel. 506/653-1102
www.bbcostarica.com

HIDDEN COAST REALTY
Tamarindo area; there's another branch in Santa Teresa
tel. 506/653-0708
fax 506/653-0849
location@racsa.co.cr
www.hiddencoastrealty.com
Joost Hauwert, Hans Veeken, Maarten Kampen, Mariano Caffaratti

MAPACHE GROUP
toll-free tel. 800/606-3564
www.grupomapache.com
A group building housing developments mostly in Playas del Coco, Playa Ocotal, and the Liberia area. Basic condos and duplexes go for moderate prices.

REMAX OCEAN SURF REALTY
Tamarindo area; other Remax branches in Brasilito, Playa Panama, and Playa Hermosa
tel. 506/653-0073
fax 506/653-0074
csimmons@racsa.co.cr
www.remax-oceansurf-cr.com
Chris Simmons

REMAX RESORT PROPERTIES PAPAGAYO
Playas del Coco area
tel. 506/670-1129
cell 506/392-7111

fax 506/670-0825
mailloux@racsa.co.cr
www.costa-rica-real-estate1.com
Iris Mailloux

THE CENTRAL AND SOUTH PACIFIC

Regional Information
PUNTARENAS
www.puntarenas.com

DOMINICAL
www.dominical.biz

QUEPOS/MANUEL ANTONIO
www.quepolandia.com

SOUTHERN COSTA RICA
www.exploringcostarica.com
www.ecotourism.co.cr

WOMEN OF THE OSA
www.womenoftheosa.org
This association has written a handbook, *Living in the Jungle,* a guide to sustainable living "off the grid" in the tropics.

Real Estate Agents
PREMIER REALTY
Jacó area
506/643-5252
www.premierrealtyincostarica.com
Canadian Catherine Fitton and Italian Christina Senigaglia have been doing business in this area for many years.

THE CARIBBEAN COAST

Regional Information
TORTUGEURO
www.geocities.com/tortugueroinfo/main.html

ATEC–ASOCIACIÓN TALAMANQUEÑA DE ECOTURISMO Y CONSERVACIÓN
Talamancan Association of Ecotourism and Conservation
tel. 506/750-0398
tel./fax 506/750-0191
atecmail@racsa.co.cr
www.greencoast.com/atec
Director Alaine Berg presides over this grassroots community organization in Puerto Viejo; they work to promote ecological and socially responsible tourism in the Talamanca area. The office is also a kind of community center with Internet access and a small bookstore; you can book a variety of eco-friendly tours there.

Real Estate Agents
CARIBE SUR REAL ESTATE
Southern Caribbean coast area
Manuel Pinto
tel. 506/759-9138
cell 506/826-3998
info@caribesur-realestate.com
www.caribesur-realestate.com

Internet Resources

ENGLISH WEBSITES

LIVING ABROAD IN COSTA RICA
www.livingabroadincostarica.com
The author's website, with information on everything from real estate to yoga retreats

A.M. COSTA RICA
www.amcostarica.com
Online news, in English, about Costa Rica

COSTA RICA BULLETIN BOARD
http://punkhart.net/CostaRica
Useful and varied message board where you can post questions about Costa Rica

INSIDE COSTA RICA
www.insidecostarica.com

LANIC
www1.lanic.utexas.edu/la/ca/cr/
The Latin American Network Information Center has a wonderful array of links to all things Costa Rican, from government agencies to educational travel programs.

MAPTAK
www.maptak.com
Excellent source for online maps of Costa Rica

THE TICO TIMES
www.ticotimes.net
Online counterpart to the most widely read English-language weekly in Costa Rica

SPANISH WEBSITES

LA NACIÓN
www.nacion.com
Web version of the most respected Spanish-language daily in Costa Rica. It also has a weekly roundup of stories in English.

TIQUICIA
www.tiquicia.com

Forums, articles, and many useful links; frequently updated

INTERNET RESOURCES FOR LIVING ABROAD

AMERICAN CITIZENS ABROAD
www.aca.ch

CIA FACTBOOK
www.cia.gov/cia/publications/factbook
Detailed profiles of all countries

CULTURE BRIEFINGS
www.culturebriefings.com
Subscription-based service offering reports on various countries and cultures

EXPAT COMMUNITIES
www.expatcommunities.com

EXPAT EXCHANGE
www.expatexchange.com

EXPAT EXPERT
www.expatexpert.com

EXPATICA
www.expatica.com
Focuses on Europe, but has some good general information no matter where you plan to live

JOURNEYWOMAN
www.journeywoman.com

LIVE ABROAD
www.liveabroad.com

OVERSEAS DIGEST
www.overseasdigest.com

PRACTICAL NOMAD
www.practicalnomad.com
Emphasizes independent and responsible travel

TRANSITIONS ABROAD
www.transitionsabroad.com

Excellent resource for anyone who wants to work, study, or live abroad. It also has an in-depth monthly magazine.

WORLD CITIZENS GUIDE
http://worldcitizensguide.org/
Especially useful is this site's free downloadable guide for students traveling the world. Offering succinct tips like "Slow down" and "Be quiet," this brief guide helps travelers of any age have a richer trip and leave a good impression.

WORLDWIDE COST OF LIVING SURVEY
www.finfacts.com/costofliving.htm

INTERNET RESOURCES FOR RETIREES

AMERICAN ASSOCIATION OF RETIRED PERSONS (AARP)
www.aarp.org

ELDERHOSTEL
www.elderhostel.org

THIRD AGE
www.thirdage.com

TRAVEL WITH A CHALLENGE
www.travelwithachallenge.com
Global travel resource aimed at people over 50

Glossary

aguacero: downpour
aguinaldo: Christmas bonus
ballena: whale
boticas: pharmacies
buzón: mailbox
chapulín: tractor
chicha: corn liquor
cochino: "piggy," dirty
colón: Costa Rican currency
correos: post office
estranjero: stranger
farmacias: pharmacies
fútbol: soccer
grano de oro: coffee ("grain of gold")
impuesto de ventas: sales tax
lluvia: rain

mayor: main
menudo: loose change
pensionado: pensioner/retiree
personas de la tercera edad: senior citizens
polacos: roving vendors
polideportiva: sports center
precaristas: squatters
presupuesto: cost estimate
pueblo: town
pulpería: general store
puro Tico: pure Costa Rican
quebradas: creeks
residenciales: gated communities
sabanero: cowboy
soda: café/restaurant

GLOSSARY OF REAL ESTATE TERMS

Before you dive into the world of Costa Rican real estate transactions, you'll need to learn a whole new vocabulary. Here are some of the terms you're likely to encounter.

Spanish	English
activo	asset
agencia inmobiliaria	real estate agency
ajuste	adjustment
alquilar	to rent
amortización	amortization
anticipo	advance payment
apreciación	appreciation
arrendador	landlord
arrendatario	tenant
asignar	to assign, to transfer
avalúo	appraisal
bienes	personal assets
bienes inmuebles	property
bienes raíces	real estate
capital	equity
carta de crédito	letter of credit
cedente	assignor
cesión	assignment, transfer
cesionario	assignee
cierre	closing
comprador	buyer
concesión de crédito	extension of credit
confiscación	forfeiture

construcción en progreso	construction in progress
contraoferta	counteroffer
contrato de arrendamiento	lease
corredor de bienes raíces	real estate broker
desvalorización	depreciation
deuda	debt
embargo fiscal	tax lien
escritura de traspaso	deed of transfer
estatuto	bylaw
garantía	collateral
gastos de cierre	closing costs
gastos de mudanza	moving expenses
gravamen	encumbrance, lien
hectárea	hectare (10,000 square meters or about 2.5 acres)
hipoteca	mortgage
hipoteca colectiva	blanket mortgage
hipoteca con tasa de interés fija	fixed-rate mortgage
hipoteca en primer grado	first mortgage
hipoteca en segundo grado	second mortgage
hipoteca sin límite de importe	open-end mortgage
impuesto	tax
impuestos territoriales	property taxes
incumplimiento de pago	failure to pay
ingresos por arrendamientos	rental income
instalación	fixture
interés compuesto	compound interest
inversión	investment
investigación de título	title search
linea de crédito	line of credit
manzana	7000 M2 or about 1.75 acres
oferta en firme	firm offer
opción de compra	option to buy
pago inicial	down payment
patrimonio	owner's equity
pedir prestado	to borrow
peritaje	survey
permiso	permit
plazo fijo	fixed term
precarista	squatter
precio al contado	cash price
precio de lista	list price
precio máximo	maximum price
precio real	actual price
prestamista	lender
préstamo	loan
préstamo bancario	bank loan
préstamo hipotecario	mortgage loan
prestar	to lend
prestatario	borrower
propietario registrado	owner of record

prórroga	extension (of time)
promesa reciproca de compra-venta	reciprocal promise to buy and sell
Registro de la Propiedad	National Registry property section
Registro Nacional	National Registry (or Public Registry)
Registro Público	*See Registro Nacional*
respaldo financiero	financial backing
seguro contra incendio	fire insurance
seguro contra robo	theft insurance
seguro contra inundaciones	flood insurance
seguro contra riesgo	hazard insurance
servicios públicos	public utilities
servidumbre	easement
se alquila	for rent
se vende	for sale
sociedad anónima (S.A.)	corporation
tasa básica	base rate
tasa de interés	interest rate
tendencias del mercado	market trends
tenencia conjunta	joint tenancy
terrenos sin mejoras	unimproved land
tipo (or taza) de cambio	exchange rate
tipo de interés preferencial	prime rate of interest
título	deed, title
título de propiedad or *libre de gravamenes*	clear title
traspaso de propiedad	transfer of title
valor de mercado	market value
valor declarado	declared value
valor del avalúo	appraised value
valoración	appraisal
vendido	sold
zona maritimo	maritime zone
zona pública	public zone
zona restringida	restricted zone
zonificación	zoning

Spanish Phrasebook

PRONUNCIATION GUIDE

Spanish pronunciation is much more regular than that of English, but there are still occasional variations.

Consonants

c — pronounced like 'c' in "cat" before **'a,' 'o,' or 'u';** like 's' in same before 'e' or 'i'

g — pronounced like 'ch' in Scottish "loch" before 'e' or 'i'; elsewhere pronounced like 'g' in "get"

h — always silent

j — pronounced like 'h' in "hotel," but stronger

ll — pronounced like 'y' in "yellow"

ñ — pronounced like 'ni' in "onion"

r — always pronounced as a strong 'r' as in "red"

rr — a trilled 'r'

v — pronounced similar to 'b' in "boy" (not as an English 'v')

y — pronounced similar to an English 'y,' but with a slight 'j' sound. When standing alone, it's pronounced like 'e' in "me."

z — pronounced like 's' in "same"

b, d, f, k, l, m, n, p, q, s, t, w, x — pronounced as they are as in English

Vowels

a — 'ah' as in "father," but shorter

e — 'eh' as in "hen"

i — 'ee' as in "machine"

o — 'oh' as in "phone"

u — usually 'oo' as in "rule"; when it follows a 'q,' the 'u' is silent; when it follows an 'h' or 'g,' it's pronounced like 'w'—except when it comes between 'g' and 'e' or 'i,' in which case it's also silent (unless it has an umlaut, when it's again pronounced as English 'w')

Stress and Accent Marks

Words in Spanish follow a few basic rules as to which syllable is stressed (emphasized).

1. Words ending in a vowel, -n, or -s are stressed on the penultimate (next to the last) syllable, as in *nada (NA-da), origen (o-RI-gen),* or *esto (ES-to).*

2. Words ending in any consonant except -n or -s are stressed on the last syllable, as in *doctor (doc-TOR), ciudad (ci-u-DAD),* or *comer (co-MER).*

3. When rules 1 and 2 above are not followed, a written accent is used as in *rápido (RÁP-i-do), compró (com-PRÓ),* or *limón (li-MÓN).*

4. Written accents are also used to differentiate between words that are pronounced the same but have different meanings:

si — if
sí — yes
el — the
él — he

5. Remember that emphasizing the wrong syllable of a word can turn it into another word entirely. Consider the word *animo.* With stress on the first syllable, we have the noun *Á-ni-mo,* meaning 'spirit, intention, or courage'. With stress on the second syllable *(a-NI-mo),* we have the first person present tense form of the verb *animar,* meaning 'to encourage'. Finally, with stress on the final syllable *(a-ni-MÓ),* we have the third person preterite form of the same verb.

NUMBERS

0 — *cero*
1 — *uno (masculine)* or *una (feminine)*
2 — *dos*
3 — *tres*
4 — *cuatro*
5 — *cinco*
6 — *seis*
7 — *siete*
8 — *ocho*
9 — *nueve*
10 — *diez*
11 — *once*

12 — *doce*
13 — *trece*
14 — *catorce*
15 — *quince*
16 — *dieciseis*
17 — *diecisiete*
18 — *dieciocho*
19 — *diecinueve*
20 — *veinte*
21 — *veintiuno*
30 — *treinta*
40 — *cuarenta*
50 — *cincuenta*
60 — *sesenta*
70 — *setenta*
80 — *ochenta*
90 — *noventa*
100 — *cien*
101 — *ciento y uno*
200 — *doscientos*
1,000 — *mil*
10,000 — *diez mil*
1,000,000 — *un millón*

DAYS OF THE WEEK

Sunday — *domingo*
Monday — *lunes*
Tuesday — *martes*
Wednesday — *miércoles*
Thursday — *jueves*
Friday — *viernes*
Saturday — *sábado*

TIME

Latin America mostly uses the 12-hour clock, but in some instances—usually associated with plane or bus schedules—the 24-hour military clock may be used. Under the 24-hour clock, for example, *las nueve de la noche* (9 P.M.) would become *las 21 horas* (2100 hours).

What time is it? — *¿Qué hora es?*
It's one o'clock. — *Es la una.*
It's two o'clock. — *Son las dos.*
At two o'clock. — *A las dos.*
It's ten to three. — *Son tres menos diez.*
It's ten past three. — *Son tres y diez.*
It's three fifteen. — *Son las tres y cuarto.*
It's two forty-five. — *Son tres menos cuarto.*

It's two thirty. — *Son las dos y media,* or *Son las dos y trienta.*
It's 6 a.m. — *Son las seis de la mañana.*
It's 6 p.m. — *Son las seis de la tarde.*
It's 10 p.m. — *Son las diez de la noche.*
today — *hoy*
tomorrow — *mañana*
morning — *la mañana*
tomorrow morning — *mañana por la mañana*
yesterday — *ayer*
last night — *anoche*
the next day — *el día siguiente*
week — *la semana*
month — *mes*
year — *año*

USEFUL WORDS AND PHRASES

Most Spanish-speaking people consider formalities important. When approaching someone for information or any other reason, do not forget the appropriate salutation—good morning, good evening, etc. Standing alone, the greeting *hola* (hello) may sound brusque.

Hello. — *Hola.*
Good morning. — *Buenos días.*
Good afternoon. — *Buenas tardes.*
Good evening. — *Buenas noches.*
How are you? — *¿Cómo está?*
Fine. — *Muy bien.*
And you? — *¿Y usted?*
So-so. — *Más o menos.*
Thank you. — *Gracias.*
Thank you very much. — *Muchas gracias.*
You're very kind. — *Muy amable.*
You're welcome — *De nada* (literally, "It's nothing.")
yes — *sí*
no — *no*
I don't know. — *No sé.*
It's fine; okay — *Está bien.*
good; okay — *Bueno.*
please — *por favor*
Pleased to meet you. — *Mucho gusto.*
Excuse me (physical) — *Perdóneme.*
Excuse me (speech) — *Discúlpeme.*
I'm sorry. — *Lo siento.*
Goodbye. — *adiós*

See you later. — *hasta luego (literally, "until later")*
more — *más*
less — *menos*
better — *mejor*
much; a lot — *mucho*
a little — *un poco*
large — *grande*
small — *pequeño; chico*
quick; fast — *rápido*
slowly — *despacio*
bad — *malo*
difficult — *difícil*
easy — *fácil*
He/She/It is gone; as in, "she left" or "he's gone." — *Ya se fue.*
I don't speak Spanish well. — *No hablo bien el español.*
I don't understand. — *No entiendo.*
How do you say. . . in Spanish? — *¿Cómo se dice. . . en español?*
Do you understand English? — *¿Entiende el inglés?*
Is English spoken here? (Does anyone here speak English?) — *¿Se habla inglés aquí?*

TERMS OF ADDRESS

When in doubt, use the formal *usted* (you) as a form of address. If you wish to dispense with formality and feel that the desire is mutual, you can say, *Me puedes tutear* (you can call me *"tú"*). Also see below for a special note on *vos*, an alternative for *tú* that's common in Costa Rica but rarely taught in Western classrooms.

I — *yo*
you (formal) — *usted*
you (familiar) — *tú or vos*
he/him — *él*
she/her — *ella*
we/us — *nosotros*
you (plural) — *ustedes*
they/them (all males or mixed gender) — *ellos*
they/them (all females) — *ellas*
Mr.; sir — *señor*
Mrs.; madam — *señora*
Miss; young lady — *señorita*
wife — *esposa*

husband — *marido; esposo*
friend — *a*migo *(male)* or *amiga (female)*
sweetheart — *novio (male)* or *novia (female)*
son — *hijo*
daughter — *hija*
brother — *hermano*
sister — *hermana*
father — *padre*
mother — *madre*
grandfather — *abuelo*
grandmother — *abuela*

GETTING AROUND

Where is. . . ? — *¿Dónde está. . . ?*
How far is it to. . . ? — *¿A cuanto está. . . ?*
from. . . to. . . — *de. . . a. . .*
highway — *la carretera*
road — *el camino*
street — *la calle*
block — *la cuadra*
kilometer — *kilómetro*
north — *norte*
south — *sur*
west — *oeste; poniente*
east — *este; oriente*
straight ahead — *al derecho; adelante*
to the right — *a la derecha*
to the left — *a la izquierda*

ACCOMMODATIONS

Is there a room? — *¿Hay cuarto?*
May I (we) see it? — *¿Puedo (podemos) verlo?*
What is the rate? — *¿Cuál es el precio?*
Is that your best rate? — *¿Es su mejor precio?*
Is there something cheaper? — *¿Hay algo más económico?*
single room — *un sencillo*
double room — *un doble*
room for a couple — *matrimonial*
key — *llave*
with private bath — *con baño*
with shared bath — *con baño general; con baño compartido*
hot water — *agua caliente*
cold water — *agua fría*
shower — *ducha*
towel — *toalla*

soap — *jabón*
toilet paper — *papel higiénico*
air conditioning — *aire acondicionado*
fan — *abanico; ventilador*
blanket — *frazada; manta*
sheets — *sábanas*

PUBLIC TRANSPORT
bus stop — *la parada*
bus terminal — *terminal de buses*
airport — *el aeropuerto*
launch — *lancha; tiburonera*
dock — *muelle*
I want a ticket to. . . — *Quiero un pasaje a. . .*
I want to get off at. . . — *Quiero bajar en. . .*
Here, please. — *Aquí, por favor.*
Where is this bus going? — *¿Adónde va este autobús?*
round-trip — *ida y vuelta*
What do I owe? — *¿Cuánto le debo?*

FOOD
menu — *la carta; el menú*
glass — *taza*
fork — *tenedor*
knife — *cuchillo*
spoon — *cuchara*
napkin — *servilleta*
soft drink — *refresco*
coffee — *café*
cream — *crema*
tea — *té*
sugar — *azúcar*
drinking water — *agua pura; agua potable*
bottled water — *agua en botella*
beer — *cerveza*
wine — *vino*
milk — *leche*
juice — *jugo*
eggs — *huevos*
bread — *pan*
watermelon — *sandía*
banana — *banano*
plantain — *plátano*
apple — *manzana*
orange — *naranja*
meat (without) — *carne (sin)*

beef — *carne de res*
chicken — *pollo; gallina*
fish — *pescado*
shellfish — *mariscos*
shrimp — *camarones*
fried — *frito*
roasted — *asado*
barbecued; grilled — *a la parrilla*
breakfast — *desayuno*
lunch — *almuerzo*
dinner (often eaten in late afternoon) — *comida*
dinner; late-night snack — *cena*
the check; the bill — *la cuenta*

SHOPPING
I need. . . — *Necesito. . .*
I want. . . — *Deseo. . . or Quiero. . .*
I would like. . . (more polite) — *Quisiera. . .*
How much does it cost? — *¿Cuánto cuesta?*
What's the exchange rate? — *¿Cuál es el tipo de cambio?*
May I see. . . ? — *¿Puedo ver. . . ?*
this one — *ésta/ésto*
expensive — *caro*
cheap — *barato*
cheaper — *más barato*
too much — *demasiado*

HEALTH
Help me, please. — *Ayúdeme, por favor.*
I am ill. — *Estoy enfermo.*
pain — *dolor*
fever — *fiebre*
stomachache — *dolor de estómago*
vomiting — *vomitar*
diarrhea — *diarrea*
drugstore — *farmacia*
medicine — *medicina*
pill; tablet — *pastilla*
birth control pills — *pastillas anticonceptivas*
condom — *condón; preservativo*

SPECIAL NOTE: *VOS*

In Costa Rica, as well as in several other Central and South American countries, the pronoun *"tú"* is not frequently heard. More commonly used, and rarely taught to Westerners in their Spanish classes, is *vos*.

Essentially, *vos* is used in the same instances as *tú,* that is, between two people who have a certain degree of casual familiarity or friendliness, in place of the more formal usted. The vos form is derived from vosotros, the second person plural (you all) still used in Spain. However, vosotros is not used in Latin America, even in places where vos is common.

For all tenses other than the present indicative, present subjunctive, and command forms, the *vos* form of the verb is exactly the same as *tú.* Hence: *tú andaste/ vos andaste* (past tense), *tú andabas/vos andabas* (past imperfect), *tú andarás/vos andarás* (future), *tú andarías/vos andarías* (conditional).

In the present indicative, the conjugation is the same as with *tú,* but the last syllable is stressed with an accent. The exception is with *-ir* verbs, in which the final *"i"* is retained, instead of changing to an *"e."* Hence: *tú andas/vos andás, tú comes/vos comés, tú escribes/vos escribís.*

In the present subjunctive, the same construction is followed as with the normal subjunctive, except the *vos "á"* accent is retained. Hence: *tú andes/vos andés, tú comas/vos comás, tú escribas/vos escribás.*

In radical changing verbs like *tener, poder,* or *dormir,* the *vos* form does not change from vowel to *dipthong (tienes, puedes, duermes)* in the present subjunctive form. Hence: *vos tengás, vos podás, vos durmás.*

Vos commands are formed by simply dropping the final *"r"* on the infinitive and adding an accent over the last vowel. Hence: *vos andá, vos comé, vos escribí.* When using object pronouns with *vos, te* is still used. Hence: *Yo te lo escribí a vos.*

One common irregular *vos* form is *sos,* for *ser (to be).* Also, because the conjugation would be bizarre, the verb *"ir"* is not used in the *vos* form. Instead, use *andar: vos andás.*

Suggested Reading

There is no shortage of books on Costa Rica these days, from glossy coffee table tomes to nuts and bolts travel guides. Here's a small sampling of what's on offer.

GUIDEBOOKS AND NATURAL HISTORY

Alvarado, Guillermo. *Costa Rica: Land of Volcanoes*. Cartago, Costa Rica: Editorial Tecnología de Costa Rica, 1993. A detailed and fascinating look at the fiery mountains that are still shaping Costa Rica. With maps and color photos.

Baker, Christopher P. *Moon Costa Rica*. Emeryville, California: Avalon Travel Publishing, 2007. One of the most comprehensive guidebooks on the market. Lots of good background information, and a lively writing style.

Bernhardt, Ed. *The Costa Rican Organic Home Gardening Guide*. New Dawn Center, 2003. The founder of the New Dawn organic farm and education center (www.newdawncenter.org) gives practical and comprehensive advice about starting an organic garden in Costa Rica.

Carr, Archie. *The Windward Road*. Gainesville, Florida: University of Florida Press, 1955. A book about sea turtles in Central America by the man who not only pioneered the study of the creatures but also founded the Caribbean Conservation Corporation.

Cole-Christenson, Darryl. *A Place in the Rain Forest: Settling the Costa Rican Frontier*. Austin, Texas: University of Texas Press, 1997. A remarkable account of pioneering in the southern region now known as Coto Brus. Stick with it and you'll find out a lot about farming, squatters, and how very remote this area was just 50 years ago.

De Vries, Phillip. *Butterflies of Costa Rica and Their Natural History (Volumes 1 and 2)*. Princeton, New Jersey: Princeton University Press, 2000. The real deal for butterfly fanatics. Lots of color plates.

Evans, Sterling. *The Green Republic: A Conservation History of Costa Rica*. Amarillo, Texas: University of Texas Press, 1999. Detailed account of the history of the national park system and the rise of ecological awareness in Costa Rica.

Forsyth, Adrian and Ken Miyata. *Tropical Nature: Life and Death in the Rainforests of Central and South America*. Touchstone Books, 1987. Very readable account of the wonders of the rainforest from two tropical biologists.

Mayfield, Michael, and Rafael Gallo. *The Rivers of Costa Rica: A Canoeing, Kayaking, and Rafting Guide*. Birmingham, Alabama: Menasha Ridge Press, 1992. Takes on Costa Rica's major navigable rivers.

Parise, Mike. *The Surfer's Guide to Costa Rica*. Los Angeles: Surfpress Publishing, 1999. *The* guide for surfers traveling to Costa Rica. Information on 70 breaks on both coasts and more than 100 hotels nearest the breaks. Tips on what to pack, how to pack surfboards, and how to get to remote places.

Pariser, Harry. *Explore Costa Rica*. San Francisco: Manatee Press, 2007. A 600-page guide with a strong author's voice and comprehensive background information.

Stiles, Gary, and Alexander Skutch. *A Guide to the Birds of Costa Rica*. Ithaca, New York: Cornell University Press, 1989. The birder's bible, with color plates.

Wainwright, Mark. *The Natural History of Costa Rican Mammals*. Distribuidores Zona Tropical, S.A., 2003. There are many books on Costa Rican mammals, but this one really stands out. Compact enough to be a field guide, it is nevertheless quite comprehensive, with not only color plates of the animals, but also drawings of scat and tracks. Wainwright provides details of dens, range, vocalizations, derivations of common and scientific names, evolutionary history, even local folklore and mythology. The book has 400 illustrations and is written in a very clear and sometimes witty style. A joy!

Wallace, David R. *The Quetzal and the Macaw: The Story of Costa Rica's National Parks.* San Francisco: Sierra Club Books, 1992. A very readable history of the formation of the country's park system.

HISTORY, POLITICS, AND CULTURE

Biesanz, Mavis, Richard Biesanz, and Karen Biesanz. *The Ticos: Culture and Social Change in Costa Rica.* Boulder, Colorado: Lynne Rienner Publishers, 1999. An excellent book for those who want to understand Costa Rica and its people. The authors take on everything from history to "marital relations and gender roles."

Coates, Anthony G., ed. *Central America: A Natural and Cultural History.* New Haven, Connecticut: Yale University Press, 1999. Chapters by different authors, most authorities in their fields, take on geological origins, differences between the surrounding oceans, the importance of natural corridors, the history of native people and colonizers from pre-Columbian to modern times, and current conservation issues.

Edelman, Marc, and Joanne Kenen, eds. *The Costa Rican Reader.* New York: Grove Weidenfeld, 1989. A collection of articles by diverse authors, covering many aspects of Costa Rican history and politics. Includes the text of President Oscar Arias

Sánchez's 1987 peace plan, for which he won the Nobel Peace Prize.

Helmuth, Charlene. *Culture and Customs of Costa Rica.* Westport, Connecticut: Greenwood Press, 2000. A useful and very readable introduction to Tican culture, including chapters on visual arts, performing arts, and literature.

Honey, Martha. *Hostile Acts: U.S. Policy in Costa Rica in the 1980s.* Gainesville, Florida: University of Florida Press, 1994. Account of U.S. influence in the isthmus during the tumultuous 1980s. The author lived in Costa Rica from 1983 to 1991 and brings an insider's view to the subject. Arguing that Costa Rica should be the best example of the type of country the U.S. government says it is trying to foster, Honey shows how U.S. actions actually undermined the country until Costa Rican president Arias stood up to U.S. pressure, providing a regional solution with his Central American Peace Plan.

Lefever, Harry G. *Turtle Bogue: Afro-Caribbean Life in a Costa Rican Village.* Selinsgrove, Pennsylvania: Susquehanna University Press, 1992. A professor records the folk history of the Caribbean coast town of Tortuguero.

Molina, Iván, and Steven Palmer. *The History of Costa Rica.* San José, Costa Rica: Editorial de la Universidad de Costa Rica, 2002. A short and readable introduction to the country's history.

Paige, Jeffery M. *Coffee and Power: Revolution and the Rise of Democracy in Central America.* Cambridge, Massachusetts: Harvard University Press. 1998. Central American politics and development, as seen through the lens of the all-important coffee business.

Palmer, Paula. *What Happen: A Folk History of Costa Rica's Talamanca Coast.* Publications in English S.A., 1993. The author, a North American sociologist, has collected fascinating oral histories from the Afro-Caribbean people who settled the towns of Cahuita, Puerto Viejo, and Manzanillo on Costa Rica's Atlantic coast. Out of print, but not impossible to find.

Palmer, Paula, Juanita Sánchez, and Gloria Mayorga. *Taking Care of Sibö's Gifts.* San José, Costa Rica: Editorama S.A., 1993. One of the few books on indigenous Costa Rican culture by indigenous authors.

Stuart, Jo. *Butterfly in the City: A Good Life in Costa Rica.* 2006. Short essays, originally published as columns in amcostarica.com, that take on aspects of being a single woman expat living in San José. You'll get a good sense of the everyday life of the city, from shopping to fiestas to standing in line to do your banking. Order from the author: jocstuart@racsa.co.cr.

FICTION AND TRAVELOGUE

Benz, Stephen. *Green Dreams: Travels in Central America.* Oakland, California: Lonely Planet, 1998. The section on Costa Rica explores the gap between the country's ecological aspirations and its need for economic development.

Club de Libros. Costa Rica's first online literary magazine (www.clubdelibros.com), founded in 2002, has a wealth of articles about Costa Rican and international authors (in Spanish).

León Sánchez, José. *God Was Looking the Other Way: Thirty Years on the Devil's Island of Latin America.* Boston: Little, Brown and Company, 1973. The English version of this book is unfortunately out of print but can be found if you look hard. It's worth it for this gripping account of a man condemned to life imprisonment on San Lucas Island, off the coast of Costa Rica and until 1989 a no-

torious penitentiary. The book is a fictionalized account of the author's time as an inmate there.

Ras, Barbara, ed. *Costa Rica: A Traveler's Literary Companion.* Berkeley, California: Whereabouts Press, 1994. Short stories and novel excerpts by Costa Rican authors, organized by geographical zone.

Theroux, Paul. *The Old Patagonia Express.* In this book about riding the rails from Massachusetts to the tip of South America, only two chapters are set in Costa Rica. But what a pleasure to hear about the now-defunct train from San José to Limón and the still-functioning line from San José to Puntarenas, from the best curmudgeonly travel writer alive today. Don't expect travel-brochure bromides: Theroux elevates crankiness to an art.

Weisbecker, Allan C. *In Search of Captain Zero: A Surfer's Road Trip Beyond the End of the Road.* Los Angeles: JP Tarcher, 2002. Chronicles the author's trip through Mexico and Central America in search of good waves and an old friend who has disappeared. The "end of the road" turns out to be on the Caribbean coast of Costa Rica, and there are some nice descriptions of the famed Salsa Brava, a wave near Puerto Viejo that draws highly skilled and adventurous surfers.

Young, Allen. *Sarapiquí Chronicle: A Naturalist in Costa Rica.* Washington, D.C.: Smithsonian Institution Press, 1991. Travelogue of northern Costa Rica.

For more books by Costa Rican authors, see the *Literature* section of the *People and Culture* chapter.

CHILDREN'S BOOKS

Baden, Robert. *And Sunday Makes Seven.* Morton Grove, Illinois: Albert Whitman & Co., 1990. Folk tales for kids 4–8.

Forsyth, Adrian. *Journey Through a Tropical Jungle.* Englewood Cliffs, New Jersey: Silver Burdett Press, 1996. A lighthearted romp through a Costa Rican forest.

Henderson, Aileen. *The Monkey Thief.* Minneapolis, Minnesota: Milkweed Editions, 1998. A 12-year-old boy visits his uncle in Costa Rica and learns about monkeys, smugglers, and the rainforest.

Norman, David. *Costa Rica Wildlife* and other titles. World Wildlife Fund (WWF) coloring books with descriptions of the plants and animals pictured.

DRIVING TO COSTA RICA

Nelson, Mike. *Central America by Car.* Wanderlust Publications, 1997. "Mexico Mike" gives advice on how to navigate the isthmus from behind the wheel of your car.

Pritchard, Raymond. *Driving the Pan-American Highway,* 6th edition. San José, Costa Rica: Costa Rica Books, 1997. An old classic (now edited by Chris Howard) that needs updating, but it offers tips on border crossing and sightseeing. Available from Costa Rica Books, 800/365-2342 or at www.driveto centralamerica.com.

Wessler, Dawna Rae. *You Can Drive to Costa Rica in 8 Days.* Harmony Gardens Publishing, 1998. Tales and advice from two non-Spanish-speaking surfer gringos who made the trip in their 22-year-old VW van.

MISCELLANEOUS

Hasbrouck, Edward. *The Practical Nomad.* Emeryville, California: Avalon Travel Publishing, 2007. A cult classic and deservedly so, this book helps you think about the world and how to best move through it. Great practical information (on airfares, for example) and even better philosophy (just what do we mean when we talk about first, second, and third worlds?).

Kohls, L. Robert. *Survival Kit for Overseas Living,* 4th ed. Yarmouth, Maine: Nicholas Brealey/Intercultural Press, 2001. Offering up a fascinating look at culture shock and cultural bias, this book helps readers take inventory of their own cultural "baggage" before venturing abroad. Short on practical detail about individual countries but long on strategies for developing intercultural communication skills, no matter where you plan to go.

Oliver, Scott. *How to Buy Costa Rica Real Estate Without Losing Your Camisa.* San José, Costa Rica: WeLoveCostaRica. com, 2005. A 200-page booklet with a lot of very useful and specific information about real estate in Costa Rica, by British expat and real estate agent Scott Oliver, who lives in Escazú and runs the WeLoveCostaRica.com website.

Petersen, Roger A. *The Legal Guide to Costa Rica.* San José, Costa Rica: Amerilatin Consultares, 2002. Covers everything from property rights to extradition. You can order a copy at www .costaricalaw.com.

Rupp, Rebecca. *Home Learning Year by Year: How to Design a Homeschool Curriculum from Preschool to High School.* New York: Three Rivers Press, 2000. Many expats, especially those living outside of the Central Valley, are interested in homeschooling their kids. Just exploring Costa Rica and learning Spanish provide quite an education, but this book, by one of the best known homeschool authorities, will help parents devise a more structured educational plan.

Woodman, Josef. *Patients Without Borders: Everybody's Guide to Affordable, World-Class Medical Tourism* Chapel Hill, North Carolina: Health Travel Media, 2007. One of the first comprehensive books on this growing trend.

Suggested Films

Caribe (2004), directed by Esteban Ramirez, was the first Costa Rican film to be submitted to the Academy Awards; competing against more than 50 other movies from around the world, it was not nominated. The story is of a love triangle, with a subplot about a beach town trying to stop an oil company from despoiling its shore. Filmed in and around Puerto Viejo in reportedly only five weeks, Caribe gives you a nice long glimpse of the less-visited Atlantic coast of Costa Rica and an introduction into some of the environmental issues there.

The Blue Butterfly (2004), directed by Lea Pool, stars John Hurt as an entomologist who leads a wheelchair-bound boy dying of cancer into the rainforests of Costa Rica to find a blue morpho butterfly. Their search is an arduous one; I guess they didn't know that blue morphos can be seen all over the place, including in the Butterfly Garden in downtown San José's National Museum. Filmed in Limón and Puerto Viejo.

Rosita (2005), a documentary by Barbara Attie and Janet Goldwater, looks at a recent case in which a nine-year-old Nicaraguan girl became pregnant as a result of a rape. Her parents—illiterate Nicaraguan campesinos working in Costa Rica—seek a legal "therapeutic" abortion for their child, which pits them against the governments of Nicaragua and Costa Rica, the medical establishment, and the Catholic Church.

Carnival in Costa Rica, directed by Gregory Ratoff in 1947 and filmed in Costa Rica, stars Cesar Romero in a tale of star-crossed lovers trying to thwart an arranged marriage. As with most comic films of the period, hijinks ensue.

Given Costa Rica's reputation for great surf on both coasts, it's no surprise that many surf films are filmed at least in part in Costa Rica. These include **Step Into Liquid** (2003), filmed in part in Mal País; **Costa Rica: Land of Waves** (2001); **Endless Summer 2** (1994); **Endless Summer Revisited** (2000); and **Zen and Zero** (2006), directed by Michael Ginthor, a documentary in which writer/surfer/ex-Pavones resident Alan Weisbecker plays himself.

Many other movies not necessarily about Costa Rica are filmed—at least in part—here. In **The Celestine Prophecy** (2006), about a search for a sacred manuscript in the Peruvian rainforest, was actually filmed in Costa Rica, Puerto Rico, and Florida. Some of Mel Gibson's **Apocalypto** (2006) was filmed here, and Tico actor Mauricio Amuy plays a Mayan chief in the film. In 2005 Costa Rica was the filming location for **Death to the Supermodels** ("they're drop-dead gorgeous" is the movie's tagline), directed by Joel Silverman. **Silverman's Surf School** was also filmed here.

The first **Jurassic Park** (1993) snagged some jungle scenes from Costa Rica, and Costa Rica stood in for Africa in Frank Marshall's 1995 film **Congo. Spy Kids 2: The Island of Lost Dreams** (2002) was filmed here, as was 1492: **Conquest of Paradise** (1992), directed by Ridley Scott and with Gerard Depardieu as Christopher Columbus. And who can forget **Tropix** (2002), directed by Percy Angress and filmed in Guapiles, Playa Escondido, Parque Este, and San José. The film's tagline: "Come to Costa Rica. See endangered species. Become one. More than Paradise... will be LOST!"

Index

Acknowledgments

Big thanks go out to so many people who've been generous on many levels, including Emily Fintel of AVINA, Arturo Condo of INCAE, Royce Slape at The Julia and David White Arts Colony, Kirt Wackford for his invaluable help in understanding the Costa Rican school system, Stephen and Kathleen Duplantier for sharing so much about their lives and the process of building their home, Alex Murray (writer and proprietor of Casa Mañana B&B near Tilarán, who seemed to take it as his personal mission to introduce me to everyone in town), Michael Caggiano and staff at Hotel Alta, Elaine Chalmers at the Beauty Club in Escazú for making me presentable after weeks on the road, Mary Ann Jackson for her friendship and ongoing hospitality, Lisa Brunetti for the amazing hand-drawn map of San Miguel, Beth Frischberg and Andrew Mastrodonas at Angel Valley Farm B&B, Ryan Piercy at the ARCR, Scott Oliver of welovecostarica.com, Jay Brodell at amcostarica.com, Boaz Raufman and the rest of the crew at Lands in Love, Stephen Denton and Anahi Contreras of Villa Alegre B&B, Greg Bascom in Escazú for throwing me such a great party, Jo Stewart, John McCuen of 7th Street Books, Harvey Haber, Christopher Baker, Josh Berman, Donn Wilson and Juan Caldera of Nica Development in San Juan del Sur (Nicaragua), Jacqueline Passey, Wendy Tayler for her time and warmth, Brenda Burnside in Nosara, Alaine Berg of ATEC, Loren Thomas of Monteverde Friends School, Catherine Fitton and Christina Senigaglia of Premier Realty in Jacó, Steve Broyles of Bratton Broyles & Associates in Tamarindo for being so cool under the pressure of a backwoods breakdown, Ellen Zoe, Doña Margarita Arroyo at Mapache and Ernesto for driving me around, Andrés Zamora and Raymond Cruz of Remax Lider, Victoria Schwarz, Gerry Aust and Sarah Murrillo of Toucan Realty, Iris Mailloux of Remax Resort Properties Papagayo, Chris Simmons of Remax Ocean Surf Realty, Manuel Pinto of Caribe Sur Real Estate, Lilliam at the Hotel Le Bergerac, the Hotel El Octotal Beach Resort, Robyn White and Henry Kantrowitz, Kremena Kroumova in Montezuma, Sebastian Elizondo at Villas del Mar near Tambor, Jennifer Lind at Hidden Coast Realty, Bettina del Rio at Amor del Mar Realty in Santa Teresa, Juan at Tropico Latino, Scott Serfas for his amazing photograph of Rodrigo Miranda surfing Playa Junquillal, Rodrigo Miranda for his amazing surfing of Playa Junquillal, Shifi Ettinger for her time and her great photos, Scott Pralinsky and Isaac Garcia Gutierrez, Daryl Loth for sharing the photo of his daughter, Ronald Artavia for putting me up in Jacó, Jesús Villareal and Susan Chavaria in Guatíl, writers and environmental educators Alexis Fournier and Sandra Shaw Homer, Ed Yurica of Fuentes Verdes in Tilarán, Dan Spreen and Roberta Ward Smiley in Arenal for showing me their native species seedlings and to Roberta for sharing with me her lovely hand-drawn book of birds of the region, Chuck Tonies for the loan of *Atlantis in the Americas*—I still plan to return it!

Thanks, too, to the crew at Avalon Travel Publishing, especially editor Sabrina Young, photo editor Tabitha Lahr, copy editor Deana Shields, map editor Kevin Anglin, and tireless publicist Hannah Cox.

And special thanks to Gianna De Carl and Kathy Mueller, my mother, for coming to my rescue when I needed them most, and to Houman Pirdavari, for helping out on every front imaginable, especially with his evocative photographs and his homemade chicken pot pies.

To everyone else who lent me a hand and helped me see how varied a country Costa Rica is, *un abrazo, y mil gracias.*

www.moon.com

For helpful advice on planning a trip, visit www.moon.com for the **TRAVEL PLANNER** and get access to useful travel strategies and valuable information about great places to visit. When you travel with Moon, expect an experience that is uncommon and truly unique.

HANDBOOKS • OUTDOORS • METRO • LIVING ABROA

MAP SYMBOLS

▭▭▭	Expressway	○	City/Town	✗	Airfield	⬟	Archaeological Site
▭▭▭	Primary Road	◉	State Capital	✈	Airport	▮	Church
▭▭▭	Secondary Road	◉	National Capital	⚓	Port of Entry	▮	Gas Station
- - - -	Unpaved Road			▲	Mountain	▭	Mangrove
··········	Ferry	★	Point of Interest	♠	Park	▭	Reef

CONVERSION TABLES

°C = (°F - 32) / 1.8
°F = (°C x 1.8) + 32
1 inch = 2.54 centimeters (cm)
1 foot = 0.304 meters (m)
1 yard = 0.914 meters
1 mile = 1.6093 kilometers (km)
1 km = 0.6214 miles
1 fathom = 1.8288 m
1 chain = 20.1168 m
1 furlong = 201.168 m
1 acre = 0.4047 hectares
1 sq km = 100 hectares
1 sq mile = 2.59 square km
1 ounce = 28.35 grams
1 pound = 0.4536 kilograms
1 short ton = 0.90718 metric ton
1 short ton = 2,000 pounds
1 long ton = 1.016 metric tons
1 long ton = 2,240 pounds
1 metric ton = 1,000 kilograms
1 quart = 0.94635 liters
1 US gallon = 3.7854 liters
1 Imperial gallon = 4.5459 liters
1 nautical mile = 1.852 km

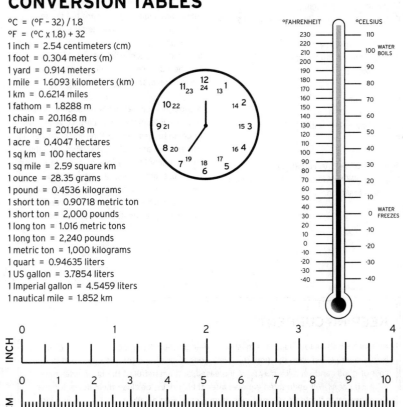

MOON LIVING ABROAD IN COSTA RICA

Avalon Travel Publishing
a member of the Perseus Book Group
1400 65th Street, Suite 250
Emeryville, CA 94608, USA
www.moon.com

Editor: Sabrina Young
Series Manager: Elizabeth McCue
Acquisitions Manager: Grace Fujimoto
Copy Editor, Proofreader, and Indexer:
   Deana Shields
Graphics Coordinator: Tabitha Lahr
Production Coordinator: Tabitha Lahr
Cover Designer: Tabitha Lahr
Map Editor: Kevin Anglin
Cartographers: Kat Bennett, Mike Morgenfeld

ISBN-10: 1-59880-007-8
ISBN-13: 978-1-59880-007-4
ISSN: 1549-1412

Printing History
1st Edition – 2004
2nd Edition – September 2007
5 4 3 2 1

Text © 2007 by Erin Van Rheenen
Maps © 2007 by Avalon Travel Publishing, Inc.
All rights reserved.

KEEPING CURRENT

Although we strive to produce the most up-to-date guidebook that we possibly can, change is unavoidable. Between the time this book goes to print and the time you read it, the cost of goods and services may have increased, and a handful of the businesses noted in these pages will undoubtedly move, alter their prices, or close their doors forever. Exchange rates fluctuate – sometimes dramatically – on a daily basis. Federal and local legal requirements and restrictions are also subject to change, so be sure to check with the appropriate authorities before making the move. If you see anything in this book that needs updating, clarification, or correction, please drop us a line. Send your comments via email to feedback@moon.com, or use the address above.